Faith and Science in an Unjust World

FAITH AND SCIENCE IN AN UNJUST WORLD

Report of the World Council of Churches' Conference on Faith, Science and the Future

Massachusetts Institute of Technology
Cambridge, USA, 12-24 July 1979

Volume 1: Plenary Presentations

Edited by Roger L. Shinn

Church and Society
WORLD COUNCIL OF CHURCHES, GENEVA

52267

Cover design: John Taylor

ISBN No. 2-8254- 0629-5

Printed in Switzerland by Imprimerie Corbaz, Montreux

Table of Contents

10. Perspectives in Industrialized, Market-Economy Societies

11. Perspectives in Industrialized Socialist Countries

PART THREE: PARTICULAR PROBLEM AREAS

12. Economics of the Just and Sustainable Society

13. Energy for the Future

APPENDICES

Foreword

The report of the conference on Faith, Science and the Future, convened by the World Council of Churches in 1979, comes in two volumes. Volume 1 consists mainly of the addresses in plenary sessions, with some summaries of plenary discussions and responses of the conference. Volume 2 contains the reports of the working sections and the recommendations and resolutions.

The speakers represented in this volume—in their professional skills, geographic and cultural settings, religious and ideological commitments—brought diverse experiences and abilities to the conference. They were sometimes chosen to present a controversial position or to contribute to a debate. They were invited to speak their own minds freely. When they were persuasive, their ideas often influenced the section reports and the recommendations of the conference.

The WCC Working Group on Church and Society has asked me to edit this volume. That job has been both a joy and a weighty responsibility. The addresses are not simply isolated essays; their context is the whole conference and the continuing process leading to it and following from it. Therefore, with the approval of the Working Group, I have written an introductory chapter to the book, plus introductions to each chapter and summaries of discussions following the addresses. Those parts of the book not attributed to specific authors are my work, which involves both reporting and interpreting.

Inasmuch as one of the themes of the conference was that the purported objectivity of science and technology is often deceptive, I cannot claim that my editing is objective. I have *tried* to be fair. I have had the helpful counsel of Metropolitan Paulos Gregorios, Moderator of the conference, and of Dr Paul Abrecht, WCC Secretary for Church and Society. But my opinions and interpretations are in no way "official".

I have also had the job, often painful, of fitting the materials into a reasonable space. This has meant abridging almost all the texts—and major abridging of the longer ones. To abridge is to risk skewing the author's intentions. I have been guided here by two main principles: (1) the emphases of the speakers themselves in their oral addresses, including often their own abridgments of written texts; (2) emphasis on those themes that brought the most response from the conference itself, either in plenary sessions or in section discussions and reports. The authors have been consulted about abridgments and have been given the opportunity to make changes.

As far as possible, the speakers submitted their texts in advance, so that these could be translated by the WCC's Language Service into the official languages of the conference and distributed to participants, either concurrently with the address or soon after it. Many speakers, asking the audience to read their addresses, used their platform time for extemporaneous comments about their addresses and responses to preceding speakers. The texts printed here are those submitted by the speakers, occasionally with minor revisions made after the conference. When no text was submitted, the address was transcribed from a recording. When additions to or departures from the text seemed especially important, these are noted in the introductions.

I have edited with a very light hand. I believe that writers' styles as well as content are their own and that most editorial attempts to improve style involve distortions. This is nowhere more the case than in international and intercultural conversations, where editorial revisions are often simply one more form of cultural imperialism.

The sequence of this volume follows, for the most part, the schedule of the conference itself. The programme was planned with a logical-chronological structure. But because the actual schedule sometimes was a compromise between the logical structure and the logistics of a complicated international conference, the book sometimes revises the order of the schedule in favour of the logical structure. The actual schedule of the conference is printed as an appendix to this volume.

I would like to thank the Geneva staff of the World Council of Churches for the arduous work of preparing the copy for the press.

R.L.S.

1. Introduction

Any conference of the World Council of Churches is a remarkable blend of harmonies and dissonances. A conference on faith, science and the future multiplies the notes and overtones. The 1979 conference was, among many other things:

— an experience of worship where a congregation faced leaders in the resplendent robes of a Roman Catholic cardinal, the vestments of Orthodox bishops from Russia and India, the garments of English and African Episcopalians, the garb of a New Zealand Maori clergyman and an American pastor of the United Church of Christ—and the blue jeans of a young woman graduate student from Colombia;
— music—vocal and instrumental—and films from many, many cultures;
— students telling teachers that the teachers were miseducating them;
— an African challenging an idealistic American: "Why are you so worried about the proliferation of nuclear materials? It is you, not we, who are terrorizing the world";
— a Latin American telling a gentle European scientist: "You are our oppressors";
— a university cafeteria revising its menus so that rice would be served daily;
— a man rising to speak from the floor after many days of polemics and jolting the assembly with his mild but brave declaration: "I am an officer of a transnational corporation";
— a computer terminal at which anyone might operate a keyboard and summon up information and pictures about themes of the conference;
— a graffiti board mixing, with both wit and seriousness, scientific formulas, theology, politics, artistic efforts and personal opinions;
— the humbling experience of being challenged, kidded and insulted—all within the context of a shared Christian faith—day after day for almost two weeks.

It may be, as some said, that this was "the most diverse gathering in the history of the World Council of Churches". About 900 people converged on the campus of the Massachusetts Institute of Technology. The official participants, most nominated by their churches but some invited by the WCC, numbered 405 people from 56 countries. Of these 91 were students. The planning committee succeeded, at least approximately, in its aim that half of these should be physical scientists and technologists; the other half were church leaders, social scientists, theologians, people from government and industry. The planning committee did not succeed in its aim that at least a third should be women: some member churches met that goal, but the total was almost a fifth.

Participants came from all the continents (except Antarctica) and from islands of the Pacific, the Indian Ocean and the Caribbean. They came from both member and non-member churches of the WCC (Protestant and Orthodox), from Roman Catholicism, and from Buddhist and Muslim communities.

The Moderator was Metropolitan Paulos Gregorios of India; and the Vice-Moderator was Prof. Charles Birch, an Australian biologist. Five co-presidents came from Canada, Egypt, Nigeria, the Soviet Union and the United Kingdom.

There were disappointments, reflecting the political tensions of the contemporary world. One Cuban woman, expected to be a co-president, had to cancel attendance at the last minute; and five scientists from the Soviet Union, some scheduled to give major addresses, withdrew in the final days before the conference—although the Russian Church was well represented. Even so, most of the major ideological accents characterizing our world were heard.

Attending plenary sessions, in addition to the official delegates, were consultants and invited visitors, staff of the conference and the WCC, stewards (volunteer youth from around the world), more than 200 accredited visitors who attended plenary sessions and organized their own programme, and an international press and radio-television corps of about 150.

Time and place

History conspired to throw into prominence the theme of the conference. As the delegates arrived on Tuesday, 10 July, the press and radio were filled with the latest estimates about when and where Sky-Lab would fall to earth; when the conference started on Wednesday, everyone knew that the space vehicle had dumped its wreckage in Australia. United States President Carter had recently returned from Strategic Arms Limitation Talks with Soviet President Brezhnev in Vienna and international economic talks in Japan. As the conference opened, he was conferring with advisers at Camp David. On the first Sunday night, 15 July, conferees clustered around television sets to hear him address the nation on its energy crisis and spiritual malaise. Thus nobody could miss the importance of disarmament, the energy problem, the international economy, the perils of new technologies—all major themes of the conference.

The location was the Massachusetts Institute of Technology, one of the world's great centres of scientific-technological research. People asked: was the Church invading the inner sanctum of technology, or was the Church being coopted by the principalities and powers of technology? Somebody wrote sceptically on the graffiti board: "To have a conference on technology and a just society at MIT is like having a conference on disarmament at the Pentagon." To that, somebody else added: "Or God becoming human."

And that incarnational theology characterized much that happened at the conference.

MIT, of course, was the host, not the co-sponsor of the conference. But as host, it pleased and surprised some delegates. Some of the sharpest criticisms of rampant technology and some of the most powerful pleas for disarmament came from faculty and students of MIT. Participants could visit its nuclear reactor, its fusion experiment and biological laboratories between debates on these issues. The beautiful Kresge auditorium, where the conference met in plenary sessions, was an innovative architectural-technological achievement, superbly equipped for such a meeting. But during one rainstorm the moderator of that particular session, himself a professor at MIT, announced that the roof was leaking and wittily called for an old-fashioned bucket—thus pointing to the fallibility of technology. Although the auditorium was comfortably air-conditioned, the dormitory rooms where most participants slept were not, and people suffered in the intense July heat. That was a useful reminder that energy-consuming technologies have their limits. It was also a reminder of human frailty, as delegates occasionally realized that a conference of the World Council of Churches might be more sensitive to its own minor discomforts than to massive starvation in Cambodia and elsewhere.

The conference itself was a technological achievement. It was possible only because of aeroplanes and international telephone operations. Ingenious apparatus facilitated simultaneous translation of speeches into many languages. Television cameras on the floor, coming from both North America and Europe, were a reminder of the potent technologies of communication. Participants saw films produced by a computer animation system.

Various events around the edges of the conference reminded delegates of the kind of history they were living through. Protesting pickets from right-wing religious groups demonstrated against the World Council of Churches, which they thought was too radical. Other groups feared that the conference would not be radical enough. The Greater Boston Mobilization for Survival demonstrated for a ban on nuclear power and armaments, and distributed fliers attacking MIT. "Plowshare"—a coalition organized by the MIT chaplains and other organizations, and funded by a grant from the National Endowment for the Humanities—set up a "listening-post/discussion centre" with television broadcasts of plenary sessions and discussions with conference speakers and other guests.

In these many ways, time and place contributed to the embedding of the most esoteric issues of science and the commitments of faith in the social life of the present.

The conference theme and its evolution

The title of the conference, "Faith, Science and the Future", was a shorthand for its real theme: "The Contribution of Faith, Science and Technology in the Struggle for a Just, Participatory and Sustainable Society". That theme has a history within the WCC.

The address of Philip Potter, General Secretary of the WCC, printed in Chapter 2 of this book, tells how the WCC from its beginning had this concern. The more recent history might be traced from the Conference on Church and Society (Geneva, 1966), which had the theme: Christians in the Technical and Social Revolutions of Our Time. It became obvious there that the ecumenical movement was more adept in conversations about social revolutions than in thinking of scientific-technological revolutions. The physical scientists and technologists there were very few in number, as they reminded the conference. One result was that the Geneva meeting urged the WCC to give more attention to the relation of science and technology to human values and social structures.

The Fourth Assembly of the WCC (Uppsala, Sweden, 1968) endorsed further work in this area. And the WCC's Central Committee (Canterbury, England, 1969) encouraged the proposal of the Working Committee on Church and Society to undertake an ecumenical study on "The Future of Man and Society in a World of Science-Based Technology".

Almost immediately after that, an issue—not entirely new but certainly new to wide public awareness—struck the WCC study project and all similar projects in the United Nations and everywhere with an explosive power. It was the insistence of many physical and social scientists, armed with massive data, that the human race was consuming resources and harming its environment at a rapidly-increasing rate that would eventually lead to environmental collapse.

The Working Committee met the issue at a meeting, chaired by economist Samuel L. Parmar of India, in Nemi, Italy, in June 1971. Two visitors, who soon won increasing fame, made the point. One was the British economist, E.F. Schumacher, who presented the theme of his book, not yet published, *Small Is Beautiful*. The other was Jørgen Randers, co-author of another book, then in press and soon to startle the world: *The Limits to Growth* (the first Report to the Club of Rome). Both speakers, despite sharp differences between them, made the case that the world could not maintain its present growth in production and consumption.

That thesis challenged the hopes and expectations of many people. To whatever extent it was true, it meant that prospects for ending poverty by economic development along traditional lines were fallacious. Those prospects had already been challenged by many critics, who showed that exploitative economic growth simply widened the gap between rich and poor nations. But the new thesis, if persuasive, meant that even plans for social revolution to be followed by economic development were at best problematic, at worst futile or destructive.

From that time the Working Committee on Church and Society has sought to relate the traditional concerns of the WCC for social justice with the newer ecological concerns. It has insisted that ecology must not become the new fad of people bored with social justice and seeking an escape from its demands. It has argued that any notion of limits on production makes more urgent the requirements of just distribution, not only of consumers' goods but also of the economic power of production.

The Working Committee on Church and Society initiated and continued a series of its own meetings on the subject. It sponsored regional conferences in West Africa (Accra, Ghana, 1972), in Asia (Kuala Lumpur, Malaysia, 1973), and for North America and Europe (Pont-à-Mousson, France, 1973). It then called a world conference on Science and Technology for Human Development: the Ambiguous Future—and the Christian Hope (Bucharest, Romania, 1974).

The Fifth Assembly of the WCC (Nairobi, Kenya, 1975) heard reports of this continuing work. Charles Birch, who had contributed much to the process, gave a major address at the assembly in which he united the themes of justice and sustainability. The assembly endorsed a continuing WCC programme in this area, and the following year its Central Committee decided that "The Struggle for the Just, Participatory and Sustainable Society" should be one of the four major programme emphases of the WCC. It simultaneously authorized the Working Committee on Church and Society to plan the 1979 conference.

There were other, more specialized events leading up to the 1979 gathering: a consultation on genetics and the quality of life (Zürich, Switzerland, 1973); a meeting on science and theology (Mexico City, 1974); a hearing on nuclear energy (Sigtuna, Sweden, 1975), and a second consultation on nuclear energy (Bossey, Switzerland, 1978); a consultation on political economy, ethics and theology (Zürich, 1978). The documents coming out of these meetings have been published in the many issues of *Anticipation*, an occasional bulletin of Church and Society, WCC. Two books, coming from the studies on genetics and on nuclear energy, are mentioned in Chapters 13 and 14 of this book. Three other books, either sponsored directly by the study programme or indirectly related to it, are: Thomas S. Derr, *Ecology and Human Liberation* (Geneva: World Student Christian Federation, 1973 and Philadelphia: Westminster Press, 1974); Paulos Gregorios, *The Human Presence: an Orthodox View of Nature* (Geneva: WCC, 1978); and Charles Birch, *Confronting the Future* (Ringwood, Vic.: Penguin Books Australia Ltd., 1976).

Against this background the Working Committee structured the 1979 conference programme around four themes:

1. The relation between science and faith as forms of human understanding and the role of faith in determining the right use of science and technology.
2. The analysis of ethical problems resulting from present and prospective developments in particular areas of science and technology.
3. The economic and political problems relating to world resource use and distribution, and the more equitable sharing of science and technology.

4. The new expressions of Christian social thought and action, which are both attentive to the promises and threats of modern science and technology and engaged in the search for a just, participatory and sustainable society.

The 1979 conference was thus in one perspective a culmination of one series of activities, while it was in another perspective a germinal occasion for new programmes still to be defined.

Communication

Predictably, the conference was an exercise in the delights and frustrations of communication. It worked in five official languages, with simultaneous interpretation in plenary sessions: English, French, German, Spanish and Russian. In addition, Dutch, Japanese and Portuguese were sometimes used, with *ad hoc* arrangements for interpretation. The interpreters performed valiantly, especially since speakers used technical vocabularies (both scientific and theological) as well as conversational idiom. In informal conversations people naturally talked mostly with others who used the same languages.

Despite the best planning and devices for interpretation, it must be admitted that people familiar with English had an advantage. When speakers addressed the meeting in English, fewer of the audience reached for earphones and relied on a translated version. The sections worked mostly in English, although there was simultaneous translation in some of them, and Section II drafted its report partly in German and partly in English. There were times when the Babel of many languages turned into a Pentecost of common understanding; but there were times when communication was hard.

Fully as difficult as the diversity of languages was the variety of worlds of discourse among participants. Theologians, for the most part, do not have much experience in talking with geneticists; social scientists have different vocabularies from physicists. How does a biology student from Ghana enter into conversation with a computer specialist from MIT? Or how do an Orthodox priest from Russia and a geneticist from western Europe come to understand each other? How do those drilled in precise quantitative reasoning communicate with poets? How do mystics get through to technologists who are used to testing ideas by controlled experiments? One discovery in the planning of the conference was that, for the most part, leaders and staff of the member churches do not know who the scientists are in their membership and rarely call on the scientists to contribute as scientists to the life of the churches.

Much of the conference was an effort, with considerable success and some failure, to do what the world at large seems unable to do: establish a shared world of discourse. Most of the delegates were not what Philip Potter sometimes calls "the old boys and girls" of the ecumenical movement. To be sure, old friends did greet each other in the early days. But more of the participants than in any other large meeting of the World Council of Churches in recent years had never attended an ecumenical gathering.

So, especially in the first week or so of activity, the question was heard: will the conference and will the sections "gel"? The question was asked both hopefully and fearfully, for as people sought some coherence, they resisted premature patterns that might exclude more turbulent ideas. One purpose of such a conference is to move people to shared understandings and even some shared conclusions; another purpose is to keep alive the interchange of opinions and to raise sensitivity—and even confusion—to a higher level.

What helped most in communication was the widely and deeply shared commitments of participants. Delegates repeatedly had the experience of (1) listening to talk that to them seemed foolish or offensive, (2) yet realizing that it was uttered in good faith by intelligent people, and (3) coming to a moment of illumination when a new insight broke conventional patterns of understanding.

Social occasions helped. There were big occasions, like the reception to which the MIT Corporation invited participants on the first afternoon. Or the buffet luncheon on the first Sunday noon, in the beautiful Boston Public Library, hosted by the Massachusetts Council of Churches and the Ecumenical Commission of the Roman Catholic Archdiocese of Boston. Or the Saturday afternoon-evening excursion to Cape Cod with its laboratories and recreational beaches. There were the many lesser occasions: the coffee breaks, the three daily meals, the conversations between and after meetings when people talked to others whose experiences they had never shared.

So the achievements of communication were real. But no conference can in twelve days break through all the obstacles that culture, economics, politics, theology and professional specializations have been building for generations. This was not a conference for people who love tidiness. Its activities and its findings were more stimulating than definitive. Most participants, coming with urgent agendas of their own, found those agendas extended and complicated rather than reduced by the conference.

The function of plenary meetings and of sections

The conference met in both plenary sessions and in ten working sections. In the early days the plenary meetings predominated, with section meetings discussing plenary addresses. Gradually the balance shifted to the work of the sections, until the final days when the sections reported their findings to the whole conference in plenary meeting.

The purpose of the plenary addresses was to bring before the conference ideas and information on issues that concerned the conference as a whole. The sections did more specialized work in specific areas. There was deliberate overlapping of functions, as some plenary sessions provided background for the work of specific sections, especially when those specific topics had universal importance.

In the early days of conference planning, the question was asked: "Do we assume that this group of people are an ignorant public who must sit and listen to experts telling them new things?" The answer of the planning committee was that all who came to the conference would be expert on some subjects and ignorant on others. It might be quite important for a theologian to get some information on the ethical issues arising in the latest biological research, for the biologist to learn from the nuclear physicist, for all these to learn from economists, and so on. It might be equally important for people in different geographical and ideological contexts to hear some sustained argument from those living in quite different contexts. In a fragmented world some common experiences seemed important. The plenary addresses contributed to the common educational impact of the conference. It is those addresses that constitute most of this volume of the conference report.

But although it was the plenary addresses that got most of the attention of the press, the greater part of the actual work was done in the sections and their sub-sections, meeting not only at scheduled times but often, in drafting groups, far into the night. The ten sections had the following topics:

I. The nature of science and the nature of faith
II. Humanity, nature and God
III. Science and education
IV. Ethical issues in the biological manipulation of life
V. Technology, resources, environment and population
VI. Energy for the future
VII. Restructuring the industrial and urban environment
VIII. Economics of a just, participatory and sustainable society
IX. Science/technology, political power, and a more just world order
X. Towards a new Christian social ethic and new social policies for the churches

The section reports and the actions of the total conference are in Volume 2 of the report.

The role of the arts

WCC conferences produce a lot of words. Language is a human gift, and important issues are at stake in verbalization. And since words are easy to reproduce in print and to circulate in books, they may get an exaggerated importance in conference reports like this one.

But any report on the 1979 conference must mention, although it cannot reproduce, the arts. When linguistic communication failed, for the reasons already mentioned, artistic communication sometimes leapt across the gap. The conferees heard kinds of music they had never heard before. Some might be familiar with drums, conch shell, and African woodwinds; others with strings and brass; others with Russian Orthodox chants, German chorales or folk songs of many peoples; others with organ and piano; but for all there were echoes of familiar traditions and new experiences. Much of the music contributed to worship (see Chapter 7). Some of it expressed—and produced—sheer enjoyment, excitement, celebration.

One such event was the concert on the first Sunday night, "Voices of Black Persuasion", by a choral and instrumental group from the National

Centre of Afro-American Artists. On the following Sunday afternoon two MIT artists, the Erdely Duo, played a concert for the conference in the Kresge auditorium. Papa Oyeah Mackenzie of Ghana, who contributed to worship on several occasions, played an evening outdoor concert on his drums, bells, calabash pods and balaphone.

Films, arranged by John Taylor of the WCC staff, were an integral part of the programme. Several were short, animated cartoons, fitted into plenary meetings at appropriate times. One, produced by Taylor and called *Helping Hand*, satirized those programmes of economic aid to developing countries that, through stupidity or design, do more for the donors' purposes than for the recipients. Longer films were announced for various times between formal meetings. Devotees who took advantage of every opportunity could see about fifty films.

Kinetic sculpture in the Kresge auditorium symbolized the intimate relations between art and science. Other artistic exhibits on the MIT campus and in the Boston area accented themes related to the conference.

Some of the uses of art were clearly instructional—usually with a quality of wit and insight that plain exposition rarely achieves. Some had no instructional purpose, but left delegates aglow with exuberance or sensitive to the mysteries of human life, as impressive in this technological age as in the biblical era.

The contribution of students

Students were a large, articulate, impressive part of the conference. In the earliest stages of planning the Working Committee on Church and Society endorsed the idea of an ecumenical conference of science students as part of the total programme. A decision soon followed that the students would be full participants in the conference, with all the rights of other participants, but would also have the privilege of organizing their own programme, concurrent with other programmes, to whatever extent they chose.

In order for students to have a major part in planning their programme, the WCC invited a small international group of them to meet, long before nominations had come from the churches for the larger number of participants. This planning group favoured the idea of a student conference with its own identity, but did not want it to reduce student participation in the total conference. So it proposed (1) that a student conference meet for several days prior to the bigger conference, and (2) that the students then join the main conference. Their proposal was quickly accepted.

Another proposal of the students was that the main conference give attention to issues of scientific education. As a result one of the ten sections at MIT (Section III) concentrated on those issues.

The students met on the campus of Wellesley College in Wellesley, Massachusetts, 6-11 July, for their own conference. Then on 11 July they went to MIT where they joined the other arriving participants.

The Wellesley meetings were the first ecumenical experience for almost all the students. They faced the same problem that the larger conference was to face: establishing a world of discourse among people of diverse languages, cultures, professional specialties and ideologies. And they had a shorter time to do it. They experimented with ways of working together, defining issues, formulating position papers. They made major strides at Wellesley and continued their work at MIT.

At MIT the students participated vigorously in the plenary sessions—on most subjects but especially on those where they had already begun to form a consensus. In each of the ten sections, a student was vice moderator, thus assuring a student voice in the organizing of the work of the sections as well as in their continuing discussions.

The 91 students—overwhelmingly science students but with a few from theology and the social sciences—came from 55 countries. They were, to whatever extent they chose to be, by far the largest "bloc" among the 405 official participants. In one sense they were a larger part of the conference than the bare numbers suggest, because almost all of them were present throughout the entire meeting, whereas many of the older participants were present for shorter times. On many an issue the opinions of students were as diverse as those of other delegates, but when they reached or neared a consensus, they influenced the conference significantly.

Their presentation to the conference in plenary session is described in Chapter 18. The extensive document they produced is printed in Volume 2.

It is probably fair to say that the continuation of the work begun at Wellesley meant that many of the students could not participate in the sections as fully as they might have. At least, some section convenors felt that their sections would have been stronger with fuller involvement of the student members; and some students found themselves torn between the work of the sections and the student programme. But their influence on the sections was significant, and the influence on the plenary sessions was still greater.

Many, many students said that the conference had brought them a new realization of the social responsibilities of scientists. Such testimonies came in part from students of the developing nations, where—as they put it—scientists sometimes become an elite, detached from service to the real needs of the whole society; it came also from students in the industrialized nations, where—again, as they put it—they came to see how the momentum of science and technology sometimes moved in indifference to the impact of its achievements on the nation or the wider world.

Clashes and consensus

In the discussions and debates of the conference, people sometimes changed their minds on some subjects. Or they saw an issue in a new light. Sometimes, also, they left the conference more convinced than when they arrived that they were right on some specific issues and that their parliamentary opponents were wrong. Conferences are like that.

What is remarkable is the strong consensus among participants, even though many were chosen in order to stimulate a provocative debate, on some big issues. Three points are worth noting.

1. By the end (possibly even at the beginning) there were no "scientific utopians" evident. That is, in contrast to a considerable literature of the past century, nobody was confident of a "technical fix" for the basic problems of societies and individuals. Nobody expected to overcome world poverty by multiplying industrial production or achieving old-fashioned economic development. Some participants clearly loved scientific inquiry and hoped for great things from it. But none argued that a technical fix would, of itself, solve even such single problems as the energy problem, to take a prominent example. There were widely varying degrees of expectation for help from various programmes of Research and Development. But there appeared to be universal recognition that the world's major problems require changes in social structures and in the values and commitments embodied in those structures.

2. In similar fashion nobody was confident of a "religious fix" for the basic social problems of this century. That is, nobody proposed that a sufficient number of religious conversions or heightened commitments would relieve the human race of poverty, hunger or disease—apart from the working out of difficult scientific, technological, economic and political issues. There was no claim that the churches were able to tell scientists the ethical formulas that would make their work benign.

3. No major arguments shaped up in which the scientists and the theologians confronted each other in opposition. In the big debates—and there were some—scientists and theologians stood together on *both* sides of the issue. When this point was mentioned in a press briefing, reporters wondered whether the scientists were a selected group. In certain respects, they were. Most were chosen by their member churches. Others, invited because of specific abilities, were not church members or believers in any of the historic religions, but they had an interest in human values and an ethical commitment. In part, of course, they were self-selected: not every scientist is willing to give up two weeks of precious research for a conference on faith, science and the future. At a minimum, the scientists present had a serious concern for the human uses of science. That, rather than a credal conformity, was the distinctive character of this group of scientists—a characteristic they share with many though not all scientists, as a sampling of scientific literature readily shows.

From those three points of consensus people might move to many differences on specific issues. There were, for example, sharp clashes on nuclear energy (see Chapter 13), on genetic experimentation (see Chapter 14), on the ethical validity of abortion (see Chapter 14 and the report of Section IV). More pervasive than these were two big differences that emerged repeatedly in the conference and that tell something about a cultural situation that influences our whole world.

The first of these differences centres in two pictures of science. It emerged early on (see Chapters 3 and 4) and never faded. In one picture science is a search for knowledge and a method for solving problems. Scientific honesty means a readiness to follow the evidence where it leads, to accept correction from others, to give up treasured ideas when experiment refutes them. Its methods break superstition and dogmatism. Applied to human problems, those methods bring healing of diseases, relief from drudgery, more and better foods, enhancement of human capabilities. But the motivation of science is never solely practical; in fact, even practice suffers if scientists give up the freedom for pure exploration and enlargement of understanding.

In this picture there is ready recognition that science can be misused. There is criticism of the fact that so much scientific work is funded by industries and governments for the sake of profit or military prowess. Dr Hanbury Brown, one of those who communicated this picture of science, was also one of the most emphatic in showing how industrialism and militarism had distorted science. But, in this picture, the glory of true science is to keep alive the quest for understanding.

In the other picture science is primarily power—power over nature and power over people. It is power in the hands of the powerful; it makes them more powerful at the expense of the weak. It is an instrument of conquest and exploitation. Its purported objectivity is a deceptive veil that—until it is ripped away—conceals its real intent and drive, a force which has plundered the earth and plundered people. There is no point in talking about an idealized science that gets distorted in practice. Science is what scientists do in the social situations where they work. Science and scientific technologies—they are virtually the same in this picture—are forces that protect privilege, impose oppression, and in our experience have inflicted pain and death.

The two pictures, put so baldly, drift towards caricature. But debate, whether in ecumenical conferences or elsewhere, usually includes some caricature. The two pictures appeared often in the conference. Sometimes they met in explicit clashes; frequently they were the determinative background for other clashes on more concrete issues.

The persuasiveness of either picture depends partly upon personal and social experience. One who has felt the thrill of scientific discovery or the esthetic lure of a new theory responds to the first picture. One who has experienced science as the tool of a conqueror or oppressor responds to the second. Some people respond to both.

The advocates of each picture met each other repeatedly in the conference. In discussion they made some concessions and reached some understanding. But it may be accurate to say that in the end each side felt that its position had not really been understood or appreciated by the other.

However, to repeat a point, the argument was not between scientists and theologians. Some scientists criticized science as emphatically as any theologians—or politicians or revolutionary ideologists. And some theologians rose repeatedly to affirm the values of science in the face of its critics.

The second big difference has some relation to the first. It might be called, too simply, the difference between the fighters and the inquirers. So stated, it is outrageously simple, because everybody in the conference was on some questions an inquirer and on some questions a fighter. But the simplification has its values in clarifying discussion.

The fighters, for present purposes, see the injustices in the world and take the side of the victims. The fighters see the intricate ways in which injustice is concealed. They want to expose it and oppose it. Any prolonged inquiry into the complexity of issues is a delaying action that hinders urgent effort to set things right. When argument is prolonged and complicated, the fighters want to know who is taking advantage of whom, who wants to drag out the argument and prevent action, whose power should be taken away. The fighters, at the conference as elsewhere in the world, tended to move every issue rather quickly into a political issue. If the talk was about science and the future, they moved the argument quickly to talk about justice, power and the future.

The inquirers, again for present purposes, say that effective action had better be intelligent action. They expect that the fighters may, in the grip of urgency, hurt people whom they want to help, like a medical student hastening to practise surgery without sufficient knowledge or skill. Agreeing that all acts take place in social and political contexts, they argue that understanding the risks of radiation or the biology of genetic diseases is a complex issue, in which accurate inquiry is important before one enters into political struggle. They see an ethical flaw in the craving for simple answers to complex questions, in commitment without adequate information and theory.

The conference debates were never so simple as to ask people to choose between fighting and inquiry. The issue was always what blend of two attitudes to work out. It was the question of which issues are calls to struggle and which are calls to further inquiry. The conference faced the predicament in several of its own decisions. For example, on the issue of disarmament it declared itself clearly and urged immediate action (see Chapter 16). But on several issues connected with biological research, abortion and medical practice it asked for a continuing study (see Chapter 14). And on the issue of nuclear energy it took an intermediate position, recommending an immediate action (the moratorium) for the purpose of further study as a basis for later decisions (see Chapter 13).

Section X, Towards a New Christian Social Ethic and New Social Policies for the Churches, identified this issue—the relation of forthright action and continuing inquiry—as one that surfaced repeatedly in the conference (see Volume 2, Report of Section X, sub-head "What certainties are possible in Christian ethics?").

The achievements of the conference

There is something both scientifically and theologically rash about claiming achievements for conferences. Scientifically, social causation is so intricate a subject that nobody ever knows, for certain, what the results of any conference are. Theologically, the most Christians can do is try to act in intelligence and faith, offering their actions to God to over-rule them or let them flourish.

But people do not go to conferences unless they hope to accomplish something. This conference was an attempt, both modest and bold, to help the churches face up to issues of faith, science and the future.

Its authority was primarily the persuasiveness of its findings, and that remains to be determined. Its formal authorization, from the Central Committee of the WCC, was fairly explicit:

1) to receive reports from sections and groups and commend them to the churches;
2) to make recommendations to the World Council of Churches;
3) to issue statements in its own name on topics pertaining to the agenda of the conference.

The conference did all these things. It did not and could not make policy for the WCC or for the churches.

The results of the conference can be considered in three categories. First, there are specific organizational consequences. The World Council of Churches, through the Executive Committee of its Central Committee, has already approved its resolution on disarmament (see Chapter 16) and distributed it widely. The WCC will be acting on other recommendations. If past experience is any guide, the conference will be one influence shaping WCC policies and programmes in coming years.

Likewise, member churches of the WCC are responding to the conference. Some are continuing its work with further programmes of their own, and some are incorporating its concerns in church school curricula and other educational activities. Both regionally and denominationally the work goes on.

Second, the conference has had some public impact. Press, radio and television coverage were extensive, especially in Europe and the United States. For the public at large such news is only a ripple in the flood of mass communications in our time. But it is at least a reminder of the moral and religious element in the continuous activities of society. To people who take for granted the technological changes that are influencing their lives, news about the conference is a stimulus to recognition that the uses of technology are not automatic, that people and societies decide how to incorporate technology in their lives, that important ethical decisions are often hidden under technical guise.

Some of the recommendations of the conference may also contribute a nudge to public opinion on some big issues. The resolution on disarmament, to take a single example, is getting wide circulation not only in church groups but also in scientific and technological organizations. It strengthens other groups working on the issue and, along with their efforts, it becomes one modest influence in the vast processes that form public opinion and national policies.

Third, the conference, with the many events leading up to it and the publications coming out of it, has an immeasurable effect upon the participants and, through them, on the churches and the public. It is primarily an educational event, leading to heightened awareness of what is going on in the world and how faith can meet that world. It leads people to do new things and change old ways of doing things. For example, a world famous scientist returns home from a WCC meeting and for the first time institutes a course in his university on ethical aspects of his science. Several other scientists, after drifting away from the churches of their childhood, find a new interest in the Church because they realize that the Church is interested in them and their work. A prominent African scientist readjusts a busy schedule to get to the conference, explaining: "People here listen to me, as they do not in other international gatherings, when I explain what technological and economic changes are doing to my country." Teachers of theology and ethics go home to revise their courses, set their students on new inquiries, write new books. Professional associations of teachers arrange programmes around themes of the conference. Requests come to Geneva from unexpected places and in unexpected numbers for copies of *Anticipation* and other publications of Church and Society.

Because scientific and technological change are going on everywhere, public education would take account of it quite apart from conferences of the WCC. But in ways both obvious and invisible the conference and the programmes surrounding it frequently heighten, sharpen and deepen attention.

In retrospect, certain events stand out as landmarks—or, better, timemarks—in the contemporary history of the churches. That was surely the case, we now know, with the Geneva Conference of 1966. A decade or two from now, the churches will know better how to assess the conference of 1979.

For the time being, let it be recorded that the conference is, at a minimum, an impressive testimony that the churches and the world have an immense stake in the uses of science and technology. As Humberto Cardinal Medeiros said in his opening welcome (of which excerpts are printed in the next chapter): "A Christian faith that ignores or disregards the marvels of scientific technology in agriculture, medicine and energy is unworthy of the name religion, and even more unworthy of the mystery of the incarnation." Both the burden and the promise of science and technology were the concern of the incarnational faith that motivated the conference on faith, science and the future.

Part One
Basic Issues

2. Expectations

Introduction

The conference began with an act of worship on Thursday morning, 12 July. The presiding leader was Metropolitan Paulos Gregorios of India, conference Moderator. The ecumenical spirit became evident immediately in the music: the stirring African drums and conch shell of Papa Oyeah Mackenzie of Ghana, the sounds of Bach from the baroque organ of MIT's Kresge auditorium, the choral music of Vaughan Williams sung by the men and boys choir of St Paul's Cathedral, Boston. Participants of several nations, churches and languages read the Scripture and led the prayers.

The opening meditation of Metropolitan Gregorios, based on Colossians 1:15-20, is printed in Chapter 7, "The Conference at Worship".

Following the worship and the opening greetings, Dr Philip Potter, General Secretary of the World Council of Churches, gave the keynote address on the topic: "Science and Technology: Why Are the Churches Concerned?"

Several messages of greeting expressed the high expectations for the conference. Chancellor Paul E. Gray of MIT, who has since been elected President of that institution, brought greetings from the host school and, speaking to the theme of the conference, said:

> "Meeting these challenges will require on our part an even greater consideration of human values and societal priorities in the application of science and in the development of engineering solutions to critical problems. And it will require on the part of theologians, I do believe, more flexible linkages with science and perhaps a greater willingness to accommodate its different point of view. This convergence, as I see it, is an experiment in that kind of collaboration. And it would be my hope that out of this collaboration, and out of this shared focus, could come for all of us new ideas and insights, new effectiveness in working together, and a renewal of faith."

Humberto Cardinal Medeiros, the Roman Catholic Archbishop of Boston, expressed gratitude that he had been invited by the leaders of the Protestant churches in Massachusetts to bring greetings from the churches of the area. Emphasizing the importance of the conference theme, he said:

> "Both science and faith are committed to the 'never-ending restlessness of man' which is the quest for truth. For too many people, religion and science have been contrasted and judged for too long to be two estranged or even alien methods of searching for the truth.

"A Christian faith that ignores or disregards the marvels of scientific technology in agriculture, medicine and energy is unworthy of the name of religion, and even more unworthy of the mystery of the incarnation. A technology that ignores or disregards the questions of Christian ethics, especially the value it places on man, will quickly reduce the earth to a desert, the person to an automaton, brotherly love to planned collectivization, and introduce death where God wishes life."

Claire Randall, General Secretary of the National Council of Churches of Christ in the USA, came to the conference from meetings with President Jimmy Carter at Camp David. She said:

"I believe that largely because of science and technology we have crossed a line in history, a line to where we humans have to live in a new dimension of the possibility to destroy our earth and to destroy human existence. This has raised many new and dramatic questions which have to be dealt with about life in the future as well as the present. It calls upon us to think in new ways about coming generations as well as about ourselves. It causes us to look in new ways at science and technology from the perspective of our faith...

"We are late, I believe, in discussing as broadly and as seriously as we must the issues you are addressing here. Thank God you are getting on with this urgent task."

President Carter was not able to accept an invitation to address the conference. Nor was Vice President Walter Frederick Mondale. Mondale's message of greeting, which arrived mid-way through the conference, follows:

"I wish to congratulate you on holding this remarkable conference. The speed of scientific discovery sometimes outpaces the speed of human understanding, and we must all work to close that gap—to make sure that humanity makes wise and peaceful use of the wonders of technology.

"From all over the world you have come to Cambridge to take up this task. Your commitment is as deep as your purpose is urgent. I wish you the very best for a successful conference."

Following the worship and the opening greetings, Dr Philip Potter, General Secretary of the World Council of Churches, gave the keynote address on the topic: "Science and Technology: Why Are the Churches Concerned?"

Dr Potter showed that the World Council of Churches and its predecessor movements, beginning with the Universal Conference on Life and Work (Stockholm, 1925), had expressed concern for a just human society and for the role of science and technology in producing such a society. He placed the theme of this conference within the general programme theme of the WCC, adopted at the Nairobi Assembly in 1975: Towards a Just, Participatory and Sustainable Society.

Striking a chord that was to resound often throughout the next two weeks, Dr Potter showed the ambivalence that the Church and much of human society feel towards science and the technologies related to it. On the one hand, he paid tribute to those values in science that echo deep traditions of the Bible and Christian faith: its "rigorous and relentless examination of reality to see what it yields", its "commonwealth" of sharing and mutual correction transcending national and ideological boundaries, its abilities to transform the world and lead to a better life. On the other hand, he showed that science always works within political and economic systems, that it brings more power to those who already have power, that it makes urgent the efforts for a society that is just and participatory and sustainable.

As one example of this theme, Dr Potter spoke of the close relation between the scientific-technological enterprise and the production of armaments. This issue was to emerge as one of the focal concerns of the entire conference.

Science and Technology: Why Are the Churches Concerned?

PHILIP POTTER

It is with awe and anticipation that I welcome you, on behalf of the World Council of Churches, to this conference. Awe, because never before have we had such a large company of scientists in a world ecumenical conference. Anticipation, because we have great expectations of this conference. The issues of faith, science and the future are burningly with us and we are looking for insights and answers for our world today.

This is a curious reversal of roles. You have been accustomed to clergy posing as pundits on all human questions and dilemmas. The laity have been regarded as recipients of their wisdom, not as partners in the search for truth in God's world. The curious thing is that, whenever clergy have felt unable to cope with issues put before them, they are very apt to say: "I am only a layman on this matter." That very phrase gives us away, because we clergy are only saying that we are ignorant and do not dare to speak with authority. We are, of course, also saying that on matters of theological and ecclesiastical importance we are the authorities and lay people are ignorant and unable to make a significant contribution. Nevertheless, thanks to the ecumenical movement, we have learned that *laos*, laity, means the whole people of God, and that we clergy constitute less than one per cent of the people of God. We have become more humble, and not least because of the power which natural and human scientists wield in today's world. Hence the feeling of awe and anticipation with which we approach this meeting. We have all come here to deliberate together on the central realities of our existence—God, humanity and creation and the inextricable relations between them.

It is scientists who pose ethical questions

The question I have been asked to wrestle with is why the churches are concerned about science and technology. In a way the churches are shy about science and technology because of the long and persistently negative attitude they adopted towards science since the sixteenth century, due to a false interpretation of Scripture.

It is, nevertheless, true that the application of scientific methods, from the nineteenth century, to the criticism of the Bible has helped to bring about a more tolerant attitude towards science. The Bible has been seen to be evidently not a book of science. It was also discovered that scientific enquiry was in the spirit of the biblical message that humanity is called to fulfil the mandate given by God to comprehend and master creation, to bring the unbridled forces of nature under human control and to replenish the earth. And all this is for "good", the wellbeing of all. During this century Christians have learned a great deal from science and scientists: the rigorous and relentless examination of reality to see what it yields; the commonwealth of science which knows no national or ideological frontiers and in which there is a mutual sharing of ideas and discoveries and mutual correction where wrong or false turnings in research have been detected; the monumental fruits of scientific enquiry and technological application which have transformed our world and opened out possibilities for a better life.

Moreover, scientists have become more modest in their claims than, say, before World War II. Albert Einstein, the hundredth anniversary of whose birth we celebrate this year, agonised over the uses to which governments were putting the results of atomic research. After the bombings of Hiroshima and Nagasaki, it is reported that Nils Bohr hurried to his bishop in Copenhagen and exclaimed: "I have come to ask pardon for being alive." Scientists and technologists are much more conscious of their social responsibility than in the past. Indeed, it is they who are posing acute ethical questions to the churches and theologians, whose traditional categories of thinking are hardly adequate for such an enterprise. This conference is taking place after years of fruitful encounter between scientists and theologians. There is a long hard road before us, and this meeting is a milestone on the way.

Perhaps it is because of these developments in a better understanding between faith and science that the churches and particularly the ecumenical movement have devoted far more emphasis to the uses to which people put the artefacts of science-based technology and to what end. The ecumenical movement, which is concerned about the purpose of God for the *oikoumene*, the world of human beings, has concentrated its attention on what kind of world of human beings is compatible with the Gospel of the Kingdom of God and his justice.

From individual enterprise to a just, global society

The Universal Conference on Life and Work, which met at Stockholm in August 1925, endorsed the aspirations of people for a "just and fraternal order, through which the opportunity shall be assured for the development, according to God's design, of the full manhood of every man". There is not much difference between this stated goal and the major programme emphasis agreed to by the WCC Central Committee after the Fifth Assembly at Nairobi in 1975: Towards a Just, Participatory and Sustainable Society.

In 1928 the International Missionary Council met in Jerusalem and gave much attention to "the Christian mission in relation to industrial problems in Asia and Africa". It said: "The Christian will welcome the triumphs of science and technical skill by which the resources which God has given to his children have been made more fully available for the service of all. But he will regard material wealth as an instrument, not as an end... He will desire that economic interests shall be, not the master, but the servant of civilization." The Council went on "to emphasize its conviction that the advancement, by thought and action, of social righteousness is an essential and vital part of the Christian message to mankind".

After several years of study, the 1937 Oxford Conference on Church, Community and State, had much to say about the existing economic order which had revealed its true character through successive technological improvements. This important conference declared:

> "It was thought at one time that the development of this new economic order would not only improve the material conditions of life but would also establish social justice. This expectation was rooted in the belief that a pre-established harmony would so govern the self-interest of individuals as to create the greatest possible harmony of society as a whole. 'Each man, seeking his own, would serve the commonwealth.' Today this belief is largely discredited... The same forces which had produced material progress have often enhanced inequalities, created permanent insecurity, and subjected all members of modern society to the domination of so-called independent economic 'laws'... Industrial expansion and technical progress have tended to defeat their own ends... Christians have a particular responsibility to make whatever contribution they can towards the transformation, and if necessary the thorough reconstruction, of the present economic and political system..."[1]

It will be noticed that in those early years of ecumenical social thought, science-based technology has always been related to the aims and actual performance of economic and political systems. This was summed up by the First Assembly of the World Council of Churches in 1948 in its analysis of the contribution of the "undirected developments of technology" to the disorder of society. It went on to speak of the need for a "responsible society" which it defined as follows:

> "A responsible society is one where freedom is the freedom of men who acknowledge responsibility to justice and public order, and where

[1] *The Churches Survey Their Task*. Report of the Conference on Church, Community and State, Oxford, 1937, Vol. VIII. London: George, Allen & Unwin, 1937, p. 99 f.

those who hold political authority or economic power are responsible for its exercise to God and the people whose welfare is affected by it."[2]

The Assembly was tacitly calling for responsible science and technology. In the following years ecumenical discussion paid increasing attention to the role of science and technology in shaping or re-enforcing the power structures of society. At the World Conference on Church and Society in 1966 much was said about the new kind of world being created by modern technology. It stated:

> "Technological society is based on a continuous and consistent process of change which affects all men. It leads to a concentration of power in the hands of relatively few with the danger of its misuse by privileged groups and the destruction of democracy by a decision-making technocracy. At the same time, as technological change advances, its complexity demands interdepèndence and cooperation. If technological change is to serve human needs, the rate of change must be governed by a primary consideration for human welfare... —At its best, technology can be part of man's historic search for truth and justice, and from this search it derives its real meaning... —Political power plays a crucial role in determining the pace and purpose of technological development. Today such power is exercised not only by public officials but also by technologists, even though they may be reticent to admit it. When technologists advise politicians or make policy themselves, they are making political decisions and must do so within a just and viable decision-making system... —We suggest that the just and humane use of technology requires that every individual participate in the decision-making system to a degree commensurate with his capacity to do so."[3]

Two years later the Uppsala Assembly of the World Council bravely launched an appeal for rapid world development through the transfer of technology from the rich to the poorer nations. It was soon discovered that this was an inadequate way of proceeding because it left the unjust structures of society and of relations between nations untouched. The 1974 world conference on Science and Technology for Human Development recognized the problem and spoke of the "need for the invention of social mechanisms which will enable science and technology to serve social justice at all levels". At the Nairobi Assembly, in the section on "Human Development: Ambiguities of Power, Technology and Quality of Life", a strong warning note was struck:

---

[2] *The First Assembly of the World Council of Churches, Amsterdam, 1948.* Ed. W. A. Visser 't Hooft. London: SCM Press, 1949, p. 77.

[3] *Christians in the Technical and Social Revolution of Our Time.* World Conference on Church and Society, 1966. Geneva: WCC, 1967, p. 188 ff.

"It is the considered view of many scientists and technologists that the world is on a catastrophic course leading to mass starvation, global depletion of resources, and global environmental deterioration. The responsibility that now confronts humanity is to make a deliberate transition to a sustainable global society in which science and technology will be mobilized to meet the basic physical and spiritual needs of people, minimize human suffering, and to create an environment which can sustain a decent quality of life for all people. This will involve a radical transformation of civilization, new technologies, new uses for technology, and new global economic and political systems."[4]

Control of technology gives control of development

It is in the light of this long development of thought on the place of science and technology that this conference on Faith, Science and the Future has been planned, in the framework of an overall programme emphasis on "Towards a Just, Participatory and Sustainable Society" in God's design. The issues of faith and science have to be seen concretely in that context. Any attempt to articulate afresh a doctrine of creation and of humanity must be done in the context both of God's revelation in history and of the actualities and longings of creation and humanity in history.

How, then, are we to approach our work during this conference? There can be no doubt about the profound contribution of science and technology in alerting us to the urgent necessity to create "a sustainable global society in which science and technology will be mobilized to meet the basic physical and spiritual needs of society". We are particularly grateful to all those who, through the World Council's programme on Church and Society, have hammered out this basic concept of a sustainable society during these past ten years or so. There can be no just society which is not sustainable, that is, which does not nourish a creation which provides the means by which people can truly share the inheritance of the earth so that each and all can fully be and maintain themselves in freedom and community. We have received a massive documentation on this matter. We shall be hearing many speeches on it. We shall also be discussing it in our sections and groups. The question is: Can science and technology fulfil the role which they project for themselves? That is a question which people are asking all over the world. It is important for us to face the limitations of science and technology as they are carried out at present.

The report to the Club of Rome, *Reshaping the International Order*, under the guidance of the famous Dutch economist, Jan Tinbergen, who has been active in our ecumenical discussions, states:

---

[4] *Breaking Barriers, Nairobi 1975*. Ed. David M. Paton. London: SPCK & Grand Rapids, Mich.: Wm B. Eerdmans, 1976, p. 125.

> "Nowhere is the disparity between the industrialized and third world countries more marked than in the field of scientific research and technological development. Although 90% of all the technologists and scientists that have ever lived are alive today, over 90% are at work in the industrialized countries. Over 90% of their activities are concentrated on research for the rich world and on converting their findings into protected technical processes. The rich minority thus commands an overwhelming proportion of techno-scientific development."

Furthermore, it is said that over 50% of scientists and technologists are engaged in arms research and development. Arms production wastes the resources of the earth. It takes away from the production of goods which would meet the needs of the people. Such arms research and development is carried out in secret and the cost is kept secret from the people.

Participation essential for sustainable society

These facts beg the question: Who decides the areas of scientific research and development and the use of the results of such research and development? The general impression one gets is that only governments and big corporations can provide the necessary funds and facilities for scientific and technological research and development. How free then are scientists and technologists? The traditional posture of scientists is that it is only in freedom that they can work and that the results of their work are public. Their raison d'être is the search for truth in the Greek sense of *aletheia*, that which is not hidden and confined, but which is disclosed and open for all to see. Or, if we use the Hebrew sense of *'emeth*, that which is true to itself, which is trustworthy and faithful to one's being. It is interesting to note that the Hebrew word for righteousness, justice, *sedeq*, means the ability to maintain oneself, to act according to one's nature, to have firmness and strength, integrity of character. In its social application, it means mutual acknowledgment of persons, mutual maintenance of each other's honour and integrity, enabling one another to maintain themselves and to play their full part in the life of the covenant community. Truth and justice are therefore closely related, as the Psalmist sings: "Truth will spring up from the ground, and righteousness, justice, will look down from the sky. Yea, the Lord will give what is good, and our land will yield its increase" (Ps. 85:11-12). Sustainability depends on truth and justice and the gift of what is good. It has been rightly said that "the good" is that which increases communication and multiplies responsibilities.

What I am trying to hint at is that a just and sustainable society is impossible without a society which is participatory. In the present situation of science and technology, they are not really participatory, or rather they are forced to be biased on the side of those who wield economic and political power. There is little sign that they are on the side of the oppressed, the deprived and the marginalized, or simply the people. Science and technology might claim to be objective and universal, but this claim is not borne out in reality. The whole drift of ecumenical social thought, especially in recent years, is that participation in decision-making is an essential dimension in the cause of justice for all and for fullness of life for all.

A paper presented to the Central Committee of the World Council of Churches earlier this year described participation as follows: "Participation calls for a recognition of everybody's right to be consulted, to be heard and understood, whatever their political, economic or social status may be in society. Everyone must be involved in planning and action, giving as well as receiving. Participation means that each one takes initiative in formulating or changing policies and becoming involved in directing their implementation." What does that mean concretely when we consider the highly complex situation of science and technology? I will attempt to give a few quick examples.

Implications of participation for science and technology

Fourteen years ago we had the meeting of the Executive Committee of the World Student Christian Federation here in MIT. We were trying to understand how this world renowned institution works. One celebrated professor in the social sciences told us of a research project which he and his colleagues did for the US government. They were asked to study certain trouble spots during those stormy years of the civil rights movement. They chose Watts County in California. They accurately predicted that, in view of the total situation of discontent, which they described in detail, there would be riots during the hot summer. The report was duly handed to the government. Nothing was done about it. The riots took place, as predicted. Could not that report have been given to the public by the professor, or at least to those in California, both black and white, who could have done something about it? The professor was himself convinced that had there been participation of a wide variety of people at different levels of power something could indeed have been done.

We have been talking a great deal about the acceleration of arms production and of the arms race. This is par excellence the field in which scientists and technologists are most involved. They know what is going on. They know the wastage of resources and the need to switch arms industries into socially viable projects. There is a certain mystification surrounding arms production. The public is kept in ignorance about the real costs and the purposes of the spiralling arms race. And yet, research institutes and the special session of the UN last year have demonstrated that if the community were better informed and were allowed to express themselves on options for their nations, there could be a way of halting the arms race and achieving genuine disarmament. After all, the decisions about arming are taken by human beings. Disarmament could also be willed by human beings. What is the role of science and technology in helping to demystify the situation, and dispelling the feeling of helplessness and hopelessness which is so widespread?

One of the issues which will certainly be highlighted at this meeting is nuclear energy. It is well known that scientists and technologists are not agreed about the safety of nuclear power stations. It is equally evident that the problems are probably soluble. Nevertheless, people have been kept in ignorance about the hazards involved. They have not had a chance to discuss the issues and make responsible decisions about them. Therefore when accidents occur both the authorities and the scientific establishment are brought into question. The WCC sub-unit on Church and Society did an excellent job in bringing together a wide variety of people, including top scientists, and making known for discussion the options before people in Christian perspective. The debate has been fierce, but it is a genuine debate about real issues.

For some fifteen years now the World Council has sponsored a programme called Urban and Industrial Mission, with over 2,500 contact groups around the world. These are groups of workers or unemployed who organize themselves in people's movements to affirm their rights to work, to a decent wage, to adequate living and working conditions, and to a technology which is appropriate for meeting the needs of the people. It has proved extremely difficult to have any viable dialogue with the town and industrial planners and the science-based technologists. This lack of dialogue invariably brings about frustration and anger on both sides, with the powers using harsh methods to silence the people. Thus science and technology are seen by the people to be on the side of oppression and injustice.

Medical science has tended to concentrate on highly sophisticated and expensive plants and expertise. But it is estimated that, especially in the poorer countries of the world, only about 7% of the community is served by hospitals in which all this equipment and expertise are centred. The World Council's Christian Medical Commission has been experimenting on community health care, which includes involving the people themselves in delivering health care as far as their knowledge and experience will permit, using and improving through medical science the local medicines, and concentrating on the people as a healing community. This is an example of how participation of both the community and medical scientists can transform the situation of health and healing, especially when coupled with the participation of the people in their own development in self-reliance.

These examples or stories point to the necessity for participation as the way of sharing power towards a more just and sustainable society. Science and technology are not neutral or value free, but are instruments of power, and that means political power. How, then, can science and technology become the vehicles, not for legitimizing and perpetuating the structures of injustice, but for opening up the possibilities for structures of social control, which include all the people? To my mind, this is the central issue before this conference. It is the issue because we are concerned about faith and the future.

Faith is first of all a call to repentance, *metanoia*, the radical change of our thinking and outlook, of our style of life and, indeed, of our whole being towards God in Christ and towards our fellow human beings. It is an act of sharing in the death of Christ—the crucifixion of our self-regarding existence, and in the resurrection of Christ—the affirmation of the impossible becoming real, of life being wrested from death. Faith in the crucified and risen Lord is, therefore, a radical break with a static understanding of our existence into dynamic living and daring God's future. To have faith is to hope and to act in hope through love. Such faith, hope and love liberate us to struggle for a just, participatory and sustainable society. That is our calling as Christians and as scientists and technologists. May I end with the words of the first series of consultations on our theme in 1971: "May the Christian hope in the Creator, the crucified and risen Lord Jesus Christ, and the continuing work of the Holy Spirit, be the dynamic inspiration for our plans, our visions, and our active responsibility for the future."

3. What Is Science?

Introduction

As the conference entered into its work, it inquired into the meaning of two of the words in its title: science and faith. The preparatory work for this inquiry included the following: (1) a WCC consultation, "Science and Faith", Mexico City, 1975, recorded in *Anticipation*, No. 22, May 1976; (2) a second WCC consultation, "The Ideological and Theological Debate about Science", Cambridge (England), 1977, recorded in *Anticipation*, No. 25, January 1979; (3) Chapter 2, "Faith, Science and Human Understanding", in the preparatory book, *Faith, Science and the Future*. Some of the participants, of course, had engaged in long studies of the issue and had involved themselves in many of the world's studies of faith and science.

Beginning with the definition and interpretation of science, the conference called on the eminent Australian astronomer, Hanbury Brown, to interpret the nature of science. In the light of subsequent discussions, two of Brown's themes took on special importance.

First, he showed the meaning of science in view of recent changes in its milieu. He began with the classical understanding of science as the search for objective, verifiable truth. Then he described how the " industrialization" of science—its alliance with political and economic institutions—has modified the classical understanding. But he then reaffirmed, in a qualified way, the importance of objectivity and verifiability. And he testified that the value of science is its understanding of the world, both "for its own sake" and for the sake of human progress.

Second, Brown emphasized that scientific concepts are metaphors and abstractions related to an essentially mysterious reality. Within science itself, differing metaphors and abstractions are recognized to be "complementary" not antagonistic. On a similar basis, he argued, a duly modest science and faith can be appreciated as complementary responses of persons to the ultimate mysteries of existence.

The programme provided for two responses from the platform to Brown. The first was from Rubem Alves, Brazilian theologian and social philosopher. In a dramatic confrontation he stated that science, objectively understood, must be recognized in its social, practical functions and that these are, in fact, destructive to the interests of many of the world's peoples.

The second response came from Kenyan scientist, W. Mutu Maathai. She described the eagerness with which much of the Third World welcomes science, even while asking for its redirection. Later in the conference she spoke forcefully on the misuse of science in armaments, but her initial statement included probably the most enthusiastic endorsement of science, at its best, in any of the plenary meetings.

The Nature of Science

ROBERT HANBURY BROWN

Science is a word that worries me. Like the word Art it shows signs of wear: it has been used for too many things. Many of us, I suspect, especially when we go round galleries of modern art, have misgivings about the meaning of the word art. I often feel the same way about science. Advertisements reassure us that some toothpaste or patented medicine has been "scientifically" tested, or we are told that scientists have discovered this or that, the origin of the universe or how to grow bigger tomatoes. I often wonder what we mean by science.

To those of you who are not working scientists, let me say that science, like religion, needs to be lived. It is easy to present the body of science without the spirit, to show the dry bones without the sense of excitement, of community and progress and of the dedication which science inspires in so many of its followers.

What, then, is this thing called Science?

A conventional description of science—the sort of thing one reads in a book on the philosophy of science written a few years ago—goes like this:

1. Science, viewed as a process, is a social activity in which we seek to discover and understand the natural world, not as we would prefer or imagine it to be, but as it really is. The characteristic method of science is the rational, objective, and as far as possible impersonal, analysis of problems based mainly on observational data and experiment.

2. Science, viewed as a product, is the public knowledge of what we have so far found out, and about which the scientific community has agreed. Scientific knowledge is therefore limited to statements on which agreement can be reached and is always open to verification or disproof by anyone. A scientific fact can never be "original" in the same sense as a work of art; only its discovery can be truly original.

3. Science, viewed as an ethical paradigm, is, so Merton[1] tells us, a community governed by four imperatives—universalism, communalism, disin-

---

[1] R.K. Merton: *The Sociology of Science*. Chicago: Chicago University Press, 1973.

terestedness and organized scepticism. Universalism implies that science is independent of race, colour or creed; it is essentially international. Communalism implies that scientific knowledge is public knowledge: disinterestedness is, so to speak, the opposite of propaganda: organized scepticism requires each individual to accept nothing simply on the word of authority.

Now, many working scientists, not counting amateur philosophers of science, would probably accept this conventional description of science as a fair picture. They might perhaps think of it as being a bit old-fashioned, even romantic, but nevertheless, on the right track. The trouble is, of course, that players often see least of the game, and the nature of science is changing. In fact, it has changed so much in recent years that the conventional description now applies only to that minor, but very important, part of science which seeks to understand the world, rather than to change it. I shall call this fundamental science to distinguish it from applied science.

Industrialized science allied with power

To arrive at a more realistic description of modern science, we must take notice of the fact that in the past few decades science has been industrialized and has allied itself with power. In changing the world it has changed itself, so that the manifest, dominant activity of science is no longer the disinterested pursuit of knowledge but the pursuit of knowledge for industry and other social purposes, such as defence, agriculture, health and so on. I won't weary you with statistics, but less than 5% of the world's expenditure on science is now devoted to fundamental science. The vast majority of scientists are busy applying science to reach material and social goals, and their work is largely controlled by governmental agencies serving national, military and civil interests and by large industrial firms serving the market.

The industrialization of science has transformed not only the goals of science, but also the practice of science as a craft. Scientific research has taken on many of the features which we usually associate with industrial processes; much of it is done by large teams using large and expensive machinery. As a consequence, research tends to concentrate in the highly developed countries. It has been estimated that only 4% of the world's research and development is conducted in areas of the world where 70% of the population live. This change in the craft of science is also true of most fundamental research. You only have to compare the discovery of moons of Jupiter by Galileo in 1610 with the recent observation of these moons by Voyager I, or to visit a modern high-energy physics laboratory to see how these parts of science have taken on the character of an industry.

Industrialization has also transformed the ethos of much of science, as modern critics, such as Ravetz, Roszak, Habermas, Marcuse, Hilary and Steven Rose are so fond of telling us. The four imperatives which we have listed cannot possibly be obeyed by most of those engaged in applied science. Universalism, communalism and disinterestedness are inconsistent with most military or industrial research. Thus much of science has lost some of those precious qualities which flow from the four imperatives. Inevitably, the public respect for science has declined and this, in turn, has weakened its authority. This is one of the many reasons why we must always preserve a significant body of science which is not controlled closely by agencies primarily interested in its application.

Bearing in mind these recent changes in the character of science, I will now discuss some of the principal points which seem to me to be particularly relevant to the relations between science and faith. I shall not be able to give much time to the economics and politics of science.

All science is based on observation and experiment

First let us look at the role of observation and experiment. Histories of science are usually written in terms of outstanding people like Newton and Einstein, and they give the impression that the progress of science depends largely on the development of new theories. It would be nearer the truth to say that all science, both fundamental and applied, depends largely on the development of new instruments. The progress of astronomy, for example, owes more to two technological inventions, the telescope and the spectroscope, than to any other factor, and yet very few astronomers could tell you who invented them. Likewise, biology and medical science would not have got very far without the microscope. In our own day, the revolutionary knowledge of the structure of complex proteins and the mechanisms of heredity owes much to the X-ray diffractometer and the computer. Science and technology have always gone forward hand in hand. J.B. Conant[2] once said: "Science owes more to the steam-engine than the steam-engine owes to science."

Our knowledge of the world is often initiated, and always limited, by our present tools of observation. It is true that theories often precede and suggest observations, but, in the long run, all theories must be consistent with observations if they are to survive.

Science and values

Our conventional description says that science is based on the impersonal analysis of observational data. This leads to the question, how much of our scientific picture is impersonal and how much does it reflect our own values? Any student of history knows part of the answer. Science is a social activity and its history cannot be separated from the history of anything else.

Quite clearly the choice of topics of science is strongly influenced by our current interests and values. At any given time, our scientific picture shows some aspects of nature in much greater detail than others because they are of greater current interest; they may perhaps be relevant to industry or war. In the fifteenth and sixteenth centuries, for example, when the world was being

---

[2] J.B. Conant: *Science and Common Sense*. New Haven: Yale University Press, 1961.

explored and opened up to trade, there was a strong mercantile interest in developing navigation, which necessarily involved quite abstruse and fundamental studies of the motion of the moon and the distance of the sun.

In our own times we do not have to look any further than space research to see the connection between our detailed knowledge of the surface of the moon and military interests. In the civil field only a small fraction of the world's research and development is directly concerned with the needs of the poorest, but relatively large, fraction of the world's population.

Before we leave this point, I would like to draw your attention to a paradox in the pursuit of relevance. The demand that science should be more relevant to the things which society values and that scientists should be more socially responsible is, I believe, usually justified and certainly to be expected as the cost of science to the community increases. There is, however, one problem which is so often overlooked. The relevance of scientific work can only be judged on a short time scale; over long periods it is impossible. It takes roughly one generation for the results of new experimental science to reach application and much longer for new mathematics. Thus most of the recent ideas of modern physics depend upon mathematics which was invented, but not applied, in the previous century. I doubt whether many of the discoveries on which modern science rests, such as the discovery of the electron, would have been funded by agencies assessing their relevance. Paradoxically, our interests are best served, in the long run, by research which is guided largely by its own internal logic and not by our immediate needs. We must seek to understand the world for its own sake, not just for ours. Necessity is the mother of invention but not of discovery.

It is also clear that our values influence what we accept as "scientific knowledge". Thus the history of the theory of the heliocentric universe, from Copernicus onwards, reflects on one side a religious preference for a man-centred universe, and on the other a mystical idea about the central importance of the sun coupled with a preference for conceptual economy. Nearer our time there is the opposition to the probabilistic ideas of quantum mechanics, for example by Einstein, on the grounds of a prejudice against a universe ruled by chance. In the comparatively immature, but extremely complex, science of genetics, we can point to the well-worn example of the theories of environmental genetics advanced in the 1940's by the agronomist T.D. Lysenko, ideas which were accepted as science largely because they were politically and ideologically welcome. Judging from recent controversies in the USA it is still difficult to get value-free science on analogous questions of heredity and environment.

In brief, at any given epoch, the process and the product of science are both coloured by the current values of society.

The nature of reality

Let us now look more closely at what, in conventional description, is implied by discovering and understanding the world "as it really is".

A stone is real, not imaginary; it is a solid, inert lump which, if thrown through a glass window will break the glass. And yet modern science tells us that the inside of this stone is mostly space, very peculiar space filled with vacuum fluctuations and "virtual" particles; and in this space there are protons, electrons, and so on which sometimes behave as waves and sometimes as billiard balls and which may, themselves, be made up of other mysterious entities called quarks. To be sure, science agrees that our stone is inert and, if we want to throw it back, we can predict its path precisely by Newton's laws of motion or, even more precisely, by Einstein's general theory of relativity. But this apparently simple quality of inertia is itself a mystery; some scientists think that it depends upon the interaction of the stone with all the other bodies in the universe, and some do not.

Clearly our concept of a "real stone" is an abstraction from the wider properties of stones based on our experience of seeing and feeling stones. It is a metaphor which, in terms of our everyday experience, describes something more fundamental, more complicated and essentially mysterious. Broadly speaking, we can think of the whole scientific picture of the world in the same way, as a metaphor which describes and relates the abstractions we make by observation from a more complex, possibly infinitely complex, reality. These abstractions are chosen and limited, partly by our own theories and values and partly by our tools of observation. So our picture of reality is necessarily incomplete and provisional. It can never claim to be absolute truth; but it is the best picture we have.

Does "reality" reflect the structure of our minds?

There is another more profound question which we can ask about the impersonal nature of scientific knowledge. But first, may I remind you of Eddington's[3] story of the ichthyiologist who explored the life of the ocean with a net which had a two-inch mesh. He came to the conclusion that all fish are longer than two inches. This little parable prompts us to ask to what extent scientific knowledge is shaped and limited by the structure of our minds.

Our experience of physics in this century has made us cautious of answering this question. We have found that all the phenomena of nature cannot be explained or described in terms of our familiar, common-sense concepts of space, time, causality, identity, and even of locality. Common sense cannot interpret the behaviour of objects which are very small, like atoms, or very large, like the universe, or moving with speeds approaching the velocity of light. To bring this behaviour within the discipline of science we have had to learn to think in new ways. A good example is to be found in quantum mechanics where we have had to exchange certainty for probability. We have reached the remarkable conclusion that it is fundamentally impossible to pre-

---

[3] A.S. Eddington: *The Philosophy of Physical Science*. Cambridge, England: Macmillan, 1939.

dict what an individual particle or proton will certainly do, no matter how much we know about it. We can only predict what it will probably do by a calculus which involves waves of probability. These waves of probability cannot be detected by any physical observation; they exist, so to speak, only in our mathematical minds.

What, we may ask, must the world be like, in order that man may know it? Shall we always be able to develop uncommon-sensical concepts to relate and predict phenomena as yet undiscovered? It remains to be seen.

Is the observer part of the picture?

There is yet another question which brings out the nature of scientific knowledge rather well. How does this knowledge depend upon the act of enquiry? Is the observer, so to speak, part of the picture? The common-sense answer is obviously "yes" when we are looking at living things, especially at ourselves; but it is "no" when we are looking at the inanimate world. We think of stones as having objective existence which is quite independent of us. As Gertrude Stein might have said: "A stone is a stone is a stone."

One of the great surprises of the present century has been to learn from physics that this common-sense view of our relations with the inanimate world is wrong or, to be kinder, is only an approximation to the truth. Our concept of a "thing" is based on a limited set of abstractions which we ourselves choose to make from a more complex reality. Thus the concept of a thing, and the intrinsic properties which we ascribe to it, depend upon what particular set of abstractions we select; in other words, it depends on the particular class of observations which we choose to carry out and therefore also on the theory which guides our choice. One of the most common intellectual errors is to confuse a concept or symbol with reality and to use it outside its proper domain of validity; in religious terms this is the sin of idolatry.

In the present century physicists have come to realize that by making different abstractions from reality it is possible to arrive at quite different, even contradictory, concepts of the "thing" which is being observed. A familiar, but not unique, example of this remarkable fact is to be found in the theory of light. As you will know, the modern theory of light accepts that light behaves either as an indubitable wave or as an indubitable particle, depending on the type of observation we choose to make. We have given up trying to make common-sense out of its properties, and if asked what light is really like, we can only answer "light is like light" and offer a mathematical theory which will predict its behaviour in any given situation. The point is, of course, that light is neither a particle nor a wave, but something infinitely more complicated, something we cannot visualize in terms of everyday experience. And yet these two concepts, the particle and the wave, are both valid within their own limited domain; physicists call them complementary.

It does not follow that scientific knowledge is subjective. Admittedly, the observer does enter our picture of the world by selecting the particular set of abstractions on which the picture is based. Furthermore, these abstractions cannot be thought of as being intrinsic to the thing itself; they are interactions between the thing and the observer. Nevertheless, the actual observations of these interactions, the data on which our picture is based, remain truly objective. They are independent of the particular observer and can be verified by anyone, even by a machine. In brief, they are public knowledge.

Before we go any further, may I draw your attention to two important, and unfamiliar ideas, in this discussion of scientific knowledge. Firstly, that a particular concept of reality is valid only in a limited domain. Secondly, that it is possible to arrive quite objectively at two contradictory, but nevertheless, complementary concepts of the same thing, both of which are valid within their own field. Truth, indeed, has many faces.

Does science progress?

[Here Dr Hanbury Brown, in a part of his paper omitted in the public presentation, argues that science, although it may never "converge on some central truth", progresses in two ways: (1) it solves many specific problems, and (2) it develops "more and more powerful generalizations, laws of nature, which extend our ability to explain, relate, and predict the diverse phenomena which mark the frontiers of science". In this way it gives "progressively truer images of the world".]

Why bother about science?

Why should we bother about science? Most people, if asked that question would, I guess, talk about the practical uses of science. They would point to the very real contributions which science and technology have made to our health and wealth. No doubt they would also point to some of the things they fear like pollution, nuclear power, genetic engineering and so on. Some, perhaps rather few, would point to the contributions that science has made to our culture in the same way as music and painting. Science, they would say, is worthwhile for its own sake—*ars pro gratia artis.*

In my view, these arguments for science are too shallow. Science is not just a modern cargo cult; nor is it just an ornament of society; nor is it just an intellectual pastime. Modern science is one of the greatest achievements of the mind and spirit of man; it is not to be treated simply as an instrument of social and political purpose. It is one of the main, indispensable pillars on which our civilization and our hopes for the future rest. May I point to some of the reasons why I believe this to be true.

SCIENCE AND RIGHT ACTION

To act rightly we must always be making value judgments in which we weigh profit and loss, freedom and justice, beauty and truth; and to do this we need all the science we can get. Most of the problems of the modern world involve detailed scientific knowledge, and it is the obvious responsibility of scientists to alert us to the social implications of scientific advances and to help us, in terms we can understand, to apply them wisely. As William Blake wrote: "He who would do good to another must do it in Minute Particulars. General Good is the plea of the scoundrel, hypocrite and flatterer, for Art and Science cannot exist but in minutely organized Particulars." (I hope, by the way, that you will not misinterpret that quotation as being a general attack on the possibility or on the value of trying to do Good!)

SCIENCE AND "WELTANSCHAUUNG"

Let us now turn to the influence of science on our world-view. One of the four main elements in the ethos of science, as I said before, is "organized scepticism". We must remember that one of the dangers to any society, especially since the development of mass communications, is that it might become credulous. The antidote to credulity is scepticism.

Anyone who has studied the trial of Galileo, the controversy over evolution between Wilberforce and Huxley or the "monkey" trials at Dayton, will know that human institutions preserve ideas as rocks preserve fossils. One of the principal cultural functions of science is to prevent this happening, and to keep our ideas flexible and, above all, realistic by pointing continuously to the way the world, to the best of our current knowledge, actually is. In doing so, science fulfils the classic role of destroying superstition.

Consider, for a moment, the profound changes in our world-view brought about by Copernicus when he removed the earth from the centre of the universe, and by Newton when he developed the science of celestial mechanics. In the present century we have seen equally great changes. The earth is now a planet of a minor star in a galaxy of billions of other stars, and the galaxy itself is one among millions and millions of other galaxies which stretch away as far as our most powerful telescopes can see. The same sort of readjustment of perspective has taken place in time. Modern cosmology has given us an immense past and an equally immense future. Astrophysics has shown us how the heavy elements of which we are all made were evolved in stars from primeval hydrogen. Thus astronomy, geology and biology have placed the evolution of the earth and of the human being in a vast tract of time. What effects this new perspective will have on our culture it is still too early to say; but one thing we can already see. All modern science, the whole study of evolution from the Big Bang to man, points to an old and powerful idea, to the unity of human beings and their environment, and to their need to live in harmony with it. And there is more to come; what, for example, will be the effects on our society of understanding the mechanism of heredity, the mechanism of mind? Or even, perhaps, communication with other worlds?

If our ideas about ourselves and the world we live in are to be flexible and realistic, then we shall have to keep an eye on the picture of the world presented by science. We must always be prepared to revise our ideas in the light of what we see; and this, of course, applies equally well to the teaching of the Church.

Science and imagination

I now want to say a word about imagination, because the prophets of the counter-culture (e.g. T. Roszak[4]) are always telling us that science is an enemy of the imagination, and I believe this to be profoundly untrue. To be sure, wisdom and vision both need imagination, but history shows us clearly that imagination must always retain contact with "objective truth", the sort of truth which science offers. Beliefs and institutions guided by unrestrained imagination go stale and, sooner or later, turn into fantasy—and very nasty fantasies too. Consider, for example, the religious practices of the Aztecs. Not only does science keep imagination's feet on the ground, but it enriches it because, as Bronowski[5] was so fond of pointing out, "the strength of the imagination, its enriching power and excitement, lies in its interplay with reality—physical and emotional". No one could have foreseen or imagined the beauty and the complexity of nature as revealed by science.

Science and faith

How, in our own times, can we make it easier for faith and science to work together as faith and art have done in previous centuries? Newton certainly thought that it could be done in his day and so did the Deists after him. But it did not take long for science and religion to become enemies—what went wrong? The fault, needless to say, lay on both sides. In their enthusiasm for celestial mechanics or for the theory of evolution many scientists, like Laplace, saw no need for God. The supporters of religion, on the other hand, confused the powerful symbolic ideas which they had inherited from the past with reality, and so they fought a losing battle with science. Thus, Thomas Huxley won his battle about evolution with Bishop Wilberforce. No doubt he should have won but not, I think, so easily.

To this day there are people who carry on these old battles, but fight under different banners and on different grounds. Some, for example, tell us that the ideals of science have been so eroded by its alliance with power that it has little to offer us, apart from material goods. This argument, I suspect, we have heard before in the context of the Church. To save time, I suggest that it is no more a valid reason for turning away from the values of science than it was for turning away from the Christian Faith.

Others attack science because they say it removes the sense of mystery from the world and dehumanizes us by its emphasis on objectivity. But I think that we must dispel the idea that science removes mystery from the world. It is true, of course, that science does remove minor mysteries, such as the mechanism of heredity, but in doing so it shows us where the major mysteries really are.

---

[4] T. Roszak: *The Making of a Counter Culture*. London: Faber, 1970.
[5] J. Bronowski: *A Sense of the Future*. Cambridge, Mass.: MIT Press, 1977.

As I said earlier, our scientific knowledge is based on abstractions which we choose to make from a more complex, essentially mysterious, reality. All our ideas about the world, about time, space, fundamental particles, light and so on, are therefore symbolic entities which are themselves mysterious. As for the great mysteries which stand in the shadows of all human thought, such as the origin and purpose of the world, modern science cannot be accused of sweeping them away. The mystery of Creation is intact, pushed back by twenty billion years, but, nevertheless, where it always was—in the beginning. Nor has science anything to say about the purpose of the world. In brief, everything we know is bounded by mysteries. Science relates us to these mysteries impersonally through objective knowledge; art and religion relate us to them personally through beauty, meaning, and purpose. Thus in the domain of science, as the critics rightly point out, there is no room for the supernatural; what they overlook is that the natural is mysterious enough.

Secondly, I think we must accept that the scientific vision of the world is neither a rival nor an alternative to any other point of view. It is an essential part of learning to be at home in this mysterious universe and of making the best of it and of ourselves. At the same time, we must recognize that this "public" vision of the world is not the only one. Modern physics has demonstrated, for all to see, the importance of complementarity in human understanding. It seems that there are many things, perhaps everything, which cannot be understood from one point of view. It is therefore essential to explore other points of view but, as science tell us, it is equally important to realize that every point of view has a limited domain of validity.

Finally, I suggest that we should accept the pursuit of science as a moral duty. Not only is it essential to making a better world, but it is a dynamic revelation of the marvellous and mysterious world in which we live.

As a poet[6] has written,

> Unless the eye catch fire,
> the God will not be seen,
> Unless the ear catch fire,
> The God will not be heard,
> Unless the tongue catch fire,
> The God will not be named,
> Unless the heart catch fire,
> The God will not be loved,
> Unless the mind catch fire,
> The God will not be known.

Modern science can, I believe, help Faith to set the mind on fire.

---

[6]T.S. Eliot: *Where the Wasteland Ends*. New York: Doubleday, 1973.

On the Eating Habits of Science
A Response by Rubem Alves

Let me tell you a parable. Once upon a time a lamb, with a love for objective knowledge, decided to find out the truth about wolves. He had heard so many nasty stories about them. Were they true? He decided to get a first-hand report on the matter. So he wrote a letter to a philosopher-wolf with a simple and direct question: What are wolves? The philosopher-wolf wrote a letter back explaining what wolves were: shapes, sizes, colours, social habits, thought, etc. He thought, however, that it was irrelevant to speak about the wolves' eating habits since these habits, according to his own philosophy, did not belong to the *essence* of wolves. Well, the lamb was so delighted with the letter that he decided to pay a visit to his new friend, the wolf. And only then he learned that wolves are very fond of barbecued lamb.

First lesson

If you want to learn about wolves, do not ask them to say what they are. This is a basic principle of sociological analysis, and the central point of the parable. For one to have an objective understanding of behaviour, be it of individuals or institutions, one must suspect the individual explanations and collective ideologies of those whose behaviour is to be explained. Why? Because these explanations, for psycho-social reasons, are not objective knowledge but rather attempts to legitimize what people are doing. So, if you want to know about religion, be a bit suspicious of what religious people say. If you want to know about politics, be a bit suspicious of what the politicians say about themselves. And if you want to know about science, beware of the explanations provided by scientists. Usually they say nothing about the scientists' eating habits. Most of the explanations that science proposes about itself are not only untrue; they are dangerous.

1. The ideology of science affirms that science is nothing less than the value-free, disinterested pursuit of truth.

Is this true? From what I know of psychology and sociology, specially the sociology of knowledge, knowledge is always a function of practical interests. If science denies this, when it thinks about itself, we are forced to propose the hypothesis that science is trying to hide from itself the practical interests which are at its foundation. Max Scheler, for instance, suggests that all the methods developed by our science result from a specific form of will to power—the will to dominate, the will to control, the will to manipulate, which emerged with the emergence of the bourgeois class.

2. This ideology of science affirms, also, that it is after truth for truth's sake and that all expansion of knowledge is good. But is it empirically true that every expansion of knowledge is good? This belief is rather functional to the interests of scientists, because it allows them to become involved in any

kind of research without asking embarrassing questions about the possible bad consequences of their work.

3. It is also stated that "our interests are best served, in the long run, by research which is guided largely by its own internal logic and not by our immediate needs". Is this empirically true? What about $E=mc^2$ and the A-bomb? It seems to me that this is not a statement of fact but rather the expression of a hope. "Our interests..." Whose? Who is the subject? The scientist? The rich nations? The multinationals? The super-powers? The poor and marginalized? Who is speaking?

4. "Science is one of the main indispensable pillars on which our civilization and our hopes for the future rest." But is this objectively true? Is it not exactly from science that the possibility of global annihilation came? Or do the A-bomb and intercontinental rockets not belong to the essence of science?

5. "Most of the problems of the modern world involve detailed scientific knowledge, and it is the obvious responsibility of scientists to alert us to the social implications of scientific advances and help us, in terms we can understand, to apply them wisely."

This is the myth of the *expert*. Since the problems of our world are extremely complicated, it belongs to the experts to interpret them to the ignorant public. The world is divided between those who know and those who don't. And everybody knows that decisions must be made by those who know. But one could ask: "If they know, why should they waste their time convincing a stupid public?" Do we not find here certain authoritarian implications? On the other hand, I must confess that I never saw scientists giving advice to the poor and oppressed. Advice is always given to the hands which feed them, viz. those who have political and economic power, those who pay the bills.

6. This ideology states that science performs the social function of organizing scepticism. Is this really so? "Human institutions preserve ideas as rocks preserve fossils", it is said. I agree. This is true of *all* institutions—science included. But the paper says something different: it sees science as an institution based on scepticism. If this were true science would be a social institution above and outside society. Indeed, scientists believe very often that science has found a method which puts them above common human beings.

7. This ideology, moreover, is based on the tacit assumption of the superiority of the western civilization, the scientific civilization. Its historical project is the final assimilation of all non-western, non-scientific cultures into ours. It thus dismisses as superstitious the beliefs of other peoples, considered primitive. Science, it is stated, brings superstition to an end: "Consider, for example, the religious practices of the Aztecs"—I would add: consider the military, political and economic practices of our scientific civilization. No superstitious culture has exceeded us in insanity.

Well, it could be replied that all these instances do not belong to the *essence* of science. They are simple accidents. I will reply: this is a gross superstition. What I would demand is that we be a bit more scientific as we try to understand what the essence of science is. And science, as a social entity, is nothing less than the total amount of its social relations and results. If these empirical facts are ignored we cannot claim to be speaking about science.

Second lesson

Lambs know more about wolves than wolves do. A wolf is, to a lamb, what the wolf *does* to the lamb and not what the wolf thinks he is doing. If you ask any dictatorial regime to describe itself, the answer will be a marvellous one: nothing more benevolent, nothing more democratic, nothing more committed to the welfare of the people. But if you go to the jails of political prisoners and ask the same question, the answer will be totally different.

Science has developed a series of accounts of what it is. These accounts, most of the time, hide its eating habits. These habits, say the philosophers, do not belong to the *essence* of science. Thus very often scientists do not say a word about the objectively given, testable, concrete, empirical social results of their work. "This does not belong to the essence of science," they say. "What matters is what the scientist affirms about what he does."

You may see that I had great difficulties with Dr Hanbury Brown's beautiful paper. I would indeed like to believe what it affirms about science. But I cannot. From my angle of vision, the angle of the social sciences, this paper reveals very much about the scientists' habits of thought about themselves but very little, if anything, of science as a social reality. But science exists only as a social entity. Natural scientists insist on the fact that one must be objective. But science is objectively given only as a social entity. It exists through a language, has developed a set of rules, has an ethos (Merton), makes truth dependent of interpersonal testing, works on account of social stimuli (money, prestige, power, Nobel Prize, etc.), is closely related to political and economic interests: this is what science is, as an objectively given entity.

The God-Like In Us
A Response by W. Mutu Maathai

All of us in this conference base our comments on our own experiences and expectations. As I respond to Prof. Brown, I am looking for answers and suggestions for problems posed by faith and science for people in the developing world, the so-called Third World.

In the Third World science does not worry us. It excites us because it seems to prophesy and to signify the goods and the goals that we think we must achieve.

When science pursues certain objectives like, for example, the Skylab, most people in the Third World are told: this is not what we should look for in science; this is the false image of science. But what is the truth of science? What kind of science are we to expect in the Third World? We are not expected to be in Skylab, so where should we be? Are we the ones to seek for the truth, the real goods of science?

The Old Testament says that man was created in the image of God. I think that when a scientist inquires, discovers and enjoys the sheer feeling of understanding the world around him, he is at that moment testifying to the God-like in man. For what else is God-like in ourselves? A scientist seeks to understand; and I think that to that extent he is fulfilling and encouraging faith. For he can only pursue the truth and then marvel at the Creator and the Master.

A scientist does not try to be the Master. He can only admire and humble himself in front of the Creator. To that extent science only reveals the greater glory of God.

The industrialization of science has changed our world. In the Third World it has produced colonialism. It has brought exploitation of the people. It is gradually destroying our environment, and is even destroying our confidence and our personality. But at the same time it seems to bring faith, hope and comfort. It is gradually helping us to value ourselves, even when sometimes we are advised not to value ourselves too much.

Where do the responsibilities lie?

Who shall say what is good and what is bad, so far as science is concerned, so that the Third World will accept what is good? Who will provide the scale and who will be the judge?

In the Third World the aims of science should be mostly the basic needs. These are for food, shelter, education and health. But these are not really the values of the society in which we live. Or are they?

We have people dying every day of malnutrition, and yet we can afford the extravaganza of lasers going out there in space. How can we tell the people that the future is in their hands when Skylab yesterday was threatening the Australians? Should scientists concentrate on the basic needs of humanity, or should they pursue the thrills of super-technology? Where shall we get the martyrs in science, people who work for the good of mankind?

Surely it is in the nature of man to query. That is one mark of a scientist. He must also marvel, and that is the reason why he will continue to believe in a God, to believe in a master.

So science will have to continue, and we would be cheating ourselves if we were to find a way of stopping scientists. Even the space lasers will have to continue. But in seeking the unknown, we have to look for solutions to the many problems facing us.

The responsibility should not be left to the theologians. It can also not be left to the scientists. I wish to suggest that we have left one group, and these are the futurists. And I would like to suggest further that these are the politicians.

Many decisions are made by the politicians, and too often the future depends very much on these decisions. I hope that through this conference we shall find a situation or a path or a platform in which these three groups—the theologians, the scientists and the futurists (a better word for politicians)—shall work together for the betterment of mankind.

Reactions and Comment

The addresses provoked lively responses from the platform and the floor. Brown replied to Alves that the wolf in the parable is human nature, that the misuses of science are no more reason to reject science than the misuses of religion are reason to reject faith, that the answer to the problems posed by Alves was the transformation of human nature. Alves replied that the point of his parable was that no group or person should be trusted to define itself and that the functioning of science in society is a better guide to its real nature than the explanations of scientists.

The theme of the complementarity of science and faith, as advocated by Brown, did not become a major issue in the plenary sessions. But it was a major issue for Section I of the conference (see the Report of that Section in Volume 2).

However, the issues raised by the two conceptions of science, as put forward by Brown and Alves, reverberated through the plenary discussions and section meetings until the end of the conference. If some participants found ways to narrow the differences or to find a complementarity in the two positions, others remained partisans of one or the other position. At the end some participants still felt that one or the other of the two positions had not won an adequate hearing (see Chapter 19). And many concurred in Maathai's emphasis that science should cause both fear and excitement.

4. What Is Faith?

Introduction

From the consideration of the meaning of science, the conference turned to a comparable inquiry into the meaning of faith. Metropolitan Paulos Gregorios, of India, a theologian and bishop of the Orthodox Syrian Church of the East, gave the major address. He was already well known to many of the participants for his contributions to the Consultation on Nature, Humanity and God (Zürich, 1977) and his book *The Human Presence: an Orthodox View of Nature* (Geneva: WCC, 1978).

Metropolitan Gregorios interpreted the "semitic" meaning of faith, as understood by the Oriental Orthodox churches, as distinguished from various meanings of faith in the Roman Catholic, the Protestant and the European Eastern Orthodox churches. He revealed certain similarities and differences between faith, thus understood, and science. And he called on both scientists and theologians to revise some of their traditional ways of thinking.

In a platform response, Rosemary Ruether, professor in the Garrett-Evangelical Theological Seminary in the USA, offered a feminist response to the theme of the conference. And D.H. Verheul, professor of physics in the Free University of Amsterdam, gave a scientific affirmation of certain values in science and the importance of continuous conversations of church people with scientists.

Science and Faith: Complementary or Contradictory?

PAULOS GREGORIOS

Science is a human enterprise, and purports to deal with reality in a reliable meaningful way. Faith, too, has the same basic purpose, though its approach is different.

Our attempt here is *(a)* to point to certain misunderstandings about the meaning of faith, *(b)* to restore a more semitic conception of faith, *(c)* to deal with the question of truth in faith and in science, *(d)* to clarify what it is that constitutes the object or subject of faith, *(e)* to help see the unitive-participatory rather than the encounter stance of the believer, *(f)* to point to some similarities between faith and science, and finally *(g)* to suggest some tentative conclusions and questions for further exploration.

The words "science" and "faith" have at least five different meanings each, depending on the context:

Faith	*Science*
1. The act of believing.	1. The method of knowing in science.
2. The consequences of faith, religious practice as a way of life.	2. The scientific enterprise; its application and practice in technology.
3. Different faiths (Christian faith, Bahai faith, Jain faith).	3. Different disciplines in science: the sciences, physics, biology, sociology, etc.
4. Statements of faith (creeds, theologies).	4. The cumulative and growing corpus of tested and acknowledged propositions and hypotheses in science.
5. Faith organized institutionally and communities of faith.	5. Science organized institutionally and the scientific communities.

We will have to limit ourselves to an examination of how faith and science function in relating themselves to reality, touching upon the other aspects only where necessary.

Three misunderstandings of faith

There are several ways in which faith has been understood or misunderstood. In the Christian churches especially, there seem to have occurred three wrong emphases—on the intellectual, on the subjective and on the individual. Only a recovery of the ancient semitic understanding of faith can correct these three wrong emphases.

The Roman Catholic, the Protestant, and the Eastern Orthodox traditions in the Christian faith have all at one time or another been guilty of a one sidedly intellectualist orientation in their understanding of faith.

The intellectual over-emphasis occurs where faith is conceived as giving assent to what is proposed as dogma by the official magisterium of the Church. It also occurs when faith is regarded as "a steady and certain *knowledge* of the divine benevolence towards us, which being founded on the truth of the gratuitous promise in Christ, is both revealed to our minds, and confirmed to our hearts by the Holy Spirit" (John Calvin). The same intellectualist distortion is made by the Eastern Orthodox churches also when they regard faith as acceptance of the dogmatic definitions of the seven ecumenical councils.

All three traditions stand in need of correction by reappropriating the classical semitic understanding of faith and truth.

An over-emphasis on the subjective element is characteristic of the existential approach to faith, e.g. in Kierkegaard or Bultmann.

Søren Kierkegaard, the Danish philosopher-psychologist, claimed to be breaking with 1800 years of tradition, when he interpreted faith as a "leap into the unknown" in "fear and trembling", a "believing against the understanding". Kierkegaard upbraids science for seeking to objectify the truth and that is the point of his major essay, *Concluding Unscientific Postscript*. Truth is always on the side of the knower and not of the known, at least "for anyone who has not been demoralized with the aid of science".

> "An objective uncertainty held fast in an appropriation process of the most passionate inwardness is the truth, the highest truth attainable for an existing individual... The truth is precisely the venture which chooses an objective uncertainty with the passion of the infinite."[1]

If we take Merton's criteria of universalism, communalism, disinterestedness and organized scepticism as four main elements of science, then Kierkegaard would want to emphasize the opposite, i.e. the particular, the personal, the passionate and the unquestioning. Kierkegaard, in swinging away from the intellectualist, quasi-scientific approach to faith characteristic alike of medieval Catholicism and post-Reformation Hegelianism, tended to emphasize the volitional (the will to believe) and the emotional (passionate). Moving away from the intellectual over-emphasis in this case has led to a falling into the subjectivist trap. Here, too, the recovery of the classical semitic biblical tradition can serve as a corrective.

The third misunderstanding of faith has been also a consequence of the existential approach. For Kierkegaard faith is an encounter of the alone with the alone, in fear and trembling. Martin Buber has taken him to task for this in his memorable essay: *The Question to the Single One*. But even Buber fails to do justice to his own semitic tradition by failing to go all the way to rediscovering the community element in all faiths.

I wish to underline very strongly the community aspect of faith. It is not my belief and your belief and someone else's belief that matters. In my case I can affirm quite unequivocally that my faith is the faith of the Church. I participate in a community with an unbroken tradition through the ages. Just as in science, which also is a community activity with a tradition in which every scientist participates, I do not start from scratch on my own, trying to re-establish everything that my predecessors have found true. I know that many of my predecessors in faith have held to things which are not true. But this is true also of science. And yet I know how to sift that which is *reliable* in the tradition, only by participation in the community of faith. Neither faith nor science is an individual activity, but a community enterprise.

The semitic understanding of faith

Fortunately all of you know sufficient Hebrew and Aramaic to know the semitic etymology of the word "faith". You may have difficulty in saying

---

[1] English text in Bretall (ed.): *A Kierkegaard Anthology*. Princeton, 1951, p. 214.

Amen to my statement; but only until you know that *Aman*, from which *Amen* comes, is the root of the word: to believe. *Aman* means to confirm, to support, to nourish. The verb in its simple *qal* form refers to the activity of a nurse or a foster mother *(ōmeneth)* or of pillars *(ōmenoth)*.

The *hiphil* form *he'emin* is the Hebrew word for believe. And it means to allow oneself to be supported and nourished, to be confirmed and established. But then God's character itself is faith or reliability *(ha-el-ha-ne'eman)*, and by being supported, nourished, confirmed and established by him and in him, human beings come to have God's quality of *ne'eman*, i.e. firmness, reliability, strength, faithfulness, truthfulness, etc.

As Isaiah said, *Im lo' ta'eminu bi' lo' te'amenu* ("If you do not become supported and nourished by me you will not be confirmed and supported", Isa. 7:9[b]). Faith is not so much an emotional-intellectual commitment of the will to someone who stands over against you, as an allowing oneself to be trustingly carried, nourished, supported, by God, and the consequent strengthening and transformation of human personality and society.

When Isaiah says: "I am laying in Zion a foundation stone, a tested stone, a precious corner stone, of a sure foundation; he who believes will not run scared" (Isa. 28:16), that is what the prophet has in mind: "He who believes will not run scared" *(hama'amin lo' yahish)*.

Faith thus means being established on a firm foundation which supports and nourishes one, so that one does not have to run scared. It is not a mere subjective determination in passionate clinging to the incredulous. It is rather a peaceful, joyful, restful abiding in that which is firm, dependable, nourishing and guiding.

The question of truth in faith and science

What is this firm foundation on which one abides in faith? If it is only a subjective creation of our minds and wills, it would be neither firm nor dependable.

It is interesting to note that the semitic word for "truth" also comes from the same root *Aman*. In Hebrew, the word for truth is *emunah* or *emeth*, the reliable and supportive reality—the *Amen*. As the Psalmist puts it:

> "The Lord is my light and my salvation; whom shall I fear? The Lord is the stronghold of my life: of whom shall I be afraid?" (Ps. 27:1).

This idea that God is a rock and a fortress (e.g. Ps. 18:2; 31:3; 37:29; 43:2; 46:1) is a recurring theme in the Old Testament. Psalm 46 says:

> "God is for us a refuge and a fortress; found to be a mighty help in troubles. Therefore we do not fear though the earth is displaced, though the mountains reel into the midst of the sea; though its waters roar and foam; though the mountains shake... God is in her midst; she (the City of God) shall not totter."

In an apocalyptic age such as ours this kind of faith in a dependable, rock-like, reliable reality, takes on a new significance. To trust in God is not to panic, even in the midst of ecological catastrophe.

This truth of faith, as contrasted with scientific truth, is not primarily propositional. Truth is reality, not statement. For faith, truth is not dogma, but reality—that which is and always will be—not a *description* of that which is.

Science is concerned with ways of stating how reality behaves, in order to explain, understand or operate upon reality. But the reality which science tries to understand and state is empirical time-space reality, which it regards as self-consistent, dependable, and predictable to a large extent.

The definition of truth in science varies from culture to culture. For Anglo-Saxon philosophers of science, truth has been defined by A. Tarski as a correlation between facts and statements, in a purified meta-language, i.e. in a meta-mathematical set of symbols where facts and statements have commensurable symbols of denotation. Truth is a quality of a mathematical or logical hypothesis or proposition in which the statement corresponds to fact, is consistent with itself, and can be operationally verified.

This intellectualist-operational definition of truth is amended by Marxist philosophy of science, where:

> "Truth is the process of the reflection in human consciousness of the inexhaustible essence of the infinite material world and the regularities of its development, which at the same time implies the process of man's creation of a scientific picture of the world emerging as the concrete historical result of cognition that is constantly developing on the basis of socio-historical practice which is its highest criterion."[2]

Here truth is not statement, but a process of reflection in consciousness of the material world, through dynamic interaction with it in organized social labour, and through creating a more and more accurate picture of material reality. Truth is thus subjective-objective, theoretical-practical, personal-social interaction between humanity and the rest of material reality. It is a dynamic process of action-reflection through socially organized labour and socially conditioned perception and reflection.

Faith in what?—The object of faith

What is the object of faith? In the Christian faith at least, we see three different but inter-related objects of faith: (a) faith in a proposition; (b) faith in a promise; (c) faith in a person.

---

[2]G.A. Kursanov: "The Problem of Truth in the Philosophy of Marxism", in *Philosophy in the USSR: Problems of Dialectical Materialism*. Moscow: Progress Publishers, 1977, p. 205.

Of these the third is primary and fundamental, and marks in some sense the specificity of semitic faith—i.e. faith in Judaism, Christianity and Islam. In Buddhism, Hinduism and Taoism faith in a person is not mandatory or even advisable, and to that extent the word "faith" is hardly applicable to East Asian religions.

The Christian faith is, in its classical form, faith in a perfect personal community, namely the Triune God. This Triune God manifests himself, according to Christians, in a particular historical person. Jesus of Nazareth, who is identified as the Second Person in the Triune Community, and also in the continuing operations of the Third Person of that Triunity—the Person of the Holy Spirit.

Faith in the promises of Jesus Christ, as well as in propositions concerning him, is derivative from faith in his person. Because we trust the Person of Jesus Christ, his promises are also regarded as trustworthy, e.g. that evil shall be finally overcome and the good separated from it on the last day, the day of judgment; that the Holy Spirit will be with the community of faith, guiding it into all truth; that sin will be forgiven where persons repent and have faith in Christ. From our trust in the Person of Christ and in the apostolic testimony to that person, certain propositions about him are also derivable, e.g. that He was incarnate of the Blessed Virgin Mary, that He taught and served the needy, that He was condemned to death, hanged, rose again and ascended into the "heavenly realm", that He is there seated "at the right hand of God", that is, seated on the throne of authority exercising the power of God, guiding the universe to its destiny, that He will, at the end of history, be manifested in the fullness of his glory, and that at that time He will reconcile the universe within itself as well as to God.

The object of Christian faith is thus primarily the Triune God, manifested in Christ Jesus, and secondarily his promises and certain propositions about him and about reality.

Faith—union-participation or encounter?

In the Roman Catholic and Orthodox traditions the element of union-participation in Christ gets heavier emphasis, while in the Reformation tradition the emphasis falls generally on the human person's encounter with Christ, trusting in him, surrendering to him, and committing oneself to obeying him and following him.

The difference between man as the subject of faith and Christ as the object of faith is maintained in three different conceptual patterns. In the Reformation tradition the element of union with Christ in faith is not rejected; but Christ and the believer are kept distinct and different. In the classical Roman Catholic tradition, Christ has a divine-human nature, and it is with the human nature that man is united; but because the human nature of Christ is inseparably united with his divine nature, the believer participates in the divine nature through Christ's human nature. The believer does not participate directly in the divine nature. In the Oriental Orthodox tradition, since

Christ's nature is one composite divine-human nature, the believer, by being united with Christ through faith and baptism, participates in that divine-human nature. This element of union-participation in faith is of fundamental importance for the semitic understanding of faith as being supported and nourished. The relation between the believer and the believed-in becomes thus not of subject-object but of mutual inter-subjectivity. What is impossible for man becomes possible, when God works in, with and through him. "Without me you can do nothing... Abide in me and I in you, and you will bear much fruit" (John 15:5).

Faith is not thus a mere human act. The Holy Spirit makes it possible that God can act in a human being without suppressing his or her own subjectivity. It is only when one allows the Spirit of God to take possession of our subjectivity, that the activity of faith, i.e. being lifted up, undergirded, supported and nourished by God, becomes possible. The union between Christ and the believer by the Holy Spirit is what opens the way for faith. In fact faith is that inter-subjective union—rather than an act of intellect, will or feeling. It is an action of the Holy Spirit which makes joint action between God and man possible without suppressing the subjectivity of either.

Science, on the other hand, has for a long time sought to keep the subject and the object separate. In fact, the ideal of objectivity has often been misunderstood in science as the elimination or reduction of the subjective element. The introduction of certain public criteria of checking and verification does not, however, eliminate the subjective element in scientific knowledge. Especially at sub-atomic levels of reality it is obvious that the observer and his measuring apparatus are in some sense constitutive of the reality as apprehended, and one does not "know" any objective reality completely independent of the observer and his equipment for perception and measurement.

In science too, encounter with reality is the occasion for scientific perception and knowledge. The knowledge yielded is a composite creation of the observing equipment and the observed reality. But there seems to be a fundamental difference between the two sets of relations, observer-observed and believer-believed. In the latter relation, the believer-believed relation leads to a status-change or ontological transformation in the believer, who is now transformed from a foundationless, floating, insecure being "running scared" to a firmly founded, peaceful and joyful being.

In the scientific encounter of observer-observed, the observed comes under the comprehension and control of the observer. But here too there is a status-change on the part of the observer. His being is now extended to include the known object, which he is now able to control and use as an extension of himself. There is a difference between the two status changes to which we shall revert in the conclusion.

Faith and science—similarities and differences

Faith is not identical with science, numerically or generically. They are two ways of dealing with reality, with some elements in common.

The similarities between faith and science can be listed somewhat as follows:

1) both are human ways of relating themselves to reality;
2) both have a subjective as well as an objective pole;
3) both have cognitive as well as practical content;
4) both are community enterprises;
5) both go beyond the self-evident and the common-place to unveil the hidden structure of reality;
6) both have been capable of working enormous changes in the human reality and the relation of humanity to the observable world;
7) both have an element of tradition in which each new generation does not start from scratch, but proceeds on the basis of the inheritance from the past;
8) both have an element of progress in understanding and practice, and have anticipations of a higher degree of perfection in both cognition of and relation to reality; but can act usefully on the basis of present imperfect cognition and practice;
9) both are now institutionally organized and in that process make serious compromises which involve unfaithfulness to the best convictions and principles of each;
10) both have been unforgivably arrogant in the past and presumed to think that each had an exclusive access to the knowledge of reality, and a capacity to state the truth verbally and finally.

But the differences are crucial. Faith has a fundamental role in changing the ontological status of man which cannot be duplicated by science.

In science, *experiment*, not *experience* has for a long time been the main tenet of its methodology. Experiment means that the experimenter remains as far as possible outside the experiment, in order to keep subjective variables from interfering with the "objective" understanding of the matter under observation. It is precisely this objective-subjective distinction which has been rendered obsolete by the new perceptions in quantum mechanics. As J.A. Wheeler puts it:

> "The quantum principle has demolished the once-held view that the universe sits safely 'out there', that we can observe what goes on in it from behind a foot-thick slab of plate-glass without ourselves being involved in what is going on. We have learned that to observe even so minuscule an object as an electron we have to shatter that slab of glass. We have to reach out and insert a measuring device. We can install a device to measure position or insert a device to measure momentum, but the installation of the one prevents the installation of the other. We ourselves have to decide which it is that we will do. Whichever it is, it has an unpredictable effect on the future of that electron, and to that degree the future of the universe is changed. We changed it. We have to cross out that old word 'observer' and replace it by the new word 'participator'. In

some strange sense the quantum principle tells us that we are dealing with a participatory universe."[3]

The implication is that knowledge cannot be independent of the knower's subjective decisions and choices—that experiment cannot be separated from experience. If this is so, then that must bring science and faith closer together, because both are ways of dealing with reality in which preconceptions, experiments, experience, reflection and practical consequences are closely interwoven. Science is already abandoning its claims to objectivity in the sense of total independence of the observer. Faith too is now seen to be something that happens in the world of experience, an experience of the reality that confronts us.

Some tentative conclusions and questions

Science, until recently, had nurtured the illusions that objective, proven knowledge of the "external" world was possible; that this knowledge would lead to a complete mastery of "external" reality; that all worthwhile knowledge can be linguistically formulated. None of these illusions is tenable today, though many still unreflectively hold on to these illusions.

But from the perspective of faith a number of questions have to be addressed to science:

1. Is it not necessary that scientists themselves take the lead in dispelling the illusion prevalent among many that science is the only responsible and reliable way to the apprehension of truth?

2. Has not science proceeded on a paradigm which is in substantial need of revision? Our present paradigm is too fragmentary and incoherent—clusters of theories in different disciplines without any single coordinating scheme for a holistic approach to reality. The new paradigm should at least accomplish four things:

i) provide a framework for coordinating the central theoretical insights of the various scientific disciplines;
ii) provide a meaningful pattern in which perceptions such as religious, mystical, paranormal and other non-ordinary phenomena can also be incorporated and not arbitrarily ruled out simply because they do not fit into present theory;
iii) provide some indication of ways of transcending the emergent paradoxes in current theory, for example the Einstein-Podolsky-Rosen paradox where the incredible and presently inexplicable situation obtains of a physically isolated system being affected by a choice of measurement on another physical system having no observable physical interaction with it;

---

[3] "Superspace", in R.P. Gilbert and R.G. Newton (eds): *Analytic Methods in Mathematical Physics*. The quotation is from Wheeler's article in *American Scientist*, 62, November-December 1974.

iv) provide for the emerging fact that man and universe are inextricably inter-related and that the subject-object, knower-known dichotomy is ultimately untenable.

3. Can science continue to short-circuit the questions of origin and destiny of the universe and man by assuming them to be auturgic, self-existent and self-regulating? Has not science now the task to admit publicly that its assumption of only two realities (the conscious self as knower-subject and the rest of the universe as known-object) is scientifically untenable? Why does science have to insist on its secular assumptions, just because the Christian Church was once science's enemy and persecutor? Has not science sufficiently come of age to realize that the secular or deist world-view in which science first developed was an accident of history? Is it not possible for scientists and philosophers of science to develop a new overall paradigm in which consciousness of the universe is recognized as a manifestation of a higher consciousness within which both our consciousness and the universe as it appears to consciousness subsist, and that this higher consciousness is one with which the human consciousness can be united in faith?

4. The fourth question is addressed to the intellectual establishment in the Christian faith, to that lazy coterie of theologians among whom I count myself. Have we awakened to the fact that space, time and causality are themselves doubtful constructs of our human consciousness and that we cannot creditably discharge our task by providing theologies which explain the universe and man as sequentially "caused" by a creator who is temporally prior to the universe and spatially distinct from it? Do we not have a lot of homework to do yet, in coming to terms with the universe as science knows it today, and in providing for a non-conceptual apprehension of the ground of the universe, not in theology but in a hymn of adoration which does not conceptually explain God, but responds to that ineffable reality in worship through symbols of hope and love, faith and trust?

Such a non-conceptual apprehension cannot short-circuit or bypass the conceptual problems of science and its paradoxes, but must pass through them into the "cloud of unknowing", through the "taught ignorance" that goes beyond conceptual knowledge into silent adoration. Faith needs science, must come to terms with it, and work for new perceptions in both faith and science, through respectful collaboration and healthy self-criticism.

A Feminist Perspective on Religion and Science

A Response by Rosemary Ruether

In both the dominant religious consciousness(es) and the dominant scientific consciousness(es), with few exceptions, women have been situated on the underside of history. Both religion and science have located women in the realm of matter, of body, of earth; matter over against Spirit, body over against mind; earth over against heaven.

The Judaeo-Christian tradition

In the Hebrew tradition God is imaged as a ruling class male, a great patriarch in the sky who, like the patriarchs of earth, dominates and rules a *familia* of dependent persons, women, children and slaves. The creaturely as the creation and the community (Israel) of this divine patriarch are imaged either as a community of sons (daughters are completely invisible) or as a community of servants or, collectively, as the wife of the patriarch; in other words, as the dependent persons within the patriarchal family.

In the Greek tradition, the Divine is imaged as a transcendent male Mind which exists eternally outside of and independent of matter. This eternal male Mind creates the material, visible world by a process of devolution. This divinity retains its purity and integrity by a process of radical separation and flight from the material to the immaterial, from the visible to the invisible, from sense to Mind, from the mutable to the immutable.

Christian theology was fashioned by a fusion of these two traditions; Hebrew patriarchalism and Greek dualism. It should therefore not surprise us that women have never been allowed to represent the God of this tradition or his Christ. This leaves the suspicion that this God and his Christ do not, in fact, actually represent women. Rather their imagery has been shaped in antagonism to women, as sovereign over or in flight from Matter or the Mother (etymologically connected terms). Even the incarnation does not really allow women to represent Christ since it comes to be imaged as incarnation into a certain kind of male whose headship over the body of creation, the Church, is the model for male headship over the female (Eph. 5; compare with Matthew 23:1-10 where Jesus says to call no man father, master or rabbi because the model for Christ and his followers is service and not mastery).

In this religious tradition of what comes to be dominant Christianity, women can be imaged in two ways: *(a)* as the feminine; that is to say, as submissive, docile, receptive and sublimated (unsexual) body totally at the disposal of divine male demands; or *(b)* as the female: that is to say, as carnal, revolting, demonic body, which is the antithesis of the male quest for redemption through denial of his roots in the mother, in matter, in finitude and in mortality.

The western scientific tradition

The scientific tradition appears at first to be a repudiation of the otherworldly religious tradition. Science comes on the scene (or rather separates out of theology) as a return from the other world to this world, a turn from spiritual concerns to material concerns. At its extreme, as scientific materialism, it even declares that nothing exists except matter. But, on closer examination, we see that a new god has been put in the place of the old one or, to put it another way, a new clerical caste in service of the political powers is replacing the old one. This new priestly class is the scientist and the technologists (see Comte and St Simon in the early nineteenth century) and their god is the god of scientific reason. Like the old God, the god of scientific reason situates itself outside of matter, independent of it, sovereign over it (or her), knowing, dominating her from outside.

Historically speaking, this kind of scientific consciousness has been the tool of a white western ruling class male elite, which has used its knowledge, through technology, to exploit the material resources and labour of the rest of the world (human and non-human) for the power and profit of the colonizers. This is the *key* to the rapacious use of technology. The rest of the world has been dealt with as resources (material resources and labour) for the profit of the few, not as fellow beings who are to share equally in the development and benefits of the new power. Women have been both symbolically and actually a part of that other world as basic resources under male power. They still belong predominantly to the world of exploited labour, in the double sense of reproductive labour (and all the unpaid domestic work connected with it) and the low paid, low status labour that constitute the lowest rungs of the economic system: the day care workers, the domestic workers, the clerical workers. They deal with the babies, the dirt and the papers that are the bottom of the hierarchy of power and profit. Not surprisingly, then, we image the exploited earth as a raped female.

Feminist consciousness as revolutionary ecological consciousness

What perspective can the raped ones bring to religious and scientific traditions? First of all, let me say emphatically that this cannot be simply the romantic anti-scientific and anti-technological primitivism which has so often been the educated western male response to his own self-alienation. "Back to nature" in this romantic, anti-technological sense can only land women back where they have ever been, barefoot and pregnant in the kitchen baking the wholewheat bread for the "simple livers". Nor can we simply be content with that kind of conservationism (in religious circles called stewardship) which amounts to the freezing of the present system of injustice.

Rather women, in solidarity with all those who belong to the world of exploited labour, must look to the thoroughgoing conversion of the world system. This is the conversion which Christianity promised when it spoke of the new humanity in Christ "in which there was neither Jew nor Greek, slave nor free, male nor female", but which it has betrayed historically. This is the conversion which science promised when it spoke of the progress of humanity towards equality through truth and education. The conversions of God into flesh, mind to earth have been the great promised revolutions of Christianity and science, betrayed through their continued alliance with the male ruling classes.

Now the conversion of God to flesh and mind to earth cannot simply mean the reduction of God to flesh or mind to matter, for that is simply to jump to the opposite pole of the same alienated dualism. The revolutionary task, constantly betrayed, is to convert both sides of the dualism into a new whole. This means the thoroughgoing conversion of both the consciousness and the practice of religion and science.

There is no time in this brief presentation to spell out in greater detail what this might mean, but let us just consider the basic paradigms of each tradition:

Religion: Might we think about God, not as alienated male ego outside the visible world, but as Divine Matrix (Logos-Sophia) of existing beings—not just in the sense of the Ground of Being of what is, but of what might be, and has not yet been—the inexhaustible font of potential being, through which we both come to be and are continually renewed—the font of creativity and possibility through which we can begin again to renew and recreate the world we have so grievously misused?

Science: Might we think of Reason, not as the sovereign consciousness of an elite, linked with the western male ruling class, or even of all people, male and female, thinking together (although that would be a most profound revolution), but as the thinking dimension of all being—which should not separate male from female, advantaged from disadvantaged—or even humans from plants, animals, earth, air and water, but which should bind us together. Once we are converted from the elite arrogance of thought as the source of hierarchy and domination, we can recognize that consciousness exists in humans, not to dominate, but to *serve* the whole. Can we experience and use consciousness as the consciousness *of* earth, the consciousness *of* matter, to be used to refine, enhance and renew the great harmonies that bind animals and inanimate together in one ecology, which must either learn to become a just, sustainable society of ongoing renewing life, or else all die together? (Perhaps, as Bishop Gregorios was suggesting at the end of his paper, we should recognize that the Reason of science and the Logos-Sophia of religion are finally One.)

In conclusion, we have begun to sense, in the religious community and in the scientific community, the need for this type of conversion, a conversion of men to women, owners to workers, rich nations to poor nations, humanity to the earth. It is the purpose of this conference (I hope) to explore concretely—both from the religious and the scientific side—what this conversion might mean, both as new consciousness and as new practice.

Some Questions to Metropolitan Gregorios
A Response by D. Hendrik Verheul

In these short comments I want to put certain questions to Dr Gregorios. The first concerns his analysis of the words "faith" and "science". He traced back the history of these terms and concluded that they were inter-related. But this means that for the purposes of this conference certainly, something is left out of the analysis. Both faith and science deal with the future. Scientists, you might say, work for the future. They aim at a better understanding of nature in the future or a better understanding of creation, perhaps by dint of knowing more about the creator and finding more possibilities in nature, possibilities given there which can serve mankind positively, as we have seen over and over again in the history of mankind.

And, last but not least, scientists work for the future beyond nature; they want to know nature better, since a better understanding of nature will tell them better how mankind should behave in harmony with its surroundings and with itself.

Faith, too, deals with the future. Dr Gregorios's omission of this aspect of faith and science may be significant. It might mean that we are so impressed by the negative aspects of the application of science which are in evidence nowadays that we are in danger of forgetting the positive aspects of science.

My second question to Dr Gregorios concerns his discussion of the semantics of the term "faith". After an excellent historical discussion, which I much appreciated, Dr Gregorios says that faith for him is "not so much an emotional-intellectual commitment of the will to someone who stands over against you, as an allowing oneself to be trustingly carried, nourished, supported, by God . . ." Again, he says later "my subjectivity is supported and nourished by a transcendental subjectivity". And now, for the scientist, especially scientists from the West, certain questions arise. Are we now coming back to some neo-Platonic mythical way of identifying God and mankind by somehow taking away the boundaries between them? Why should we stop at only gods and mankind and not include nature as well? And if we take into consideration nature itself and blur the boundaries between God, mankind and nature, what does this mean for science? What does it mean for doing science as a scientist? And, a different kind of question: Isn't this in striking contrast to the psalmist singing about God in heaven and man on earth?

My last question, Dr Gregorios, concerns what seems to me to be your somewhat negative feelings about science, though you must correct me if I have drawn the wrong conclusions. But something could be done, especially by churches and faith communities—this conference organized by the World Council of Churches is a very good example—such as the following. If people think that scientists are doing the wrong job, taking the wrong decisions, going the wrong way, then as scientists we say: Please come and talk with us; talk firmly about your worries and we will tell you what we are really doing, what the mysteries are in our sciences, what we are certain of and how uncertain we are, especially since Heisenberg. I can say that fairly confidently, as a physicist. And these discussions should not come too late. They should not wait till the results, the fundamental results, can no longer be kept bottled up but will be used by us or others, now or later, but certainly used. If people have questions please come earlier to talk with us.

Scientists, especially scientists who are church members, are open to mutual criticism. And however complicated the matter may seem to be, the most fundamental aspect really needing to be discussed—namely, what the new orientation of a certain kind of scientist from a certain discipline should be—can be discussed more intelligently if people are interested. But if their interest only begins at the moment the genie we have known of for a long time is about to emerge completely from the bottle, then I think the discussions are taking place too late. And then we are told that we are not experienced and don't know how to live with it. And I agree. We don't. But where did we make the mistake?

If we want to learn a lesson from this history, it is that we must begin earlier the concrete discussion of the subjects for fundamental research. This is not planning in the short term but planning in the long term.

Reactions and Comment

The issues before the conference were now immense. The keynote address by Philip Potter and the major addresses by Hanbury Brown and Paulos Gregorios, along with the platform responses to them—all in the first day—obviously constituted a heavy agenda.

For this reason, tacitly understood by all and explicitly stated by some, the questions and comments from the floor dealt mostly with specifics rather than with the grand issues that would preoccupy the entire conference. Some participants defended positions that Metropolitan Gregorios had criticized. Some wondered whether Gregorios had limited faith too narrowly by appealing to its semitic meaning in the face of other cultural and religious interpretations—an ironic situation, since the speaker already has a reputation for insisting on the importance of insights in Oriental religions for the discussions of the World Council of Churches.

The major discussion of the addresses took place not in the plenary session but in section meetings the following day. Two themes from the day's meetings became focal points for the continuing work of the sections. Section I, on "The Nature of Science and the Nature of Faith", worked throughout the conference on the issues of the methods, the concepts of truth, the similarities and divergences between science and faith. Section II, on "Humanity, Nature and God", discussed in depth the second question presented by Verheul to Gregorios: How should Christian faith relate the distinction and the identity of God and humanity (see the section reports in Volume 2).

The feminist concerns presented by Rosemary Ruether were continued in a later plenary address by Karen Lebacqz (see Chapter 14 of this volume) and by several of the sections.

5. Rethinking Theology

Introduction

After considering science and faith as human activities, the conference in its second day moved to a consideration of the content of Christian theology in its relation to the issues of a just, participatory and sustainable society. As background for this discussion it had Chapter 4, "The Biblical Interpretation of Nature and Human Dominion", in *Faith, Science and the Future*; and, behind this chapter, the work of the Consultation on Humanity, Nature and God (Zürich, 1977), reported in *Anticipation*, No. 25, January 1979.

Three speakers in the morning plenary session presented three quite different theological approaches. Charles Birch, Australian biologist and Vice-Moderator of the conference, advocated the "process theology" that is influential in much of the Anglo-American world. In his address Birch made many extemporaneous responses to the immediate situation, including the earlier speech of Rubem Alves (Chapter 3). Birch's text, printed here, is in some ways an extension of his earlier address to the Nairobi Assembly of the WCC (1975)—a speech which did much to alert the ecumenical movement to the problem of sustainability and its intimate relation to social justice.

Gerhard Liedke, pastor and theologian in the Federal Republic of Germany, specifically criticized process theology and its "organic image of nature, man and God"—to the delight of some delegates and the distress of others. Instead, he offered a revision of Protestant continental theology, which he found thus far inadequate to the issues of the conference, by a reinterpretation of key biblical texts and by attention to contemporary theories of conflict coming from the social sciences.

Protopresbyter Vitaly Borovoy of the Russian Orthodox Church traced the loss of faith, within technological societies, in both God and humanity. He called for a reappropriation of classical theandric theology (with its emphasis on the divine-human unity), as it has been daringly related to modern technology in some strains of recent Orthodox theology.

These three addresses, and the earlier address by Metropolitan Gregorios with its advocacy of Oriental Orthodoxy, provided four focal points for the conference deliberations.

Nature, Humanity and God in Ecological Perspective

CHARLES BIRCH

There may yet be time to discover a vision of reality appropriate for our time and to engineer steps to bridge the chasm between the vision and its realization. Once we hoped for utopia. Now in a more chastened mood we can at best hope for a reprieve "lest the stone age return on the gleaming wings of science" (Churchill). As someone has said, had the dinosaur learned the art of prayer, his only sensible petition would have been to go down on his scaly knees and beg: "Lord give me another chance."

I have eight theses to my argument. They are in order as follows:

1. The world-view derived from science reflects the sort of society in which science is practised. The dominant scientific-technological world-view of today has been inherited from a society bent on mastery over nature. It mirrors its origins.
2. In this view the universe and all that is in it, including living organisms, is conceived as contrivance. It has led to a factory view of nature with humanity pitted against nature.
3. Christian theology, particularly in the West, accommodated itself uncomfortably to the mechanistic cosmology of science, thus detaching still further nature and humanity and, as well, God.
4. The dominant mechanistic world-view, whether theistic or not, has proved itself quite unadapted to our age. It is unecological and dehumanizing.
5. This dominant scientific-technological world-view is challenged by personal encounter with the universe in all its wonder and mystery. This challenge is coming largely from without science and Christian theology.
6. To meet with that challenge so that we may discover a more relevant ecological view of nature, humanity and God requires a change in the relationship of faith and science that has been dominant in the past.
7. The new partnership of faith and science that is emerging acknowledges the unity of the creation, that is the oneness of nature, humanity and God. It takes seriously both the insights of science and the special characteristics of the human.
8. This ecological view of nature, humanity and God implies a life-ethic which embraces all life as well as all humanity in an infinite responsibility to all life. This new ethic and the new vision provides a foundation on which to build the ecologically sustainable and socially just global society.

1. Science as a social construct

The dominant world-view derived from science reflects at any one time the sort of science that is practised. The sort of science that is practised is not, as so many like to believe, an untarnished reflection of the objective world. It is a reflection that mirrors the sort of society we live in. Science and the world-view we derive from it are neither value-free nor as objective as we once thought. The Newtonian apprehension of nature was conditioned by history and culture. Frances Yates, in a biography of Giordano Bruno, traces the peculiarly mechanistic framework of modern science as a reaction to a world of magic and superstition: "The basic difference between the attitude of the magician to the world and the attitude of the scientist to the world is that the former wants to draw the world into himself, whilst the scientist does just the opposite; he externalizes and impersonalizes the world... Hence, may it not be supposed, when mechanics and mathematics took over from animism and magic, it was this internalization, this intimate connection of the *mens* with the world, which had to be avoided at all costs. And, hence it may be suggested, through the necessity for this strong reaction, the mistake arose for allowing the problem of mind to fall so completely out of step and so far behind the problem of matter in the external world and how it works... This bad start of the problem of knowledge has never quite been made up."[1]

The various revolutions in biology can also be interpreted as reactions to a particular social context. I have myself wondered, as an evolutionary biologist, if Charles Darwin would have pondered evolution so deeply had he not been brought up in an uptight Victorian culture, been required to pass an examination in Cambridge on William Paley's *Natural Theology* about which he said: "I do not think I hardly ever admired a book more than Paley's *Natural Theology*",[2] and then spent four years cooped up on the good ship "Beagle" with that repressed Victorian fundamentalist Captain Fitzroy. It is a common error to say that Darwin showed there was no purpose in nature. He showed that existing views were invalid.

These examples are details of a general phenomenon of how society shapes science. From its modern origin to our time, science was moulded by a society that sought to master nature for "the relief of man's estate", to use Francis Bacon's phrase. It was a science that produced the industrial revolution and the factory was in turn itself a product of these developments.[3, 4] It is little wonder that the dominant concept of nature and humanity that arose from it was a technocratic one. We have inherited that scientific technological world-view.

2. The dominant scientific technological world-view

What do we mean by a scientific technological world-view? Science is not simply a collection of facts any more than a house is a pile of bricks. The

---

[1] Quoted from Everett Mendelsohn: "The Social Construction of Scientific Knowledge". *Society and the Sciences,* 1:3-26, 1977.

[2] F. Darwin: *Life and Letters of Charles Darwin.* Vol. II. London: Murray, 1961.

[3] H. Butterfield: *The Origins of Modern Science.* London: Bell & Sons, 1950.

[4] J. Bronowski & B. Mazlish: *The Western Intellectual Tradition.* London: Hutchinson, 1960.

framework within which facts are set provides science with its world-view or cosmology.

Now the dominant scientific technological world-view of today is not the view held by the greatest of thoughtful scientists who are impelled to explore the mystery of the universe and to find deeper meaning every day. The dominant scientific world-view is quite inconsistent, for example, with modern quantum theory and with the ideas of those explorers in biology who are brave enough to put mind and consciousness back into the equation of living organisms.

But few scientists know or care about these deeper issues. Most scientists think about the world about as much as bank clerks do. Many Christians are the same. They pour the new wine of science into old wine skins which cannot contain it. The old wine skin is the dominant scientific technological world-view. It is the cosmology of mechanism in which the universe is conceived as a gigantic contrivance grinding on its way relentlessly to an uncertain eternity. Its component parts, be they nebulae, planetary systems, atoms or living organisms are themselves mechanisms.

With this model to guide us we should hardly be surprised when at the end of astronomer Stephen Weinberg's description of the evolving universe in his book *The First Three Minutes* we find his conclusions thus: "The more the universe seems comprehensible the more it also seems pointless."[5] Biologist Jacques Monod came to much the same conclusion from the ideology of mechanism in his book *Chance and Necessity.*[6] The only purpose he could find in life was that the organism was the DNA molecule's way of perpetuating itself, a theme which was more recently developed in Dawkins' book *The Selfish Gene.*[7] The purpose of our lives is to perpetuate our DNA. In this view physics and chemistry are the fundamental sciences since all else is to be reduced to their terms.

3. Christian theology and the dominant scientific world-view

One might have imagined that Christian theology would have resisted the mechanistic interpretation of the world and all that is in it. On the contrary. Indeed, mechanism's most famous metaphor of the universe as a clockwork with God as the clockmaker was given to it by a bishop, the Frenchman Nicole Oresme, in the fourteenth century.[8]

According to Lynn White the schism between our understanding of nature and our understanding of human nature as detached from it began

---

[5] Steven Weinberg: *The First Three Minutes: a Modern View of the Origin of the Universe.* New York: Basic Books, Inc., 1977, p. 154.
[6] Jacques Monod: *Chance and Necessity: an Essay on Natural Philosophy of Modern Biology.* New York: Alfred Knopf, 1971.
[7] R. Dawkins: *The Selfish Gene.* London: Oxford University Press, 1976.
[8] Lynn White: "Christians and Nature." *Pacific Theological Review*, 7:6-11, 1975.

650 years ago in a theologically motivated effort to salvage revelation as essential to the Christian life. Most of the steps were taken by good Christians, not least by Sir Isaac Newton.

4. The misfit of the dominant scientific world-view to the twentieth century

The concept of the universe and humans as mechanisms served science admirably in its early struggles against magic and superstition. It may even have served religion in its break away from animism. Science has made its great advances by studying atoms and organisms as if they were machines. It is quite another step, a metaphysical one, to assert that they are machines, period. I put my trust in the surgeon who understands the mechanism of my pumping heart and its valve if I am to have my valves replaced. However, I do not trust so well the surgeon who regards me as a machine.

Mechanism as a world-view has let us down. The critical social context for science and religion today is not the world as a factory but the world in ecological crisis. Yet the dominant scientific technological world-view is not an ecological model at all. It is anti-nature. It provides a factory view of nature. Nature is there to serve us. If nature lets us down, the only alternative we leave ourselves is a faith that technology will prove equal to all problems and challenges, provided the imperatives of economic growth are not sicklied over with the pale cast of conservationist thought!

The dominant scientific technological world-view is not only anti-nature. It is anti-human because it fails to capture what matters most about the human in its mechanical images. A. N. Whitehead once remarked that a scientist imbued with the purpose of proving that there are no purposes is an interesting object of study.

To bring the human into the picture is to bring in mind and consciousness and purpose, sensations of red and blue, bitter and sweet, suffering and joy, good and bad. Exclusive mechanism cannot deal with these human qualities.

So we find that critical facts about nature and critical facts about the human cannot be fitted into the old framework of exclusive mechanism. Where does that leave us?

Now is the fullness of time for science and religion to react to the social context of our time and together produce an image of nature, humanity and God that speaks to the needs of this age.

5. Personal encounter with the universe

The dominant scientific technological world-view is challenged by personal encounter with the universe. The challenge comes largely from outside science and theology.[9, 10] The paradigm of such encounter is Job's interrogation of the suffering that encompassed him and his image of the God of that world.

---

[9] B. Easlea: *Liberation and the Aims of Science: an Essay on Obstacles to the Building of a Beautiful World.* London: Chatto & Windus, 1973.

[10] Henryk Skolimowski: *Ecological Humanism.* Tract 19 & 20, 1977, pp. 3-41.

It is God whom Job questioned. Did God then vouchsafe to him a revelation to solve the mystery that so oppressed him? In the reply of Yahweh there is nothing but an injunction to open his eyes and look abroad over the grandeur and the mystery of the universe of which man is but an item. Job thought he knew what was divine power and governance and the meaning of justice. He was wrong. His conceptions did not fit the facts of life.

> And Yahweh said to Job:
> "Who is this obscuring my designs
> with his empty-headed words?
> Brace yourself like a fighter;
> now it is my turn to ask questions and you to inform me.
> Where were you when I laid the foundations of the earth?
> Tell me, since you are so well-informed!
> Who decided the dimensions of it, do you know?...
> Have you journeyed all the ways to the sources of the sea,
> or walked where the Abyss is deepest?
> Have you been shown the gates of Death
> or met the janitors of Shadowland?
> Have you an inkling of the extent of the earth?
> tell me all about it if you have!..."

Job 38. *The Jerusalem Bible*

Some of these questions are questions to us, though not all. For we have more than an inkling of the extent of the earth, even of the universe. Someone has counted the number of electrons in the universe and has come up with the round figure of 10^{80}! We have journeyed all the ways to the sources of the sea and beyond to the moon. We have walked where the abyss of the sea is deepest and now we plan to dig it up. We think we know something about the beginnings of the universe and the beginnings of life. But our dominant scientific technological world-view and a good deal of the Christian theology that accompanies it provides no framework within which we can find comprehensible answers to questions of point and purpose.

What then might Yahweh say to the modern questioner?

> Who is this obscuring my designs with his mechanistic models of the universe so that there is room neither for purpose, mind nor consciousness?
> Brace yourself like a fighter, for now it is my turn to ask questions and yours to inform me.
> Where were you at the Big Bang?
> How is it that out of a universe of pure hydrogen you have come into existence?
> Did life begin when the first cell came into existence or do elements of life exist in the foundations of the universe?
> How can you be so sure that all is contrivance? How can mind grow from no mind? How can life grow from the non-living?

Do people grow from blind mechanism? Is not a universe which grows human beings as much a human or humanizing universe as a tree which grows apples is an apple tree?
Or do you think that figs grow on thistles and grapes on thorns?
Does the life of Jesus not tell you something about the life of the universe? Was He not there in some sense from the foundations of it all?
You who live in rich countries, can you not see how every increase in your standard of living reduces that of someone in a poor country now as well as threatening the survival of future generations? Who is madly Christian enough amongst you to cut his standard of living by a third for the sake of the poor?
Do you think that the world and all that is in it is simply for your use? Has it no other value?
Are plants that grow and flower in the desert, where no man is, of no value?
Because there are accidents and chance in the world, why do you think there is therefore no room for purpose? Can you not have both?
And when you have analysed life down to its molecular building blocks in DNA, why do you think you have discovered the secret of life when you have not yet discovered the source of love and all feeling?

And why do you want to make of me either an all-powerful engineer or an impotent non-entity when I am neither?

To all of which we can only reply as Job replied:

"I have been holding forth on matters I cannot understand
on marvels beyond me and my knowledge.
I knew you then only by hearsay;
but now, having seen you with my own eyes,
I retract all I have said, and in dust and ashes I repent." Job 42

That is an encounter of the ultimate kind. Intelligence is almost useless to those who possess nothing else. Confession of incompetence, according to the book of Job, is the beginning of wisdom.

6. The role of science and faith in constructing a world-view

The report of the Commission of the World Council of Churches on Faith and Order entitled "Christian Hope and the Natural Sciences"[11] presents one view of the relation of science and faith. Science, we are told, gets its information by studying nature. Christian theology gets its information from revelation; this is found in history as recorded in the Bible. This dichotomy in the way things are known leads to dichotomies in what is known, as for example between God and nature, living and non-living and human and non-human life. For the purposes of this discussion I shall refer to this view as the *disjunct view* of nature, humanity and God.

---

[11] *Anticipation*, No. 25, 1979, pp. 75-78.

Quite a different view of nature, humanity and God is represented in most of the remaining articles in the same issue of *Anticipation*. In this other view all knowledge and understanding, whatever their source, contribute to its cosmology. An essential component of knowledge of what nature is comes from science. But it is not the only source. There are other sources of human experience and understanding that come, for example, from communities of faith, Christian or otherwise, and from the Church fathers or from the modern philosophical analysis of religions. In this view knowledge is not divided between science and revelation. All truth is inter-related so we must concern ourselves with everything. There are philosophical criteria for sifting the irrelevant from the relevant, the superstitious from the real. Science has rendered religion, perhaps even revelation, a service by helping in this sifting and adjudicating process. Continuities between the different ways of knowing lead to continuities in what is known, as for example between nature and God, the living and the non-living and the human and non-human life.

This approach is as old as the disjunct approach. It can be found in the biblical record and the writings of early Church fathers. Gregorios writes that Gregory of Nyssa had "the intellectual courage to say that humanity and even the cosmos itself, participate in this infinity (God) ... and we can know God, both through his activity ... which is everywhere in the universe and by understanding ourselves as we gradually become more conformed to his image". Further, he writes that it was Gregory of Nyssa's view that "the universe reveals its full nature only when it brings forth man; therefore only through looking at man do we see purpose in the universe".[12] For the purposes of this discussion I shall refer to this unitary approach as the *ecological view*.

7. The ecological view of nature, humanity and God

Today the *ecological view* of nature, humanity and God has developed as a reaction firstly to the ecological crisis, secondly to the inadequacy of the *disjunct view* to provide a guide to the ecologically sustainable and socially just society, and thirdly to the failure of the scientific technological worldview to account for that which is most important in life. Its modern development, in which science is taken with great seriousness, is due to A. N. Whitehead and his students.

The view from within: Human experience is a high level exemplification of reality in general. There the subjective world of feeling is real for us. But that world extends beyond the human when we see everything through this window, be it cats or elephants or electrons. That is a challenge to the imagination. The biologist primarily responsible for the eradication of the malarial mosquito from the coast of Brazil was a good ecologist. He said that to

---

[12]Paulos Gregorios: *The Human Presence: an Orthodox View of Nature.* Geneva: WCC, 1979, pp. 57 ff.

understand a mosquito you had to try and think like a mosquito and that is what he did. What emerges in the human we weave back again into the total process. The world then becomes more life-like than matter-like. It is not as tame as our sluggish convention-ridden imaginations imply. Mind is no longer just in a corner of nature. It is part of all nature.

In human experience we consciously touch God or God touches us through the values of existence. But God is involved in all that exists in a radical way. Harry Emerson Fosdick used the ocean as a metaphor to depict the relation of humanity, nature and God. There is a near end of the ocean which I experience and know when I sail in it, swim in it and get to love it from sunrise to sunset. But beyond my shore the ocean extends to reaches I have never explored away beyond the horizon. Every drop in the wide ocean is continuous with the ocean I know on my shore.

A universe that produces humans cannot be known apart from this fact. It is a humiverse. We only begin to know what it is by what it becomes. We do not start with electrons and atoms and build a universe. We start with humanity and interpret the rest in terms of this starting point.

When we realize that things not only meet each other externally but take account of each other internally as well, ecology takes on an additional connotation. To be related in any real meaning of the word is to be not only an object to some other entity but to be also a subject. The inner reality of entities is analogous to our inner reality, which is our subjective life which we know as feelings, perceptions, taking account of things. We are members one of another. The present for any entity, including ourselves, has two components. It is born out of the womb of the past and anticipates the future. Or as Whitehead put it: "The present is memory tinged with anticipation."[13] Real being is concrete feeling. In the ecological view this is a feeling universe.

To know only the outer aspect of things is to know them only as objects. It is a one dimensional perspective of reality. It is to mistake the abstract for the concrete, the menu for the meal. To really know we have to be involved subjectively.

The view that subjectivity does not exist is the doctrine of materialism. The view that subjectivity exists in some entities and not in others is dualism. In the ecological view subjectivity exists in all evolved entities. It is the most thoroughgoing attempt to see the universe as a universe and not a multiverse.

That all actual entities have an inner reality as well as an outer reality is a rational basis for our sense of kinship with all things.

> And never for each other shall we feel
> As we may feel, till we have sympathy
> With nature in her forms inanimate,
> With objects such as have no power to hold
> Articulate language. In all forms of things
> There is mind.
>
> Wordsworth, "Tintern Abbey"

---

[13] A. N. Whitehead: *Process and Reality*. London: Macmillan, 1929.

We desperately need an interpretation of "experience" that will apply up and down the line from protons to people. What we superficially see as static entities are on analysis processes. A statue preserves its shape whereas a fountain actively performs it. All created entities from protons to people are like fountains. They perform their existence.

This view of nature, humanity and God finds support in physics from scientists such as Heisenberg and Bohm, in biology from Sewall Wright, Waddington and Rensch and in philosophy and theology in the process school of thought from Daniel Day Williams, Charles Hartshorne, John Cobb and Schubert Ogden.

The nature of order: A central problem of cosmology is the nature of the order of the universe. Nature, including the human, is a mixture of order and randomness. In the ecological view, order is not a consequence of one all-powerful orderer, a view which has led to a hopeless impasse in understanding disorder and evil. There are many creators, for all created entities have a degree of freedom to respond appropriately or not. Because God is not in complete control of the events of the world, genuine evil is not incompatible with God's beneficence.

How can there be order with a multitude of creative agents? Without some sort of coordination there would be chaos. It is unlikely that a committee could have painted a *Mona Lisa.* It is all the more unlikely that a multiplicity of creators could have produced cosmic order. What is required is some all pervasive influence that will give shape and direction to things.

Consider a lecture theatre full of students, each a creative agent and each capable of doing many different activities during the lecture hour. Each student in the theatre is a potential source of disorder. If the class is ordered it is not because it is controlled by an all powerful controller. It is ordered because it is persuaded by the lecturer or the common purpose that has brought the students into the theatre. Order is anarchy tamed. So it is with the universe. The potentiality for disorder with a multitude of creative entities is immense. But they are brought under control by persuasive lure of their inner life which lure is God.

What happened in evolution? In the ecological view the cosmos is a fighting frontier of progressive integration or order. The struggle at one time was at the level of electrons, protons and the like as they formed atoms. That frontier is now passed. That association now has a stability it did not have some eight billion years ago. Billions of years later there was a time when the association of atoms into complex molecules, proteins, and DNA was the fighting frontier. Stability is now achieved at that level, but not yet so fully established. Complex molecules became organized into cells. Here and there are still considerable possibilities for misfits and miscreations. Cells became organized into complex organisms, animals and plants, whose stability is less than that of cells. The creation is yet more delicately poised than it had ever been. When we come to human societies, this is where integration is least achieved, where disintegration and chaos are widespread and perilous. Is not this now the fighting frontier of progressive creativity in the universe? Here the existing creation is groping in the realm of possibilities where undreamed of values of God have their being. The universe has got to where it is without us. Now it needs us. The creative challenge to the human is from his spiritual environment, the realm of values not yet realized. For the Christian the human response of Jesus to God was complete. Our failure to respond is not just a personal deficiency. It is a cosmic tragedy. The ecological and economic crisis is part of that tragedy. They are examples of the ambiguity of creative advance. With each new advance there is a cost. The cost is a cross. The new brings with it new possibilities, new freedoms, new stimuli, new intensities of experience and new hopes. It also brings with it new risks, new sufferings, new tragedies and new evils. That is what the fall symbolizes. The major advances of civilization are processes that all but wreck the societies in which they occur. The symbol of the fall is always with us. It identifies the occurrence of a new level of order and freedom bought at the price of suffering. There can be no realistic vision of evolution without some sense of tragedy. The cross pattern is woven deeply into the fabric of nature.

We are not alone. In the ecological view the universe feels God in its creative advance. And God feels the universe in its joy and its agony as it evolves. God not only gives love but God is responsive to love because God is love.

8. A live-ethic

The ecological model of nature, humanity and God implies an ethic that embraces the whole of the world of value, especially the value of life. Western ethics is radically anthropocentric. The only argument western ethics has for conserving nature is that we should take care of the habitat because it takes care of us. It is counter-productive to destroy it. In short, it is a principle of good management to take care of our resources. So, in the final analysis, the ecological habitat becomes a resource that people use. Our conservation ethic is purely an instrumental ethic. We recognize a silo value of nature; nature as a source of food, clothing and other products we need. There is the laboratory view of nature espoused by scientists who want to study the kangaroos and elephants in the wild. There is the gymnasium view of nature as a place for recreation and athletic activities. And there is the cathedral view of nature that provides opportunities for esthetic delights and spiritual renewal. These are all part of the instrumental value of nature. But is that all? Is the only value of plants and animals their value to us? Have they no value in themselves for themselves and for God? What could give them such value? It is the knowledge that other humans enjoy experience and hence have value in and for themselves that gives our sense of obligation towards them. Only sentience or feeling gives intrinsic value. This is the strong meaning of intrinsic value.[14] In an ecological universe every created entity has intrinsic value

[14] John B. Cobb: "Ecology, Ethics and Theology." In Herman E. Daly: *Toward a Steady State Economy*. San Francisco: W.H. Freeman & Co., 1973.

because all are subjects as well as objects. And whatever has intrinsic value has some right to exist and to prosper. Here then is a substantial basis for an ethic of life that embraces all life. Jesus seemed so to think when he said: "Not a sparrow falls to the ground without your father knowing." Albert Schweitzer said: "Ethics is the infinitely extended responsibility towards all life."[15]

If sentience be the criterion of intrinsic value, then there must be a hierarchy of intrinsic value from lesser creatures through mammals to the human. "Are you not worth more than many sparrows?" asked Jesus. A complete life-ethic would take into account the hierarchy of intrinsic value and instrumental value. No one has yet attempted to do that systematically. But the immediate point of importance for us is that in the ecological view of nature, when the interests of people and elephants and kangaroos come into conflict, the non-humans count for more than zero in the equation.

But can we persuade people to act with consideration and restraint and compassion with respect to non-human creatures when they are so blind even to anthropocentric values? Perhaps the shift in attitude is too drastic, too unthinkable to persuade most people. They will not change without a change in their deepest convictions about the meaning of life after an encounter of the ultimate kind.

Life is to be sustained because of its intrinsic value and also because all life has instrumental value, if not to humans then to other life. Though we are to value all life we shall be most conscious of value as it affects human life. An earth which is so managed as to be ecologically sustainable is of more value to humanity than one which is ecologically unsustainable. An ecologically sustainable earth is a necessary requirement for distributive justice. There is no possibility of justice in a world in which the rich exploit resources at the expense of the poor and of other life. The ethical consequence of the ecological crisis is that the rich world reduce its present level of exploitation of the earth in order that most of the world, which is poor, may share more than the few percent of the products of the earth which are at present theirs. The only way this can come about is for the rich world to reduce its standard of living. A world cannot sustain all the world as rich as the rich world. Justice requires that the rich become the poorer that the poor may survive. The arithmetic has been done. At least for me the consequences are clear. The alternative is ecological unsustainability and yet greater injustice. The two go hand in hand.

We have been warned as Noah was warned. Sceptics laughed and ridiculed then as they do now. The sceptics drowned and Noah the original prophet of ecological doom survived. We are warned that a flood of problems now threatens the persistence of our industrial society. But this time the ark cannot be built of wood and caulking. Its foundations will be a new aware-

---

[15] Albert Schweitzer: *Civilization and Ethics*. London: Adam & Black, 1949, p. 241.

ness of the meaning of life, of the life of all creatures, both great and small. Its name will be the ecologically sustainable and socially just global society. If this ark cannot be made watertight in time, industrial society will sink, dragging under prophets of doom as well as sceptics and critics.

We do not have to be victims of circumstance. In the ecological view the future is not predetermined. It is radically open. Through its openness to the lure of God the self becomes freed from total preoccupation with itself. Its concern becomes the world. That is still possible for each one of us.

Solidarity in Conflict

GERHARD LIEDKE

To subdue the earth, to have dominion over the non-human creation even to the point of destroying it—such is the mark of the relation between man and creation in the period of history in which we live.

This attitude of man to the non-human creation presupposes the separation, or rather the rupture, of man from nature. René Descartes, with his separation of *res cogitans* from *res extensa*, stands as its symbol. The edifice of modern western science and technology rests on that rupture, and the ecological crisis of our world is the unwelcome consequence of that separation. Western Christendom has made a decisive contribution to this development.

The pattern of separation between nature and man has penetrated so deeply into the modern theology of the West that this theological tradition can only with difficulty correct it. The most that has been done within its framework is probably Karl Barth's account in §69 of the *Church Dogmatics*: The non-human creation is the "stage and setting" of the drama of reconciliation and consequently linked with man and his history with God. But that is not enough. Western theology must therefore seek other sources for dealing with the problem, above all the main source of theology, the Bible. A beginning has been made in preparation for the present conference, particularly at the 1977 Zurich consultation, by the papers of John Austin Baker and Claus Koch and Section III of the report (*Anticipation*, No. 25, p. 29 ff).

My contribution will attempt to take up these biblical ways of approach and carry them further at three points:

— reflections on Romans 8:18 ff. can be deepened;
— Genesis 1 and 9 can be referred more precisely to the ecological problem;

— the aspect of conflict between man and non-human creation can be stressed.

The groaning of the creation and its hope

In the description of the "new life" (Rom. 8), Paul cannot leave the non-human creation out of account. In this he is entirely in line with the Old Testament (cf. Isa. 11), in contrast to the western theology of recent centuries.

For us, his starting-point in Romans 8:18 is extremely topical: suffering. The Christian theological sense of suffering must be grasped; we are not yet living in the consummation, as Christian enthusiasts dreamt then and have repeatedly done since. The new life is present only under the conditions of this time. Suffering, however, is no reason for resignation. On the contrary, the sufferings of Christ, the sufferings of Christians, the sufferings of the creation all mark the discordance between the utter insufficiency and need of this world and God's salvation, and consequently point to the coming glory. In verses 19-22, the suffering and longing of the non-human creation is described. As Ernst Käsemann has shown, *ktisis* means primarily the non-human creature. According to Romans 8, therefore, man and the non-human creation share a common fate, or more exactly, a common suffering. Christians, like the non-human creation, "wait with eager longing" for glory to be revealed. Both "do not recognize the existing earthly state of affairs" and so are "in search of eschatological freedom" (Käsemann). Because both are looking out for "liberation from the constraints that do violence to them", they have hope in the midst of hopelessness. Christians and non-human creation therefore form not merely a community of suffering but rather a community of hope.

There is, of course, a difference between Christians and non-human creation in one important point. Only the Christians "have received the first fruits of the Spirit". The Spirit of God and his hope of freedom comes to the non-human creation through the Christians, who suffer as children of God.

This goes far beyond the Old Testament definitions of the relation between man and nature; it is a christological and pneumatological transformation of the *dominum terrae* of Genesis 1 and 9. Certainly the Spirit-endowed Christians do not redeem creation. But the creation looks anxiously and longingly to the Christians. By the way in which we Christians deal with suffering, the creation is shown how its hope stands, whether it is an illusion or not. If we human beings increase the suffering in the world—that of men and of the non-human creation—then the hope of the creation sinks. If we aggravate the conflict between man and nature and the conflicts between human beings, then the creation falls into hopeless resignation. If, on the other hand, in solidarity with the non-human creation we reduce suffering, then the creation's hope of freedom awakens to new life.

As the envisaged goals of the sustainable society consist in reducing suffering of both the human and the non-human creation, they can—according to Paul—help Christians to be the great promise of the creation.

Creation — flood — renewal of the creation

The relation of Christians to the non-human creation is not, however, identical with that of mankind to nature, for it is not mankind that is the bearer of the Spirit of God, but only the Christians living in Christ. If we want to find something from the Bible about the relation of men to the rest of the creation, we must inquire of the Old Testament and in particular Genesis 1 taken in conjunction with Genesis 9. The difference between the two is that Genesis 1 shows how God really meant his creation to be, while Genesis 9 shows what in fact became of it after the eruption of deeds of violence into the world (Gen. 6). One cannot appeal directly to Genesis 1 ("Subdue the earth!"), but only through the intermediary of Genesis 9, the new regulation of the *dominium terrae* after the flood. Failure to take account of this difference has often led to wrong conclusions in Christendom.

Reflection on Genesis 1 must start with a reference to the ecological structure of this creation narrative. Hannes Odil Steck has shown that in the second to the fourth works of creation the habitats (*oikoi*) are created, in the fifth to the eighth works, the living creatures belonging to each. The stars (they are, according to the ancient conception, not dead bodies but living beings) inhabit the heavens, the aquatic animals the sea, the birds the air, and land animals and men together inhabit the earth. The fact that in the fourth work of creation the earth is arrayed in a clothing of plants underlines the ecological meaning of this creation narrative: only an earth covered with vegetation is a dwelling-place for men and land animals; neither man nor beast could live in a desert.

The ecological structure of Genesis 1 is furthermore the main point of connection for the scientific point of view. Evolutionary research shows us in its attempts at reconstruction the way to the ecosystem which Genesis 1 presents. As long as the attempt was made to establish a parallelism between the order of the days of creation in Genesis 1 with the chief steps of evolution, the theology of creation and natural science came into insoluble contradiction. The ecological view appears to be the point at which the two outlooks meet.

Genesis 1 is therefore less a document of rudimentary natural science than an assignment of the creatures to their places in the habitats created for them by God. We note that each kind of living creature has its own habitat — the stars, the heavens, the aquatic animals the sea, the birds the air; there is no overlapping. Only in respect of earth as habitat is there a difference. There two kinds of living beings, the land animals and human beings, have to share one habitat.

Everyone knows what that can mean. There can be disputes about living-space and food. We hear nothing in Genesis 1 of this latent conflict breaking out. God's good creation has inbuilt mechanisms which still prevent the conflict. The first of these is the different distribution of food for men and animals, Genesis 1:29-30. The animals are to eat "every green plant", that is to say, plants that grow of themselves, which do not have to be cultivated. Man, on the other hand, is assigned corn and the fruits of trees, that is to say, plants that need cultivation and tending. According to Genesis 1, man does not eat animals; he is a vegetarian. This vegetarianism is not given any metaphysical basis, but represents the ecologically significant avoidance of conflict in the situation of Genesis 1. God's command "Subdue the earth!" (1:28) is in the first place simply an authorization to man to engage in agriculture, which is needed to ensure the prescribed food-supply. On the other hand, the mandate to have dominion over the animals (1:26, 28) means that if there are matters in dispute between animals and men in their common habitation—after the food arrangements have been made—then men must decide. For man is, and this distinguishes him from the animals, the image of God. Just as God rules his world with care, so man is to rule the animals and cultivate and preserve the earth. The *dominium terrae* therefore places a responsibility on man for the non-human creation; it does not give him unrestricted power of disposal over the non-human world. The creed of modern times that the world is only material for man, has, therefore, no biblical sanction. Claus Westermann notes: "A relation of domination in which the ruler simply enjoys the benefits provided by his subjects, is unthinkable in the Old Testament. The relation always includes in some way an existence for the subjects."

Genesis 1, and also the creation story in Genesis 2, describe the world as God its creator meant it to be. We all know, and the Bible knows, that in fact the creation is not like that. The world in which we live is the world "after" the so-called Fall of man (Gen. 3), "after" the fratricide and the revenge (Gen. 4), "after" the flood (Gen. 6-9) and "after" the dispersion of the peoples (Gen. 11). At the beginning of the story of the flood (Gen. 6:11), we read: "Now the earth was corrupt in God's sight, and the earth was filled with violence." Violence—not sexuality—is the characteristic of sin for the priestly narrator. Violence is the outbreak of the possibility of conflict about living-space that was latent in God's good creation. There is no speculation in Genesis about the origin of evil. This much can be said, however: The scope for freedom and responsibility given to man in the creation contains the possibility of conflict; that is why Genesis 6:13 says: "The earth is filled with violence through men." That is, of course, a way of looking at it that cannot be directly harmonized with the views of evolutionary research. But neither is there any contradiction. The understanding of the Genesis texts that I have outlined is in agreement with the views of evolutionary research in that in evolution possibilities are increasingly realized.

As a result of violence the earth now perishes in the great flood. The story of the flood is probably the most important text ecologically in the Old Testament. It is not a report of a unique event in the mists of antiquity, but the powerfully significant symbol for the threat to a creation in which violence has spread. It shows that the Creator has the power to revoke his creation (Westermann). Nevertheless, it is repeatedly—not only in the case of Noah—God's merciful will that the world, men and animals, should be brought safely through the violence as though in an ark. That is why the blessing is renewed in Genesis 9:1-7 after the flood. Thus man's dominion over earth and animals is regulated anew, but now with the condition of violence on the earth. The relation between men and animals is spoken of realistically as a war. "Fear and dread" are upon the animals now; that is the formula with which God makes Israel's foes tremble. The animals are delivered "into the hand" of man; that is the victor's formula in the Holy War. The conflict will cease only at the end of the ages when men and beasts live together in harmony as Isaiah 11 foresees. In our world, however, man's *dominium* is in fact full of violence, conflict is the fundamental form of relation between man and the non-human creation. The sufferings of the creation which Paul names in Romans 8 are caused by this conflict.

In Genesis 9, man is permitted to eat flesh-meat and consequently to kill animals. The difference between Genesis 1 and 9 in this respect shows that it is not in accordance with the true will of the Creator that animals should be delivered up to men's violence and even to slaughter. The blessing of the creation is renewed after the flood, and we all live on it, but it is realized now at the expense of our fellow-creatures.

However, Genesis 9 does not stop at realistic observation of the fact of conflict between man and the non-human creation, for measures are taken which protect each of the partners in the conflict, so that the worst, mutual annihilation, is avoided.

Protection of the animals from men is served by a restriction placed on the permission to kill animals. The blood of the animals is not to be consumed with their flesh (9:4). As the life of a living being is in the blood, the flesh of animals may be eaten, but not their life, which according to Genesis 1:24 has come from the earth. It must be given back to the earth in the outflowing blood when they are slaughtered. Judaism has scrupulously observed this prohibition of blood. Claus Koch pointed out in Zurich that Christian theology was not well-advised to dismiss this prohibition as a ritual law without devising some equivalent protection of non-human life. For it is with this commandment that in Genesis 9, despite the killing of animals, the blessing of the whole creation is maintained, even though in conflict.

Conversely, man's protection from the animals is served by God's promise (9:5) that he will require a reckoning for the blood of men even from the animals themselves.

Another important observation must be made here. In the setting of this regulation the priestly narrator mentions for the first time of the threat to human life from other men. Conflict between human beings, social conflict, is therefore in Genesis 9 a part of the ecological conflict. The ecological conflict is the framework to which social conflict belongs. Both are ultimately conflicts over distribution. Consequently the two adjectives in the formula "sustainable and just society" should be set in close relation to each other. It cannot be that the ecological conflict is concerned only with sustainability and the social conflict only with justice; both conflicts are about both.

Solidarity in conflict

This interpretation of the *dominium terrae* has employed the category of "conflict" and elements of conflict theory. This is exegetically legitimate, provided it is done deliberately. No interpretation can dispense with the use of present-day words and categories. Only in this way is it possible systematically to unfold exegetical observations. I use in particular some elements from a theory of conflict formulated by Johan Galtung.

Galtung distinguishes between symmetrical and asymmetrical conflicts: "When we speak of a symmetrical, balanced conflict, we mean a conflict between two parties that are of equal rank, that is, they are both of the same kind, e.g. nations, and have the same resources. An asymmetrical, unequal conflict arises between unequal parties, who are not on the same level, do not have the same resources and may even be different in kind. A dispute between slave-owners and slaves, for instance, would be an asymmetrical, unequal conflict."

For regulating conflicts there are in principle, according to Galtung, two strategies, the dissociative strategy, which separates contestants and keeps them apart (e.g. the earlier system of "natural frontiers" between nations), and the associative strategy, which aims at bringing the parties as close together as possible (cf. alliances between states or formations like the EEC).

If the two distinctions are combined, the following rules emerge: In symmetrical conflicts associative techniques should be employed. In asymmetrical conflicts, however, associative techniques only increase the power of the stronger; in these conflicts a two-phase strategy is appropriate: first a dissociative phase, which allows the weaker to achieve survival, self-regard and autarchy, until the confict has become symmetrical, when an associative phase can follow.

But how can an asymmetrical conflict be made symmetrical? By strengthening the weak, e.g. by the coalition of many weak (formation of trade unions by workers) or, what is almost utopian, by the strong themselves strengthening the weak (parents their children).

The conflict between man and the non-human creation—originally in Genesis 1 almost symmetrical, but then in Genesis 9 perceptibly asymmetrical—has in the last few centuries through western science and technology become extremely asymmetrical. Destructive man faces a nature that in many of its domains has been laid waste, and he is in possession of many powerful means of continuing this process.

Nature is no longer regarded in any sense as a rival partner, but as dead material at man's disposal. To restore nature as party to the conflict is therefore the first act of the ecological interpretation of the *dominium terrae*. Then it is possible to see that the conflict is asymmetrical. This then, according to the principles of conflict-theory, forbids an associative treatment of the conflict, a harmony between men and nature. The only meaningful thing is to maintain the dissociation and find means of strengthening the weaker partner, nature. The goal of these attempts cannot be the achievement of complete symmetry. Genesis 1 and 9 rightly see that the asymmetry of the conflict cannot be removed in our eon. Consequently they, and especially Genesis 9, choose a path which is well-advised in conflict-theory. They devise defence mechanisms especially for the weaker part, the non-human creation. The fact that we human beings in modern times have no longer provided this protection to the non-human creation is the transgression of divine commandments.

This points the way, then, for an ecological ethics:

1) to take nature seriously as a partner in the conflict;
2) to work against extreme asymmetry by redevising defence mechanisms chiefly to protect nature from men.

The ecological conflict is complicated by the often disregarded fact that man is a part of nature, so that together with nature he is exploiting and expressing himself by acting on the western interpretation of the *dominium terrae*. That means that ecological ethics always includes taking man seriously and protecting him from himself. Georg Picht describes the connection between *dominium terrae* and man's membership of nature as follows: "The concept of dominion over the earth has as it were two poles. Earth is the nature which is mastered, of which man as an organism is a part, to which he himself belongs, and which he bears in himself. Dominion, however defined, constitutes a responsibility for whoever is master. Responsibility for nature presupposes a certain measure of freedom from nature... Consequently the responsibility has a different origin from the phenomena of nature which man masters."

To sum up, there is required of us solidarity of men with the non-human creation in the conflict between man and nature. From Christians, more than that kind of solidarity is required, because according to Paul they have to make visible the great promise of eschatological freedom for the non-human creation. What forms this solidarity will take must be investigated and implemented by specialists, politicians and the electorate. The theological grounds for that solidarity are once again clear when we realize that God's relation to us human beings is likewise one of solidarity in conflict. By voluntary renunciation of his power, God in his Son Jesus Christ has put himself in solidarity with us and so resolved the conflict. Man as image of the merciful God is called to the same kind of solidarity in regard to the non-human creation. God will give us the strength for it if we ask him for it.

That is how I see the connection between God, man and the non-human creation in the age of the ecological crisis. To my mind these considerations are sufficient effectively to justify a new way of dealing with the non-human creation. It is not necessary to devise a new ontology or a process theology; it is not necessary to work out an organic image of nature, man and God (Birch). Such a picture easily makes us underestimate the difficulty of the problem. Backed by the biblical texts we must correct the mistake of separating too deeply man and the non-human creation in the western tradition of philosophy and theology. The contra-distinction of man, God and nature must not be blurred, however. Until the end of time conflict will remain the fundamental character of these relations. But ecological theology has to work out and announce the manifold signs of hope in this conflict, and so make solidarity in conflict possible. This will then be a contribution of theology and churches to the construction of a just and sustainable society.

Christian Perspectives on Creation in a Time of Ecological Unsustainability

VITALY BOROVOY

In every respect—not only socially, economically and ecologically but also culturally, ideologically and spiritually—the contemporary world is marked by crisis. Everything has become problematic. The world has entered into a liquid state; there are no longer solid bodies in it; it is experiencing a revolutionary era, internally and externally alike—it is the era of spiritual anarchy.

Humanity lives in fear (*Angst*—Kierkegaard) which is greater than ever today; it is under constant threat; it is suspended over an abyss (*Grenzsituation*—Tillich). Contemporary humanity has lost the faith which in past centuries it tried to substitute for the Christian faith. It no longer believes in progress, humanism, the saving power of science, nor in the saving power of democracy; it knows the falsehood and injustice of the capitalist system but at the same time has lost its faith in the utopia of a perfect social order. It is not only its belief in God which has been considerably weakened but also its belief in itself, and in humanity's creative power, in the human cause in the world. The dominating principles in the socio-political movements are the principles of violence and power.

Humanity seems to have tired of spiritual freedom and to be willing to surrender it in exchange for a power which will settle human life both internally and externally. Humanity is tired of itself, has lost its self-confidence and seeks backing in something supernatural, even if this something supernatural is social and collective.

Technology as faith

Our age is rejecting many old idols but creating many new ones. Human nature is such that we can live either by our faith in God or by our faith in ideals or idols. In fact, it is impossible for us to be persistent and absolute atheists. When we deviate from belief in God we fall into idolatry. In every sphere, in science, art, the state, national and social life, we can see idols being created and worshipped.

Contemporary humanity's belief in anything at all has weakened. In one respect, however, contemporary humanity is full of optimism and faith. To one idol it sacrifices everything. Contemporary humanity believes in the power of technology, of machines and of science. It sometimes seems as if this is the only thing in which humanity still believes.

There would appear to be very serious grounds for this optimism. Man is profoundly—shockingly—impressed by the might of technology which has revolutionized his life completely. It is humanity's own product, the creation of its own genius, a child of the human spirit. Humanity has succeeded in setting free and using for its own purposes the hidden forces of nature. But humanity has not succeeded in possessing and controlling the results of this process. Technology has become stronger than humanity and enslaved it. Technology provides humanity with a formidable power by which humanity itself in its entirety can be destroyed. Once such a formidable strength is given to humanity, the fate of mankind becomes dependent on our spiritual state as human beings. The destructive technology of war, threatening every living thing with disaster—this alone demonstrates how urgent the spiritual problem of technology is.

Technology implies the domination of man not only over nature but also over man; domination of life, of freedom and of the human spirit. Technology can be made to serve human welfare, the general good, but it can also be used and very often is in practice used to serve evil purposes, destruction, enslavement, exploitation, to achieve diabolic purposes in respect to individuals, social groups, nations, and even humankind.

How do we as Christians view this crisis, this agonizing over these extremely urgent problems confronting humanity? Is this a crisis of the non-Christian world or even of the anti-Christian world which has betrayed the Christian faith? Or is it also a crisis of Christianity? Christians share the world's destiny and its responsibilities. They cannot pretend that all is well with Christianity, with Christendom, now or in the past. A judgment is taking place on the world, but it is also a judgment on historical Christianity. The ailments of our world today are not due only to a falling away from Christianity or to a weakening of faith but also to the ancient ailments of the human expressions of Christianity. Christianity is universal in its significance and everything comes within its orbit. Christians must thus understand the spiritual condition of the contemporary world and that of Christianity itself.

Weakness of the Christian response

We must define the meaning of the world crisis as an event within Christianity itself, within Christian universality. Christians have proved completely unprepared for any assessment of technology, science, the machine. The Christian conscience does not know how to respond to the introduction of technology and the machine into human life. The natural world in which humanity was accustomed to live in the past no longer has the character of an eternal order. We live in a new world which is no longer the world of the new

Christian revelation, no longer the world of the apostles, fathers and teachers of the Church, no longer the world of Christian symbolism.

In its conception Christianity was intimately related to the soil, to a patriarchal way of life. But modern technology tore humanity away from the soil and finally destroyed the patriarchal way of life. In a world in which everything is constantly changing, Christians can live and act only by practising a double rhythm: the secular rhythm and the religious rhythm. In the former, they participate in the technization of life unsanctified by religion, whereas in the latter they turn away from the world to God, in the numbered days and hours of human life. What remains unclear is what this newly conceived world means in religious terms. The reality born of modern technology must not be identified with the former reality of the physical world, the reality studied by mechanics, physics and chemistry. It is a reality which did not exist prior to the human discoveries and inventions which heralded its coming in history. Technology has a cosmogenic significance. It creates a completely new reality.

Modern technology signifies the transformation of all human existence from something organic to something organized. Humanity no longer lives in an organic order. The great cultures of the past were still surrounded by nature; people loved gardens, flowers, animals; their link with the rhythm of nature was still unsevered. The feeling for the soil generated a telluric mysticism. Humanity came from the soil and returns to it. With this is linked a profound religious symbolism. Fertility rites played a very important role. The life of the individual and of society was viewed as organic and similar to that of plants. The life of the family, society, the state, the Church was organic. Society was seen as an organism. An organism is something born, not something man-made. It is the product of natural cosmic life.

Technology tears humanity from the soil, transfers it into space, gives it the sense of the earth as a planet. Technology radically changes humanity's attitude to space and time. It is hostile to any organic embodiment. Here lies the major problem. The organization into which the world is moving—the organization of great human masses, of scientific activity, of the economy, of technology, of life—is one of great difficulty for humanity's spiritual life, for its infinite life, and produces an inner religious crisis.

The elements of organization have existed since the dawn of civilization and so have the elements of technology. But the principle of technical organization was never dominant and all-embracing. Many things remained in an organic state. Organization related to technology is the rationalization of life. But human life cannot be subjected to a total rationalization; a mystery always remains. The universal principle of rationalization receives its reward. The rationalization which does not fall under the highest spiritual principle leads to irrational consequences. A universal rationalization, a technical organization which repudiates the mysterious foundations of life, leads to the loss of the old meaning of life, generates a sense of nostalgia and the possibility of suicide. Humanity cannot itself turn into a machine. Humanity is an organizer of life but in the depths of its innermost being it cannot be the object of organization: there always remains in humanity an organic, irrational mysterious element.

Christianity should define its attitude to the new reality in a creative way. It is impossible to return to the former organic mode of living, to patriarchial relationships, to the old forms of peasant life and crafts, to life with nature, with the soil, plants and animals. Nor is such a return desirable. This mode of life was based on the exploitation of people and animals. Christianity can help people to define creatively their relation to the new epoch, to master technology to serve their purposes. The spirit can be an organizer, it can master technology for its spiritual purposes, but it will resist its own transformation into a tool of the organizing technological process.

Another aspect of the contemporary cultural crisis is the democratization of humanity which is proceeding on a broad front. Culture is spreading widely, and new social and ethnic groups are beginning to share it. This process is inevitable and just. But the process of technization, mechanization and democratization leads to the transformation of culture into technological civilization. The major problem in the contemporary crisis is connected with this transformation. The striving of the individual for emancipation is more and more suppressed in a society which is dissolving into a social collective.

Christianity: answer to spiritual confusion?

The identity of humanity as the image of God is perishing, disintegrating into fragments and in this way losing its wholeness. Christianity alone can in principle solve the painful problem of the individual and society. Christianity values personality above all, the individual human soul and its eternal destiny. It excludes the treatment of the individual as a means to serve the ends of society; it recognizes the unconditional value of every individual. The individual is linked directly with God by the spiritual life, and this is the limit to the power of society over the individual. But Christianity calls the individual to union with a suprapersonal goal, to the union of every "I" and "you" with "we". It does not conceive of the individual outside the communion of all people, outside values and the eternal salvation of all people as society and "communion".

Christianity defends the individual from the peril which threatens her or him even in Christianity. The inner union of the individual with others is more possible in a relationship, a communion, in which the individual develops fully and realizes himself, on the third level, the supra-social and the supra-individual, in Godmanhood, in the Body of Christ. At the basis of Christianity lies the Godmanhood—the theandric principle, the revelation of God and the revelation of man as the image and likeness of God, the revelation of the Son of God becoming man.

Sinful human nature found it difficult to understand the fullness of the Christian revelation of Godmanhood. The Christian doctrine of man was not fully achieved in practice. Both intellectually and existentially, the organic

Christian anthropology of Godmanhood, a divinely revealed anthropology, began to be destroyed. First one half was rejected—the revelation of God. But there remained the other half—the revelation of man, the Christian teaching on man. Feuerbach, for example, denied God, but still retained the idea of the divine likeness of man. But the destruction of the Christian theandric, divinely revealed teaching continued in the process whereby modern technological civilization and society developed.

The process of technization increased in tempo, as did the process of the absorption of the individual by society. The technological and economic process of modern civilization transforms the individuality of man into its instrument and demands unceasing activity, the use of every instant of life.

The individual cannot catch up or keep up with this accelerated process and the mad speed of the conveyor of modern technology. He cannot stop to think, cannot understand the meaning of his life, because this meaning can only be revealed through its relation to eternity. Taken separately, the stream of time makes no sense. Of course we are called to be active, to work, to create. The idea of labour and of a working society is basically a Christian one. As the image of the Creator, the human being is a living being with a capacity for creation. But the activity demanded by modern civilization is actually a denial of this creative nature as well as of humanity as such. Human creativity presupposes society as the aim, but at the same time it presupposes the preservation of the peculiarities of the creative identity of humanity. It presupposes the distinctive combination and inter-relatedness of action and contemplation, of time and eternity, of matter and spirit.

This is the essence of the contemporary crisis, the crisis in the human being, the crisis of humanity itself, the crisis which is religious, the crisis of Christendom as such.

The world crisis is a judgment not only on the secular, non-religious, non-believing world, but rather and primarily on our historical Christianity. The major problem of today does not imply God, as many are in the habit of thinking—including those Christians who call for a religious revival. The problem of today is the problem of humanity, the problem of saving the human individual from disintegration; it is the problem of the vocation and goal of humanity, the problem of solving urgent questions of society and culture in the light of the Christian truth about humanity. This truth must be realized in life. But the problem of realizing this Christian truth is the most difficult and the most complicated problem, not just in the history of Christianity but also in the history of humankind in general, since it points to and calls for the solution of the question of the inter-relationships between the individual and society. This question is organically related to and integrated with the question of the inter-relationship of humanity, nature and God.

Christian understanding of creation in Russian religious thought

When at the present time of ecological unsustainability we are faced with the need to reconsider the Christian idea of creation as a problem of the relationship between nature, man and God, the contribution of Russian theological, religious, philosophical and social thought can be fruitful for our discussions. Because of the limitations of time, let me draw your attention to just one thinker who is not yet very well-known. I refer to Nicolay Fedorov (1828-1903). He was a librarian of the Moscow Public Library. Fedorov was a deeply religious Christian, faithful to the Orthodox Church and a strict ascetic in his personal life. He was one of the most original of Russian thinkers, combining with his genius as a thinker and his profundity as a philosopher an incredible knowledge of the exact natural sciences. As the teacher of the founder of modern space exploration and of the science of space, Tsiolkovsky, he can be regarded also as one of the fathers of space exploration. An official Soviet textbook on the history of Russian philosophy says that "some ideas of space philosophy of Tsiolkovsky are very close to the guesses and 'regulative' projects of Fedorov".

Fedorov's main work, the two volumes of his "philosophy" of the common cause, was published after his death. Fedorov presents a profound and original conception of Christian revelation combined with a moral and practical striving for the transformation and transfiguration of the world.

For him the task of philosophy does not lie in contemplating and understanding existence but in "projection", in the affirmation of its perfectibility. All his writings are in the form of "projects" for the salvation of the world. The thinking of Fedorov is somewhat reminiscent of the French "utopian socialists", such as Fourier and the St Simonists, and to some extent of contemporary Marxists. But his "projects" are much more daring and his radicalism is grounded in an interpretation of Christian revelation. This is very clear in his conception of eschatology and in his interpretation of the Apocalypse. Russian apocalyptic thinking had a dual character, with both revolutionary and reactionary aspects, but a passive conception of apocalypse was undoubtedly uppermost. What the Apocalypse prophesies will happen to humanity, but humanity is not the active agent in the fulfillment of the prophecies. The Apocalypse is understood as a divine *fatum*; human freedom plays no part here. Fedorov's conception of the Apocalypse is radically different. The apocalyptic prophecy about the reign of the anti-Christ, the end of the world and the Last Judgment, is understood by Fedorov as relative, as a threat. There is nothing inevitable or fateful about them. If people will unite for the "common cause", for the existential realization of Christian truth in life, if they will struggle against the elemental, irrational, death-dealing forces of nature in brotherly union, then there will be no reign of anti-Christ, no end of the world, no Last Judgment, and humanity will pass straight into eternal life. Everything depends on the activity of man. And Fedorov preaches an as-yet unheard-of activity for humanity which must overcome nature, organize cosmic life, conquer death and raise the dead.

This "common cause" presupposes as an essential condition brotherly relations among men, the cessation of strife, the realization of brotherhood among men, but it is realized by means of science and technology. Fedorov believed that technology, if used by a humanity united in brotherhood, can perform miracles, can even raise the dead. He conceives of philosophy as "project". Philosophy must not only perceive the world but must also change it; it must create a project for the salvation of the world from evil and suffering and, above all, from death as the source of all evil. The life of the world is ruled by the irrational "elemental" forces of nature. These forces must be regulated, subjugated to reasons and knowledge. Fedorov calls humanity to cease struggling against each other and to unite for the struggle against the elemental forces of nature.

Typical of Fedorov is his extreme activism, his belief in the mighty power of technology, his teaching of a collective common cause, his preference for a regulated planned economy, for a cosmic extension of his projects, for speculation divorced from practical action, and a recognition of labour as the basis of life. Soloviev wrote in a letter to Fedorov: "I have read your manuscript with eagerness and enjoyment of the spirit. It has taken me the whole night and a part of the morning to read it. I accept your project unconditionally without discussion. Your project is the first move of the human spirit along the way of Christ. For myself I cannot help recognizing you as my teacher and spiritual father..."

Dostoievsky wrote of the teaching and the "projects" of the "common cause": "I fully agree with these thoughts." Tolstoy speaking of Fedorov said: "I take pride in the fact that I am living in the same time as such a man." Tsiolkovsky recognized Fedorov as a "remarkable philosopher". Gorky called him a "remarkable thinker".

For Fedorov, the Gospel was not just simple "Good News". It does not provide knowledge only but is also a programme for action. Ideas are not subjective or objective, they are "projective". Fedorov went so far in this conception that he considered it is given to us to know the universe, to possess it. We are destined "not only to explore but to inhabit the whole cosmos". "This is what humanity is created for," concludes Fedorov.

And it is to this that the great Russian scientist, thinker, philosopher and theologian calls all humanity.

Reactions and Comment

It was immediately evident to the conference that all three addresses, in addition to the preceding day's address by Metropolitan Gregorios, agreed on one central theme: the dominant theological traditions of modern times have not only been inadequate to the social issues coming out of science and tech-

nology but have in some ways been responsible for the human misappropriation of technology. That consensus is of considerable importance to the history of modern theology. It remains to be seen how widely it will be shared by churches and theologians at large.

However, this agreement within the conference led to great differences in the proposals for theological reconstruction. While all the speakers found biblical bases for their theological proposals, they diverged in their uses of the Bible, tradition and contemporary scientific knowledge.

Discussion on the floor of the plenary session and in the section meetings raised many questions. Some participants defended the Faith and Order documents that Birch had criticized. Some questioned whether Liedke's biblical exegesis, in which neither people nor animals ate flesh before the human introduction of violence into creation, could be related to an evolutionary understanding of natural history. The most persistent questions and arguments centred on the continuities and discontinuities of humanity with both God and the non-human creation—an issue earlier raised in the discussions between Gregorios and Verheul (Chapter 4). This issue got further attention in several sections, most notably Section II (see Volume 2).

6. Science and Technology as Promise and Threat

Introduction

As the last phase of the investigation of basic issues during the opening two days, the conference turned its attention to the promises and threats of science and technology. The preparatory work for this theme had been summarized in Chapter 3 of *Faith, Science and the Future*, whose title is identical with this chapter of this book. The same theme had also been explored, and was to be further explored in this conference, in WCC work on such specific issues as genetics and nuclear energy. It emerges in many of the section reports in Volume 2.

Jerome R. Ravetz, reader in the history and philosophy of science at the University of Leeds (United Kingdom), gave the first address on "The Scale and Complexity of the Problem". He emphasized the paradoxes inherent in the subject. Science, he argued, has not only brought to humanity new knowledge and power, it has also contributed to the ethical virtues of freedom and tolerance. However, its threat is not only its potential physical destructiveness, but also the ethical vices of deception and the cover-up, when science becomes deeply allied with government and industry. He held out the possibility that scientific knowledge might become "a good servant rather than a bad master", but concluded that since "human reason alone" cannot solve our problems, faith "comes in as the link between science and the future".

Manuel Sadosky, a mathematician at the Central University of Venezuela, used the Latin American experience as an example of the way in which science and technology, controlled by the world's great centres of power, have imposed dependence on "the peripheral world". While echoing some of the themes of Rubem Alves (see Chapter 3), he became an advocate of "basic science" in ways that Alves had not been. He maintained that the "peripheral world" should develop research and education, both in basic science and in technologies appropriate to its situations, but said that this could not take place without fundamental changes in the international economic order, a task as formidable as it is urgent.

Bo Lindell, Chairman of the National Institute on Radiation Protection in Sweden, took an entirely different approach. Avoiding polemics, he spoke on specific issues of risk assessment and management. Using as examples the risks of radio-active and carcinogenic materials, he looked at the problem of developing a society of high technology which is authentically participatory. Although Lindell avoided the intentionally provocative styles of Ravetz and Sadosky, he concluded on a deeply foreboding note.

The Scale and Complexity of the Problem

JEROME R. RAVETZ

Wherever we look among the interactions of our science and technology with its natural and human environment, we find problems. These grow in scale and complexity (sometimes quite suddenly), and their individual practical solutions seem to recede in a fog of political and economic constraints, coupled with further problems associated with any projected solution. The current fuel crisis is an example of a trend.

Indeed, for me the most significant phenomenon at present is the widespread sense of bewilderment at the onset of so many problems and dilemmas all together. This is seen most dramatically in the reaction of Americans to the present shortage of motor vehicle fuel. There is a general sense of incredulity; in the classic words of the loyal citizen picked up by his own secret police: "There must be some mistake!"

These mass phenomena are the most obvious and well-known. They indicate a crisis in science itself, where by "science" I understand both research and application, in the total, unified system on which our daily lives depend. What we are seeing is the development, in ways partly anticipated by the ecological critics, of a crisis in this system as a means of controlling the natural world for the satisfaction of human purposes. It is vital for members of this conference to appreciate that there is *no mistake*. This deepening crisis is all quite natural. And by readjusting our image of "science" we may first understand how our science (as a total system of knowledge and belief) got us here, and thus perhaps be better equipped to cope with what may come. Our whole dominant concept of social amelioration and moral progress had depended on an increasing power of "the productive forces" (as our Marxists brethren call them). Should this increase be halted as now seems likely, that centuries-old programme is thrown into disarray.

Think of a sample question. If progress depends on standard of living, and that is measured very well by automobile ownership, then how will the world sustain a billion private automobiles? If it cannot, we are doomed either to a permanent gross inequality or to a sharp decline in standards in the West. For with some five billion people, we have a billion families, more or less; and which ones should be refused the car? Neither prospect—permanent inequality or decline—is attractive; but who can see another?

Let me now introduce my main theme, which is the crisis of scientism as it is revealed in the social practice of science. My way in here will be through an analysis and social criticism of science. For the image of "the scientist" as dedicated lone researcher, analogous to a saintly hermit, is now dangerously obsolete.

A preliminary word of warning is necessary. I will say some very harsh things about "science" and "scientists", even speaking of reprehensible practices like "corruption" and "cover-up". Please understand that I am *not* accusing the vast majority of scientific research workers of malpractice, conscious or otherwise. I must show, however, that there are some tasks of science that do lead their practitioners into severe temptations; and that, in the absence of any preparation in the social and ethical aspects of science (conspicuously absent from all university science teaching), they are ill-equipped to resist or even to recognize the danger to their integrity. The example of the recently revealed ignorance and incompetence of nuclear power scientists and engineers, as at Harrisburg, the misleading and manipulated scientific information being presented to the public, and the growing suspicion of corruption in a long-standing systematic cover-up of serious hazards in that field, will serve as examples.

All this may be very shocking to many of you. The idea of a scientist being a deceiver, or corrupt, is very nearly a contradiction in terms. How can a searcher after knowledge be a party to its distortion or suppression? If you are thus bewildered, take it as a warning that your concepts are now obsolete. Until they are changed, you will be able neither to understand how science works today, nor to appreciate the real role of faith in resolving the crisis we face.

What I shall do is to sketch the different sorts of tasks that scientists may have, be they scientific research, technology, or "government"; and to show how a popular image of "science" that may have been appropriate when the main activity was research, is now a real hindrance to effective thinking about science.

The phenomena

We must start with paradoxes. Unless we soon learn to assimilate paradoxes, we are lost. The first paradox is too obvious: we now depend on science-based technology as on air. A sudden collapse in any part of that complex vulnerable system of artefacts, attitudes and beliefs would easily bring the whole world to the state of, say, Lebanon, or perhaps Kampuchea.

Moreover, we have all absorbed the vision of the good social and political life that was first popularized by prophets of science in the eighteenth century. Not only material protection and comfort, but the virtues of freedom and tolerance can be traced largely to them. Now even the head of the Roman Catholic Church has proclaimed these virtues. And for this improvement in social and religious life, I would argue that the scientific movement deserves at least as much credit on a world scale as institutionalized religion.

Yet this same wonderful science now threatens to destroy us, in all dimensions of our existence. The cosmic obscenity of weapons of mass annihilation is still with us; and, I ask, when did some established scientific society last do something to avert that horror? Now we have new industrial revolutions springing up all around, kept beyond social control by the manoeuvres of their promoters in science and industry. Genetic engineering is promised to be intensely powerful for industry but yet so harmless as to need no serious regulation. Microprocessors will assuredly lead to the redundancy of humans on a mass scale and to the convulsion of all industrial-based societies; yet the official media permit only anodyne reassurances to reach the public.

These are only external phenomena, particular examples of what happens when technical progress is shaped to serve only particular institutions and people. But the severe difficulties of social control in each case stem from weaknesses in science, weaknesses that were hardly imagined in the student days of leading scientists of the present. Let me analyse these weaknesses; with an appreciation of them we might yet make scientific-technical knowledge a good servant rather than a bad master.

I have already indicated them, in connection with the nuclear example; they are, first, ignorance in scientific research; second, incompetence in science-based technology; and finally, corruption in science policy.

Ignorance becomes a serious weakness because students are not taught to recognize and cope with it. We teach facts, not their limits and their pitfalls. In the scholastic style now dominant, the student is kept ignorant of his ignorance. Thus he has not learned the first lesson of real education, and is in this respect a skilled barbarian. The same style continues in the sort of research called "normal science", which T.S. Kuhn has so eloquently described as "the strenuous and devoted effort to force Nature into the conceptual boxes provided by professional training".

Although technology purports to have closer contact with the uncontrolled external world, this is still partial and dependent on the traditions of each field. In the nuclear case, we find a long history of carelessness about the problems of what happens when things go wrong. Running an industrial installation well when things go right is rather like being an investor in a rising stock market: you can't lose, but you are a lot less clever than you may think. The illusion of competence may persist a long time, but is finally exposed by blunders, incomprehension and incompetence when a real accident finally occurs, as at Harrisburg.

This weakness is a result partly of arrogance, of experts choosing to recognize the convenient or profitable problems and ignoring the others. This arrogance is also bred into them by the *ethos* of research science. A most eloquent statement of this Faustian ruthlessness was given in connection with genetic engineering, by a leading researcher, herself a person with a strong social awareness:

> "The consequences of attempts to restrain the search for knowledge have been even more fearsome than the science fiction scenarios construct-

ed by genetic fearmongers. Besides, such attempts are certain to fail. They will fail, first, because we are not smart enough to foresee what we will or will not learn from a given line of research. They will fail, second, because we are not smart enough to foresee all the future applications of the knowledge. They will fail, finally, because the indomitable forces of nature oppose such attempts. The acquisition of knowledge by the human brain is part of protean nature. Biologists and poets alike know this."[1]

This arrogant and blinkered approach to the study and control of nature has produced vast material gains; so long as things go well the scientists involved have no reason to be troubled. But when decisions and choices need to be made, particularly when things begin to go wrong, then problems of my third sort, science policy, arise. And the underlying weaknesses of scientists' outlook easily give rise to corruption. This is most readily seen in cases where embarrassing accidents, or incidents, occur in some area or installation. Should they be revealed, to be taken by unsympathetic news media to an ignorant public? Or are they better handled with "discretion"? Thus, all too naturally, starts a cover-up. Loyalties to employing institutions, and sanctions imposed by them, are usually far more impressive than abstract considerations of publicity of knowledge or a generalized public welfare.

I believe that ordinary forms of corruption, as embezzlement, nepotism, or non-work, are less important in this sphere than cover-up. For this latter sort can entrap the most intelligent and industrious of people. Yet its consequences are as deadly as those of any other sort.

Perhaps you are wondering whether I am still talking about science, whose defining ideal is "public knowledge". But then ask yourself: For those twenty-one years after the Soviet nuclear disaster of 1957, who in the nuclear field was kept ignorant, who chose to remain ignorant, and who merely posed as ignorant? Then ask again whether a nuclear-energy Watergate is inconceivable.

An analysis

In order to make these phenomena more comprehensible, I shall go into a little more detail about the three sorts of scientific activities I have mentioned: research, technology and government.

In the traditional propaganda for science, research has a saintly image, and is also taken to stand for all of science. In this lies a two-fold distortion. First, when we recall the image of "the scientist", dedicated, otherworldly, interested only in truth, we can detect an assimilation of this contemporary role to that of the traditional saintly hermit. But the similarities, however real, are misleading. In particular, there is nothing that moves the research

---

[1] Maxine Singer: "The Involvement of Scientists." *Research with Recombinant DNA*, Academy Forum, March 1977. Washington: National Academy of Sciences, 1977, p. 29.

scientist to follow Bacon's injunction to "cultivate truth in charity". The arduous isolated work may well be only a means to fame, fortune and power.

Even the act of research itself can involve insensitivity or cruelty (to sentient experimental subjects), exploitation (of laboratory staff and families), selfishness (in the choice of problems), deceit (in the "improvement" of data), and dangers to the public (through laboratory hazards). I am not saying that all this is common or characteristic; only that it can and does happen.

Further, the community of science stands to the creative research scientists rather as an established church to its genuinely holy people. In both cases, these persons are at the core; without them the whole structure would quickly rot. (And on this essential point, I am in full agreement with Prof. Hanbury Brown.) But to assume that every PhD or professor is a searcher like a Faraday or an Einstein would be as naive as to assume that every employed churchman is another St John of the Cross. I would not say that science has yet developed to the point of having the equivalent of "Borgia popes", but the possibility cannot be excluded on logical grounds alone.

Hence when we think of "science", even the research section, we do best to conceive it *first* as a part of the white-collar, bureaucratic world of work; and *then* to consider the special features that make it particularly interesting and valuable.

When we come to science-based technology, the demystification is not so difficult. It is a long time since we became aware of the passing of the fabled lone inventor, working in his garret on making that better mousetrap. But here we must reckon with the paradoxes that lie very deep in our style of technology. A liberation—yes; an enslavement—also. It depends on whom, when, where and how. We cannot turn back the clock in the world colonized by Europe; and their previous conditions were not really Arcadian ideals. But we cannot appreciate our own "developed" technology in its world context without recalling the rape of resources and cultures in South America, the genocidal slave-trade in Africa, and the barbarously intolerant destruction of sacred customs and beliefs all over. Now the third world peoples are left in a hideous mess, social, intellectual and spiritual, thanks to that European imperialism whose material benefits we have taken for granted until very recently.

All this may be familiar to many of you. My third point, however, about science-policy decisions in government, derives from very recent experiences in attempts to control and regulate science and technology. I think it is fair to say that this area, rather than innovative research, is now the crucial one for human survival. A person of only modest competence may (so it seems) build or operate a nuclear reactor in many countries; but the recognition of the various risks inherent in all phases of the nuclear fuel cycle has required the combined wisdom of scientists, regulators, and independent critics as well.

Let me use this example a bit longer. The person who assures you that a particular mode of nuclear power production is "safe" may have a PhD in science and may indeed have performed experiments and calculations. But to consider him as a "scientist" doing the same sort of job as the traditional researcher can be disastrously (literally so) wrong. The differences are so many and various that I can indicate only two essentials.

First, whereas traditional scientific research is well described as "the art of the soluble", this "policy science" is better called "the art of the unavoidable". The investigators here do not choose problems because rigorous solutions are possible; rather, they study those where practical decisions are urgent. Typically they lack *both* hard data *and* effective theories. Inspired guessing may be the only justifiable course, where "research" means groping through a morass of ignorance and incompetence.

The research problem that best conveys the character of this sort of science is a second-order study: to assess the quality of particular quality-control procedures upon which depends the prevention of accidents or disasters. Such work requires virtues of imagination and courage in ways that are not normally fostered in academic research.

Now in some speculative fields of basic research the scientists are working far beyond the limits of objectivity and certainty; but then they have the luxury of admitting it. Researchers in this area of policy-science must provide *an answer* for use by decision-makers, however shaky its foundations. Worse (and here is the second essential difference), their social situation is frequently totally different from that of the old-fashioned scientist. They may be employees, and not scholars; their research results may appear in private "in-house memoranda" rather than published papers; their product is not so much "public knowledge" as "corporate know-how".

I must emphasize that the scientific side of the work of regulation of technology is largely in the hands of such intellectual workers. I cannot discuss here how individuals can really retain their integrity in such a role. They can, indeed, though sometimes needing to pay a higher price than academic scientists could possibly imagine. And I should remark that this problem of integrity is much more subtle and difficult in the case of an academic scientist who maintains unannounced ties with industry through research contracts or consultancies, as we have recently learned occurs among leading persons in nuclear physics and genetic engineering. In either case, this "science-policy" work is a totally different social and ethical experience from the traditional activities of the advancement and diffusion of scientific knowledge.

My final observation about "policy science" is that there is a constant and inevitable tendency by employed experts and their masters to reduce every problem to the technical, preferably quantitative dimension. Thus we, that is the public, are criticized for failing to recognize the "acceptability" of the risks of nuclear power, given the small size of the estimated probabilistic damage. This effort not only conceals the social aspects of the problem, including those political power struggles involved in every determination of a technological risk. Even more significant, it attempts to remove questions of value and commitment from the problem altogether. And it is on this point, the values implicit in *every* technological policy decision, large or small, that the scientistic programme of our high-technology civilization has finally shipwrecked.

For now we have a paradoxical inversion of the classic programme of scientism. Whereas before there was a faith that human values could ultimately be derived from scientific knowledge, be it Newtonian physics or Darwinian evolution, *now* we see that the crucial problems of choice and of quality control, in technology and in socially significant scientific research too, depend on values held by the community that *cannot* and *will* not be reduced to scientific facts.

Perhaps here, even more than in the simple temptations to cover up, lie the roots of the dangers of corruption of those involved in science-policy matters. For the biggest secret needing a cover-up is this: science is not, and *cannot be*, self-sufficient in determining policy decisions and in managing risks. Those processes are basically political and ethical; to attempt to proceed otherwise is to enter a technological fantasy world that is fully as dangerous as its most notorious part, "nuclear deterrence".

Some lessons to be drawn

Thus we see that in this age of increasing instability and turbulence, the basic concepts that have shaped our thinking for generations must now be held up for scrutiny. When we think of "scientific research" we might change our type-case from the discovery of, say, polio-vaccine, to that of the determination of the carcinogenicity of, say, saccharine.

For "the scientist", we bid farewell to the lone researcher as the type case, and consider one sort or another of white-collar worker. And a scientist who is advocating a case in public (particularly for an employer or a corporate client) should be viewed precisely in that role: an advocate or lawyer, or perhaps diplomat.

Seeing this change in historical perspective, we notice the loss of a plausible claim by science to the sole possession of truth. Speaking figuratively, we may refer to God coming in again from the gaps. When the salient problems of science are not the discovery of new facts about nature, but are rather the coping with new crises afflicting mankind, then values cannot be ignored or simply assimilated to facts. If we understand "faith" as an awareness of a realm beyond that of "sense-data" and logic, a realm which gives our lives their particular meaning and value, then "faith" is firmly back on the agenda of discussions of science.

No one can now effectively pretend that the experts know best, in providing us with technologies guaranteed safe, clean and cheap, and from which we will all derive material happiness and personal fulfilment. Decisions on technologies involve commitments to the definition of the good life: what we are willing to risk, what is essential to our human purposes. And this is where faith, as I understand it, comes in to view.

Let me remind you that the building, or even the definition, of the elements of a "just, participatory and sustainable society" (in the World

Council's admirable phrase) has not yet been accomplished. It is, I suspect, a task that defies all expertise in natural and social science. Let me remind you again of those billion cars that could be necessary for a global "fair shares" at present levels of material aspiration. The transition from our present one-sided and self-destructive material and intellectual order, to that other, quite staggers the imagination. Those who thought they saw it starting to happen in one or another far-away country have all been cruelly disillusioned.

Perhaps here, then, is the last lesson to be drawn in this contribution. The scientistic style, having got us into these straits, is not likely to get us out. The really contradictory idea of our time is "blue-print for survival". Rather, we might, while keeping our scientific skills and critical faculties fully intact, proceed in humility and charity to prepare ourselves and our neighbours to flow with those great revolutions which now seem ever more imminent. The scale and complexity of the problems are so great that human reason alone will not conquer them; it is here that faith comes in as the link between science and the future.

Some Aspects of the Problem in Latin America

MANUEL SADOSKY

Continuing progress in science and technology has been instrumental in widening the gap between rich and poor countries. More and more people agree that this gap can no longer be widened without resorting to brutal forms of political coercion.

In a world plagued by hunger, poverty, disease and ignorance, modern science and technology might offer solutions to the great problems of mankind. At the same time, the threat of global catastrophe looms large: ecological disaster is an immediate possibility; non-renewable natural resources have been depleted; environmental pollution is out of control; radio-active waste constitutes an ever-present danger.

According to one form of reasoning, the dilemma of underdeveloped nations is thus a painful one: how can they undertake urgently needed scientific, technological and industrial development in the face of such a threat, yet how can they avoid continued dependence if they do not?

This argument allows only for a choice between false options. In what follows we try define as rationally as possible the real problems posed by the development of science and technology in dependent countries; discuss certain factors which have contributed to the present situation; and suggest alternatives for the future. While we will talk primarily about Latin America, much of what is said applies equally to other parts of the world.

The assumptions on which our arguments are based

1. "Underdevelopment" is not a stage prior to development but rather the result of an unjust division of labour among nations. Some people appear destined to provide raw materials and cheap manpower to others; as the owners of science, technology, industry, and international commerce, these others sell their expertise and manufactured products at prices of their own choosing. The sources of this unjust division of labour are historical: in different countries, industrial revolutions occurred and foreign markets were conquered at different times and at different rates. Since much has been written about this matter from many points of view, we will simply enumerate some of the questions which students and writers have sought to answer: Why did Europe give birth to modern science while civilizations like that of China, which flourished at other times in history, experienced nothing comparable to the sixteenth century European Renaissance? Why did the Iberian empires have no industrial revolution? How can we explain the genocidal Hispanic conquest of America—the destruction of civilizations and use of antiquated institutions as vehicles for cultural development? Why was England the first country to undertake an industrial revolution, the first to conquer world markets, and the first to organize a great capitalist empire? Why did Germany delay so long before attempting to do the same? By what means and exactly when did the Soviet Union achieve status as a world power after the 1917 Revolution? How did Germany—one of the most culturally advanced nations in the world—reach the extremes of degradation represented by the barbaric practices of Nazism? How did Japan succeed in solving the problems of underdevelopment under absolutely unique conditions? How did an underdeveloped country like Vietnam win a war against an army equipped with the most sophisticated technology? Needless to say, these questions are of paramount importance, since they deal with the events and processes which together have shaped the world we live in.

2. Underdevelopment is a reality of the dependent world, where it appears in varying degrees and gives rise to different levels of backwardness, poverty, disease and ignorance. But the essential feature of underdeveloped countries is their lack of decision-making power; they cannot give direction to their foreign policy; determine how or at what pace their natural resources should be exploited; establish priorities for the development of their scientific, technological and industrial potential; or even organize advanced research in the sciences.

I do not hold the central nations alone, or other external forces such as the transnational corporations, responsible for our continued dependence. Responsibility lies in some cases with a native oligarchy; in others, with a middle class resistant to change, or with an army which has relinquished its national character in the defence of foreign causes; and in general, with those economically privileged sectors eager for a place in the "consumer society". Integrated first into a colonial and then into a neo-colonial structure, these sectors now take part in a process of "denationalization" which serves in turn to consolidate an international order bent on perpetuating the unjust division of labour.

The changes which have taken place in Latin America for over a hundred and fifty years "so that nothing would change" are unmistakeable. Even during the wars of independence which enabled the Latin American nations to sever their ties with the Iberian monarchies, England was planning its balkanization of the subcontinent, organizing its trade, advocating an economic order in which Latin America would produce raw materials and consume the goods manufactured by the empire and its allies.

From the mid-nineteenth century, the United States of America extended its imperial rule, especially in Central America and the north of South America. Together with England, whose influence was especially strong in the south, the United States set out to stifle even the slightest tendency towards independence. As the old colonial structures crumbled, the imperial powers replaced them with new forms of international relations, giving rise to the phenomenon known as neo-colonialism. As methods of foreign interference became more subtle, the governments of the peripheral countries acquired somewhat greater freedom in the handling of domestic policy; to a certain extent, they could even engage in discussions regarding the prices of their raw materials and begin to industrialize. But none of this really meant an end to dependence. The central powers dictated foreign policy; provided the armies with weapons and ideology; guided scientific development; sold technology, thus directing industrial development to suit their own purposes; and, through continued economic and financial control, maintained their influence over educational, informational and cultural institutions.

The transition from colonial to neo-colonial structures did not take place in the same way and at the same time all over the peripheral world (in Africa, the colonial system persisted until after the end of the Second World War); neither did the transition from neo-colonial structures to the process of "denationalization", which became characteristic of dependent countries following the arrival of the transnational corporations. The Second World War, the Chinese revolution, and the Vietnam war produced changes in the world which transformed international relations. The dictatorships currently in power in the south of Latin America, with their fascist-like repressive tactics and virulent anti-Communism, see themselves as the "guardians of the free world". The transnational corporations, loyal only to capital and increasingly independent of their countries of origin, need the products of the peripheral countries and, above all, their cheap manpower and technical potential or craftsmanship.

3. During the sixties, the so-called "developmental paradigm" enjoyed great popularity in international organizations and in many peripheral countries. The notion that underdevelopment was a stage in the development process and, in particular, that science and technology kept that process going, was still fairly widespread.

In Latin America, the Alliance for Progress, UNESCO's literacy and educational programmes, the Economic Commission for Latin America's teachings in the economic field (designed to promote industrialization with import substitution as its goal) are all examples of the unsuccessful application of developmentalist concepts.

During the same period, major private US foundations and organizations connected to the US Department of Defence pressed for the creation of research groups and centres of higher education by providing research grants. Ostensibly, recipients of these grants were free both to choose their topics and to acquire the equipment needed for their research; in reality, they remained tied to the centres of power by more or less ambiguous contracts which limited their independence.

Many Latin American scientists have studied at well-known universities and laboratories in the central countries, where their training was geared towards the solution of problems of interest to the universities and laboratories in question. Thus Latin America has produced research of use in the development both of foreign space programmes—hardly a relevant concern anywhere in the area—and of more effective means of reducing demographic growth. Interestingly, it was in Argentina and Uruguay, both *underpopulated* countries, that major studies were conducted on the applications of physiology to contraception.

In several countries in the south of Latin America, this period brought significant progress in university teaching and in the technological organization of industrial and agricultural production. However, the fallacious nature of developmentalist illusions was later revealed.

That the developmentalist road has not led to development in peripheral countries is now apparent from both an international and a domestic perspective. The overall results have been described by Argentine economist Raúl Prebisch, first Executive Secretary of ECLA and an expert on present-day Latin American economics. In a paper entitled "Critique of Peripheral Capitalism", published in the ECLA *Review* for the first semester of 1976, he says: "...great hopes of a few decades ago have been shattered as peripheral capitalism has evolved. It was [once] thought that [if peripheral capitalism] were left to operate according to its own dynamics, penetration by the technology of the industrial centres would gradually spread its fruits over all strata of society, and that this would contribute to the progress and consolidation of the democratic process. The facts no longer permit us to harbour such illusions. Development tends to exclude a sizeable portion of the population. Its benefits are felt mainly in higher income sectors where the consumer habits of the centres are increasingly imitated. The consumer society exacts a very high social and political price: the social price of evil and the political price of dashed hopes."

In other countries developmentalist illusions have been even more violently destroyed: attempts to achieve progress in science and technology did not have the desired effect in societies whose efforts to adapt national economies to the requirements of present-day world capitalism led to political degradation.

4. Since the decline of developmentalism in Latin America, many of the real scientific and technological gains of that period have been lost. With the complicity of reactionary governmental groups, valuable programmes and projects have been eliminated, restricted or ignored, especially at the universities of Buenos Aires, Montevideo, Brasilia and Santiago de Chile. Nevertheless, the frustration of the sixties also underlies the productive efforts of several groups of Latin American scientists who, over the last ten years, have rethought the problems of the region within the context of our continuing struggle for independence. They saw that science and technology were in themselves no guarantee of independent development; they were merely a link in a much more complex chain.

A group of Latin American economists broke with orthodox thinking at a time when the latter enjoyed unprecedented prestige. In 1977, a Brasilian economist, Celso Furtado, characterized that approach as follows: "By emphasizing the idea of transformation and resistance to transformation, this Latin American structuralist thought approaches a dialectic view of social process, in contrast to the neo-classical functionalist view and the ahistoricism of contemporary European structuralist thought."

However, social scientists were not the only ones who decided to search for new solutions. Researchers in the exact and natural sciences also came to understand that unless their work was part of a national plan undertaken with national interests in mind, they were destined to be "second rate" researchers; only if their efforts were supported by a consensus broad enough to encompass the economically less privileged classes might they hope to match the achievements of scientists in the central countries, with their superior working conditions and unparalleled opportunities. In other words, it was understood that if the struggle for independence must be primarily a political one, in which scientists and technologists have their place, it is also true that political, economic and cultural independence go hand in hand.

5. An essential part of national independence struggles is the restructuring and strengthening of educational systems. In Latin America and in peripheral countries in general, rapid demographic growth and the peculiar nature of our societies have aggravated the problem of explosive increases in student enrolments at all levels.

In our dependent countries, universal education through the secondary level is more urgently needed than is development of higher education. Proper channelling of available resources for that purpose would make it possible for the vast majority of the population to participate effectively in the preparation and implementation of national plans. Primary and secondary education must be substantially modified: the curriculum must be updated and its content more closely related to the experience of our students. The effort should be to educate in such a way that knowledge acquired in the classroom can be put to good use elsewhere.

At the secondary level, teaching must be diversified and more attention paid to technical, industrial and agricultural training. At the same time, we must be careful not to make of such vocational training an academic "dead-end street"; access to higher levels must be possible at every stage in the educational process. When we refer to secondary education, we include the training of middle-level technicians, whose assistance is invaluable in any process involving the adaptation or renovation of technologies.

Special attention must be paid to the training of primary and secondary school teachers. The teaching profession will attract fewer and fewer young people if it does not regain the prestige which it has lost everywhere.

This problem warrants the immediate attention of our governments, and as much effort as is required to solve it.

In reorganizing higher education, we should keep in mind many of the matters previously discussed. A critical question is how to prevent technology from becoming an instrument of perpetuating dependence. Aware that technology imported to facilitate import substitution had precisely this damaging effect, a number of well-intentioned but poorly-informed Latin Americans have called for the creation of an "independent" or an "autochthonous technology".

There is no reason why any country should have to do without scientific knowledge embodied in technology, since that knowledge belongs to all mankind. Of course, another part of technology involves the research conducted in the central countries which is protected by patents, trade marks or manufacturing secrets. However, when technology becomes merchandise, the important thing is that its purchase include all the knowledge required to use it, *plus* the right to adapt and to improve upon it. The technology which increased our dependence was not chosen but imposed from abroad; for the most part, it reached our industrial establishment in the form of "black boxes"; and our very costly purchases—modestly referred to as "transfers"—included no right either to adapt or to improve upon what we had bought.

Anyone familiar with Latin American universities will understand the magnitude of the challenge. Nevertheless, it is encouraging to note that a number of Latin American social scientists and technologists have developed lucid and original analyses of the problems of technological marketing and the production of technology in the region.

6. Unfortunately, unilateral remedies will not work in situations as unjust as the one created and perpetuated by the present international order.

In recent years, there has been much talk about the urgent need for a new international economic order—one in which a more equitable division of labour among nations would be possible and governments could begin to attack the poverty, disease, ignorance and backwardness that afflict two-thirds of the human race.

The deprived masses of the world can no longer overlook the selfish refusal of wealthy countries and third world bourgeoisies to abandon their wasteful habits. However, they still do not fully understand why they are denied more generous access to the fruits of science and technology. They are victims of a sinister hoax: so much is squandered in preparation for war.

Harvey M. Sapolsky, a professor at MIT, says in his paper on "Science, Technology and Military Policy": "At present, and this has been true for three decades, the search for more and ever more terrible weapons is of first priority among scientists and engineers all over the world... No other activity absorbs a greater proportion of the total investment in research than that activity spent on the progress of science and technology for war. According to Forsberg, one third of the total world expenditure for research and development goes for military matters. The number of scientists and engineers involved in military projects is estimated at one million."

Equally deceptive are the sums drawn from the budgets of peripheral countries (often by means of loans from international banks or the arms-producing countries which add greatly to dependence), used to equip national armies for internal repression or participation in conflicts usually involving not their own interests, but those of the central powers.

Alleged concern over the "non-proliferation of atomic weapons" is manipulated just as deceitfully. More often than not, it is invoked to prevent dependent countries from undertaking research on the peaceful applications of atomic energy.

Generally speaking, the same lack of sincerity surrounds the handling of ecological issues. Many processes prohibited by law in "advanced" countries because they result in pollution are employed with no misgivings in peripheral countries by the very same transnational corporations which were prohibited from using them at home. By now the citizens of dependent countries are hardly surprised when they discover that their lakes and rivers have been hopelessly polluted, their forests destroyed, or their non-renewable natural resources definitely depleted; such news has become commonplace rather than exceptional.

We would like to reiterate however, that in such instances most of the responsibility lies with us—at least, with the more affluent sectors of our dependent societies, who are committed to maintaining the *status quo*.

What we can expect from scientific and technological progress

While we realize that scientific and technological progress is no guarantee of independence, such progress is a *sine qua non* for peripheral countries interested in development and the acquisition of decision-making power.

In a paper on "The Philosophy of Scientific Research in Developing Countries", Mario Bunge says the following about Latin America: "...it is widely believed in our countries that science is a luxury, and that therefore technology should take precedence over pure science. This pragmatist thesis overlooks the fact that modern technology is applied science... The same pragmatist thesis fails to note that social problems such as crime are solved not by increasing the size of the police force, but by carrying out economic, social and educational reforms; and that to be effective, the planning and implementation of these reforms must be based on economic, sociological and psychological studies. In short, the pragmatist thesis is hardly practical. By emphasizing praxis over theory, it invites failure and encourages improvization. Pursuing its goals with no attention to means, excessively preoccupied with things, it forgets about people."

We cannot abdicate either our right or our duty to study and to teach pure science. We still hope that scientific knowledge will enable us to improve the overall situation of mankind; that it will become the basis for rational and harmonious education; that its technology will offer solutions to major problems of housing, health and labour; and that these solutions will be suited to the specific needs of our countries.

We also hope that collaboration between natural and social scientists will result in greater awareness of intellectuals; that through the mass media and the educational process, such collaboration will foster a sense of responsibility among the people as a whole; that it will convince them that they can and should participate in political decisions. We hope the increased understanding of our problems will result in strong and united opposition to any new attempts at balkanization of the periphery by the central powers.

In Latin America, the ideal of integration which was courageously upheld by men like Simón Bolívar was cast aside and trampled upon in artificial conflicts among sister peoples. We hope, through increased public awareness and political participation, to transcend the narrow definitions of territorial sovereignty.

High on our list of hopes is a change in attitude on the part of our colleagues in the developed world. Of course, we do not expect the economists of the Chicago school who advise Latin American governments to recommend policies antagonistic to the interests of the transnational corporations, or to propose popular measures aimed at improving living conditions of the poor. Nor do we expect those who advocate the massive purchase of cheap blood drawn from the veins of the Haitian people to be uncomfortable about their complicity with one of the most sinister governments in the hemisphere. We do not expect those who plan and carry out sterilization experiments on entire communities of Latin American women and men to be aware of the criminal purpose which they serve. Nor do we expect the pharmaceutical laboratories to stop using our people as "guinea pigs" in experiments with drugs whose use is prohibited in the central countries. We are too realistic to believe that we can substantially modify a situation based on such vast interests. What we *do* hope is that scientists in the central countries who share our concerns, and who are as reluctant as we are to see their knowledge misused, will succeed in making themselves heard and seek more authentic forms of collaboration.

The hazards of scientific and technological progress

At this point in history we know that the vast possibilities which science and technology offer are at the same time fraught with danger. The scientists themselves are the best qualified to assess the dangers. By virtue of our professional expertise, we have the responsibility of informing the public about the hazards of scientific and technological development. These include potentially harmful techniques or practices, such as the development of more and more lethal weapons; the indiscriminate utilization of pesticides or defoliants; the use in foods and medicines of chemicals whose effects are insufficiently understood. It also entails discussion of the dangers inherent in certain scientific solutions and technological advances which, while contributing to progress and ostensibly to development, can aggravate already existing problems. Atomic research and agricultural genetics, for example, are universally dangerous. Other types of dangers threaten our dependent countries in particular.

The habits of consumer society find their way into peripheral countries, creating fictitious needs, favouring only the economically privileged sectors, and thereby deepening the injustices already present in anachronistic social systems.

The computer—which was introduced into our countries via the transnational corporations and not via the universities—has become a marketable gadget, more often used to create a mystique than to solve real problems. Lack of organization is frequently characteristic of peripheral countries, and attempts are often made to compensate for this by installing costly electronic equipment. Things continue to be badly done, only faster.

Another consequence of the pressure to imitate which accompanies consumerism is the enthusiasm with which poor countries have greeted the invention of colour television. They would do better to concern themselves with the quality of their programmes—usually imported and full of violence—which destroy national cultures by imposing foreign values.

Modern medicine helps to widen the gap between different sectors of peripheral societies. While slum-dwellers lack vaccines, basic medicines, healthy food and safe drinking water, elsewhere private hospitals comparable to the best in the developed countries serve the needs of proportionately minute priorities. As J.L. McKnight, of Northwestern University, said in a paper entitled "Cancerous Development in the Field of Health: the Case of North American Medicine": "The promise of medicine has become a sizeable justification for maintaining social injustice."

However, all is not lost if we keep in mind the following ambitious but attainable goals:

A. A new and productive role for the scientists and technicians of our peripheral societies in the struggle for independence. Scientists and technicians can cooperate in drawing up and implementing national plans worthy of support from all sectors of the population.

B. Substantial modification of educational systems aimed at raising general cultural levels rather than preparing elites whose work—however successful by international standards—may isolate them from national and regional realities. Priority should be given to the development of primary and secondary education—with special emphasis on technical, industrial and agricultural training—and to the preparation of primary and secondary teachers. The task of training negotiators and legislators knowledgeable about technology must be undertaken at the third level.

C. Development of a technology "of our own", keeping in mind that this is not the same as an "autochthonous technology". The concept of an autochthonous technology is absurd; the knowledge embodied in all technology should be available to all mankind. Technology can be of value in achieving independence, if it is properly purchased and distributed, and carefully adapted to national and regional needs.

D. The end of the paralysing pragmatism characteristic of politicians, business executives and academics who erroneously believe that good technology can be developed and good technicians trained in a setting where only applied research is conducted. The widespread notion that research in the pure sciences can be dispensed with is fallacious: without pure science there is no such thing as applied science or technology; and without applied science and technology there is no such thing as independence. There can be few truths as valid as the one attributed to Kant: "There is nothing more practical than a good theory."

All of this is more easily said than done; the task of creating a new international order will be formidable indeed. To be of assistance in such an enormous undertaking, each one of us must seize every available opportunity of thought and word to serve our imperfect and corrupt societies. There are no pre-established standards for possible action. As the Spanish poet Antonio Machado put it: "Caminante no hay camino, Se hace camino al andar." ("Traveller, there is no path, One cuts a path as one goes.")

Ethical and Social Issues in Risk Management

BO LINDELL

The purpose of this plenary session is to examine the predicament of people faced by modern science and technology. How real is that predicament and how shall we evaluate it? Have we reached the point where we might have to call a halt to technological development in certain fields? In a situation where only a small number of technical experts can truly assess such risks, what are the implications for popular participation in determining technological policy? These are big and important questions, but the answers are not readily available.

The technological society

"Technological society" has a dual meaning. It could mean a technologically organized society in the widest sense, or it could mean the sub-population which is able to understand and control the tools of science and technology, beyond comprehension for the majority of the population. The two are not compatible. The present gap between technological and non-technological sub-populations seems to lead to disastrous confusion.

No one claims that it is acceptable to have a society split into one literate and one illiterate sub-population. Certain abilities—to read, to swim and even to drive a car—are encouraged in technologically developed countries. Problems arise when the majority do not have the basic knowledge and terminology to understand the specialists. The popular participation in determining technological policy in a democratic society is therefore often limited to crude "yes" or "no" decisions based on perceived consequences. Long-term planning is difficult, particularly if politically elected decision-makers give priority to immediate results.

One may argue that there is a limit to the demands society can put on the average citizen. Can we afford a technologically developed society if it takes a lifetime to understand how it functions? On the other hand, the specialists have not always helped understanding. There is a lot of jargon and terminology which may be a help to the initiated but which is certainly an impenetrable barrier to the layman. The communication gap is one important hindrance to meaningful participation in decisions.

The substitute discussions

There is a tendency not to discuss the major problems directly. We live in a world where people die of poverty, starvation or violence, a world that is constantly threatened by new wars and weapons, the ultimate horror being nuclear warfare. To starving people discussions of a technological society may seem a mockery. Those fortunate enough to have time and resources to participate in such discussions seem to shrink from the major problems. We prefer to talk about substitute problems.

Rather than considering how we could launch an attack against poverty, starvation, violence, terror and warfare, we discuss society's "demand" for energy. Instead of being frightened by the world's stockpile of nuclear weapons, we worry about the possibility that nuclear power technology may proliferate these weapons. Until Harrisburg, the attention we paid to radioactive waste disposal was out of proportion to the attention we gave the possibility of large reactor accidents. We discuss nuclear power rather than the technological society in general. However, we do not explicitly discuss the consequences of introducing the breeder technology (which would solve our energy problems for a millennium at the cost of a more advanced and perhaps more risky technology), but limit ourselves to the question whether or not we should reprocess the spent fuel from our present reactors (for which available uranium would only last a few decades).

Before we engage in any new discussion we should ask ourselves if we have, in fact, chosen the most relevant subject.

Risks and consequences

The word "risk" is given different meanings by different authors. It is always related to an undesirable effect, e.g. an injury. In the sentence: "What is the risk in crossing this street?", the word is used to indicate the type of effect, and the answer may be: "You might be run over and killed." The next question may be: "How large is that risk?" In that sentence "risk" is the probability of the harmful effect and the answer may be: "The risk is small, probably only one in a million."

In the following, I shall let "risk" mean the probability of a specified harmful effect. This is the usual meaning in, for example, radiation protection.

If only one person is subject to a very small risk, the odds are that there will be no harmful consequence. For example, for any given person selected in advance, the odds are that he will not be killed in a traffic accident during the next year. The individual risk is rather small. In Sweden the average annual risk is of the order of one in ten thousand, which may be written 1:10,000 or 0.0001 or 10^{-4}.

If many persons are subject to the same small risk, however, the odds are that there will be some harmful effect. In Sweden the product of the annual risk of 1: 10,000 and the number of Swedes—which is about 10,000,000—is 1,000, which is the expected number of Swedes killed in traffic accidents each year.

To assess the total consequence, one considers all types of harmful effects. These may not be directly additive; for example, the expected number of cancers from the release of a carcinogenic substance in the environment represents different consequences depending upon whether the type of cancer is skin cancer, which is easy to cure, or lung cancer, which is difficult to cure.

The International Commission on Radiological Protection (ICRP) has introduced the word "detriment" to denote the total consequence obtained as the sum of the expected number of affected persons after weighting each harmful effect for its severity. For example, ICRP gives each lethal effect the weighting factor 1, but gives other effects weighting factors less than one. Because of its curability, skin cancer has been given a weighting factor of 0.01. If the consequence of exposing a large number of persons to a cancer risk is calculated to be 10 cases of lung cancer plus 100 cases of skin cancer, the detriment in the ICRP sense would be $1 \times 10 + 0.01 \times 100 = 11$ cases of lethal injury.

Risks in perspective

It is not unusual that the public or labour unions demand a zero risk from a certain source of potential harm. However, no human activity carries a zero risk. Our interest should be to protect against any significant increase in overall risk and to eliminate substantial contributions to that risk.

One easy observation is that we tend to forget that our total risk of death in a given year is quite high. Since the mean life expectancy in a technologically developed country is about 70 years, the average annual risk of dying is 1:70. Even in the teens, at the minimum risk, the annual risk of dying is as high as 1:3,000.

If we ask for information about our risk of dying next year and are told that it is about 1:100, we are not likely to request more precise information, e.g. to know whether it is 1:98.72 or 1:100.89. It is not likely that we would consider a change of the order of 1% of the risk a significant change. However, we might not be agreeable to the introduction of a number of new risks, even if each one of them were insignificant alone. This means that we might be willing to neglect new types of risks, which we cannot control, only if they increase our risk of dying by less than, perhaps, one tenth or one hundredth of 1%. If the new risk is temporary, or if we feel that we can control it, for example by accepting it voluntarily, we may then accept some much higher risks.

Quantitatively, this means that we might accept a new type of risk if it is of the order of 10^{-7} to 10^{-5} per year and that, in some cases, we might accept voluntary risks of the order of 10^{-4} to 10^{-2}. This assumption may be compared with the ICRP assumption that public risks of the order of 10^{-6} to 10^{-5} per year might be acceptable. It may also be compared with the fact that the voluntary risk of smoking is a death risk of about 10^{-3} to 10^{-2} per year. In both cases there is the complication that there is a time lag of perhaps twenty years between the exposure and the manifestation of the risk.

What, then, is the conclusion of this? In my view, it is that a number of common risks are at present being controlled at a level which is low enough to prevent substantial changes in our life expectancy. We therefore have no reason to be concerned because of individual fear of any particular source of risk. However, we might be concerned lest the number of risk sources increase to such an extent that our overall risk situation changes significantly. To prevent that, we have to be more cautious with regard to each source than is justified by the risk from that source alone.

The relative-risk approach also tells us that an extra annual dose of 0.1 millisievert (mSv)—10 millirem in the old units—could not possibly change our overall risk situation significantly, since we receive at least 1 mSv annually from natural radiation sources and this natural exposure is most certainly not the dominating cause of human death. Only at the level of an extra 1 mSv per year would we conceivably have a reason for concern, and then only because of our wish to keep the number of risk sources under control. A radiation source that is not expected to cause exposure over more than a few years would be less objectionable. The present ICRP dose limits for individual members of the public are 5 mSv a year and, in the case of lifelong exposures, an average of 1 mSv per year. The main recommendation, however, is that all doses should be kept As Low as Reasonably Achievable (the "ALARA" principle).

This rational and quantitative approach, however, is not always understood or accepted. Few persons are trained in quantitative thinking and "a risk of 10^{-5}" says nothing to the great majority. Many persons have a fatalistic or superstitious approach to risks and to statistics in general. The pessimistic slogan among nuclear safety experts that anything that can happen will happen is also often the fatalistic, non-quantitative view of the individual member of the public.

The source-related consequence

In principle, individual risks can always be controlled by means of dose limits, i.e. the radiation dose or the toxic or carcinogenic substances to which the public may be exposed. If the dose is low, the corresponding risk may be small enough to be considered negligible. It is a common mistake to believe that this also means that the source is acceptable because of negligible consequences. This is often not the case.

Let us assume, for example, that I am an official of the US Lottery Inspectorate and that I am asked to license the following practice. Each year one American will be selected at random and executed in Yankee Stadium for public entertainment. I would, of course, reject this proposal as an outrageous violation of human decency and ethics. The proponent, however, may say: Why worry? The risk to all involved is only about 1:200,000,00, which is less than 10^{-8}. Surely all Americans can agree that one life per year is negligible in comparison with the millions of lives claimed by other causes each year.

The explanation of the paradox is that the only thing that is truly negligible to each individual is his own personal risk. The proposed practice would with certainty kill somebody every year. That is a consequence that is not in proportion to the "benefit" of the practice.

The justification of a practice must be related to the benefit of the same practice in a risk-benefit analysis. (It should be noted that "risk" in "risk-benefit" means harmful consequence and not probability of harm as in my presentation.) To compare the consequence of one practice with the consequence of other practices does not tell anything about the justification of the practice.

This all seems fairly obvious, but it is usually not appreciated. For example, a practice may cause a consequence which is not in balance with the benefit and is therefore not found justified. This does not necessarily mean that it causes significant individual risks. When a protection authority takes steps to reduce or eliminate unwarranted consequences, the public often erroneously concludes that the individual risks must be significant. This leads to unnecessary anxiety and sometimes to misguided action.

There is only one case where the information of the relative consequences of various practices is relevant. That is where society wishes to set the order of priority for efforts to reduce the consequences of existing practices which have already been judged justified.

A licence to kill?

Someone may ask: Can a practice ever be considered justified if the expected consequence is that a number of persons will die?

On that basis, are automobiles, railroads and aeroplanes justified? Is it justified to employ people in construction work or in any industry? Our technological societies have accepted such practices because society has found their benefits outweigh their harmful consequences, even including deaths. It may be said that technological society, bought at the price of these consequences, may cause less premature death and suffering than any conceivable alternative.

If a society permits some practices which cause harmful effects, should we not put such stringent limits on exposures that these effects are prevented? Is not a dose limit which would not entirely eliminate all harmful effects equivalent to a licence to kill? This would be true if there is a threshold dose below which harmful effects cannot occur. However, the internationally adopted cautious assumption is that there are no such thresholds and that the risk may be proportional to the dose down to the lowest doses. The costs and efforts of applying very low dose limits would also be unreasonable if the same resources could save more lives if used for other purposes. This is why protection authorities refer to the ALARA principle to keep doses as low as reasonable achievable.

The two basic requirements that all practices should be justified (risk-benefit evaluation) and that all doses should be kept as low as reasonably achievable (optimization of protection, cost-effectiveness assessment) could seem to be enough. Is there still a need of a dose limit if the practice is justified and the doses reduced as far as reasonable? Yes, because in most cases the population at risk is not identical to the population which benefits. Dose limits are then necessary to guarantee a sufficient degree of safety to all individuals.

Biological assumptions on dose-response relationship

Within reasonable over-simplification, radiation effects on man may be divided into stochastic and non-stochastic effects. The non-stochastic effects do not occur until the radiation dose has exceeded a threshold value and will then show a severity that increases with the dose.

Stochastic effects occur where the probability depends on the dose without any threshold value, but where the severity of the effects is essentially independent of the dose. The main stochastic effects are cancer and hereditary harm. The hereditary effects of ionizing radiation and mutagenic chemicals have been demonstrated in numerous animal experiments. Studies on human cells have also shown chromosome anomalies in, for example, blood cells, after irradiation. There is no reason to doubt that radiation can also cause similar effects on germ cells, thereby causing hereditary harm as in experimental animals, even though hereditary effects of radiation have not yet been shown in man.

There is good reason to assume a linear relation between the risk of hereditary effects and radiation dose. The risk of inducing hereditary harm with the exposure of a given individual would depend on the child expectancy as well as on the gonad dose. The consequence in terms of genetic harm after the exposure of many individuals would be directly proportional to the collective gonad dose, weighted for child expectancy. If the individual doses are expressed in sievert, the collective dose may be expressed in mansievert.* The present ICRP assumption is that one mansievert of collective gonad dose will cause a consequence of 0.008 future cases of severe hereditary harm, half of which would be evident in the first two generations. The average collective dose, equally distributed in a normal population of individuals of all ages, that would be needed to cause one case of severe genetic harm some time in the future would therefore probably be larger than 100 mansievert. In a population of only fertile individuals, it would be about 50 mansievert.

The carcinogenic effects of ionizing radiation, in contrast to the hereditary effects, have long been demonstrated in man. The main observations, however, are limited to relatively few groups of persons who have been exposed to high doses, e.g. the survivors from Hiroshima and Nagasaki and patients who have been treated with radiation or have undergone extensive radiological examinations. These observations make it possible to establish some points in the dose-response relationship, but not the shape of the curve that shows the cancer risk at various doses.

The problem is to demonstrate a significant net increase in the cancer risk above the background of the normal cancer incidence. Since the latter varies geographically and with each individual's living habits (food, smoking, air pollution, occupation, etc.) as well as with age and sex, and possibly also with the genetic constitution, it is always extremely difficult to find a representative "normal" population for comparison with the exposed population.

Usually, the cancer risks observed at high doses of radiation are extrapolated down to the low doses (less than 100 mSv) which are of interest in radiation protection. The extrapolation may be direct, assuming a linear dose-response relationship over all doses, or indirect, postulating some mathematical relationship between risk and dose. A common assumption is to assume linearity at low doses, so that the risk is assumed to increase in proportion to the dose up to at least 100 mSv, but to accept the possibility of a curvi-linear relationship (e.g. quadratic) at higher doses. Usually the slope of the curve, i.e. the risk per unit dose, is assumed to be the same or lower at low doses, in comparison with high doses. There is no accepted reason to assume a dose

* Number of persons receiving dose (No.) × dose received (sievert).

threshold below which the risk would be zero. At doses less than 10 mSv, however, no carcinogenic effects on man have been demonstrated conclusively, because of the large statistical uncertainties.

Since the risk per unit dose is usually assumed to be about 2.10^{-2} per sievert for lethal cancer, it would take, on average, a collective dose of 50 mansievert to cause one extra case of lethal cancer. At the dose level of 10 mSv, there would therefore be needed a population of 5,000 persons exposed, to cause, on average, one such case. In that population there would also be some cases of curable cancer. The assessment is on the assumption that the whole body is exposed. Since the extra cases of cancer could appear at any time after a long latency period, some 100,000 person-years would have to be studied long after the exposure. The normal cancer incidence in such a population is several hundred cases, which would completely hide any few extra cases.

A number of recent studies claim to prove an increased cancer incidence in some populations which have been exposed to rather low doses of radiation. But there are also some studies that have failed to demonstrate an increased cancer rate where current estimates would have predicted it.

In essence, radiation protection and consequence assessments at low doses are based on assumptions rather than proved facts. This is one explanation why so many knowledgeable persons instinctively refuse to accept the need for concern when individual doses are very low. On the other hand, many of those responsible for radiation protection, on reasonable grounds, are not willing to "wait for the bodies" before they enforce strict dose limitations. This is a field where caution has been the policy from the beginning. It remains to be seen if this caution has been proper, unwarranted or insufficient.

The commitment concept

In all assessments the total harmful consequences are important, even if the individual risks are negligible. A collective dose of 500 mansievert (50,000 manrem) would be expected to cause ten cases of lethal cancer. These are ten human lives, irrespective of where they occur. The enforcement of individual dose limits (such as the ICRP dose limit of 5 mSv in any one year) would prevent the possibility that these ten cases would be limited to a population of less than 100,000 persons. They would therefore never be detectable in the cancer statistics and would therefore never cause a societal problem, as would be expected if ten cases of cancer appeared in a population of 100. Yet they are the same number of cancers.

It is therefore not appropriate to leave out any individual contributions to the collective dose in the assessment, on the basis that they are negligibly small. They have to be included if they contribute to the total collective dose.

What we do today may cause an exposure in the future, for example, from long-lived radio-active pollutants in the environment. These future doses, to which we are committed at the moment we exercise a certain practice, have to be included in the assessment. The sum of all present and future dose contributions, including all exposed individuals wherever they are, gives the collective dose commitment.

There are three uses of the collective dose commitment. One is that it gives a measure of the total radiation detriment of the practice under consideration and hence is a relevant quantity in the justification (risk-benefit) assessment.

A second use is to see how different protective measures will change the collective dose and therefore also the detriment. The changes in collective dose commitment due to changes in the protection efforts therefore indicate how far protection can be pursued and still be reasonable.

The third use of the commitment concept is to control the future doses and avoid unpleasant surprises. By assessing the total available resources for a practice (e.g. the world supply of uranium) and setting a limit for the collective dose per unit practice (e.g. per ton of uranium used in nuclear reactors or per TWh of electricity produced in nuclear power stations), it is possible to keep future doses under control.

To set a price on collective dose

In optimizing protective measures, it is necessary to give some indication of the amount of money which it is reasonable to spend to eliminate one mansievert. There is a remarkable international agreement that this amount is of the order of \$20,000, with examples of perhaps ten times more or less in the practical implication.

The combination of \$20,000 per mansievert and a (somatic plus genetic) risk of 4.10^{-2} per mansievert for a lethal effect implies a cost of \$500,000 per life statistically saved. This "cost-effective" reasoning has sometimes been criticized as cynical and unethical. Is it not presumptuous to set a price on human lives?

Some reflection should give the answer. The over-ruling thing is not what a human life is "worth" but the fact that society's resources for protection are limited. Since we shall all die, we can only achieve a prolongation of life. We cannot save lives, but we can save days, and we can give more useful life to these days by reducing the risk of harm and anxiety. For this, however, we have limited resources. It should be an ethical requirement that we use these resources with the maximum yield. A higher ambition in radiation protection than the present \$500,000 per statistically saved life would reduce the possibility of adding days to life and life to days in other fields where the yield per dollar may be much higher.

However, it would not be appropriate to limit radiation protection on this argumentation and then waste the money saved on something less urgent.

The great catastrophe

The consequence of a given practice can be assessed as the product of the average individual risk and the number of persons exposed to that risk. The example of traffic deaths in Sweden (1,000 individuals per year) is the mathematical expectation of the number of victims. It is also the most likely of all possible numbers, the modal value or the mode. It therefore gives some guidance on the need of, for example, hospital resources.

If the mathematical expectation of the number of victims is less than one over the entire risk period, the situation is different. A person who buys a ticket in a lottery with one million tickets and only one prize, let us say one million dollars, has very little use for the fact that the mathematical expectation of the prize is one dollar. In this case the mathematical expectation and the mode are quite different. The mode is a zero prize, with a probability of 0.999,999. The ticket buyer would not be expected to plan for his use of the prize, one dollar, which he will never get. If he has a realistic attitude, he will tell himself that he will win nothing, and plan accordingly. If he is optimistic (or fatalistic, or superstitious), he will play with the idea of winning one million dollars and dream of the things he might then do.

The corresponding, but inverse, situation exists in the evaluation of the consequences of a great radiation catastrophe such as a nuclear reactor accident. The mode of the consequence, if the accident has not occurred, is zero, because the accident has a low probability. The consequence if the accident occurs may be very great. The mathematical expectation, however, has no practical meaning unless the reactor would operate over billions of years and it would be meaningful to average consequences over such periods of time, which is, of course, nonsense.

We therefore face a situation where the consequence as such is of importance. The ticket-buyer in the lottery takes an almost certain loss when he buys the ticket, merely because the possibility of the big prize means so much to him. If he trusted the mathematical expectation, he would never buy a ticket, because the ticket price is always higher than this. In fact, the mathematical expectation of the prize could be increased by paying all ticket buyers back a sum slightly less than the ticket prize and eliminating any other prize. Such a lottery, however, would not be popular. Correspondingly, the public takes fright from the possibility of the great consequence, and the probability is of qualitative rather than quantitative interest.

An additional problem is that the occurrence of a reactor accident is not a stochastic phenomenon. A stochastic phenomenon implies a purely random process, which may be approached in dealing with large numbers of identical elements such as atoms, molecules and ball-bearing balls. Some components in mass manufacture may also provide some basis for calculating probabilities based on pure randomness. The likelihood that individuals will neglect instructions or act foolishly, or that the construction did not follow drawings, etc. is not a stochastic quantity. It may be assessed subjectively and may even be given some number indicating the odds, but it is not a true probability. It can never be said that the likelihood is extremely low; any numbers below 1:1,000 must be guesswork, because of unforeseen human errors. All one can say is that probably the likelihood of an accident is apt to decrease with increasing experience. It is an irony of fate that it may not necessarily decrease with increased protection efforts. Some ingeniously devised protective arrangements may introduce new risks, if preventive protection is overdone.

Conclusion

I have tried to describe a number of problems and solutions relating to risk assessment and risk control in the use of radiation sources. Some of my examples are relevant in other sections of the technological society. They illustrate the difficulties but do not prove that there are no passable roads towards reasonable safety.

I wish to conclude by referring again to the basic problem: our tendency to shrink from the major issues. There seems to be considerable agreement that our present technological societies, with their increasing complexity and vulnerability, their steady growth and expansion, their complicated control mechanisms which only few (if any) understand, their ominous commitments for the future and their waste of natural resources and pollution of our environment, represent a development that cannot be permitted to continue. But the agreement does not extend to the possible solutions.

There are two possible reactions to the present situation. One corresponds to the instinctive reaction of a burnt child: never more to play with fire. This would mean that we change to a less complicated, essentially non-technological, zero-growth society and hope that, like the child, we shall be able to play happily again. I am not convinced that this type of society is practicable, but I am certain that it is completely out of reach unless we all cooperate purposefully to the utmost of our ability.

The other reaction is that of a more determined and curious child: to try again, more cautiously. I am not convinced that this is a practicable solution either; it is easy to see that it could lead to disaster. This reaction can only save us if we pool all our resources and cooperate, enthusiastically and with great skill, to make technology a controllable tool rather than a demanding master. And a tool for good, not for evil, to be used with wisdom, not stupidity.

The important thing seems to be to make a decision and stick to it. Whichever alternative we choose, we must work on it, jointly, all of us, the entire world. We cannot afford to hesitate. We must mobilize all our collective strength, knowledge, brain-power and best intentions to succeed. Our chances to succeed are, in my pessimistic view, very small. That, however, may be the challenge we need as motivation.

In reality, however, we do not seem able to make the necessary decision. We continue along the familiar road, like passengers in a car which approaches a road fork with increasing speed. Instead of turning into one of the possibly passable alternative roads in front of us, we all pull the steering wheel amid horrified arguments, with the result that the car continues, straight ahead, where there is no road and only certain disaster.

Reactions and Comment

While all three speeches emphasized both the promise and the threat of science and technology, the conference responded primarily to what the speakers said about threats. And the responses were still reverberating at the close of the conference. Sadosky's theme was reinforced by later speakers (see Chapters 8, 9, 12, 17, 18) and by the protest from third world delegates late in the proceedings (see Chapter 19). It also became a special concern of Sections III, V, VIII, IX and X (see Volume 2).

Lindell's concerns received special attention in the later plenary debates on nuclear energy (Chapter 13) and in the work of Sections VI and X.

The immediate responses of the plenary session centred primarily on the controversial address of Ravetz. John Turkevitch, professor of chemistry and Chaplain to Eastern Orthodox students at Princeton University (USA), replied that Ravetz's description of scientific corruption bore no resemblance to the science he had taught and practised throughout his career. David Rose, professor of nuclear engineering at MIT, made a documented reply to Ravetz's charges about cover-ups in nuclear technology. Rustum Roy, Director of the Materials Research Laboratory at the University of Pennsylvania, maintained that scientists were currently doing more than other professionals or the Church to oppose the arms race.

Ravetz replied that he could accept all these comments as one side of the paradoxes of contemporary science and that he could answer them by pointing to the other side. The paradoxes and arguments continued to dominate the conference in the following days.

The second day of the conference ended with evening meetings of the sections in which discussion of the programme of the first two days continued.

7. The Conference at Worship

Introduction

The conference engaged daily in worship or Bible study. Dr Geiko Müller-Fahrenholz of the Geneva staff of the WCC and the Rev. Jessica Crist, a chaplain at MIT, planned the morning prayers for days when the conference was in plenary session. The leaders and forms of worship represented various liturgical and ethnic traditions of member churches of the WCC. The conference sections on several occasions began their day's work with studies of biblical texts. Most days ended with evening prayers in the famous MIT chapel, designed by Eero Saarinen.

There were three major occasions of conference worship. The first was the opening service, described briefly in Chapter 1. The meditation of Metropolitan Gregorios on that occasion is printed in this chapter.

The second was on the first Sunday morning, when participants gathered with church people of the Boston area in the historic Old South Church (United Church of Christ), with its reminders of American history from 1669. (It was the congregation of Phyllis Whealey, a slave and later freewoman, and of Samuel Adams. And it was the congregation in which Benjamin Franklin was baptized.) The church displayed a huge banner, made by one of its members, decorated with symbols of science and of the WCC. The host pastor, the Rev. James Crawford, welcomed the worshippers. Together with Mr. Crawford, worship leaders included Archbishop Kirill of the Russian Orthodox Church, Canon Burgess Carr of the All Africa Conference of Churches, Metropolitan Paulos Gregorios, the Rev. Hone T.K. Kaa of the Auckland Anglican Maori Mission in New Zealand, and Ms Irma García Heredia, a Roman Catholic teacher and graduate student from Columbia. Joining in the processional was Humberto Cardinal Medeiros, Roman Catholic Archbishop of Boston, who had welcomed the conference at its opening meeting. The sermon of Bishop John Habgood of Durham, UK, is printed in this chapter.

On the second Sunday, participants worshipped in a variety of the churches in Boston and the surrounding area. Many were guest preachers.

The third major event of worship was the closing celebration. The meditation of Metropolitan Gregorios is printed in Chapter 20.

Science and Technology within the Story of Redemption

PAULOS GREGORIOS

The Son of his love
Manifest Presence of the Unmanifest God
Born before all creation
In whom all things came to be
Both within and beyond the horizon of our senses.
Realities in heaven and on earth, seen or unseen,
Ruling thrones, lordships, powers, structures of authority,
All things came to be, through him and in him.
He himself is prior to all, above all,
For in him all subsist.
He is also the head of the Body, the Church
Source-spring of the new, Firstborn from the dead
In the new creation also He is first;
In him the incarnate God-Man
The total fullness of God was pleased to dwell,
Also to re-harmonize all things to himself;
By the blood of his cross he has made the peace-offering
Through him and in him
All in heaven and on earth are reconciled. *Colossians 1:15-20*

Our humanity is made in God's image. The invisible God makes himself manifest through this image—the humanity of Christ, which is also ours. Humanity is God's Icon—the revealer of his presence. This is the vocation of the new humanity.

This new humanity, which is ours by the grace of God in Christ, has its foundation, its orienting norm, and its integrating centre, in the same Christ our Lord.

Both humanity and the creation subsist in God, in his Son. Science and technology are activities taking place within that single reality—man and world subsisting in God. It is our task here to see science and technology in this light—in that single framework: God—humanity—universe.

But our humanity is still a sin-infested reality, though redeemed. Our sin distorts science and technology, prevents it from helping the face of God becoming manifest in the visage of humanity. Science and technology would also be redeemed, when they become an instrument for manifesting the true face of humanity created in the image of God. How to lend our God-given energies to complete the realization of humanity's redemption, how science and technology, that powerful product of God-given human energies, can also be part of the story of the fulfilment of our redemption in Christ—that, it seems to me, is the task before our conference.

Faith, Science and the Future: the Conference Sermon

JOHN S. HABGOOD

Big conferences tend to drown us in words. But the words which stick, the words which rouse the heart and mind to action, usually have to be rather few and simple. We depend on symbols, images, phrases which help to focus a wealth of meaning. And if what is said inside a conference is ever to penetrate outside it, it is the symbols which have to carry most of the weight.

People who know little or nothing about nuclear energy have heard of the "Faustian bargain". Many who are only dimly aware of the mixed blessings of scientific curiosity will nevertheless talk of "Pandora's box", though they might be embarrassed if pressed to explain who Pandora was and what her box contained. And it is the same with Prometheus, and Titanism. Shorthand summaries of subtly balanced attitudes act as reference points in a debate which might otherwise seem too complex to handle. More accurate and sophisticated phrases, like our present theme of a "just, participatory and sustainable society", tend to sink like lead outside the context of the discussion which produced them.

But where are the biblical symbols in this process? Why do we have to go to Greek mythology? Is it that the biblical writers were basically uninterested in the themes which concern us now? I hardly think so, for they touch the deepest issues in the relationship between God and his creation. Or has that biblical symbolism somehow been spoilt, so that it is difficult to see beyond the interpretations which history has put upon it? This is nearer the mark, I suspect. And this is why I ask you, in hearing my text, to hear it just as it is, without imposing on it inappropriate questions from critical scholarship or misguided literalism. My concern is with a story, a symbol, which lives and grows in the pages of the Bible, and draws into itself the fundamental themes of our Christian faith: the symbol of the godlikeness of man.

Genesis 3:1-5

> Now the serpent was more subtle than any other wild creature that the Lord God had made. He said to the woman: "Did God say, you shall not eat of any tree of the garden?" And the woman said to the serpent: "We may eat of the fruit of the trees of the garden; but God said, you shall not eat of the fruit of the tree which is in the midst of the garden, neither shall you touch it, lest you die." But the serpent said to the woman: "You will not die. For God knows that when you eat of it your eyes will be opened, and you will be like God, knowing good and evil."

Note first what is said about the serpent. It is not some great demonic tempter. We are told simply that it was "subtle". This is the temptation of cleverness, which sees beyond the so-called arbitrary limits set upon human activity, and opens up vistas of power and knowledge which could set man beside God himself. "You will be like God, knowing good and evil." There is more at stake here than moral insight. "Good and evil" is a vivid phrase for "this and that", for "everything". It is the fascination of unlimited knowledge, godlike knowledge, which is man's glory and his downfall.

In one sense the promise was true. We know, and the Bible knows, that in relation to the rest of creation man is indeed godlike. Humanity, we are told, alone bears the authorized image of God. Humanity alone is given dominion over the fish of the sea and the birds of the air and over every living thing. Humanity alone shares consciously in God's activity as creator.

But equally, only human beings know that they must die. Only human beings know their separation from God, know the frustrations and limitations of creatureliness. Only human beings plunge into the abyss of rootless, unrestrained demonic freedom.

It is a familiar paradox, the same paradox that the Greeks knew only too well. But in the pages of the Bible it gains depth and power because it is set in a rich context of theological themes. One could write the story of the Christian faith around it. God became man that man might be lifted up to God. But it is man's godlike pretensions which lie at the heart of his misery. And it is in the resolution of this paradox that salvation lies. If man is godlike and can indeed share God's knowledge and power, then how does God himself exercise it? If the image of God in man is a broken and distorted one, then how dare we impose on God's creation the distortions of our own egotism?

"Who is man," asked the Jewish writer Abraham Herschel. "A being in travail with God's dreams and designs." But how embarrassing to be "a messenger who forgot the message."

Godlike knowledge

The question whether there can be godlike knowledge in science is all part of the same problem. Nowadays we are witnessing the wholesale abandonment not only of claims to such knowledge, but also of the very idea of it. Human knowledge, we are constantly reminded, is inevitably partial, limited, conditioned. Our concepts, even our scientific concepts, belong to a time, and a place, and a social setting. The search for truth in some absolute sense is a relic of the religious past still buried in uncritical western-based science. The most that any of us can have is a map of things from our own particular point of view.

But I wonder if this isn't going too far. As I understand it, science is the search for reliable knowledge. It is a search which acknowledges that in the last resort we are dependent on human consensus, yet goes on to report that in some areas of study at least such a consensus can be found. It allows that there may be other types of knowledge, less easy to pin down precisely and more dependent on personal involvement. It admits that there are differing degrees of reliability; it is compatible with a view of science in which much that is partial and provisional or plain wrong can find a place. But to assert that there can be reliable knowledge is to recognize that at the heart of orthodox scientific theory there are concepts so well tested and ideas so fundamental that we are prepared to say: "This corresponds in some fashion to the way things really are." Is this godlike?

To deny it, to deny that there are truths which we can at least approximate to, seems to me to surrender too easily to the challenge of relativism, a surrender which in the long run could have disastrous consequences for science, as well as for religious faith. Indeed, in a curious way orthodox science needs the concept of truth. It needs a kind of overarching awareness of some ultimate reality, a reality which is what it is and which is not a mere projection of our own inadequacies, a reality to which belief in God bears witness. To me concern for truth and concern for God are two sides of the same coin.

But it is important not to read too much into this. If we human beings are only in some distorted fashion godlike, if we are trapped in our own particular points of view, then it is not enough just to equate the search for truth with the search for God, or to see God as somehow in the background validating our longing to make sense of things. The way to truth, to unity of perception, is much more costly than that. God enters into our human points of view, and shares them, and slowly bridges the gulfs between them, and offers us the promise of transcending them, and bears the pain of our distortions. We are not godlike spectators searching for patterns in a universe which somehow already reflects the unity of God. We are fellow workers invited, incredibly, to share in the work of creating a universe; we have to make sense of it in the active, not just in the passive, sense of the word. And so our godlikeness must express itself, not just in the search for some transcendent truth, but in humble readiness to enter sympathetically and attentively into the diversity of things, valuing them for what they are.

"You will be like God." A terrifying responsibility. But godlikeness entails power as well as knowledge. Indeed knowledge is power, and it is perhaps in this aspect of it that we are most conscious today of the burdens upon us. How should we exercise our powers as creators, creators even of new forms of life itself? How should we use, and share, and respect, and develop the resources God has put at our disposal? How far must we work in partnership with things as they are, going along the grain of nature, as it were; or how far should we cross the grain, interfere with what is given, seek to correct by planning—fallible human planning—the complex system of checks and balances, structures and traditions, which life has evolved?

Caring means rootedness

These are some of the questions we are here to wrestle with. We know there are no general answers. But perhaps there might be a clue to the right approach to them in asking how God himself uses his powers, how he interferes, how he works within and against the forces of the world.

"God so loved the world that he gave.." To care is to interfere; but to interfere subtly, in the form of a servant, so that the bruised reed is not broken and the smoking flax not quenched. The character of God's care is that it is incarnated, localized, rooted in the world itself. And this is perhaps where some human manifestations of power reveal their failings.

Let me illustrate. I suspect there is a correlation between exploitation and mobility. Those who do not belong to a place are more likely to exploit it. Big enterprises which encourage a certain rootlessness in those who serve them are apt to breed insensitivity to local needs, and feelings and values. The lack of a close and defined social structure in which to live shifts ethical awareness from a concern for small and attainable objectives towards a generalized sense of guilt about large and insoluble problems. But "he who would do good to another must do it in minute particulars". As Christ did.

If to care is to interfere, then caring must entail rootedness. Of course we cannot really go back to our tight little social systems and our individual acts of charity. But we must know that we belong. Perhaps the way ahead is to learn to see the world itself as a local place in a universe of immensities. We have only one earth. It is up to us to cherish it.

God's power also demands responsiveness. It is the power to evoke, not the power to overwhelm. I like the notion that God acts by being believed in. It is not the whole truth, but there is truth in it. The story of faith in God is, at least in part, the story of how a vision of what might be has utterly transformed what is. Something new and vital is fed into the stream of history by those who respond to what they see as the call and presence of God. I would want to assert that the call and presence are actually there, which is why the response is effective. But for the moment, it is the element of response I wish to stress. God acts through others. And so to act with truly God-like power must surely be to evoke responsiveness in others. To follow our dreams we must not impose them, but help others to share them.

"Would you be like God?"

One final point, the point to which any Christian sermon must eventually lead. God's power is the power of the cross. This is the heart of the paradox. This is where human godlikeness brings God, and where God's humanity finds man. Here is the place of judgment and hope. And though it is here that I end, perhaps it is really here that we ought to begin.

The trouble about conferences, as I said in the start, is the multitude of words: fine words, moving words, intelligent words, words designed to change the world. But the reality I suspect we are most conscious of is ignorance and confusion. We grope our way through monstrously difficult problems, snatching at insights, carefully balancing our differences. The bigger the conference, the longer the years of preparation, the more intense the efforts, the more rich the supplies of scholarship, the more conscious we are of our ultimate inadequacy. But it is just then, in the failure of our godlikeness, that we can dare to go to the man on the cross. "Would you be like God?" he asks us. "Then you can attain it only by sharing the pain and the darkness, the self-giving and the self-restraint, of God's way of being God."

Part Two
Perspectives and Futures

8. Inter-faith Conversations

Introduction

The early days of the conference made obvious the fact that the impact and meaning of science and technology differ greatly in different social situations. The next phase—as well as some later sessions—was structured specifically to bring into dialogue a variety of human communities and societies.

One source of variety can be found in the various world religions. The planning committee early recognized the importance of including in the programme some representatives from these religions. The ecumenical Christian community is only part of the world; people of other faiths and ideologies also influence the world and determine its directions. Furthermore, some of the world's religions have insights into the issues of ecology and social justice that may correct biases that are historically associated with most western forms of Christianity.

This conference was not and could not be a congress of world religions. It was designed primarily to help and guide the member churches of the WCC. But even for this purpose some representation from other religions, although necessarily very selective, was important. For this purpose two faiths—Islam and Buddhism—were chosen. The importance of "secular" ideologies was acknowledged elsewhere (see Chapter 11).

From the Muslim world, Fouad Zakaria, Chairman of the Department of Philosophy of Kuwait University, spoke on the issues of science and faith in Islam, and O.A. El-Kholy, Assistant Director General for Science and Technology of the Arab Educational, Cultural, and Scientific Organization in Cairo, addressed the issues of technology in Muslim societies.

From the Buddhist world, Mahinda Palihawadana, of the University of Kelaniya in Sri Lanka, spoke on the historical and contemporary meaning of science in Buddhist cultures. His long and scholarly paper, distributed to the conference, had to be greatly reduced both in his presentation and in this chapter. Nobuhiko Matsugi, a Japanese novelist, spoke from the perspective of northern (Mahayana) Buddhism, especially of Zen.

The four addresses emphasized the general relation between religious traditions and scientific innovation, as well as the particular issues that arise in specific traditions.

The "Science-Faith" Issue in Islam

FOUAD ZAKARIA

In dealing with the problem of "science versus faith" in Islam, two different issues should be clearly distinguished. The first is the actual achievements of Muslim civilization in science; the second is the attitude of religion itself to science and scientific research. In this paper, we are mainly concerned with the second question; it is not our intention, therefore, to add another list to the already existing lists of Muslim scientific achievements.

The remarkable thing about the development of science in the Islamic civilization is that the actual practice of science among Muslims was not greatly affected by the theoretical considerations concerning the attitude of religious faith to science. While the opinions differed, on the theoretical level, science continued its march and achieved, in certain cases, a spectacular success. Similarly at a crucial moment in western civilization, science moved along in spite of the official rejection by the Church of the scientific endeavour in certain basic domains. If this phenomenon means something, it is that man's search for knowledge is most likely to continue regardless of the varying attitudes taken, at different moments of history, by representatives of religious faiths.

A glimpse of the situation in classical Islam

The problem of faith versus science was raised early in classical Islam. The content was purely theological. It was soon realized that the practice of science presupposes the existence of fixed laws of nature, as well as the subjection of natural events to strict determinism. To some thinkers, this seemed to be a limitation of divine power.

However, the Mo'atazilites suggested an early solution. They distinguished between a primary cause and secondary causes. While God is the primary cause of everything, natural laws constitute secondary causes which fall within the general design of divine creation. The fixity of these laws does not constitute a limitation of divine power since, after all, God is the creator of everything. Just as the divine activity is manifested through the fixed nature of things, so it is also exercised through the natural disposition of man, which drives him to investigate and observe. Thus, scientific effort does not violate the design of God, but it is rather the realization of this design.

The Asha'arites took a different position. Generally speaking, they stressed the divine intervention, not only in the original design of creation, but also in the detailed course of natural events. Within such a perspective, it would be hard to find a place for independent scientific effort.

Thus was laid the general frame of a controversy which continued for many centuries. Each of the two parties could very easily find justification for its position in Quranic texts.

Muslim scientists must have belonged, implicitly, to the former position. It seems, however, that they were not bothered very much by the gradual prevalence of the latter position in the Muslim community, particularly during periods of political decline. On the whole, the theoretical discussion did not hamper their triumphant march.

For instance, the great progress of Islamic medical science and practice continued despite the unsolved theoretical problem: Does human medical treatment constitute an interference in the work of God? If a doctor can cure a patient (who otherwise would have been dead), how much would that bear on the predetermination of human spans of life, according to Muslim faith? Such questions were easily set aside by the victorious procession of medical knowledge and practice.

Therefore, one can safely conclude that the general social and political deterioration of Muslim society in the past five centuries, and not the prevalence of an anti-scientific interpretation of religion, was responsible for the almost total paralysis of scientific thought during this period.

Differences between classical and modern situations

The modern situation is infinitely more complex. The basic elements of the controversy, laid down in classical Islam, still exert considerable influence. However, other important factors have appeared in the intervening period.

1. In its classical age, Islamic science found no great difficulty in assimilating foreign influences, particularly from Greek civilization. Conversely, the problem of adopting modern western science is still a subject of much theoretical controversy in Islamic religious circles. This difference of attitude to foreign influences may be explained by the fact that, by the time Greek scientific achievements reached the Arabs, the Greek culture itself had already come to a standstill and did not constitute a serious threat to Muslim life. On the other hand, the western civilization which produced modern science is still an active force. With its continued achievements, it raises unexpected problems and creates unforeseen situations, thus shaking the whole edifice of human values.

2. Modern western science raised the problem of man's domination of nature through technology—a problem totally unknown to Greek culture, which was basically rational and deductive. In face of the new power acquired through modern science—a power that makes human beings, in the words of Descartes, "masters and possessors of nature"—the Muslim mind felt perplexed. The modern, man-centred technology necessarily raised basic problems concerning the God-Man-Nature relationship.

3. Greek science had been pagan; hence it did not constitute any real threat to the Muslim religions, which never found serious difficulty in refuting paganism. Modern western science, however, arose in the heart of Christendom. It was positively or negatively influenced by Christian values. No wonder, then, that it raised doubt among devout Muslims. Religious and

ethical factors played a basic role in shaping the attitudes of such Muslims. Western empirical science was described as materialistic, and thus incompatible with Muslim spirituality. The negative ethical values created by the progress of science and technology encouraged Muslims to conserve authentic Muslim morality, which was threatened by the feverish pursuit of a scientific progress that takes no consideration of human values.

4. Modern western science was associated, in the minds of Muslims, with the European colonization of most Muslim countries. This factor had an ambivalent effect: it led, on the one hand, to Muslim aversion to western science, but, on the other hand, to an appeal to adopt that very science as the only means by which Muslims could fight colonizers with their own weapons.

Differences between modern Muslim and western-Christian situations

A comparison between the Muslim and Christian views of the science-faith issue in modern times reveals an equally complex picture.

In the Christian world, religious faith showed a violent resistance to modern science. Scientific truth was seen to be in direct contradiction with revealed truth. However, faith always accepted the scientific truth eventually. The resistance shown by religion continued to lessen, in its duration, and to loosen, in its intensity, until we have now reached the time in which faith accepts in advance almost all the achievements of science, endeavouring only to alleviate its negative effects. The divergence between science and faith in Christian civilization since the Renaissance represents, in general, a descending curve, although this curve shows at times cases of abrupt ascent, when a new theory shocks religious sentiment, as in the case of evolution.

In Muslim civilization, however, no such simple schema can be drawn. The situation is too complicated and the trends too divergent. Let us try to explore the causes of such a complicated situation:

1. It was Christian civilization that gave birth to modern European science and went through the first experience of an encounter between science and faith. In spite of all the bitterness of the first stages of this experience, Christian civilization learned the lesson and knew how to benefit from it in due time.

In the case of Islam, modern European science was first known after a long period in which the effects of the glorious medieval scientific movement in Islam were forgotten, and the cultural gap between Islam and the West was greatly widened. The French expedition to Egypt at the turn of the nineteenth century was the first encounter between an extremely backward Islamic society and European science. (Napoleon brought with him, along with soldiers and arms, a whole group of scientists from different fields.) This encounter was shocking to many minds. One of those most affected was the Sheikh of Alazhar (the highest religious authority in Islam) who declared that Muslims should reconsider all the "sciences" they had already acquired—a clear admission of the inadequacy of the theological science which was the only one known at that time.

The experience of modern science in the Islamic world is still young. No wonder, then, that the reaction to modern science is still characterized by the uneasiness that reminds us, in some respects, of Renaissance Europe.

2. A related factor is the degree of understanding of modern scientific theories. In western Christian circles, ultra-modern currents in science are completely assimilated, their implications objectively discussed. By contrast, Islamic religious circles restrict themselves to generalities; their knowledge is, for the most part, out-dated, their analyses superficial. As a matter of fact, many discussions in the Islamic world about the science-faith issue are still related to the very basic principles of scientific thinking, e.g. whether to accept or to reject the rational explanation of the universe, whether there are natural causes of certain phenomena, what role the supernatural plays in determining the cause of events, etc. Some well-known thinkers still denounce empirical science because it leaves no room for the "supernatural" (*Ghaib*); they "prove" the validity of the supernatural by pointing to the fact that every scientific research implies immaterial elements (such as mathematical formulae)—using the world *Ghaib* in an obviously fallacious sense. Furthermore, Islamic societies, which belong mostly to the underdeveloped world, have not yet gone through all the problems raised by recent scientific developments. Problems of the environment, for instance, rarely attract the attention of Muslim thinkers. The same applies to other problems which disturb the western conscience at the present time, such as genetic engineering, the depletion of natural resources, etc.

3. As a result of the two previous factors, the science-faith issue, in a society in which traditional values still prevail, differs completely from that in a society in which the scientific outlook is well established. In the Christian West, the problem now is: How can religious faith find a place in a society whose life is dominated by scientific thinking and shaped by technology? In Islamic society, the problem is still: How can science justify itself in a society dominated by religious values? It is faith that is fighting its battle in the Christian West, whereas in the Muslim world it is science that is still aspiring for a legitimate place.

Examples of different Muslim attitudes to science

This last fact sheds light on certain traits of the controversy over science in the Muslim world. Both sides in this controversy take their points of departure from religious faith.

A. THE PRO-SCIENCE ARGUMENTS

1. Many of these arguments start from the idea that the Quran is full of texts which encourage investigation of nature and consideration of its phenomena. This point of view may be called "progressive", because it makes scientific investigation a mark of obedience to a divine injunction, thus leaving the door open to all possible developments in science.

2. Others take their point of departure from the idea that the Quran includes, within itself, all the knowledge that can be attained by mankind, both at present and in the future. Thus a school of thought tries, by a forced interpretation, to find, in Quranic texts, the latest scientific discoveries, such as the theory of relativity, space ships and wireless communication. Even the theory of evolution, which has been under violent attack in several Muslim circles, found a writer who reconciled evolution and creation by explaining Adam's fall from paradise as the starting point of a long journey on earth, which marked the evolution from the amoeba to man.

It should be noted that this school invites Muslims to study modern science *in order to* understand the secrets of the Quran and comprehend its hidden meanings. Thus, its support of science is only a means to another end. However, this whole school was attacked by others belonging to the same camp of faith. The latter deny that the Quran is a book in physics or biology, and hold that the destiny of the Sacred Book should not be decided by the mutations of the ever-changing sciences.

3. Other thinkers support modern science on the ground that this science is indebted for its very existence to the great scientific movement that flourished under Muslim civilization, and whose influence was transmitted to Europe, particularly in the twelfth century. They stress the fact that the method of Muslim science and thought was in essence empirical, and that Muslims rejected the Aristotelian deductive method. This view is corroborated by some European investigators who admit that Muslim scientists excelled in meticulous observations and patient collection of detailed facts. It is these traits that constitute the essence of the empirical method as it was established at the beginning of the modern era.

B. The anti-science arguments

1. There are extreme cases of writings which reject modern science as such. They not only denounce Darwin and Freud as destroyers of faith, but also object to the idea of the earth's revolution and express doubts about man's descent on the moon, on the ground that all this conflicts with religious texts.

2. In other cases empirical science is associated with materialism and atheism, or with western colonial conquest. The declared aim of the protagonists of this view is to spare Muslim society the destructive effects of scientific progress in the West, particularly moral degeneration and social instability.

3. Lastly, there are those who take advantage of any weak point in science in order to make room for religious faith. This is a procedure which was, and still is, adopted in the Christian West, e.g. when the collapse of physical determinism was hailed as a great triumph of religious thinking. Thus the Muslim world has known many thinkers who seize the first sign of weakness or indecision in science in order to defend a higher source of knowledge immune to such errors. This procedure is most likely to fail in the Mus-

lim world, as it did in the Christian, because science incessantly corrects its errors and closes many of its gaps.

A synoptic view

There are basic facts about Islam which invest the science-faith issue with a special character:

1. Islam is a direct revelation. Its holy book is the literal, unalterable word of God. This belief has led, particularly in periods of decline, to an inflexible attitude towards developments outside the domain of religion.

This basic fact has led to the formation of a fixed picture of the God-World relation. In general, Muslim society cannot readily admit the fact, easily accepted by modern Christian theology, that science has changed religion. As an example, I quote from page 16 of the WCC publication *Faith, Science and the Future*: "Religions around the world have gone through many changes because of science. Even the most committed Christians, because of science, for example, read their Bibles differently from Christians in the past. They also live differently. They pray differently. They look to science to explain phenomena that they once attributed to direct activities of God. They look to technology for kinds of help that they once asked of God."

Such a text would most probably be unacceptable in Muslim circles. Anyone who wants to convey such an idea in a Muslim environment should express it with extreme caution.

2. On the other hand, Islamic civilization does not admit a basic distinction between the secular and the spiritual. Therefore it finds difficulty in accepting the manner in which science and faith were reconciled in the Christian West since the Renaissance. Europeans tended to separate the two realms so that each one would not encroach upon the domain of the other. However, Islamic civilization, which spiritualized the secular and secularized the spiritual, and thus did not recognize any opposition between a worldly order and a spiritual order, could not establish the coexistence of science and faith by setting a barrier between them. It resorted to other means, such as making science emerge from a religious injunction, or regarding science as marginal by comparison to revelation, or testing its results by religious standards.

3. Although the problem cannot find an adequate solution on the theoretical level, there is a de facto coexistence between faith and the results of science in every aspect of Muslim life. Even the most devout Muslims, in Saudi Arabia for instance, make use of the most sophisticated products of science, while intellectually rejecting European science, without being aware of the contradiction involved. What is more important, some scientists, with strong religious feelings, even combine literal faith with high-level scientific practice by simply putting each in a separate compartment.

Thus, the *theoretical* question concerning the relationship of science and faith has not yet found a satisfactory solution in the contemporary Muslim world. The only solution lies in a religious renaissance which would overcome rigidity and allow a flexible interpretation of religious ideas. Indeed, the real challenge in the Muslim world is not to defend faith *in spite* of science, but to defend faith *along with* science.

For such a change to be possible, it is not enough to call for a transformation in the attitudes and ways of thinking of Muslim theologians. What is needed, above all, is a radical social change in the Muslim world itself. The rigid authoritarian interpretation of religion is closely linked to authoritarian and oppressive regimes. Enlightenment and flexibility, on the intellectual level, are impossible without a change in the type of relationship between the rulers and the ruled in Muslim countries.

In this respect, the recent experiment of Iran constitutes a most important testing-ground. Its success would not only lead to radical changes in the politics of the Muslim world, but would also be reflected in the thinking of the ordinary Muslim and his attitudes to the facts of the age in which he is living.

Science, Technology and the Future: an Arab Perspective

O. A. El Kholy

My terms of reference are the perspective in Arab countries of the future of science and technology and the influence of Islamic values on development of science and technology.

Let me first mention some distinguishing features of the Arab region. It represents about one tenth of the area of the world, one thirtieth of its population, and only one hundredth of its revenues. About one half of the population is under 15 years of age. Life expectancy is 52.5 years. Compared to the "industrialized" world, room occupancy is four times, per capita consumption of energy 2%, the number of agricultural workers per unit arable land area 16 times, per capita share of GDP 4% (unchanged between 1960 and 1970), the ratio of manufactured products to exports less than 9% and per capita share of exports one third.

There are considerable differences among the 21 Arab states. While six are officially classified as "least developed countries", per capita GNP in two others exceeds $10,000. One state has a serious overpopulation problem, but many others are underpopulated and rely heavily on imported manpower. Some educational systems are broadly-based and have reached fairly high standards; others are still young. Illiteracy varies between 95% in one African state and 14% in a small Asian state.

The region has been the scene of almost continuous political and military upheavals. In the last thirty years it has been deeply disturbed by the Zionist challenge, which most Arabs see as essentially cultural-scientific-technological, not withstanding its geopolitical implications.

Nevertheless, the sense of identity of the Arabs is strong and talk of the end of "Arabism" is premature. There are, however, two disturbing realities of the present situation that are of relevance also to the future:

1. The region imports 50% of its food at an annual cost of about $15 billion, a sum almost equal to current expenditure on armament. Unless radical changes occur, the percentage of food imports will reach 75% of total needs by the year 2000. Yet the region is quite capable of achieving self-sufficiency and even of contributing to alleviation of the food problem in the world.

2. The region has been importing technology on a massive and increasing scale. It is estimated that the total value of foreign engineering contracts exceeds $100 billion per year. Contracts with British engineering firms have increased a hundred-fold over the last twenty years. Arab imports of heavy industrial machinery from Japan increased 2,000 times in fifteen years!

Two highly undesirable features in this trend are cause for deep concern. First, these huge contracts involve acquisition at very high cost of inappropriate products that deteriorate rapidly and plants that work inefficiently, delivered as packages in which indigenous participation is almost non-existent. It has been ironically pointed out that the extra cost to be incurred during the period 1975-1980 in the petro-chemical sector alone is far in excess of all Arab expenditure on science, technology, higher education and research since the turn of the century. Secondly, this state of affairs has been going on with remarkably little significant change for more than a century and a half. We pay more to produce less and without the benefit of building an indigenous capability.

Official Arab thinking on the role of science and technology

What is the official Arab thinking on the role of science and technology in development? Let me give some examples.

The First Conference of Arab Ministers of Science (Baghdad, 1974) declared its faith in the basic role of science in economic and cultural development, its belief that scientific progress could only be achieved in a suitable social climate, and its conviction that sound science policies are not the prerogative of particular socio-economic systems, but vary so as to achieve harmony with such systems.

Let us note here that technology does not figure in this "credo", and also the interesting disclaimer about contradiction between science policy and socio-economic systems.

Two years later the "Rabat Declaration" (1976) expressed conviction of the vital role of science and technology in development and the liberation of man. It spoke of disparities between developing and industrialized countries, of dependence, of attaining scientific and technological autonomy, of awareness of the causes that have hindered advance, of conviction that scientific/technological development in the Third World will continue to encounter obstacles. It called for creation of an "Arab Fund for Scientific/Technological Development" at an initial minimum of $500 million.

This is a distinctly different tone, reflecting new orientations and points of emphasis, even while making allowance for the infusion of UN slogans in a conference convened by UNESCO. Events between the two conferences may explain this interesting development. The full impact of the 1973 Arab-Israeli War and its aftermath has sunk home. The sharp increase of oil prices brought a new feeling of self-confidence and added responsibilities. An Arab summit meeting held in Rabat in October 1974 discussed for the first time the subject of science and technology and the future. The heads of states called for a feasibility study for the establishment of an Arab science foundation and fund for support of scientific/technological research. The result was a study on "Science and Development in the Arab Region" which included the first comprehensive plan of action.

It would certainly be a mistake to take such declarations and resolutions at their face value. In fact, little positive action has been taken on either the foundation or the fund. We now turn our attention to the attitudes of the chief actors in this field—the scientists and the decision-makers.

The attitudes of scientists and engineers

How, then, do the scientists and technologists view the role of science and technology in development? The situation here is typical of many parts of the Third World. The natural scientists have been rather isolated from the turmoil of social and economic development. Their isolation has been compounded by the realization that "big science" calls for resources and facilities qualitatively different from anything they can dream of having. Thus, scientists faced a critical moral choice. They had to choose between their attachment to science and their commitment to their own people.

Some opted to work abroad and achieved professional satisfaction and recognition. A minority started questioning the very premises on which they have based their view of the role of science in their society. The majority, however, held the view that they are victims of ill-informed societies that fail to make full use of their potentialities. I think it is fair to say that there is no clear appreciation that the fundamental cause of marginalization of science in our society is inherent in the development policies which denied Arab scientists a significant role in development.

The engineers are even worse. They are fascinated by everything "modern". They despise all traditional technological "know-how" and maintain a blind faith in the unlimited power of technology as a problem-solver. They are generally more interested in machines than in people and are insensitive to the social damage and disruption caused by their practices.

In sharp contrast are the social scientists. They have discovered, in the harsh social realities of the development "battle", the vital role that science—and particularly technology—play in the long list of problems of unsustainable development, environmental degradation, uncontrolled urbanization, social disruption, and the "double gap" of widespread poverty and increased dependence, under an unjust world economic and information order. There is among them a healthy awareness of the fact that technology is value-loaded, that its importation raises serious ethical issues related to the value system, the power structure and the foreign relations of a country.

But the gap between the social scientists and the natural scientists and technologists has yet to be bridged. Some links are being forged, and it looks as if the issue of the environment will prove to be the common ground for the first effective interaction.

I must mention here the pioneering efforts of a small number of distinguished Arabs on either side of this gap (e.g. Abdullah, Abdel-Rahman, Elamanjara, Kaddoura, Kassas, Sayegh and Zahlan, to mention only a few). I must confess, however, that they are generally better known as international figures rather than prophets in their own land.

The second and most important group of actors are the politicians and decision-makers. Here we come across two distinct features. I do not know of any Arab leader who has not expressed his firm belief that science is a key factor in development. President Sadat's slogan epitomizing Egypt as the "state of science and faith" is a typical expression of this widely-held belief. Technology, too, is featuring more frequently in political utterances, mainly to refer to the achievements of the "North", which leave the speaker spellbound and yearning to acquire the manifestations of this newly-discovered engine of development.

More important still is the tacit adoption by the minority in power, slowly being isolated from the poor majority, of the consumption patterns that make importation of technology and its products the only means of satisfying social demand. In one African Arab state, $27 million were allocated to the purchase of two new transport planes at a time when the railway transport system, so vital for agricultural and industrial development, was almost grinding to a halt.

Basically, this reflects a schizophrenic outlook which combines concern for modernization and growth with disregard for the dignity of human beings. It is related to the failure of many countries to establish some form of truly democratic participatory government. The paternalism that prevails deprives the silent and illiterate majority of the chance to know more about issues of vital concern to them.

The preceding remarks have dwelt deliberately on problems. They do not deny the important achievements of Arab development effort, nor do they imply that scientists, technologists, planners and decision-makers have deliberately chosen socially undesirable courses of action. I have not dealt with the severe constraints imposed by outside forces, be these political, economic or cultural. In the context of looking for a better future, it is necessary to look mainly at problems.

Arab perspectives on the future

Against this background, there emerged recently an Arab interest in the future—an interest that is shared both by thinkers in the oil-rich states, looking beyond the current ambitious development plans to the time when oil reserves will dwindle, and by their colleagues in the poorly-endowed countries who are already facing very serious internal problems. A number of such studies have dealt with food, industry and energy. They seem to indicate, as I have mentioned previously, the imperative need for some form of coordination, cooperation, or even integration, for the mutual benefit of all the countries involved, and they all touch upon the role of science and technology in shaping the future. One study on science and technology in the future is of particular interest to us here. The preliminary phase is concluded, and some of its main findings are these:

1. Failure of development efforts is mainly due to the adoption of an alien model, which itself is facing serious material and spiritual problems. This has perpetuated foreign intellectual and economic domination, stifled scientific initiative and technological innovation, and caused serious social tensions. There is need for another model of development, giving priority to the strengthening of our own scientific/technological capabilities and integrating them within a viable and effective system.

2. Development that is not a copy of another model, nor slave to it, is bound to be the conscious effort of an educated and well-informed society, enjoying freedom of thought and expression, unfettered by pseudo-religious obscurantism or intellectual bigotry. The "magical" view of science, in a stagnant autocratic society, leads to intellectual oppression and manipulation of public opinion. Technology also should be demystified and subjected to careful scrutiny and effective social control, not manipulated as a tool for domination and exploitation.

3. Development should aim first and foremost at meeting the essential demands of the majority, particularly food. This is an economic necessity, a condition for national survival and independence, as well as a moral duty and a guarantee for social security.

4. There is an urgent need for integrating social and physical science and technology. Technological activity is essentially social action involving the whole of society. Social science should become a full partner in formulating policy decisions, in planning and in monitoring development. This is all the more important since a new development model calls for criteria for the choice of imported and indigenous technologies, taking into account varied circumstances in each country, methods of integrating rural and urban development, through technological pluralism, and specification of adequate measures for resolving the conflicts arising between technological development, cultural heritage and social values.

5. Science in the region is being challenged both on the national and international fronts. The concentration of scientific research in certain fields

in expensive, supranational centres rules out any significant participation of scientists in the Third World. At the same time, there are several basic problems, for example in food production, water resources, health and energy, which are crucial. These problems are acquiring now a regional and, ultimately, a global dimension. Work on a regional basis is long overdue. Bi-multilateral cooperation between "North" and "South" is a better mode than current bilateral projects, which interfere with national priorities and aggravate the brain drain.

The relevance of Islamic teaching

Finally, how does a Muslim see the relevance of Islamic teachings to his work? We believe in a system in which life is treated as a whole, in one unified context that envelopes the material and the spiritual. No aspect of life is seen separately from the others. Distinction is made, however, between the basic (faith, prayer and ethics) and the subsidiary (social relations and economic transactions). While the first are unchanging, the latter undergo continuous revision and adaptation as social conditions and challenges change. This has gone as far as considering suspension of punishments prescribed in the Quran in one extreme case of natural disaster in the early days of Islam.

We have an intrinsic sense of equality, brotherhood and human dignity within a framework of social mutual reliance in which everyone is responsible for his fellow men or women in a structure of tolerance, respect and solidarity. The golden era of Islam was dominated by a spirit in which humanity was elevated above differences of race, nationality, language and even religious dogma.

Islam calls for a truly democratic and participatory society. The Prophet Mohammed was ordered to consult the people. He openly acknowledged the validity of their criticism and adopted their point of view. He said: "I am only human, you know better about your world."

Particular emphasis is placed on knowledge, learning and reasoning. The very first verse in the Quran begins with the word: "Read!" It abounds in passages urging us to think and reason. The prophet exhorted Muslims to seek knowledge "from cradle to grave" and "even if it be in China". Learned men are "prophets"; "those who die seeking knowledge enter Heaven".

The two sources of knowledge are the Quran, which is the source of values, ethics and spiritual truth; and the Universe, whose resources are at the disposal of man. Islamic epistemology enabled Muslim scholars to discover and apply what we now call the scientific method. Inductive methods and sources of knowledge were separated from the deductive; physics from metaphysics, chemistry from alchemy, astronomy from astrology and facts from values, while maintaining the supremacy of divine values.

To this effect, knowledge was considered as one integral whole. The social sciences and humanities (or the technological sciences), together with the exact and applied sciences, form one harmonious drive aiming at satisfying man's spiritual, intellectual and material needs.

Islam considers the satisfaction of the essential needs of the people the duty of the ruler. The appliance of science and technology is guided by the basic principles of the "universal common good" and "public interest". The production of goods and services should follow an order of priority which, according to the Muslim philosopher Al-Ghazali, places "necessities" as first priority, followed by "conveniences" and finally "refinements".

The concepts of "environment" and "development" are basically different in Islam. "Environment" is both the inner self and the cosmos. "Development" is selective production of goods and services, ranked according to levels of priority. It is also the spiritual growth and self-purification of individuals and society.

To me, then, there has never been any conflict between Islam and science. Islam has no dogmas to protect. Learning is respected and is a lifelong occupation. But the unifying perspective of Islam has never cultivated various forms of knowledge separately. How, then, can we move away from the western specialization and compartmentalization of science to the unity of knowledge.

Technology, however, poses more serious questions: How are we to reconcile present-day technology with our concept of the environment as the inner self, as well as the outside world; of man as the steward and trustee of God's bounty and not the possessor; of the imperative of satisfying the needs of the people as the prime responsibility of lawful government?

How can we spread human participation in technology—both in the "North" and in the "South"—so as to involve all mankind in the spirit of equality and justice, so that it becomes a tool for spiritual development as well as material improvement, a liberating force and not a means of oppression, a potential for building a beautiful and peaceful world and not a terrible weapon against life and the environment, a hope for a better future and not a progenitor of extinction?

Such are the questions we are all seeking to answer. An Arabic proverb says: "Consult the old and the young, then go back to your reason."

Buddhism and the Scientific Enterprise

MAHINDA PALIHAWADANA

Buddhism as a human enterprise

When Siddhartha Gautama, at the comparatively young age of 29, rejected the pleasures and privileges—and also the responsibilities—of an Indian *ksatriya* chief, he did so because he was wholly unable to find satisfaction in an existence in which he, like all others, was threatened by inevitable death, decay and disease. He saw man like one burning away in a terrifying night, who yet did not care to seek the light. As far as he was concerned, it was a pressing necessity to discover the light, and so he set out in what the Buddhist books call the noble quest.

We thus see that the Buddha's concern from the beginning was with the facts of man's discontent. His quest is unique among the great religions in that he did not see it as a search for God or divine guidance.

The critical-rational temper

An important aspect of the Buddha's temper of mind, the critical-rational aspect, comes to light from his later teachings. He criticized the sacrificial religious rites of the Brahmans, and their animal sacrifices were particularly revolting to him. He did not see external rites such as the fire sacrifice and ritual bathing as a means to purity. He also discouraged personal devotion to *gurus* and in fact suggested that his own conduct should be critically examined and that he should not be taken merely on trust.[1]

And again, he advised his followers to test every opinion. An explanation of anything could be accepted only if it stood verified by one's own personal experience and conviction. There was no way to sidestep the effort of understanding: solutions to one's problems do not come externally, through tradition or from authorities. Anything externally given has no validity until it is understood and interiorized and becomes part of one's own experience and judgment.[2]

The Buddha's critique of prevailing religious views touched the theistic standpoint with particular emphasis. He did not deny the existence of gods as such; in fact, the Buddhist literature reflects the acknowledgment of the presence of gods everywhere and of "planes of existence" other than this world of human beings. The Buddha even appears to have granted the possibility of there being a potent divine being whose devotees could easily "misread" the extent of his domain and function. But he rejected the notion of creation in no uncertain terms and showed the far-reaching and unacceptable implications of the doctrine.[3] To him what was of far greater moment, we might even say of cosmic significance, was the liberation of man from the bonds of suffering and ignorance.

Buddhism thus originated basically as a human enterprise. It has no external point of reference. It sets out from the existential fact of human discon-

---

[1] Cf. e.g. *Itivuttaka*. London: Pali Text Society, Sec. 92. And *Majjhima Nikaya* (PTS), Vimamsaka Sutta.

[2] Anguttara Nikaya (PTS), i.188 ff. And K. N. Jayatilleke: *Contemporary Relevance of Buddhist Philosophy*, 7. Kandy, Sri Lanka: Buddhist Publication Society, 1978.

[3] K. N. Jayatilleke: *The Message of the Buddha*. London: George Allen & Unwin, 1975, ch. 8 especially pp. 114-115. And see especially Gunapala Dharmasiri: *A Buddhist Critique of the Christian Concept of God*. Colombo: Lake House Investments Ltd., 1974.

tent. Only through the depths of the human personality are solutions to human problems discoverable.

It is important also to realize the dimensions of the social implications of the Buddha's teachings. His critique of Brahmanical ritualism went hand in hand with an unquestionably revolutionary departure from the Brahmanical social theory, based as it was on the notions of castes and caste occupations. The Buddha affirmed the fundamental similarity of all men in no uncertain terms.[4] In this he went much further than verbal criticism. The Sangha (monastic order) which he founded was open to all alike, not merely in theory but in actual practice, as we can see from the many poems written by monks and nuns of previous low social standing, joyously giving expression to the freedom which they experienced as members of the Buddhist Sangha.

The principle of "conditioned genesis"

What was necessary from the Buddha's point of view was a clear understanding of the existential predicament. To understand matter "as it exactly is" is of paramount importance. "Well-grounded thinking" leads to such understanding. For this, one had to be free of prejudices (for and against), fears and confusions; or as we would say, one had to face the problem impartially, in a tranquil and unemotional frame of mind.[5]

Setting about the task in this fresh frame of mind, what explanation of man and the world did the Buddha himself find out? It dawned on him that suffering was there as long as certain conditions existed; it was not there when those conditions disappeared. This was true of everything. Take anything, and you will find that there are certain conditions upon which its presence is contingent and upon whose disappearance its absence is contingent. This was the Buddha's famous causal principle of "conditioned genesis".[6]

The sorrows and the joys, the changing moods, and all that is there as one's inner life also are explained by this principle. It is not a case of denying the reality of matter and mind and life. But their birth and death and re-becoming take place because of the unvarying operation of this law of conditioned genesis. "Conditioned genesis" and not materialist or essentialist or theistic theories explained the flux of life in all its aspects.

The Buddha felt that the burden of his ignorance was lifted, and with this came the great change that he always sought. The natural consequence of deep wisdom is moral transformation, or as the Buddhist books say, the "influxes becoming extinct". It was a new orientation, of which the "I and

---

[4] G. P. Malalsekara & K. N. Jayatilleke: *Buddhism and the Race Question*. Unesco Publication, 1958, 35 f.

[5] *Contemporary Relevance of Buddhist Philosophy, op. cit.*, 7. And David J. Kalupahana: *Buddhist Philosophy: a Historical Analysis*. Honolulu: University of Hawaii Press, 1975, 19.

[6] See David J. Kalupahana: *Casuality, the Central Philosophy of Buddhism*. Honolulu: University Press of Hawaii, 1975. Also *The Message of the Buddha, op. cit.*, ch. 13, especially pp. 196 ff.

mine" were not the centre. The whole philosophical exercise of Buddhism was for this liberation:

As the great ocean has but one taste—the taste of salt—even so this teaching and discipline has but one flavour, the flavour of liberation.[7]

With this theory of conditioned genesis, the Buddha has clearly opted for an unchaotic world—by and large. An orderliness, a regularity operate in the universe. Its events are not haphazard but occur according to regular patterns. Nor are events and individuals isolatable; for their very existence is possible owing to others that are related to them as conditions of their coming into being. The phenomena of the mind are no exception. The present temper of a mind is a consequence of its past operations and experiences and also of its interchanges with other minds.

On the face of it, one would be tempted to understand the conditioned genesis view as one that scarcely recognizes the human will: the confluence of past and present circumstances produces new circumstances, and this will go on and on. How can one intervene to change its direction?

The Buddha has clearly said that one can initiate action. The very crucial Buddhist theory of *karma* is a theory of the possibility of meaningful action,[8] and not merely a theory that explains man's present condition as a result of his behaviour in past lives (which also it is). The principle of conditioned genesis is not a principle of determinism. It does not rule out accident, nor does it preclude free will.

Without a concept of free will the Buddhist praxis makes no sense. Man, though affected and changed by past experience, has always the capacity to choose between alternate ways of action. Any deliberate exercise of the will is an "action", and the moral significance of an action depends on the way it affects ourselves or the external world. In effect there are only six possible ways: our actions either create attraction, repulsion and confusion or they reduce attraction, repulsion and confusion. These are the so-called six "roots" (of action)—more expressively the "roots" greed, hate and confusion and the lack of each of these.

In effect the connative element of any action either increases or reduces one's greed, hate, and "ignorance". Our actions are wholesome if they reduce these, unwholesome if they increase them. And the Buddhist view is that we *can* act so as to reduce greed, hate and ignorance—or we can choose to act the opposite way. This is man's freedom of will. Morality becomes necessary not only because desire is impossibly insatiable, but also because there are moral instincts ("the wholesome roots of action") and because there is a possibility of meaningful action.

In many sayings of the Buddha we are told that what should be pursued is the good of both self and the world and what should be avoided is harm both

---

[7] *Vinaya* (PTS), II 239.

[8] *The Message of the Buddha, op. cit.*, 146 f.

to self and to the world.[9] In fact there is no conflict of interests: what the Buddha shows to be good for oneself is in fact good for the world, because it is designed to purge man of greed, hate and ignorance.

If one were to sum up the Buddha's enterprise and the "agenda" which he commended to others, one would say that they include the following as their core:

1) the awakening to the existential predicament;
2) discovery by personal effort of the realities of the situation as they exactly are: the principle of conditioned genesis both explains the predicament and then shows the way out of it;
3) follow-up action for moral transformation which is the eradication of greed, hate and ignorance (the Middle Way or the Noble Eightfold Path).

The person and the universe

The great creative periods of the classical civilization of India within which the Buddhist tradition evolved antedate the great developments of modern science. But in its great epochs, Indian civilization too achieved a scientific and technical mastery of considerable dimensions (cf. for example decimal counting, the mathematical notions of zero and infinity, achievements in metallurgy, surgery, hydraulic engineering, etc.).[10]

Indian civilization therefore cannot be called anti-scientific. Hindu and Buddhist Asia clearly chose to alter nature in order to build cities and temples and palaces, divert the flow of river waters, construct roadways and modes of travel, control disease and prolong life and produce food to feed populations inconceivable without these operations.

But the ethos of the great religious cultures in which these developments took place worked without any notion of conquest in relation to nature, animate or inanimate. As for the Buddha, he explained everything as liable to change, and also as interdependent. Things interact and become different from what they were. But since there is always change, Buddhism refuses to resort to any substantialist notions, either to explain the human personality or to explain the world. Both of these it explains in terms of conditioned genesis.

It is therefore not surprising that we do not have an exact Buddhist term to correspond to the English word nature. The western concept of nature implies a unitary essence or substance behind natural phenomena, and it also excludes man from the realm of these phenomena. Such a concept is impossible in Buddhism[11] except of course as a poetical metaphor or as a linguistic convention.

---

[9] *Majjhima Nikaya, op. cit.*, Ambalatthika-rahulovada-sutta.

[10] See B. N. Seal: *Positive Sciences of the Ancient Indians*. Delhi, 1958. And A. L. Basham: *The Wonder That Was India*. New York: Grove Press, Inc., 1959, pp. 495 ff.

[11] S. J. Samartha & Lynn de Silva: *Man In Nature, Guest or Engineer*. Colombo: Ecumenical Institute for Study and Dialogue, 1979, 32.

The complex human entity

Man is conceived of as a complex entity, being a combination of five aggregates or "systems". The first of these is all that constitutes his physical personality. And the other four comprise the phenomena of perceptivity, sensitivity, connativity and conceptuality, i.e. all phenomena of a "mental" kind.

Man, with this complex equipment, is regarded as rather high up in the scale of refinement among living beings. But on the other hand the notion of rebirth, which Indian religions accept, tends to blur distinctions: for a man today might have been a lesser being yesterday.

The physical world

So far as the world is concerned, Buddhism naturally regards its physical matter as subject to constant change. The usual definition of matter in the Buddhist texts is "what undergoes change".[12] Buddhist intellectuals reflected on matter as exemplifying the transient and unsatisfactory nature of life. In the course of these reflections they constructed a considerable theory of matter.[13] This theory views matter as made up of atoms appearing in combinations or complexes. The ancient Buddhist scholars had the notion of an infinitesimally small atom: one table puts the number of atoms in a minute speck of dust at 46,656![14] So it is not surprising that the atom is said to be beyond the range of the naked eye: it can be seen only by paranormal vision.

In keeping with the Buddhist notion of unceasing change, the atom was also conceived of in a non-substantialist way. It was held to be simply "flashing into being: its essential feature is action and function and therefore it may be compared to a focus of energy".[15]

At the other end, no less startling is the ancient Buddhist conception of the universe.[16] Although the Buddha discouraged speculation on the origin and end of the universe, the Buddhist books contain several references to the structure of the universe (which is considered to have been seen by the Buddha with his paranormal vision). Several units of this structure are mentioned, the smallest being what is called the "Thousandfold Minor World System" with "thousands of suns, moons and continents". Larger than this is the unit called the "Twice a Thousand Medium World System" and larger still the "Major World System".

It is stated that this vast universe is without a known beginning in time, nor a known end. Whether it is finite in extent, or infinite, can also not be

---

[12] *The Message of the Buddha, op. cit.*, 71.

[13] See Y. Karunadasa: *Buddhist Analysis of Matter*. Colombo: Department of Cultural Affairs, 1967. And *The Message of the Buddha, op. cit.*, ch. 5.

[14] *The Message of the Buddha*, 69.

[15] Arthur Berridale Keith: *Buddhist Philosophy in India and Ceylon*. Oxford, 1923, 161. And *The Message of the Buddha*, 67.

[16] See *The Message of the Buddha*, ch. 7.

known. However, there is a constant reference to the "evolution and dissolution" of the worlds, which clearly does not mean a definite end or annihilation.

Relationship

The Buddhist books always classify consciousness as consciousness of visible objects ("eye-consciousness"), of audible sounds, etc., and of conceivable concepts. To be conscious is to be related to the world around you. In relationship with others, the Buddha advises man to be ever mindful of one thing: that all dislike pain and relish the pleasant sensations. Knowing that others are also like oneself, one is advised never to inflict pain on others. Here the Buddha expected magnanimity on a truly spectacular scale:

> "Whatever living being there be, large, medium or small, developed or developing—may they all be at ease. Let no one humiliate or despise another, anywhere whatsoever. Let one no seek another's suffering by wrath or violent thought. Develop boundless regard to all beings, even as a mother would cherish her own only child."[17]

The Buddha's rule of the Monastic Discipline forbids monks to undertake any enterprise involving violence to living beings and plant life. He felt and expressed great ecstasy in seeing places of natural beauty. The forest was particularly attractive to him and he commended it to the monks as a source of solitude best suited to the contemplative life.

The Buddhist teaching in regard to nature and environment is not a matter for doubt. When it is said that the understanding of man and the world is in terms of conditioned genesis, it also implies this: "If when you do X the result is Y, and you find Y to be unacceptable, then you should learn to refrain from doing X. To lead an intelligent life, you must forever be mindful of how actions yield results." This is an implication which has relevance both to man's inner life as well as his relationship with nature and fellow beings.

How much mindfulness is adequate is also a point at issue. In this regard the following reference in an important commentarial work is enlightening:

> "Not only does the unwise man do unwholesome acts under the sway of hate, but also, even as he is doing them, he is not aware (of what he does). (Of course) it is not that, doing unwholesome acts, a person is unaware to the extent of not realizing: 'Here I am doing an unwholesome deed.' He is said to be unaware in the sense that he does not know: 'For this act, the consequence is such and such'."[18]

The message of this is that intellectual awareness is only the beginning of the process. From there it must deepen evermore. It is only through deepening understanding that we can dissociate ourselves from what is finally

---

[17] Sutta Nipata (PTS), stzz 146-149.

[18] Dhammapadatthakatha (PTS), on Dhammapada stz 136.

harmful and unproductive, in our relationship with fellow men as well as with our environment.

Buddhism and modern science

It was stated earlier that Indian civilization could not be called anti-scientific. Speaking specifically of a Buddhist country, Toynbee[19] in his *Study of History* refers to the Sri Lankan *tour de force* of "conquering" the dry zone of the island for agriculture by constructing irrigational reservoirs "on a colossal scale" to compel "the monsoon-smitten highlands to give water and life and wealth to the plains which nature had condemned to lie parched and desolate":

> "(In the fifth century) the Jayaganga was constructed to bring water from Kalavava to Tisavava in Anuradhapura: it was a man-made river uniformly 40 ft in width and 54 miles long. In tracing this channel the anonymous engineers... performed an incredible feat. For the first 17 miles the gradient of the channel was a steady six inches in every mile. Man-made rivers criss-crossed the dry zone, feeding tanks at different levels and supplying water to a vast area of rice fields. At the end of the tenth century such channels totalled over 500 miles."[20]

Between the modern age and this civilization lies the traumatic experience of western colonialism. The massive success of this other, and basically different, conquest owes as much to the technological superiority of cannon and gun as to the ruthless militancy of its perpetrators—which of course other warriors also had in other times and other lands.

This human sacrifice was the first homage that Asia and Africa (and the Americas) were forced to pay to the new gods of a militant technology. All this is part of history. The point is that, if only history had been otherwise, a humanistic technology might have flourished in Asia, and the traffic in knowledge might have been a happier story of give and take—instead of a dismal tale of cultural impoverishment.

Since westerners brought the *modern* scientific enterprise to Asia, its story is bound up with that of colonialism. In the wake of colonialism came the Christian missionaries. One of the first priorities of the missionaries was the setting up of schools to teach the scriptures and to facilitate colonial administration. The colonial administrators recognized and supported these schools and also set up similar schools themselves. The long process that this venture in western education set in motion finally laid the infrastructure for the introduction of scientific information, and also took away from the Buddhist Sangha their exclusive privilege in education.

---

[19] Arnold J. Toynbee: *A Study of History*. London: Oxford University Press, 1960, p. 81.

[20] A. W. P. Guruge, in *Education in Ceylon: a Centenary Volume*. Colombo: Ministry of Educational and Cultural Affairs, 1969, p. 96.

Well into the early decades of the twentieth century what came from the West was not so much advanced scientific knowledge as various kinds of *finished goods* and western-inspired attitudes. Gradually other things arrived: the commercial set-up, the agencies, the repair men, the technicians, the engineers and so on.

One of the main social changes that resulted from these developments is that a bureaucracy trained in the new schools replaced the old order of secular authorities. And, in the post-independence developments, the missionaries too, like the Sangha before them, lost their privileges in the field of education and the schools generally became secular in character. Although religious instruction occupies an important part in the curriculum, the Asian school has taken on an increasingly "modern" character.

The new emphases attract the most gifted students to medicine and the various sciences. In the old set up, it is likely that a considerable percentage of talented students would have been attracted to religious or allied studies. A fair number would have become members of the Sangha, and others would have joined the more "intellectual" of the old secular occupations. This is no longer so.

The most striking change, then, is to be seen particularly in the secular occupations—and partly also in the Sangha. The farmer today relies less on the plough and the fertility rites than on the tractor and chemical fertilizers: the cleverer and more prestigious doctor will be the product of the western-style medical school rather than the pupil of the reputed native physician. And the brilliant young man who becomes a monk is an increasingly rare phenomenon.

It is difficult to say that the Sangha is respected less. The Sangha still remains a powerful influence with the people, but some erosion of its social prestige has indeed taken place.

How science has affected the religious quality of Buddhist communities is a many-sided question. What is most obvious may be stated first: more than science itself, more than the inner nature of its methodology and its logic, it is the creeping materialism of new life-styles that has been cutting into both the visible cultural fabric and even the intangible spiritual content of the Buddhist religiousness.

Yet it is a noteworthy fact that there has been hardly any controversy between Buddhism and science. One reason for this may be the fact that as of now we have only a comparatively simple scientific establishment. But two other factors are also worthy of our attention. First, the Buddhist monk, the classical interpreter of Buddhism, has no mediatory role assigned to him. He is basically an instructor. If new explanations of nature are proposed in a strange idiom, this would not matter to the monk, because it is difficult to show that they affect the core of the Buddhist teachings. Science has obviously not banished man's discontents, nor can science convincingly prove that the "agenda" proposed by the Buddha will not work.

The other reason is that a considerable number of people, both in the scientific community and in the Buddhist, have been impressed by the critical-rational aspect of Buddhism. This evident common denominator between Buddhism, and science and modern socio-political systems like Marxism, has led several recent Buddhist scholars to treat these systems quite seriously. We can in fact say that recent studies within the Buddhist community reveal a response to scientific thought as well as to modern political thought, a certain rescrutiny of the roots of the Buddhist tradition to see how far they agree with science and political analyses like the Marxist.

We saw above the emphasis that Buddhism places on understanding the existential state "as it exactly is". There is no need to suppose that such understanding is necessary only in the case of the inner life, though in Buddhism this is primary. Anything that enlarges understanding is indeed desirable. From this, and from its use of the principle of conditioned genesis in understanding things, it can be argued that the "climate" that Buddhism creates is favourable to the scientific enterprise. But the scientific enlargement of understanding is welcome only *if* it is conducted within the framework of the value system of Buddhism. While this may be inimical to science that is linked to power and violence, it does not at all affect the vast potentialities before science to aid in the total development of mankind.

However, the Buddhist ideal of understanding "what is" has dimensions in which science in general shows no interest. The Buddha demands *a total understanding* of greed and hate, which in itself brings liberation from them for all time.

In this regard, what Prof. Thoules says about certain aspects of Buddhist and Freudian psychology may be of suggestive interest:

> "Freud's point of view was that of scientific medicine. Scientific medicine had one obvious characteristic in common with Buddhism in that it was concerned with the salvation of man from suffering. In this respect it diverged from the Jewish-Christian tradition of accepting salvation from sin as the central purpose of its system. A second respect... in which medical science shared the point of view of Buddhism rather than that of the surrounding Christian culture, was in its acceptance of the principle of cause and effect even with respect to the results of human actions. This would seem to be essentially the same as the Buddhist principle of dependent origination, and it led to similar implications for behaviour...
>
> "The orthodox medical science of the nineteenth century differed, however, from the Buddhist tradition in the fact that it recognized as causes of illness only physical causes... Freud's great contribution... was that he recognized and studied the mental causation of such disorders and introduced mental methods of treating them... There were of course differences... One of the most striking was that Freud was concerned with giving his patients sufficient peace and inner harmony to enable them to carry on the business of the present life; the Buddha aimed at relieving his

disciples from the burden of suffering of both the present life and future lives... Yet... Freud's idea of the... unconscious plays something of the same part in explaining present mental dispositions as does the *karmic* effect of past lives in Buddhist psychology."[21]

To turn to the question of technology. In the light of basic Buddhist principles, one would have to make two objections against modern technology. First, the way its products are turned out and distributed means that the human being is today subtly trapped by the greed and pride of possessing material conveniences as never in the history of mankind. For the Buddhist of course this would quite simply rule out the basic pursuit of his religious culture.

The second objection is about the scale and speed of technological progress. At the rate that modern technology goes, the human being is not left enough time to cope with the complexities it creates. We all know that it sometimes takes decades to discover the hidden ill effects of a new thing or a new behavioural pattern. To be bombarded with an unceasing volley of ever-new "gadgetry" is certainly not conducive to the self-understanding which is the foundation of the Buddhist way of life. So technology tends to increase all the cardinal evils against which the Buddhists have been warned by their religious heritage.

But of course this is not all that Buddhists would have to say. Rejection of technology is not an inevitable implication of the Buddhist teachings. As pointed out earlier, Buddhists in their own way made use of technology. The Buddha's own unmistakable advice was that reasonable comfort need not be avoided. The only requirement was that it should not rule out the *dhamma* (righteous) way of living.

And here one would like to add another word. In the Buddhist view the future cannot be regarded as settled, as determined by what has already happened. When someone said that the future invents itself, he was in a sense close to the Buddhist point of view. The future will in large measure be the result of what we choose to do, how we choose to act. And this in turn will be commensurate with how much we understand, how much awareness we possess and acquire. This is partly scientific, but largely "spiritual".

In the past the Buddhist diagnosis of the problems of man as stemming from individual greeds and desires might have appeared as a dismal analysis to many. Today, after about half a century or so of consumerism, it looks more like the unavoidable conclusion to which events point, even though it appears unpalatable. Indeed, what the Buddha taught is a severe teaching. In fact on one occasion, he himself declared: "The way I speak will be harsh and pressing. That which has pith will endure."[22]

---

[21] Robert H. Thoules: Foreword. In M. W. Padmasiri de Silva: *Buddhist and Freudian Psychology*. Colombo: Lake House Investments Ltd., 1973.
[22] See Samyutta Nikaya Atthakatha (PTS), on S.i 1.

A Contemporary Buddhist's Critical Evaluation of Scientific and Technological Culture

NOBUHIKO MATSUGI

In order to compare thought patterns of Buddhism and Christianity within a short time, I would like to explain the meaning of the phrase "the tremendous mystery of nature". This is a central phrase used by the eminent Zen Buddhist scholar Daisetz T. Suzuki in his explanation of Zen Buddhism.

Contrary to Christian thought, Buddhism does not recognize a creator of the universe or of human kind. We human beings are created and maintained by some kind of power, but Buddhists retain an understanding that is identical with Brahmanist thought forms derived from the ancient religion of India. When we seek for that reality which brings us into existence and supports us in this world, we move towards a thought sphere that centres in "tremendous mystery". Just as in the very famous painting by Gauguin entitled "D'où venons-nous? Que sommes-nous? Où allons-nous?" (Where have we come from? Who are we? Where are we going?), we Buddhists prefer to respond that all such metaphysical questions are ultimate mystery and impossible to answer. Gautama Buddha, the founder of Buddhism, kept silence when his disciples asked these kinds of questions.

The importance of relationship

In this sense, then, Buddhism participates in agnosticism. This fact, however, does not mean that Buddhism neglects such metaphysical questions. Although the responses to such questions are removed from verification through either philosophical or scientific orientations, Buddhism provides several excellent intuitive insights. In this regard I would like to point to Gautama Buddha's understanding that existence resides in "relationship". As an example, we cannot exist without air and food. In this fact Buddha points to the reality that our existence does not abide outside of relationships with otherness. The conceptualization of relationship carries with it the implication of "relationship" as expressed in this context.

The primary characteristic of Buddhist emphasis on relationship as the origin of everything is that we, as the subject, and air, as the object, are not to be recognized as singularities. In other words, I am "I" only in relation to "air", and in like manner air is "air" only in relationship with me. The Buddhist will maintain that I alone or air in-and-of-itself does not exist in actual reality, but rather the object exists only in relationship. The second characteristic relative to "relationship as origin" is a recognition that human beings, birds, beasts, insects, fish, rivers, grass, trees, and all else in this world exist in complete equality. With this kind of inter-relatedness Buddhist thought requires a respect and affection for all existence on earth.

However, all Buddhists do not worship nature as mystery or beauty as do Shintoists in Japan and Hindus in India. Contrary to this, Buddhist thought places the animals and plants in this world in a relationship of struggle in an evil world. In this regard, the Buddhist insists that plants and animals participate in a desire for liberation from suffering and bondage just as human beings seek such liberation. The very word Buddha contains the meaning, discoverer of liberation from suffering. Buddhism insists that not only human beings but animals and plants also have the possibility of becoming Buddha. Since all things retain the possibility of becoming Buddha, all things are equal. Thus Buddhists deeply respect the possibility and hope that actually exists within everything.

Since the days of Gautama Buddha, Buddhists have prohibited to themselves the killing of animals for food, because animal life partakes of the same life substance as human life. As another example of the ways in which the concept of equality has been practised, Buddhists also prohibit the throwing away of broken kernel rice. This concept of equality comes not only from the requirements of mercy inspired by suffering but is derived also from a central recognition that all things partake in the possibility of attaining Buddhahood.

The same respect for people and things

Present day Buddhism, as it has come to be practised, has lost some aspects of this asceticism. Even Zen Buddhists, holding as they do some of the most rigorous religious commandments, allow the eating of meat. But even in the act of taking the life of an animal, basically Buddhism sustains the concept that all things are equal. In the traditions of Buddhism, while it is recognized that hell is a state of ultimate pain and suffering, there is the other inherent aspect of the Buddha's world of peace as liberated from all suffering and toil. In other words, animals and plants struggle to the same degree as human beings, but they also have the same possibilities and hope for liberation from suffering and toil. Thus Buddhists worship all things with the same deep respect.

I have studied books on entomology by Jean Henri Fabre as well as other works on plants and animals. What amazes me is the fact that each of the different plants and animals have differing and specialized but mysterious abilities. For example, it is completely mysterious to me how migratory birds take journeys of several thousand kilometers without ever getting lost or making a mistake. The conclusion that I must draw is that all things are equal, based upon their differing but mysterious abilities. All things, being different from human beings, have at the same time equally mysterious abilities. When we have come to realize this central essence of reality we cannot help but nurture a spirit of tremendous mystery relative to nature in much the same manner as in Buddhist traditions. This deep respect for all living things replaces the arrogant wish to eliminate and use other things for the purposes of security and the development of an artificial man-made world. Of course other life forms and certain kinds of inanimate reality contain realities that are harmful to human beings. But when we come to appreciate and know the unique and mysterious abilities of each form of existence, it is possible to develop a humble spirit of learning and a desire for understanding relative to all forms of existence. This is the spirit of Buddhism, and all things are teachers.

To "centre on human life" proves detrimental

From a Buddhist point of view, it becomes apparent that the primary contributor to materialistic security, prosperity and rationalism in human societies has been the advent of scientific and technological discoveries and inventions supported by an attendant world-view. Over against this and as a countervailing influence we find the religious perceptions and dogmas of Buddhism and Christianity that have resisted the presently dominant scientific world-view.

As is the case with rationalism, so it is with science, technology and the use of their attendant discoveries and inventions; the basic article of understanding is the belief that, for the scientific and technological enterprise, all the results are neutral in value terms. They can be used either for the edification or destruction of society and nature. Thus the outcome of science and technology must be controlled by mankind.

In the scientific and technological cultures, the discoveries and inventions derived have been used only to increase materialistic pleasure and physical comfort. These orientations are used only for self-satisfaction in an ideology that is in fact excessively centred on human life alone. In the process we have created, in the last analysis, an extremely uncomfortable environment for all kinds of life: plant, animal and human.

The use of the phrase "centred on human life" points to an ideological orientation that affirms human existence only, through a value system that places humanity at the pinnacle above all other forms of existence. But from even this vantage point, when we take a careful look at the actual conditions of scientific and technological culture, we discover that what was thought to be "centred on human life" is in fact very much to the detriment of human kind. Because of the terrible waste of extremely limited natural resources in the pursuit of materialistic security, the human environment has been seriously polluted and compromised. Even worse, we face the impending end of the petroleum era, and we are frantically and blindly developing an atomic power technology that will pollute the future for the next several thousand years. Scientific and technological culture has created a great crisis for human life which completely ignores the development of men and women. In this framework of understanding, the ideology is not only self-centred but self-destructive. I believe that we are past the point of writing about and debating over whether there is validity in the scientific and technological world-view, but rather are faced with the final judgment as to its lack of validity in the impending and fearful destruction of life on the planet. This destructive scientific and technological culture and its world-view is strongly tied to a very anthropomorphic and self-indulgent ideology.

As I indicated earlier, Buddhism does not look on human kind as the pinnacle above all other forms of existence. From the Buddhist point of view human beings are filled with mysterious capacities, as are all other living organisms and the inanimate world. The existence of human kind is possible only through real struggle, just as is the case with other forms of life. As a matter of fact human life exists only in a devilishly pitiful set of circumstances. But as with other forms of life, human kind also strives for freedom from bondage and suffering. The present reality of human life on this planet is characterized by an excess that engenders mediocrity. It is very apparent that a concept of humanity which allows no hesitation at the destruction of other lives and the environment, and is also willing to sacrifice the future of human culture for the fulfilment of the present, could in no way be derived from Buddhist understandings.

Although Buddhists do not take the extreme position in regard to life that the Hindu religion does, so as to even allow locusts complete freedom at crop destruction, Buddhists are ascetics in that they are concerned to protect the environment, being unwilling to destroy other life for the sake of self-indulgence. Such an orientation is grounded in the Buddha spirit as this requires a wholehearted effort at being humble in the realization of the Buddha nature as this moves one towards self-transcendence.

Reactions and Comment

The presentations from Muslim and Buddhist perspectives evoked vigorous and sympathetic interest in the plenary sessions. Among the issues raised were these: What is the impulse for social action and world transformation in Buddhism and Islam? How can one account for the unusual relation between Buddhism and Japanese industrialization? What is the source—empirical, metaphysical, or otherwise—of the congeniality of Buddhism and modern science?

There was, along with gratitude for the presentations, a recognition that plenary sessions could not discuss in depth the issues raised. Nor were the sections structured to give intensive attention to interfaith dialogues, which must be continued in a more sustained process with approximate numerical equality of differing groups. Even so, the impact of this plenary session can be noted in several of the section reports, either in references to insights from world religions or in the frequent recognition that Christian churches must act within a pluralistic world.

The very real differences among the faiths represented in the conference did not obscure the convergence of ethical concerns on many issues of justice, participation and sustainability. Hence there appeared to be considerable agreement that diversity of faiths was less a divisive issue for most of the hopes of the conference than diversity—sometimes hostility—of different economic, political and cultural forces in the contemporary world.

Despite the diversity of experiences represented by the four speakers, their addresses converged on several common themes. All took up the problem of serious poverty in their nations. All saw the poverty as not merely accidental but as a deprivation and injustice within the international order. All saw a need for scientific and technological efforts, but none expected help to come from the prevailing methods of "transfer of technologies"—a theme already emphasized by Philip Potter in his opening address.

9. Perspectives in Developing Countries

Introduction

From its opening session the conference showed an awareness that science and technology function within social systems. Any attention to "perspectives and futures" must take seriously those systems and their inter-relations. For practical purposes the conference considered these systems in three groupings: (1) developing countries, (2) industrialized, market-economy societies, and (3) industrialized, socialist societies. It began with the first.

As Metropolitan Gregorios pointed out, the "developing countries" or the "Third World" might better be called the "Two-Thirds World". These countries comprise a large majority of the human race. Their needs and complaints had already found eloquent voices in Rubem Alves and W. Mutu Maathai (see Chapter 3), Manuel Sadosky (Chapter 6), and O. A. El-Kholy and Mahinda Palihawadana (Chapter 8). Now the conference experienced the concentrated impact of three speakers from widely differing societies with many similar problems. The speakers were Liek Wilardjo of Satya Wacanya Christian University in Salatiga, Java, Indonesia; Thomas Odhiambo of the International Centre of Insect Physiology and Ecology in Nairobi, Kenya; and Carlos Chagas, Dean of the Faculty of Health Sciences in the Federal University of Rio de Janeiro, Brazil, and President of the Pontifical Academy of Science. The text of Prof. Chagas is taken from the recording of his extemporaneous address.

An Indonesian Perspective

LIEK WILARDJO

Indonesia is a developing country that faces many problems, most of them common to third world countries. The population problem is due not only to the sheer number of 140 million people, but also to their very uneven distribution throughout the thousands of islands that constitute the republic. Even now that the National Family Planning Programme has been gaining momentum, the rate of growth of the population is still about 2.3-2.4%. Java is densely populated, with around 530 people per square kilometer. Assuming that the fertility rate can be reduced by 25% in the span of one generation, Java will have to stretch its carrying capacity to well above the limit, for by the year 2000 some 146 million people out of the total population of 250 million will live, or try to exist, on Java, doubling its average population density to about 1,105 people per square kilometer.[1]

With a per capita income below $300, distributed with disparity great enough to leave some 40% of the population at the absolute poverty level, it is easy to see why we have the formidable task of ameliorating the sufferings of the lowest stratum of our society, and of striving to attain some betterment in health and nutrition, employment, and universalization of primary and secondary education.

The promise of science and technology

Our state ideology, *Pancasila* (panca = five, sila = principle), is summarized in five principles, namely Belief in God, Humanity, Nationality, Democracy, and Social Justice. It has proved to be effective in uniting the members of the pluralistic Indonesian society. And that is no mean accomplishment, considering the hundreds of languages and vernaculars, the different religions and political persuasions of the people, the multi-ethnic composition of the population, and the traits and customs which vary throughout the more than 3,000-mile long chain of islands and islets making up the Indonesian archipelago.

Science provides us with options and means to attain these options. It is true that without an appeal to value-judgment it is impossible to pick out which, among the alternatives open to us, is the most desirable. But once the choice is made, then again we must turn to science for the means and the safest route to that choice. Thus, provided we are most careful in deciding which options we must take and how to develop them through research and development, we should be able to minimize the threat of science and technology.

The Indonesian people should not and, I believe, will not, resist the theme: "Science and Technology for a Just, Participatory and Sustainable Society". Subordinating science and technology to the service of mankind in a just, participatory and sustainable society is very much in line with our state ideology. Justice and democracy are among the five principles. On Java and Bali, where about 60% of the population live, there is a very popular, traditional, all-night show, called *wayang* (shadow play). In *wayang*, the *dalang* (shadow-play master) always describes an ideal society. He does this in his

---

[1] S. Djojohadikusumo: "Indonesia in 2000 A.D." *Prisma*, April 1975, p. 17.

janturan (monologue), which is sandwiched in between melodious *suluk* (chanting), before the characters begin their *antawacana* (dialogue) in the particular scene of the play. And the *dalang*'s description of the ideal society conforms exactly with the kind of world society we are all yearning for!

As I have mentioned above, among the five principles in the ideology, there are "democracy" and "social justice". Social justice and international solidarity is a *conditio sine qua non* for a just society. And it is hard to imagine how participatory decision-making could be realized unless some form of democracy is functionally in operation.

But the first of the five principles of *Pancasila* is belief in God. This principle should not be divorced from our science and technology perspective, either. Some may argue whether God is not a concept devoid of real meaning and an unnecessary hypothesis in science. Yet in keeping with the first principle mentioned above, and the goal of a sustainable society, we tend to view man as God's special creation who is bestowed with inherent need to communicate meaningfully with his fellow-beings, with nature (both the animate and the inanimate) and with his Creator.

Prior to the coming of Islam and Christianity, the Indonesian people were monistic in outlook. Our ancestors went through their rituals of sacrifice to appease the deities they believed manifested in the awesome and frightening power of nature. They sought harmony with nature, so that man and nature could peacefully mingle and become one. Nowadays, when western dualism (the clear-cut separation between man and nature in which man as the knowing subject carries out God's mandate to conquer nature as the object to be exploited) seems to have brought us various environmental problems, we should turn back to man-nature harmony, now ecologically interpreted to mean that the role of man as the responsible custodian of nature must be emphasized. The switch to the ecologically harmonious relation between man and nature will not be difficult for our society, since the influence of the ontological and functional aspects of the western culture has never been able to totally wipe the mystic belief out of the conscious or sub-conscious feeling of a large proportion of the Indonesian people.

All this must be borne in mind when we are in the process of coming to a decision as to whether or not to allocate funds for scientific research, and whether we should, or should not, develop a particular technology for practical application in industrialization for development.

Science, ethics and faith

I think only a few citizens of Indonesia would fail to sense the connection between science and technology on the one hand, and ethics and faith on the other.

Ethics gives us advice regarding behaviour. It implies, and sometimes also directly points to, the desired, good ends that will be attained if we heed the advice. But we are now in a modern world in which science is undeniably one of the dominant factors in the development. So science, too, should be regarded as a source of advice. The vast body of knowledge accumulated through centuries of gruelling efforts by the scientists in their scientific undertaking, and some of science's reliable predictions, should be accepted as additional information, in light of which the norms of ethics can be interpreted, and should even be re-examined. Only when scientific and ethical considerations are intertwined will they become more relevant, not only to global problems but also to contextual situations of people in different parts of the world. Only with ethically-responsible attitudes on the part of the scientists and science policy-makers can science hope to serve humanity.

Though science in itself may contain no normative principles dealing with ultimate goals, and religions are based on norms, it is nevertheless hard to say that science must necessarily be a religiously-neutral undertaking. This is because every scientific endeavour starts from basic presuppositions, including some which are metaphysical in nature, and because the faith perspective of the scientist influences his choice of methods and his lines of reasoning.

Every scientific activity which seeks to free itself from the religious issues of how to attempt to be responsive to God tends to enthrone human reason above everything else.

Participation

Since the adjective "participatory" qualifies the society which science and technology is supposed to serve, I would like to say a few words about what participation means to us. To build a participatory and sustainable society, participation both within a nation and between nations is necessary.

Participatory decision-making requires some form of democracy. But democracy can really function only if the education of the general public is sufficiently high, and the people know what their rights are and how they should exercise those rights. The requirement of education is particularly crucial when it comes to participatory decision-making concerning scientific and technological issues. And this is one reason why in Indonesia participatory decision-making has not been really functioning, even though ideologically we accept democracy as a principle.

The general public in Indonesia do not know for sure, for example, whether the government has decided to go nuclear. We have heard about the National Atomic Energy Commission's exploration for uranium ore, but only a few people know whether any success has been achieved. We can only guess that the likely choice will be either a light-water reactor with enriched uranium as fuel or the natural uranium-fuelled CANDU type reactor. In either case, the general public do not know what the considerations are. And neither do they know the considerations behind the choice of the site for the first power reactor which, according to some newspapers, will be somewhere in the north-eastern part of Central Java. Only a few people in Indonesia have the layman's knowledge about what a thermal reactor is, and how it differs from a fast breeder reactor, and how they compare in relative risk. Thus it is virtually impossible for us at the present time to have a participatory decision.

The above case can be easily extended to science and technology in general. If there is any hope for remedying this situation, it is only by raising the general educational level and by serious effort in presenting scientific and technological information in a popular way. And this calls for a close cooperation between the scientists and the press.

As for the participation among nations in the world, let me consider two cases only: the energy crisis and the transfer of technology.

Especially with regard to energy resources and certain basic minerals, we are entering the stage of relative materials imbalance,[2] as demand for scarce commodities meets the dwindling supply. The poor countries have been hardest hit by this situation.

So for the developing countries like Indonesia, there is no alternative but to strive for economic growth. If the depletion of fossil fuel resources should force the world to opt for the zero-growth scenario, then the rich, energy over-consumptive countries would have to compensate for the accelerating energy intake in the poor countries by learning to live with a negative rate of growth in their energy consumption. Participation and world solidarity also mean that even those poor countries which have no natural resources must be treated as full-fledged partners by the rich, technologically-advanced countries in the international decision-making process concerning the world's resources. There must be a genuine interest on the part of the developed countries to help the developing countries raise their science and technology capacity.

Until all this can be realized, there will be no real participation in the world community's quest for a just and sustainable global system. What is bound to emerge is mounting tensions and restiveness in regions where the people have long been plagued with poverty. And the world as a global system will most surely be affected by such injustices.

Science and technology fill us with a hope for a brighter future, but at the same time also frighten us with perils. It is up to us all whether we make a concerted effort to check the ever-enlarging spiral of mutual interaction between science, technology and society's greed that degrades the quality of life and threatens to damage our environment beyond recovery. If we fail to create effective channels for participatory cooperation, the vision of the just and sustainable society will be but a utopian dream, and the threat of science and technology will loom more menacingly.

---

[2] S. Djojohadikusumo: "Energy and Raw Materials, Present and Future." *First World Symposium on Energy and Raw Materials*, Paris, June 1974, p. 6.

An African Perspective

THOMAS R. ODHIAMBO

The African continent is undergoing an agonised anguish that only a few eminent African thinkers have been able to portray accurately and empathetically to their countrymen and to the world. Dr Amadou-Mahtar M'bow, Director-General of UNESCO and a distinguished scholar of Africa, said in June 1979:

> "What were the factors that enabled the modern West to subject the rest of the world to its laws? What specific historical process brought this about and how can one explain the survival of a system of cultural and economic domination which has outlived the colonial era and continues as a form of indirect dependence?
>
> "I would answer in this way. The industrial world has profoundly influenced the advance of Africa primarily because the Africans themselves have not succeeded in countering this pattern of development with an alternative model of progress rooted in their own traditions."

And in a similar vein, Chinweizu of Nigeria, in his book, *The West and the Rest of Us*, laments:

> "We need... to understand our past defeats if we want to avoid the deadly shocks our future seems to be holding in ambush for us. And to do so, it is imperative that we revise our understanding of the history of which we are products.
>
> "This book should, therefore, be seen as a long letter to... those who fancy themselves to be the African elite, pleading for a moment to listen closely and analyse the tunes being played to us by the Pied Pipers of progress from the West..."[1]

This, then, is the great dilemma of the new leadership of Africa: how to initiate and sustain development while at the same time keeping the socio-cultural fabric of the African peoples—or how to add an industrial dimension to our lives while keeping intact the essence of the African ethos.

Need for a modern technological revolution in Africa

The clamour for economic growth and social development in the Third World can be gauged from the concern of the Group of 77 for a New International Economic Order. Although they may not get substance to the dream they have dared verbalize, it is now impossible for the developed countries to blink away this dream. Apart from the many proposals put forward to share more equitably in the exploitation of natural resources, the global marketing

---

[1] New York: Vintage Books, 1975.

system, and the pricing dynamics, the Third World has come to realize more fully that the way to industrial progress is through science and technology. After the Second World War, the new nations then emerging from colonial circumstances were advised that the surest way to rapid socio-economic development was by applying the existing scientific knowledge to the problems of underdevelopment. Indeed, at that time, in the fifties and sixties, it seemed that the cry of President Julius Nyerere for the "abolition of ignorance, hunger, and disease" could be answered quickly by the application of science, which was portraying a dazzling spectacle to the world public: the race of the moon, the wonders of antibiotic drugs, and the initial push of the Green Revolution.

The assumption in the proposition was that the way to rapid socio-economic development in Africa was through the application of existing scientific knowledge to the region's practical problems, and that the technologies designed for the Developed Countries (DCs) were necessarily applicable to the Less Developed Countries (LDCs). With the benefit of hindsight, we can now state unequivocally that this is not so. In the first place, northern technology has been developed under a different cultural setting and a vastly different environment. Secondly, the Third World has become much more aware that their own particular problems may be quite new to science and that there is therefore no existing store of technological solutions. And thirdly, some LDCs have developed traditional systems of production and management that can hardly be improved technically by our present scientific experience.

An example may be given to illustrate this latter point more clearly. In large parts of Africa, shifting cultivation has been practised as a viable method of assuring yields of crops while sustaining the fertility of the rather fragile tropical soils. The Wakara, living on the small island of Ukara in Lake Victoria, had no chance to do this.[2] The island, which is about 29 square miles in size, has a highly dense population of 572 people per square mile; but in fact only 13.5 square miles of the island are arable land. Consequently, an acre of arable land supports about two people. In the face of this acute problem, the Wakara have adopted an indigenous farming system which is unique, technically highly productive, and agronomically difficult to improve upon. The system involves almost continuous cropping, which at the same time ensures the maintenance of soil fertility.

The Wakara apply heavily farmyard manure or green manure to the land every year. Cattle husbandry is therefore an essential part of their farming system: each family keeps about three stock units, which are housed in part of the family dwelling where they are fed by hand. The cattle are taken out to graze and for watering for only short periods. This number of stock units

---

[2] E.S. Clayton: *Agrarian Development in Peasant Economies*. Oxford: Pergamon Press, 1964.

enables the Wakara to apply about four tons of farmyard manure to each acre of land. In addition, a leguminous crop is grown specifically to be dug in at maturity as a green manure, and produces about nine tons of green manure per acre.

The Wakara have also devised a three-shift rotation system. In the first shift, bullrush millet is sown soon after farmyard manure has been applied to the land. After the millet has germinated, a slow-growing leguminous crop for making green manure is interplanted with the millet, which allows the latter to be harvested long before the leguminosa is dug in as green manure several months later. The leguminosa is dug in at the beginning of the second year, thus allowing the second shift of crops (millet, interplanted with groundnuts) to be sown. In the third year, millet is again sown, after farmyard manure has once again been applied, and this is later interplanted with sorghum and often also with cassava. The whole farming system is characterized by a most economical use of scarce resources and closely planned management of the land.

The Wakara farming system provides an extremely apposite instance of an indigenous technology that we should retain and further develop to meet Africa's specific needs. And there are others—in psychiatry, in traditional medicine, in pottery and other forms of artisanship—that we should equally strive to maintain and modernize.

Indeed, part of the strategy for a new technological revolution in Africa is for the scientific and technological communities to rationalize, modernize, and put on stream the continent's indigenous technologies for wider and more sustained production. This is a crucially important step, since the African has been told so many times that he has no indigenous science or technology that he has almost come to believe it. This near-belief in itself has been a major stumbling block in nurturing a scientific and technological culture in Africa.

Of all the power resources underlying international economic relations—finance, the control of markets, access to cheap manpower and to non-renewable resources—the control of technology is the cornerstone of the present-day industrial civilization.[3] Such control is able ultimately to replace all other power resources; and this technological superiority has given the North the power to dominate the rest of the world in material terms. When, therefore, the North offers to assist the South through a system of transfer of technology, one wonders if this offer is really genuine.

The mythology of technology transfer

Ever since UNCTAD III, the existing international system of transfer of technology has been high on the agenda of international conferences trying

---

[3] C. Furtado: "Power Resources: the Five Controls". *IFDA*. 7, 1979.

to establish a new international economic order. So far, we have made little impact on the original problem: to order technological matters so that the LDCs are involved in the design and acquisition of technological know-how and technological know-why; to renegotiate the patenting system so that it is of limited duration for particular innovations; and to get away from the notion that the transfer of technology implies simply the creation of local assembly or manufacturing facilities in the LDCs. As it is, the annual bill of the LDCs for technologies imported from the North is already of the order of US$3-5 billion.

At the heart of the matter is the operation of the transnational corporations (TNCs), which possess a vast inventory of technological and managerial expertise, obtained through a great deal of concentrated research, development, and design. The goals of TNCs are profits, growth and expansion of activities. Their vital assets are, then, technologies. Consequently, the TNCs are extremely sensitive about their inventories of technologies—they have an intense motivation to exploit them adequately and to be paid for them adequately. The limits to altruism are pretty clear.

TNCs tend to be conservative: while they must innovate to stay competitive, the innovative strategy is one of an incremental type rather than planning for a major breakthrough. Many of the problems of the LDCs, on the other hand, require revolutionary ideas from science and technology. For instance, there is an accumulating body of agronomic knowledge in the tropics which sustains the conviction that mixed cropping gives higher crop yields on a sustained basis than monocrop cultivation. If this farming method is systematized in the coming years, it will give Africa a basis for an agrarian revolution as well as a scientific means for conserving productive soil in the tropics. A major technological hurdle for Africa, however, will come from two sources: firstly, there is need to design and develop agricultural machinery that can work primarily under a mixed-cropping system; and, secondly, there is need to devise machinery which the individual peasant farmer can afford (in terms of capital outlay and energy requirements) and which can be adequately serviced by the village artisan. The research, development, and design of machinery for such specific purposes require a totally new approach to the methods involved in the manufacture of current agricultural implements by a variety of TNCs, whose reference has been rightly the temperate, monocrop farming system of the North. It is unlikely that the TNCs will want to invest their expertise in such a long-range objective.

It is now apparent that the concept of transfer of technology, although attractive in theoretical terms, has no chance of becoming a major avenue for the development of LDCs. In operational terms, the concept has become an apparition. The time being invested in devising new patent and licencing understandings, in planning a new code of conduct for the TNCs, and in suggesting formulae for taxing TNCs on their technological operations in the LDCs, should be recognized as merely a cosmetic operation for a much deeper problem which needs an original approach for its solution. TNCs are not humanitarian organizations; they are not technical assistance programmes; and they are not consulting bodies to the LDCs. They are organizations to produce and to market the products and services they are skilled at, and to do it for a profit over as long a period as possible.

The real question is not the transfer of technology—a mirage—on which we have already spent too much time and vast effort. The decisive issue, which is only now beginning to emerge as the core problem of development for the South, is how to overcome technological dependence of the LDCs. Put differently, how can the national scientific and technological capabilities in the LDCs be promoted?

Science and the capacity to develop

The creation of technological independence should not be translated to mean self-sufficiency. It implies the capability to assume decision-making in technological matters. But in the circumstances of Africa it also implies a strong sense of direction towards social and economic goals. Thus, the building of a scientific and technological capacity is imperative in the coming decade for four critical purposes:

1) to create a knowledge-discovering capacity, particularly for the tropical environment of Africa;
2) to develop the ability to identify priority problems of national development requiring scientific and technological solution;
3) to promote indigenous ability to choose between alternative technological pathways to the solution of these problems;
4) to create the national expertise to implement the relevant solutions, whether the technologies are indigenous or modified from foreign technologies already in the market.

Such a strategy for the long-range and self-reliant development of Africa needs a new measure of political will, including the recognition that the continent's central tactic is to develop its human resources in science and technology. For the most basic component of institutional building is not merely the physical and fiscal resources, but the availability of trained, motivated, and targeted people of talent.

In recent years, Africa and other developing regions of the world have been preoccupied with the development of a national science policy. Such a policy will not by itself solve the horrendous development problems of the South, but it is an important step in the right direction, since national science policy has to do with the policy for the allocation of scientific resources—with financial resources, research and development activities—and the scientific and technological manpower to shoulder the scientific effort.

Motivation and talent for scientific research and technological innovation are vital prerequisites for science-based development. It has been known for some time now that most of the significant research discoveries and scientific advances are made by a small minority of scientific workers.[4] And it is also well known that the average social returns from research and development are much higher than the returns from investments in physical plant and facilities. It is therefore a matter of political will, science policy, and national economic planning to invest more in research and development. Consequently, the single most vital decision that Africa must take is to establish and strengthen the domestic abilities in science and technology.

If the world community can assist Africa in achieving this crucial goal in the next two decades, it will have shown a degree of international cooperation that Africa has rarely witnessed in the past. This viewpoint was dramatically stated by the Symposium on the "Future Development Prospects of Africa Towards the Year 2000", jointly sponsored by the Organization of African Unity and the United Nations Economic Commission for Africa, in Monrovia, Liberia, 12-16 February 1979. The symposium, bringing together forty experts, reached a full consensus in these words: "So long as it has no audacious and vigorous autonomous research policy geared to the most pressing needs and problems of Africa, the continent will continue to be at the mercy of the kind of dependence that is inseparable from 'transfer of technology' policies."

Africa is conscious of the fact that the present industrial civilization of the North has brought with it many serious social problems: environmental pollution, the threat of human annihilation, the satisfaction of material well-being without a corresponding development of the human mind and human responsibility, and the inequitable satisfaction of basic human and biological needs. The new, balanced approach must be human-oriented, African, science-based development—with the prime objective of creating a material, cultural and spiritual environment conducive to creative participation and self-fulfilment. What we are talking about is a new ethical dimension to development strategy.

The ethical dimension to development

It is the practical results of science that are in the forefront of the current global debate on science and technology for development. The metaphysical bases of science are not receiving any public attention. And there is no critical reason why they should, except for two important factors. Firstly, it should be more widely appreciated that the world-view of science is limited: the validation of its findings relies on reproduceability under defined and appropriate circumstances. Precisely because of this limited view of the physical and biological world, science has been able to promote and underpin technology; and precisely because of this concentration and problem-orientation, science has always insisted on its "value-free objectivity". The

[4] J. R. Cole & S. Cole: "The Ortega hypothesis". *Science*, 1972, 178:368-374.

second factor is the world-view of the African: his view of nature is one of a continuum between the physical, biological and spiritual world, and of a holistic understanding of nature. This approach is an antithesis to the reductionist view of western science, which approaches the question of understanding nature by utilizing analytical tools and problem-solving.

The answer is not to eschew the potential for practical achievements by science. Indeed, many scientists have made too much effort to dissociate themselves from the practical results of science in their attempt to establish their status as humble seekers after objective truth. The answer, or at least an important part of the overall answer, is to take full cognizance of the power and vitality of science and technology, and to think critically about the social goals and cultural context for which they should be used.

Contrary to the belief that the advances that might stem from indigenous research and development could prove traumatic to the African people, the African social and cultural fabric has the strength to absorb these potential changes when they come. The noted African research psychiatrist Lambo has said:

> "One of the most striking features of the traditional cultures of Africa is their flexibility, adaptability and other built-in factors for maintaining a high degree of socio-cultural homeostasis in the face of many major and rapid changes. Most of these cultures seem to have a high threshold of tolerance for rate and impact of change and, measured by the rate of integration of western ways of life and values, these cultures would seem to be highly responsive to new opportunities, new demands and new experiences... The same characteristic is manifestly displayed in the basic psychological structure of the African peoples. The overpowering vitality of these cultures is reflected by the African emphasis on life and not only life *here and now* but life transcendental—the basis of ancestor worship.
>
> "This phenomenon has proved to be the determining factor for maintaining an overall good mental health within the population in spite of the continual social disruption and instability of the social institutions which are constantly under stress. This is clearly shown in the way individuals have absorbed new secular types of religions and the cultures have evolved others which are manifestly syncretic in their structure, and in the minimal psychological impact of a disruptive kind which the introduction of western educational system has had. The remarkable ability of certain Africans to assume and mimic western values and behaviour with precision in their day-to-day lives and the readiness with which these values can be shed under stress shows this attribute of the cultures clearly."[5]

---

[5] T. A. Lambo: Social and Psychological Change: Human Needs in Developing Countries of Africa. In A. Tiselius & S. Nilsson, eds. *The Place of Value in a World of Facts*. Stockholm: Almqvist & Wiksell, 1970.

The science-based development in Africa should therefore take on a new character: Africa must play a central role in the technological solutions of its own tropical problems, and it must build into the development process a social, cultural and ethical dimension. Africa faces an agonising challenge: to encourage the scientific enquiry that will solve its long-term problems of underemployment and unemployment, of meeting the basic human biological needs of the great majority (80%) of its population, of raising its annual per capita income from $365 (the lowest in the world), and of technological development directed by a higher social ethos.

Underdevelopment is not a natural state. In Africa it is largely a legacy of the past world economic system. But the continent cannot go on lamenting past misdeeds or world neglect: it has to start shaping its own destiny.

A Latin American Perspective

CARLOS CHAGAS

In 1963 I was the Secretary General of the UN Conference for the Application of Science and Technology for Development, held in Geneva. The idea behind the conference, which had stemmed from Dag Hammarsjöld and then was put to work by U Thant, was relatively naïve: it was considered that the application of science and technology could really close the gap between rich and poor countries. As we know 16 years later, nothing happened.

The conference was opportune because it came at the beginning of the era of decolonization. It was in the spirit of introducing new tools for social progress that many of the developing countries came to Geneva. However, we must consider the meeting a failure, because it became a sort of science fair where technology was displayed and sold, either for money or for political influence. Only a very small group of people really thought that development is a systemic and structural problem and that a holistic approach has to be made to all developmental activities.

From this conference came the fallacious concept of appropriate technology, which we are now unable to explain. Let me tell you of a personal experience of appropriate technology. I am in my second pace-maker. The first pace-maker was "built", as they say, in Brazil. When it failed two years afterwards, I came to a very important country where we had the pace-maker examined. We telephoned the company which manufactured it, and were told production had been discontinued ten years before. They had sold all parts to Brazil so that that country could become autonomous in producing pace-makers. This is the sort of transfer of technology that is happening, and I think this personal experience of mine is a very illustrative one.

A case study

I would like now to offer a case study of the application of science to a developing country, and naturally, because of my own experience, I will take the example of Brazil. During the whole of our colonial period we were not allowed any scientific or technological development—not even a printing press—by the Portuguese regime. A group of natural scientists could not even visit Brazil. In other parts of Latin America some universities were transplanted from Spain, but they practised the same rhetorical type of teaching as the Spanish universities at that time and, in my opinion, they did not contribute to the development of the people of the Spanish American countries.

During the nineteenth century, a very interesting personality reigned over Brazil, our second Emperor, who tried as much as possible to foster science. (Although I speak well of our Emperor, I must add that I am a member of a family who overthrew the monarchy, so I am not defending the regime at all. I am simply speaking of the man.) We have in Brazil a good example of a society facing a challenge at the end of the nineteenth century: the challenge was yellow fever, which used to kill about 10,000-15,000 people per year in Rio de Janeiro, a city with about 100,000 inhabitants at that time.

It was a Cuban scientist, Carlos Finley, who proved that a species of mosquito was responsible for yellow fever. A young man named Oswaldo Caruse took charge of eradicating yellow fever from our cities. He established the first institute for medical and veterinary research and contributed a great deal to the advancement of biomedicine in our country.

Probably the development of medical sciences in Brazil was premature in the sense that we had no scientific approach to agriculture, transportation, or housing. Health was the great challenge society was facing. Up to the thirties, we had one of the best institutes in the world in what we call now biomedical sciences.

Industrialization

Then came very sombre years, between 1930 and 1952, when there was complete neglect of science and technology. Yet in 1921, the first steps in industrialization were taken by the rich people in Sao Paulo with legislative measures to protect their interests, measures which were, in my opinion, extremely damaging to the process of industrialization.

In the period 1952-1964 science blossomed in Brazil, but mostly basic science, due first of all to the establishment of the National Research Council, and secondly to the help of the Rockefeller Foundation, and (in the latter part of this period) to the external programme of the National Institutes of Health.

Then in 1964 with the installation of the military government, the economists took over science policy and established what I would call a great many "desk priorities". They set up new programmes without any regard for the need for a critical scientific mass, without which you cannot develop any scientific or technological programme. Nobody can be against priorities. But "desk priorities", where scientific policy is ruled by economists or planners, contain the great danger that, as soon as the plan is made, the planners consider its objective already achieved.

Now I come to a more important and difficult problem: the discussion of the role the Latin American society (here I am considering the whole continent or the whole region, as we now say) has played in trying to develop science and technology. In contrast with the North American pilgrims, the Iberian Americans who came to the Spanish-speaking countries brought with them what one may call the attitude of the temporary colonizer: their aim was to make money as fast as possible, exploit the natural mineral resources as fast as possible, then return to the Iberian peninsula. This hampered our scientific and technological development considerably. It gave rise to the conception that it is much easier to buy know-how or to associate with firms to establish false Ibero-American industries than to establish an indigenous development of science and technology.

I must say that in some ways the multinational corporations have been effective in transferring what we can call the technical skills, but no multinational has ever transferred the know-how. A good example is the fact that there is only one multinational interested in the very important work done in Rio, Sao Paulo and Brasilia by a group of chemists of Brazilian origin (though trained abroad), who are developing the chemistry of natural products in our country and who can make a major contribution to our development.

Another problem arises from the fact that we are developing the industry of alcohol as an energy source. Already almost all the cars in Brazil are running on 10%-15% alcohol, and many cars have been adapted to run on 100% alcohol. Yet here again we are in danger of falling into the hands of a foreign monopoly, because it is probable that in a few months or a year or two alcohol will be produced much cheaper by DNA recombination. I am afraid that our country is still not equipped to do this kind of work.

The role of the Church

My next point is the important role that the Church has played in Brazil in changing the concept of development. I would say that, until very recently, the Catholic Church was a supporter of the high income classes, the government and the bourgeoisie.

Also until recently, the best science secondary teaching was done by religious priests, mostly Jesuits; the secular priests were obscurantists. Once one of my very dear friends, a Monsignor, came to visit me in my office and saw the portrait of Einstein. He said: "How can you have the picture of this demon in your office, being the Roman Catholic you are?" And this is a typical comment. Naturally, the secular priests feared the Reformed Church, because it was doing the social work they were not doing themselves.

Then the great change came after Vatican II with Pope John XXIII. We saw a Church which had been attached to the rich gradually drifting towards the poor and creating new aspirations and a new interpretation of what the Church and faith really mean.

You may have heard criticism of Marxist priests in Brazil. It is clear that Marxism is uncomfortable with the Catholic faith, or any type of faith and religious feeling. But one has to understand the position of those priests. They are in contact with poverty, with the great mass of the people. Brazil is a country of contrasts: we have rich people and very, very poor people. The great disease of our country is malnutrition—not malaria, not tuberculosis, not leprosy, but malnutrition. Now those priests, on account of their insufficient preparation, naturally have a tendency to use the Marxist argumentation in trying to solve the problems of society. I think you can analyse social problems in many other ways, but one has to remember that these priests are in contact with the suffering poor. Secondly, they firmly believe that faith is allied to a certain way in which people live, the praxis; I think this is quite clear also in St Thomas.

The Church has transferred the emphasis from the concept of economic development—which in our country has brought more riches to the rich and has increased the gap between the rich and the poor—to one of social development, where the human being and human values are much more important. I think this has spread all over the country.

Towards the solution

Now in closing, I would like to present what I try to call the solution. For the scientist, no doubt, quality is essential. If we do not have good science, we cannot do anything. But we cannot accept a science which bears no relation to the national problem—any kind of national problem. And even if there is a unity of sciences, which go from basic science to its application, even if a man is doing basic research which does not seem to be applicable to any specific problem, he must still be engaged in the national problem. He cannot stand aside from it.

Regarding science policy, the important thing is not to neglect the national challenges: education, health, housing, nutrition, agriculture, industrialization and so forth. I am firmly convinced that we should abandon the myth of some techniques in many fields and come back to more traditional attitudes. We should not be slaves of the fetishes of advanced technology, behind which are greed and political ambition.

The cost of a science programme in Latin America should not be a burden on our national budgets if we take into consideration what is spent on weaponry and the military establishment. Without a science programme our countries cannot achieve self-reliance and enter into a world of interconnection. In spite of some sorrowful examples nowadays, I think the world is inexorably driving towards this interconnection. To face this, we have to develop a scientific and technological base.

Reactions and Comment

The immediate response to the addresses of Wilardjo, Odhiambo and Chagas was vigorous and appreciative. The discussion on the floor produced a suggestion for an international award, comparable to the Nobel prizes, for science directed towards human need. The suggestion evoked considerable approval, along with the warning that there is presently no peer group in a good situation to choose the achievements that would deserve the award.

Continuing response to the addresses came in most of the sections. The same themes got further attention in later plenary sessions on economics (see Chapter 12) and on participation and power (see Part Four).

Many of the third world participants felt that the conference, even though it usually assented to their statements, did not really take them seriously in the work of the sections. This discontent led to a later protest and special plenary session (see Chapter 19).

10. Perspectives in Industrialized, Market-Economy Societies

Introduction

To move from the developing societies to the industrialized societies is a huge shift of perspective. Yet if perspectives make different observations possible, some realities are visible from many perspectives. The world described in this chapter is recognizably the world described in Chapter 9. There are difference of nuance and accent, but there are rather few direct clashes. Certainly there is little triumphalism among the speakers from the industrialized, market-economy societies. The problems they describe are as great as—and sometimes are the same as—the problems described by the speakers from the Third World.

The three speakers were: John Francis, a nuclear physicist and public official in the United Kingdom; Yoshinobu Kakiuchi, professor of physics and sociology of science, the International Christian University in Tokyo; and Theodor Leuenberger, professor of contemporary social and economic history, University of St Gallen, Switzerland.

Looking at the issues of a just, participatory and sustainable society, the speakers emphasized two main problems. The first was the relation between technology and politics. All three speakers pointed to the importance and the difficulty of achieving some measure of political direction of technological processes—thus hitting the themes of justice and participation. The second problem, emphasized by Francis and Kakiuchi, was the unsustainability of industrial economies built on lavish consumption of dwindling resources.

Francis, in extemporaneous remarks introducing his paper, described his personal experience in moving from scientific research into government. "The world of pure science", he said, "is a land of lotus eaters by comparison with the world of public policy." He went on to advocate political decentralization through a disengagement from "dependence on central institutions" and a "radical commitment to community self-help and resource management". The process, as he described it, would require fundamental ethical and economic transformation, as well as reliance on technologies designed to be humanly manageable and not wasteful of scarce resources.

Kakiuchi spoke from the context of the Japanese society, which has experienced a swift and tremendous achievement of economic growth in recent decades. In so doing, it has become highly dependent on imports of raw materials and energy sources, and more than most societies it faces the issue of the "ultimate shortage of available resources". He also expressed concern about the breakdown of communication between scientists and the general public, a problem that makes difficulties for meaningful public participation in major social decisions.

Leuenberger spoke of a "shrinkage of political capacity" in a world where "technical-economic processes" prove stronger than the "guidance capabilities of our political systems". He saw a difference between technological rationality (the domain of the expert) and the political process (which deals with competing values and interests). He called for a combination of political modesty (the "end of the planning euphoria") and boldness in looking for alternative scenarios for the future. Agreeing with earlier speakers from the Third World, he emphasized the power of transnational corporations and the importance for all societies of developing technological capacities.

The Transition to a Just, Participatory and Sustainable Society

JOHN M. FRANCIS

To embark on the transition to a more just, a more participatory and a more sustainable society is a task that will tax all our expertise in the natural and social sciences, and most other disciplines besides. One of the most crucial challenges before this conference is to forge a meeting place and to provide a working agenda with which to confront the world of practical politics—before it is too late and the opportunity slips from our grasp.

In most industrialized societies the increasing problems of structural unemployment and inevitable resource constraints bear down upon us. This means that in key areas of public policy pressure will be applied to our scientists and engineers to deliver us from the impending storm. But what kind of science and technology do we hope for during the remainder of this century? The answer could be "more of the same". We shall have to provide a better synthesis of ideas and inventions if we are not to add to the growing public disenchantment with the scientific endeavour. If we can show some large measure of humility and acknowledge that present patterns of production and consumption are neither just, participatory nor sustainable, then we shall have made an important beginning.

The freedom to choose

If those who control the investment in new science and technology are to be moved by this appeal for an alternative synthesis, then we shall have to be very persuasive indeed. Some years ago, when I was seated next to the biologist René Dubos at a dinner in London, we had a long and argumentative exchange of views. At the time I was quite unprepared for the thrust of his main argument. ''We can do it, we can afford to do it, but we should not do it.'' His remarks were set in the context of likely damage to the ozone layer in the upper atmosphere that would be brought about by a high volume of supersonic air transport on the North Atlantic routes. Needless to say, Prof. Dubos is strongly opposed to all forms of supersonic transport.

I want to take a closer look at his statement and see whether it has any general validity for the industrialized countries today.

''We can do it''

What are the implications of this claim? The posturing is instantly recognizable: bring us your problems and we can tell you exactly what you can do —we have the technology. What a preposterous and arrogant suggestion! Do you wish to be reminded of the risks and the uncertainties that daily confound us in so many fields: nuclear energy, air transport, building design, pharmaceutical products, to name but a few? The list is seemingly endless and goes to the very core of a technological society. Can we seriously pretend that we have satisfactory, enduring and socially acceptable solutions in any of these fields?

Far from feeling complacent about the present levels of scientific achievement, we should be increasingly chastened by the volume of human catastrophe that technological failure of one kind or another almost inevitably brings in its wake. Instead of romanticizing our short-run successes, we should be prepared to acknowledge soberly that we have *not* got the technology.

At the same time, I do not consider that the situation is irretrievable. If we have allowed ourselves to become enticed by the apparent economies of scale, of through-put and of mass distribution, then we shall have to learn to recant these principles and begin to value other factors more highly. If the economic base of our societies is not to be vastly expanded, in design terms it should still be possible to guarantee most people the energy they need for essential purposes, enabling them still to travel economically and keeping them secure in home and health. The political problem that emerges is whether we shall be prepared to settle for less than we have already. The working proposition might be set down as follows:

> If we choose we can still go part of the way down existing routes to the future. We cannot back off and walk away from our problems. The choice of the "appropriate" technologies is going to be both difficult and contentious. We cannot avoid the process of choosing and therefore we shall need to set up criteria by which effective choices can be made.

"Can we afford to do it?"

Industrialized countries in Europe and North America have enjoyed some remarkable bursts of material prosperity since the Industrial Revolution. But we can hardly pretend that we have earned our wealth with much thought for the morrow. Despite the economic expansion, deep pockets of poverty and multiple deprivation remain within our inner cities and within our proud new centres of industrial growth.

What is most worrying is that much of the wealth emanating from the increasing productivity of our manufacturing industries is dissipated in short-run, whimsical and frequently trivial demands from a rising generation of new consumers who have never had to grapple with austerity in the true sense of the word. Can we reach a consensus on what it is we should be doing at this particular crossroads in our history?

Governments continue to appeal for industrial regeneration and capitalization of the new growth industries (in micro-electronics and the like), by fostering the illusion of rising expectations. In many industrialized countries investment swings away from the traditional systems of heavy engineering—of coal and steam, of iron and steel—towards the "cleaner" production environment of the electronic computer and the micro-processor. Economists assert that the sustained introduction of the micro-processor will result in the loss of millions of jobs in the primary and secondary sectors. In a recent book a leading trade unionist has put it this way: If we fail to invest in the new technology, we shall end up with a weak economy and massive unemployment; if we choose to embark on the new technology, we shall end up with a strong economy and massive unemployment.

The underlying theory is that we must accept the social costs of this further revolution in production techniques in order to survive in an increasingly competitive world still dominated by the economic thinking of Adam Smith and John Maynard Keynes. It does not follow that we shall be able to afford the costs of re-educating and redeploying our unskilled and semi-skilled manpower. The prospective waste of human resources is highly intimidating, and no country has even suggested the semblance of a suitable working solution.

Burdened as we may be with a staggering increase in unemployment, it is possible that we could turn to good use a key evolutionary principle: diversity is strength. We might even find the collective courage to say: "We cannot afford to do it this way", and begin to distance ourselves from the gravitational pull of centralized planning and the emerging view that people are a redundant feature of the working landscape. While it is good that comparatively few people will continue to be exposed to the constant production hazards of noise, chemical pollution, dust and occupational disease, it will not be easy to create equivalent levels of useful employment under existing structures. Patterns of work-sharing, shorter working hours and earlier retirement will soon begin to herald the shape of things to come in most industrial countries. As more and more people become ideologically separated from the notion of work as something directly linked to the production of material goods, we may discover both a new sense of direction and a more mature assessment of the "needs" of an industrial society. The very nature of the production process as translated in the equation "production equals consumption" will come under close scrutiny.

You will recall that one of our few visionary economists, E. F. Schumacher, long contended that we had not solved the problem of production. He was correct but so easily disregarded because he went for the jugular vein at the very heart of all market economies. If we were to begin to determine patterns of production now in terms of "needs" rather than "wants", we should quickly find ourselves living in a materially different kind of world. The dominant ethic which is so closely related to the acquisition of things is surely only a projection of our own deep sense of insecurity. We clutch at the "having" mode because it insulates us from the discomfort and the hurt that is so much a part of our way of life.

However, should we find the necessary inspiration and disengage from this near total dependence on the fruits of production, we might be encouraged to find that human ingenuity knows no bounds. The management of the immensely complex social fabric of our towns and cities would be a challenging assignment at the best of times, and there is certainly no prospect that they could be quickly brought to a sustainable condition at considerably lower levels of consumption. That is quite simply because we have persuaded ourselves that the regeneration of our cities is totally dependent on the heavy overlay of resources brought in from the outside. Consequently, the dignity and self-respect of whole communities has become depreciated over the years, and large injections of urban aid have apparently had little effect. Yes, it is true that a certain level of resources is required to do the pump-priming and to provide a stimulus, but the real task that lies ahead is to restore the confidence of communities in the inner city and to allow them to become self-determining. I suggest that we must seek progressive disengagement from the current dependence on central institutions, together with a radical commitment to community self-help and resource management of food, energy, shelter and transport.

Within industrialized societies we have created a dynamic of dependency on our central institutions, particularly on government. By means of taxation we have institutionalized systems of housing, transport, medical care, social work and, latterly, even the processes of urban renewal and community development. In one sense each of these programmes can be regarded as an essential building block on which to found a "caring" community with a proper assessment of needs determining the order of priorities. However, the stark reality is that, despite the apparently increasing scale of this investment, many of our towns and cities are now almost literally falling apart. The paradox is that whilst the social technologies of housing, energy supply and transport are seen to be inadequate and not sustainable, the community spirit in such areas is still remarkably vibrant and full of hope. Unless we can define socially acceptable technologies to replace existing services which are already in an advanced state of decay, then—before long—the communities themselves will disappear, their hope dissipated. Surely it is possible that we could choose to focus a significant fraction of our accumulated technical wisdom and ingenuity on such problems. We can afford to do it this way—and no other. It is high time that the needs of people living in community took precedence over increasing the means of production.

"But we should not do it"—at least, not the way we have done it in the past

We now come to the point when I am obliged to put forward some criteria against which to measure the choices of the coming decades. I have no time for the neo-Luddite philosophy which characterizes so many of the mass protest movements today. That is because I was rigorously trained as a physical scientist and I regard it as my business to solve difficult and sometimes intractable problems. We need to be more constructive than to go along with the anti-technology fashion of consigning our hard-won skills in science and engineering to the rubbish heap. But the scientific community has no reason to feel complacent about its achievements to date. A great deal remains to be done, not least to convince the public that the continuing commitment to science and technology has a serious social purpose and is not the idle pursuit of knowledge for its own sake. There is a case to answer. The future direction of science and technology, therefore, could be judged by the following criteria:

1. We should not continue to subvert the cause of natural justice by assuming that the accumulation of risks must simply be accepted by the public as a necessary evil.
2. We should not promote the development of ever more centralized technology unless we are persuaded that there is no reasonable alternative.
3. We should not invest in systems of production which serve only to trivialize demand and stimulate consumption.
4. We should not continue to treat the natural environment with disregard for the long-term consequences of our actions.
5. We should not construct our towns and cities as if the everyday concerns of people living in community are matters of secondary importance.
6. We should not plan and build our roads and transport networks as if liquid petroleum fuels were an inexhaustible resource.
7. We should not propagate the idea that the production and distribution of material goods are the central feature of our economic system.
8. We should not forget the lessons of history and flounder into the future as if we had no methods of policy analysis or of social organization with which to combat uncertainty.

The kind of eight-fold path that I have just outlined is only the first crude stage in the process of selecting appropriate technologies for industrialized countries if they are to embark on the path to sustainability.

Despite the current preoccupation within these countries to hold on to at least their current economic standing, the writing is already on the wall. We could easily become immersed in the minutiae of managing our own discomfort, while forgetting that the world today is a very much smaller place than it was twenty or thirty years ago. The mirage of western affluence has introduced a grave distortion into the economies of many developing countries, and unfortunately there are all too many countries ready and willing to repeat our mistakes.

For the most part the debate within the UN and related bodies over development and the all-important transfer of science and technology has not reflected the changing climate of assessment within the industrialized countries. Development has become the greasy pole of international politics, while the recent western preoccupation with resource constraints has been part of the everyday reality of the developing countries for as long as many of us can remember. However, the prospects of economic recession and rising unemployment are not easily accommodated wherever they are encountered. It may prove to be much more difficult for people accustomed to a higher material standard of living to come to terms with this new circumstance. I am not confident that people in the industrialized world are psychologically prepared for the economic trauma that is to come. Paradoxically there may be a certain amount of truth in the old saying: "What you've never had, you'll never miss."

Even the churches seem bemused by what lies ahead. That is the most puzzling fact of all. I am not entirely persuaded that we need to thrash around for theological statements that can be shown to be compatible with the just and sustainable society. It would be far more appropriate for the churches to try and keep their collective nerve so that they can continue to offer guidance and sustenance to those feeling totally betrayed by the uncertainty of the future. A supportive and caring Church at the centre of the community will respond to that need. It will also encourage a more enlightened view of the human predicament and reinforce the need for a transition to a just and sustainable society.

There are no utopias, scientific or otherwise. We need to reconcile ourselves to the difficulties of living in an increasingly imperfect world. We know almost instinctively that there could never be any formal transition to a just, participatory and sustainable society. But this model should stand as more than a talisman as we embark on this next phase of our work together. It is in the nature of our commitment as Christian men and women that we seek for a better world where "hope" is characterized by something more than the bitter-sweet taste of the struggle to survive against all odds.

Conclusion

I should not need to remind you of the urgency of the situation both in the industrialized and in the developing countries. The mood of the recent summit meeting between leaders of the OECD countries in Tokyo was one of apprehension.

The need to forego consumption without precipitating the worst ravages of inflation and economic recession poses a real dilemma for each of these countries. The central imperative of the industrialized countries demands more than promises to resolve extravagant and wasteful patterns of resource use. The developing world waits to see whether the good and pious promises can be translated into action. And OPEC is watching.

The first faltering steps to moderate demand will be a mark of humility set against the proud achievements of the industrialized countries in this century. The illusion of mastery vested in the conception of more powerful forms of technology has dissolved for the foreseeable future. If we are dispirited enough to claim that the world is in an irretrievable condition, then we deny the basis of Christian hope. I trust that this conference will be able to respond that redemption is possible for those who are prepared to pay the price, that a constructive path to the future is still available, and that Christian hope prevails.

Hopes and Difficulties of Science and Technology in Japan

YOSHINOBU KAKIUCHI

Science and technology in the modernization of Japan

When Japan opened the door to foreign countries, it found itself engulfed by the invading flood of western powers. The leaders of the early Meiji government therefore concluded that the only way for Japan to survive and to become a member of the international community was to modernize itself by a radical westernization of its administrative, economic and educational systems. The introduction of western technology seemed almost indispensable if Japan was to catch up with the dazzling prosperity of the West. Modernization was not a natural outgrowth of Japanese society, but something deliberately promoted by government leadership. All changes and reforms were thus essentially *political* in character.

Science and technology were taught in the university by foreign scholars and engineers. Selected young people were sent to foreign universities, and on their return they soon replaced the guest teachers.

The Meiji government established two semi-governmental companies, one in the textile and the other in the iron industry, financed by loans from existing leading merchants. The rapid development of the Japanese economy was sustained by the fairly advanced educational background of those engaged in it and also by traditional Confucian teaching.[1] The first private univer-

---

[1] Seiichi Tohata: *Nippon Shihonshugi no Keiseisha* (Founders of Japanese Capitalism). Iwanami Shinsho, 1964.

sity, Keio Gijuku, was founded in 1868, and graduates of this university played a leading role in later business developments. Education in science and technology, however, was provided exclusively in the national university.

After World War I the Japanese economy achieved a considerable maturity. In the late 1910's a number of research institutes were established in private industries. The Institute of Physical and Chemical Research was founded in 1922 as a private institution. The most striking feature of this institute was the greater atmosphere of freedom in comparison with the national universities.

Considerable original research has been done in basic science. Technology relied to a great extent on imported technical know-how. Not that there was no original Japanese research in technology. Well-known examples of such research are Dr Takayanagi's studies on television and the invention of the aerial by Prof. Yagi. However, the Japanese industry lacked the necessary capacity to develop them for production on a commercial basis.

After World War II the Japanese economy took some time to recover. The production of cameras and automobiles has registered outstanding progress both qualitatively and quantitatively on the international market. Technologies developed by the armaments industry became important for the field of optics and aeronautics. The technology of battleship construction was of considerable help in the making of large oil tankers.

Atomic power and the computer industry have been developed with the strong leadership and backing of the government.

Application of fundamental research to industry

Examples of the application of fundamental research to production include: the invention of a new synthetic fibre, later known as Vinylon, by Prof. Sakurada and Mr Yazawa in the late thirties; the invention of the ferrite magnet, later commercialized as OP magnet; the development, by Prof. Kaya and Dr Taguchi, of magnetic material with a very high magnetization saturation, using rolled silicon steel, which was successfully applied to the magnet for the proton synchrotron in the High Energy Research Institute. In the field of microbiology, Dr Kinoshita developed a new method of producing sodium glutamate, a well-known chemical seasoning of Japanese invention, by biosynthesis using microbes.

Throughout the development of the Japanese economy textiles and metallurgy had been the two leading areas of Japanese industrial activity. The fermentation industry has also had a long tradition in Japan and has accumulated a wealth of experience sufficient to sustain a steady development of technology.

Problem of industrial policies

When trade with Holland was begun in the seventeenth century, the Tokugawa government's policy was to separate and exclude foreign religious and political influences and to admit only the inflow of western science and technology, and useful commodities. The Meiji government followed a somewhat similar pattern. The government was enthusiastic about importing technical expertise, but the import of goods was regulated in order to protect domestic industry and to save money for the purchase of raw materials and more sophisticated machine tools for further production. These policies were perfectly reasonable and justifiable for that period. To do exactly what the West did was the best policy for catching up with it.

The great advantage of modern science in dealing with practical problems is that scientific knowledge can be formulated in mathematical or other formal languages which are particularly suited for the transmission of information to others. This played a crucial role in liberating technology from being the business of the skilled few to being that of the unskilled many.

This is, however, only one side of the story. Our knowledge is always changing. The same is true of administrative regulations and institutions in state and society. In a stable society, the best policy is to follow the traditional pattern. Pre-Meiji Tokugawa governments had enjoyed stable political patterns based on Confucian ethics and philosophy. This tradition still persists to a considerable extent in Japanese politics and administration. It is here that industrial policy has a problem. Bureaucracy prefers to play safe and avoid risks. However, it is vitally important to invest in the exploration of future possibilities. Even primitive societies spared some grain from what was eaten each day to produce future crops.

Science policy has been widely discussed everywhere in recent decades, but the situation is changing rapidly. Science should not let itself be a mere tool for power politics. It should serve as the means for further economic and social development and for the survival of human society.

Industry and the ethos of traditional cultures

The high productivity of Japanese industry could partly be credited to the well-organized policies of government and industrial leaders, but even more to the diligent and obedient character of the employee, something inherited from our traditional culture.

There is a strong sense of social interdependence among Japanese. This dependence[2] is limited to the community, which is structurally stable and constitutes a sort of clan. Within the clan, people are more "other-directed" than "inner-directed" and will only find their identity as they remain in the clan. Outside the clan one finds oneself alienated from the outside world and this experience tends to pull people back into their mother clan. This may explain what is often described as the collectivism of the Japanese. Even the Hitachi Company, one of the main industries with technological foundations, appears to the foreigner as one big family. Employees wear uniforms

---

[2]Takeo Doi: *The Anatomy of Dependence*. Kodansha International, 1973.

with name-tags on their jackets.[3] Mr Gibney described this as *familism* and rather ironically called the Japanese group "the unlonely crowd".[4]

In his book *Ways of Thinking of Eastern People*, Prof. Nakamura defines the above situations as a *limited social nexus*.[5] There is a definite hierarchy in the Japanese clan. This could be related to ancestor and emperor worship but it seems to have developed further during the feudal period and continued for centuries under the sovereignty of warriors. The ruling class of the local community was made up of warriors led by the feudal lord. They were highly disciplined and followed Confucian teachings. The ruled class consisted of farmers and merchants who were taught to be obedient to their Lord. Such obedience was regarded as the highest virtue of the people and this, too, can be attributed to the strong influence of Confucian ethics.

The idea of objectivity: a gap still unfilled

It is surprising to note that the average Japanese has no very clear idea of objectivity. By "objectivity" here I mean objective knowledge of our external world. Many Japanese think of objectivity as meaning "not being subjective", i.e. about things independent of our personal feelings or prejudices. Hence objectivity often means no more than logical consistency.

There is a noticeable difference between our common sense feelings of the world and more sophisticated views. When we introduced modern science from the West, we almost entirely neglected the process whereby it was given shape, and the splendid final form of the system of knowledge has been accepted and applauded by the many.

Accepted as mere verbal statements, science sounds like a magic formula, "open sesame". This is simply a kind of idolatry—the worship of the form to the neglect of its meaning. We have to pay more serious attention to the fact that the general public's image of science is considerably distorted. Scientists teach students to use their own sophisticated languages, which are generally too difficult for ordinary people to understand. Scientists thus tend to be segregated from society. Situations of this kind result in an unhappy situation for the public's understanding of science and this is one of the most important subjects to be studied in coming society.

The public understanding of science[6]

To restore communication between scientists and non-scientists is certainly the problem of other industrial societies as well. If the scientific com-

---

[3] Ronald Dore: *British Factory—Japanese Factory*. University of California Press, 1973.

[4] Frank Gibney: *Japan, the Fragile Super Power*. Norton & Co., 1975. Yasuo Okamato: *Hitachi to Matsushita*. Chuko Shinsho, 1979.

[5] Hajime Nakamura: *Ways of Thinking of Eastern Peoples*. East & West Centre Press, Hawaii, 1964.

[6] United States-Japan Cooperative Science Program Joint Survey Seminar on Science and Society, 29 January-2 February 1979. *Science, Technology and Human Values*. Harvard University, Summer 1979, Issue No. 29, 27.

munity is alienated from the rest of society due to the lack of communication between them, science is left entirely in the hands of the scientists. If things go wrong and the results of the application of science turn out to be undesirable, there will inevitably be public criticism. But then it is too late. It is the responsibility of scientists to interpret science to the public to enable it to participate in the solution of the problem.

This is becoming increasingly important because the social and ethical aspects of scientific issues emerge on the scene very significantly.

The prospects

One of the most difficult problems confronting us today is how to solve the shortage of materials and sources of energy. It is especially serious for Japan because of its lack of natural resources and large population. We are learning fast that resources cannot simply be purchased for money. There is an ultimate shortage of available resources. We still hope we shall be able to solve the problem using our intelligence and our selfish desires in order to save our resources and to share them with other people on the earth, and also to make available new or potential resources.

It has been pointed out that although Japan has been the consumer of scientific knowledge established by the West and has made maximum use of that knowledge, it has not invested much money and labour for the production of new knowledge for the future. It is the time for us to change from being mere recipients of technical know-how to being a producer and supplier of new knowledge.

In the coming age of material shortage, we have to share resources with other peoples. We have to prepare ourselves for the painful sacrifice of our wealth whenever necessary. "Workoholism and living in a rabbit hutch" are not necessarily blameworthy. What should be blamed is the pursuit of one's own profit at the expense of the other party.

To share the future we have to share our past

A number of peoples in the West have become interested in eastern thought and comparative studies of the East and the West are becoming increasingly important.[7] Japanese are entitled to be proud of various past cultural achievements, but should not be so optimistic as to believe that their traditional way of thinking would be of immediate use for the solution of the difficult problems of modern industrial society. The eastern and the western cultures have their own traditional backgrounds, and in order that both the East and the West may share the present, they have to deepen their mutual understanding by sharing their past as well. Exchange of our past experience would enable us to supplement our own history with that of other peoples. And only when both become one shall we be able to share the present. Those who share the present can share the future as well.

---

[7] Hajime Nakamura: *Parallel Developments*. Kodansha International, 1975.

The Role of the State in Technological Development

THEODOR LEUENBERGER

The western pattern of development: science, industry, the idea of progress

We start from the fact that the course of our society since the eighteenth century has been determined by industrialization. In the two centuries since then science, technology, industry and the economy have emerged as the decisive forces of our modern world. Understanding, developing and controlling technology and economy has become a crucial task. Our main problems today have their roots in this process. The breakthrough of the Industrial Revolution gave rise in the West to a permanently expanding technological and industrial system. It is this continuous expansion that constitutes the true historical novelty of industrial capitalism. This type of scientific and technological dynamics is an entirely new phenomenon.

It is interesting to note that China long ago possessed a highly sophisticated body of knowledge in the field of the mechanical sciences. That knowledge, however, had little or no influence on the general level of industrial technology and economic growth. It remained the exclusive property of academics and state officials. There was no spirit of innovation; above all, there was no desire to incorporate discoveries and inventions in the production process. Knowledge and invention alone were static; only practical exploitation could have made them dynamic. But exploitation is only possible when the economic facilities are at hand.

It was only in the context of the western Industrial Revolution that the marriage of the natural sciences and industry, of science and technology, took place. The fact that it did take place had to do with a new approach to solving problems, a new readiness to experiment and new motivations and attitudes. There emerged in Europe a kind of sub-culture of economico-technological dynamics.

This new enthusiasm for innovation has to be seen against the background of the European Enlightenment and the belief in continuous upward progress. This was something new, this belief that there was such a thing as progress, that with the help of science and technology we could master the world, that furthermore this progress in the fields of science and technology went hand in hand with social progress.

Ever since the Enlightenment the belief in progress through science and technology has been gaining ground. There emerged what McClelland has called the *Leistungsgesellschaft*—the performance society or the society of achievement. The forms of production, the structures of society, practically everything now became subject to change.

Knowledge, power and politics

This modernization process was nothing else than the process of modern man's taking possession of the world. Since Descartes it has been a basic conviction that scientific knowledge signifies the domination of all reality. Everything becomes predictable and seizable. It becomes an unquestioned fact that human knowledge signifies a seizure of power over all reality.

The modern concept of knowledge is intimately linked with the goal of technological world domination. It was Heidegger who dealt in this century with the problem of the scientific-technical "will to power". One of Heidegger's basic themes is the continuity between the spirit of the modern age and that of preceding centuries in the West, the entire metaphysical structure of western thinking. He understands the technological world-view and European nihilism as the necessary conclusion of western thinking as such. Already in Plato Heidegger discerns a form of the turn towards the conviction which is the beginning of modernity. The entire western metaphysics, he argues, is in its basic tendency "humanistic". European humanism is the event which pushed man into the centre of all existing entities. It is always the question of leading man, the animal rationale, into the certitude of his destination. Everything revolves around man. European humanism is a process in which western man takes hold of himself and of his world. His faculty of knowledge is an instrument of his power. As the possessor of such knowledge he is capable of projecting his world in advance. It is in modern science that this capacity of thinking has revealed itself in its extreme possibilities as a tool of the human "will to power".

What is characteristic of the modern expansive society is the permanent accumulation of knowledge and power. These two things cannot be separated. Knowledge is the basis of power today. As Daniel Bell made clear, "what has now become decisive for society is the new centrality of theoretical knowledge". Out of this new constellation follows the modern law: every accumulation of knowledge leads to an acceleration of societal development. Every expansion of the knowledge potential enlarges the potential of expansive possibilities. Thus the permanent accumulation of new knowledge has a revolutionary quality and power. The whole development of the scientific-technical civilization is based upon this. Knowledge is potential power, because it is future-oriented. The basic pattern, in which human knowledge relates itself to the future, is the anticipation of future possibilities.

Due to the faculty of knowledge we have become capable of projecting the world in advance. History in its course cannot produce anything new that was not already encompassed by man's projecting a priori thinking. It is in modern science that this capacity of thinking has revealed itself in its extreme possibilities as a tool of the human will to power.

SCIENCE AND POLITICS

Does this mean that we have moved to a completely technological understanding of our reality? Does it mean that society and politics are dominated by the apparatus of science and technology? Is the scientization of politics already a reality? Did the scientists already seize state power? Let us first answer the following question: What are the conditions of political problem perception?

How does a problem become a political issue? How does political agenda-building or issue-formation occur? Politicians are not free to determine the political agenda of specific problem areas. On the other hand, no one prescribes the agenda. In the agenda-building different inputs count: public opinion, the press, which themselves produce and elaborate on issues. In addition, political parties and governments take part in the producing of political issues. Another important input for the issue-formation is Academia.

Scientific information is often a precondition for the perception of a problem. Science is basically regarded as capable of problem-solving. In other words, concrete political actions are based on the conviction that scientific solutions can be found, and scientists do everything to strengthen this belief.

Problem perception is indeed a function of scientific development. This does not mean that the scientific process always arrives at clear problem formulations and problem solutions. Particularly where the problems transcend the disciplinary boundaries and where there is a research deficit between the formulation and the solution of a problem, we are confronted with very different interpretations.

What does this mean for the relationship between science and politics? The scientific and political decision-making bodies do not merge. The society is not a scientific-technical apparatus. There is a built-in resistance in the political system against intellectual concepts and scientific designs. Political reality has never obeyed the scientific house of cards. Therefore one cannot rely upon completely capturing and controlling political situations through scientific means. Neither the proliferation nor the increase in intellectual technologies can ultimately determine the degree of social and political rationality. One might put it more sharply: the faith in the capability of overcoming political contradictions through scientific planning is a modern superstition. Our total option for scientific-technical progress puts a heavy burden on our governments. We still possess a thoroughly technocratic view of politics and society. Everything appears in relation to technology. This thesis of the technological problem-solving capability is an ideology which permanently overburdens the capacity of governments.

Processes versus politics

Vis-à-vis the scientific-technological processes political guidance and control appear very limited. In the relation between politics and technological economic processes, the latter prove to be more and more autonomous. But our current model of democracy still postulates that all the societal activities can and should be politically contained and controlled. Politics should control and guide economic and technological processes. In contrast to this classical postulate, we see today a shrinkage of political capacity: the technical-economic processes (for example, the actions of transnational corporations) prove to be stronger than the decision-making and guidance capabilities of our political systems. At best the speed and the effects can be contained through political action, or these processes can be slowed or accelerated, but no longer stopped.

Politics, however, are still expected to provide coherent strategies for all problems. In fact, the management of often unreconcilable conflicts has become a primary political task. But the conflicts today have globally achieved such extension that they can no longer be contained within a single coherent policy and strategy. At the same time the myth of essential political coherence continues to be proclaimed. But the self-applied laming of our political systems becomes more and more apparent. The various processes are running out of control. Politics become permanent crisis management. The outcome of these crises and self-obstruction is uncertain. Only under positive conditions of pressure will it be possible to develop new long-term strategies in order to move our political systems again.

The end of the planning euphoria

If we raise the demand for a long-term strategy, then this is not to be confused with demands for increased political planning of our development. This demand was characteristic of the sixties and early seventies. But this former planning euphoria has yielded to scepticism regarding the possibilities of such political planning. With planning it was hoped that the quality of political decisions would be improved. One intended to improve the rationality, the long-term orientation, the coordination of political decision-making. The micro-economic optimization technologies did not allow for simple transposition in the arena of political decision-making processes.

Why? This type of planning calls for *one* decision-maker who can clearly order his preferences and make them the basis of his decisions. But the political structures of our western democracies can do little with the optimization models of the micro-economy. In this case we do not have one decision-maker as in entrepreneurial management, but rather a multiplicity of interests and goals. Complexity describes the nature of political decision-making processes. It has to do with processes which, once started, can no longer be reversed, and which in their complex nature no longer obey the original intentions of those who set the processes in motion. Political action thus gets lost in the merging of conflicting and overlapping streams of intentions, reactions and reaction chains. And the broader the problem and field of interests involved, the more the course of such processes assumes its own patterns.

Long-term planning can surely consider facts and figures, but those are raw elements. We must draw the lines ourselves, they are not imposed upon us. Only within a limited political formation clearly set apart from the bulk of occurring processes can possibilities for decision-making be recognized.

THE UNCERTAINTIES OF POLITICS

Attempts to achieve a longer-term orientation of our political action have thus, for the most part, failed. This failure is not only a result of the evasive complexity of today's processes: another cause lies in the short-term calculations of day-to-day politics. The pressures for quick success lead by necessity to short-term action. The forms of our politics were not made for the solving of long-term problem complexes.

A third reason for the failure of every sort of long-term planning is the obvious ruptures and changes during this decade. These intrusions into the relative continuity of the fifties and sixties pose for us the question whether the capability for making political decisions can ever be improved by available planning models. Current models still work on the assumption that upcoming developments can be forecast. But complex processes by no means exhibit stable tendencies over the long term: intrusions, opposing developments, and tendency changes appear over and over again. We are not able to predict the time and direction of such potential tendency changes.

In other words, the prime determinant for current politics is *uncertainty*. This uncertainty cannot be covered up by planning models and forecasts. Our political and economic situations have become tendentially more open and less calculable. The factors of insecurity and uncertainty belong constitutively to political decision-making. We cannot determine our future in a fail-safe manner through proper forecasting and planning. The political-economic processes are not to be handled as a controllable system from which all data are translated into measurable information and transferred to punch cards. This technocratic conception of reality is a dangerous deception with which, for example, US-Vietnam policy in the sixties and US-Iran policy in the seventies had much to do. Our political technocrats especially, used to working within fixed systems, must get accustomed to the indeterminate character of socio-political reality. Access to this reality is not like the acquisition of a technical field of operation. Even in a society determined by science and technology choosable alternatives can be found. Ends are not absolutely prescribed: rather they must always be newly formulated, established and revised. There is always the possibility of a grasping beyond available forms and patterns. Therefore governments, legislatures and the public must support positions in which existing patterns are not accepted as unchangeable, but in which alternative action is left open.

The military-industrial-bureaucratic-scientific complex

A scientific community which is both controversial and multifaceted could serve as the basis for alternative thinking in terms of scientific-technical-political scenarios. There is an urgent need to bring alternative possibilities for the future to the attention of the public and to relativize one-dimensional politics which seek to uncritically extend present structures to the future.

Every future carries in it a "counter-future". There are always different future scenarios: necessary and unnecessary, avoidable and unavoidable, intended and unintended. When speaking of the future, scientists should especially keep the plural in mind. They should reveal the power of institutions and structures and the chances of changing them; they cannot, however, develop any ultimate norms, even though they should be capable of presenting the framework or conditions of potential developments and the consequences of specific decisions or actions.

For this purpose we do not need one centralized scientific organization speaking with one voice, but a plurality of different voices and interpretations. This demands a pluralization of scientific experts on all levels. Never should an expertocracy speak with one voice but with different voices. Only such a plural presentation allows governments and the public to reach a more independent decision about which way to take.

Political institutions comprise an arena of constant interaction and confrontation of different value systems. I refer here to the substance of Max Weber's model: the interaction between scientific expertise and political practice. He strictly separated the function of the expert from that of the politician. The politician makes use of technical knowledge, but political practice requires that decisions be made and carried out. In the last analysis political action cannot rationally justify its own premises. Instead a decision is made between competing value orders and convictions. Although the knowledge of the expert may determine the techniques, a practical decision in concrete situations is not completely ruled by reason. Rationality in the choice of means is often accompanied by irrationality in the orientation to values. The result is reflected in the present situation: we have a scientific-technical instrument at our disposal without being able to organize our world society in a responsible way. We live instead in an uncontrolled play with different huge technical power potentials.

Many therefore favour a more technocratic model. The politician would become the mere agent of the scientific community. This scientific intelligentsia would elaborate the implications and techniques as well as the optimal strategies. If it were possible to rationalize political decisions (which are mostly choices in situations of uncertainty), then the politician would be left with nothing but a fictitious decision-making power. "The politician would then be at best something like a stop-gap in a still imperfect rationalization of power, in which the initiative has passed to scientific analysis and technical planning" (Habermas).

The weakness of this technocratic model is evident. It is neither the technocrat nor the politician alone who holds power. Technocracy is not the newest mode of government. Neither is it just the "military-industrial complex", but it is a blending of economic-scientific-technological and political power. We might speak of the military-industrial-bureaucratic-scientific complex.

A typical manifestation of this techno-bureaucratic complex is the large technologically based, partly government-supported corporation or enterprise. These in fact hold today the world's high technology industries in their hands. The multinational corporation symbolizes the international dimension of this power complex. These global actors affect resources, structures, values across the old nation-state lines. They have global organization capable of initiative and transnational management. We experience today the emergence of a global techno-economic stratification system. Within this system the multinational corporation is assuming the role of an agent promoting the model of a global technological lead. But this model is carried forward by a small technological and managerial elite. Their multinational transactions make democratic participation and control even more difficult. The decision-making networks are such that it becomes increasingly unclear where real power can be located.

The inter- and transnational economy that has developed across the Atlantic and the Pacific is most powerful. The national bureaucracies and the national public have no control of these global operations. We still live from the political models of the nineteenth century. What we need is more political reflection upon a responsible relationship between a new political and a new economic world order. In the long run it is not advisable that the transnational actors of world economy move in a political vacuum.

The lack of adequate political theory and understanding has to do with the fact that the present power structures are evaluated according to traditional power models. But we are confronted with a transformation of power on a global scale. There has been a change in the nature of power. One is its diffusion, which has resulted from the increase in the number of actors and from the increase in the issues. Another change is the diversification of power. The classical use of power is the diplomatic-strategic game between nation-states. The world power system today is a multi-channel system. The same actors participate in different systems and power channels. The new major power games are the techno-economical power games.

Modern power games are very complex; they are no longer just war games. With the end of the western empires, with the internationalization of economies, with the worldwide spread of technology, the rules of the game have changed. The interdependence of all—bigger or smaller actors— is both an opportunity and a restraint. The level of interdependence is often such that one power cannot reach its own goal unless others (including the rivals) reach their own goals to a certain extent. A very aggressive use of one's own power may backfire.

Power today tends to be disaggregated into various systems of interdependence. Each one involves only a certain element of power (money, raw material, technology, skill). This fragmentation of power has brought a change in the power hierarchies.

For instance those who can handle capital-, research- and administration-intensive technology (in other words capital holder, researcher and able administrator) can strengthen their position. This is a circular process: the technology cannot operate without them, so as the technology gains foothold, it will generate everywhere more members of the CRB-complex (Capital-Research-Bureaucracy). And as this complex grows there will be more technology.

Acquisition of technological capabilities

There is no doubt that technological capability building is today crucial for every power holder. This is particularly true for third world countries. But technological capability building involves much more than the mere creation of local facilities. It involves the acquisition of manufacturing know-how and of scientific-technical design philosophy, and in general of know-why in addition to know-how. It also includes acquisition of know-how relating to management, marketing, servicing, logistics, finance. Technology transfer is today a universal social process, it is a transfer of social code, of the social cosmology behind the western technology. One might say that with this transfer a more effective westernization of the world is taking place than under colonialism, under which the third world by and large could retain its cultural orientations.

There is no way out if one enters the modernization process. The incorporation of the know-how and know-why into the stock of local knowledge will be necessary. Today a certain technological independence is absolutely crucial for economic and political independence. Technological independence should not be understood as self-sufficiency or complete autarchy. It is just a better capability for autonomous decision-making of a government.

States today have to choose among different models and strategies of development—each with its own priorities and costs. There are states in the Third World that do not want the social costs and the external dependencies of the western model. If their primary concern is social justice and national identity, and not just economic growth, then the western model is wrong. Some disconnection from the West may then be necessary. If states do not have a certain measure of domestic autonomy, the constraints of the international system are too big. And yet the concept of self-reliance and autonomy is not the ultimate word. There are poor countries in which self-reliance would not provide any real gain in autonomy. For autonomy is meaningless unless one has a certain stock of capabilities. Neither the intensifying of independence nor the accepting of interdependence is, of itself, the solution.

In every community each element needs its own breathing space, its own measure of autonomy, its protection from total dependence. Room must be made not only for more collective management through collective institutions, but also for some emphasis on self-sufficiency. A partial delinking between some poor states and the richer ones may be necessary. The objective would then not be autarchy, but the lessening of one-sided dependencies.

Of course there are objective constraints and limitations to such domestic capability building: so far technology, capital and management know-how are still dominated through the multinational corporations which offer a package deal under their own conditions. TNCs prefer to maintain full control by insisting upon a package of technology, capital and management with minimal interference from the host country in technological decisions.

Real acquisition of technological capability demands the capacity to understand the complexity of present technology; it demands the acquisition of basic data and know-why. The TNCs have little interest in helping to build up technological capability of host countries, since real diffusion of technology know-how weakens their own privileged position.

At present there is still absolute control from the classical industrial centre, USA, Europe, Soviet Union and Japan, and the control is built around the research component of technology. It must be clearly seen that technology building means building one's own research capacity. The corporation power is not just based on its marketing success but on its ability to generate new technologies. Third world countries have to realize the importance of technology, associating Research and Development (R & D) laboratories and engineering design organization with the acquisition of technology. This process must be strengthened, in spite of the heavy cost of developing know-how. The cost of not developing know-how is even higher.

The TNCs try to perpetuate the mystique of sophistication with regard to technology development. It can be said that once a national decision is made to develop a product or a process, it is not so difficult to develop the necessary know-how.

First world states and technology development

It is characteristic of science and technology that they created new types of problems for the political systems in the West. This is not to say that the only major political problems are caused by technology but the interaction between politics and technology is a key question today.

There exists a major commitment in western governments to foster science and technology (science includes the social as well as the natural sciences, and technology refers to such social technologies as systems analysis as well as engineering, etc.). After World War II there emerged a kind of symbiosis between government agencies and private business. A contract system has made available to government almost all of the nation's scientific and technological capacity.

The phenomenon of the "military-industrial-scientific-bureaucratic complex" did not come until World War II. Peace-time research funding for private business began in the late 1940's. The establishment of full military industrial cooperation came very strongly with Robert McNamara's "system management" in the early 1960's. A crucial part of the public-private defence industry is aerospace and electronics; this is part of the whole range of modern scientific and engineering business including computers, calculators, semi-conductors—in other words, the whole technology industry. The aerospace component has today the largest concentration of research and development money of any industry in the United States. The technology industry in California presents a huge innovative ferment on a scale without precedent in industrial history.

Particularly defence contractors are in a very strong economic position. They depend upon public money from a Washington fountainhead that never runs dry. Adams refers to this alliance between government and the technology business as follows: "Here government not only permits and facilitates the entrenchment of private power but serves as its fountainhead. It creates and institutionalizes power concentrations which tend to breed on themselves and to defy public control... The complex is a natural coalition of interest groups with an economic, political, or professional stake in defence and space. It includes the armed services, the industrial contractors who produce for them, the labour unions that represent the workers, the lobbyists... and the legislators who for reasons of pork and patriotism, vote for the sizeable funds to underwrite the show..."

Thus we see that the expansion of Big Technology is not just the result of the inner dynamics of private economy. The management of national security had an immense impact on the development direction of the national economies.

The present strength of the USA derives from the accumulation of scientific and technological "capital". This potency of technology as an instrument of national power was first recognized by the military establishment. Even today military and closely related projects account for a large percentage of the government-funded R & D in the USA.

The crucial question for the coming decade will be how governments and parliaments are able to control the technology development. If a state is at the forefront technologically, how does it help steer technology? We have to recognize that neither national nor international joint steering may help much to control the situation.

We must do what we can today, but there is a limit to what our generation can do. The international fragmentation of power, the general insecurity stand against the urgent need to tame technology.

If we are thinking in terms of a world order policy we have to create stronger ties—a worldwide application of the "theory of the net" (Stanley Hoffman). This means creating a dense web of ties, a code of behaviour which corresponds to minimum common values. One might object that if we stress the minimum we avoid the real hard issues. This is not the case.

We need to separate two political processes: agreements on framework and arguments on dynamics. Commonly agreed frameworks are no guarantee of success; but if the framework is agreed upon, then there is some pressure to fill this framework. If most states are caught in a dense web of agreements, then there is less chance to break out of the net. The drama of world order lies in its interconnection. There is no simplifying formula. There are no easy achievements.

Reactions and Comment

The three addresses evoked many immediate questions in the plenary session. Is the decentralization, desired by Francis, really possible in an intricately interconnected world, where events in one area have repercussions far away? Has science become so specialized that no amount of communication can overcome the alienation, described by Kakiuchi, between scientific elites and the public? Did Leuenberger distinguish too sharply between technological and political processes? Is it possible that both alike are the tools of groups in power?

The conference gave further attention to some of these issues in later plenary sessions (see Chapters 12, 15, 17). And, as usual, discussion in depth of the issued raised in this plenary session had to await section meetings. Some of the consequences appear in reports of Sections V, VIII and IX.

11. Perspectives in Industrialized Socialist Countries

Introduction

From the beginning the design of the conference included a dialogue between people living in socialist and in market-economy societies. The Christian churches live in many kinds of social systems. Much of the world is, at this stage of history, committed to one or another style of economic system, and much of the world is in the process of deciding what system or combination of systems to adopt. Both the old, persistent issue of social justice and the newer concerns about ecology bear upon discussions of economic systems.

The final planning meeting of the WCC Working Committee on Church and Society, a committee of twenty representing six continents, convened in Erfurt, German Democratic Republic, in August 1978, for the specific purpose of drawing into discussion a larger number of East European church leaders and scientists than can usually participate. One decision was to include in the programme a number of Marxist speakers living in socialist societies—in addition to the Christians from socialist societies and the academic socialists from outside the socialist world, who would be present in any event. The last-minute withdrawal of expected speakers from the Soviet Union and Cuba (see Chapter 1) frustrated this aim of the conference.

Participants were able to hear, according to plan, Ernest Petric of the Faculty of Sociology, Political Science and Journalism of Ljubljana, Yugoslavia. He addressed the issue of the just, participatory and sustainable society with specific emphasis on the current worldwide debates about the "limits to growth". He showed how the issue calls for changes in both traditional capitalist and traditional socialist thought, and he emphasized the capacities of Marxism to deal with the issue.

The conference also called on two Christian church leaders living in East European socialist societies. Both disclaimed any intention to represent Marxist thinking, but spoke of the opportunities and problems of the churches in Marxist societies. Heino Falcke, Superintendent of the Erfurt region of the Federation of Evangelical Churches in the GDR, spoke from the background of a paper prepared by the Church and Society Committee of that church, a paper earlier published in *Anticipation* (No. 26, June 1979). Karoly Pröhle, General Secretary of the Ecumenical Council of Churches in Budapest, spoke from a comparable experience in the Hungarian Church.

Because of the adjustments necessary to plan this set of addresses, they were scheduled later than originally intended and did not, in fact, all occur in the same programme (see the conference schedule at the end of this volume). That delay made it possible for Falcke to refer to the address of Herman Daly (see Chapter 12). However, the addresses are printed at this point in this volume, to correspond to the logical structure and plan of the conference.

These addresses should be related to Chapter 19, "The Environment and Social Production: a Soviet View", in the preparatory book, *Faith, Science and the Future*. That chapter was written by Pavel Oldak, a professor of Novosibirsk State University in the Soviet Union.

Some Remarks on Marxism and Limits to Growth

ERNEST PETRIC

When I spoke six years ago at the WCC North American-European Conference on "The Technological Future of the Industrialized Nations and the Quality of Life", I started by saying that "the tremendous technological change of today, with all its promises and threats, is a universal process, a world scale problem".[1] I can reaffirm that today. The problems connected with science and technology are not, and should not be, only the problems of the so-called developed West.

Of course, much could be said here of the problems and ways, successes and failures of socialist countries, and my homeland in particular, in connection with the complicated and complex problems of contemporary human society and the role of science and technology in it. We have to share—and we do—our experiences, our understanding of problems and our knowledge. I will try here to present shortly and superficially the thinking in the part of the world to which I belong—Yugoslavia—on the limits to growth.

Everybody here would probably agree that we would have much less doubts about science and technology if it were possible simply to go on growing and expanding—and also exploiting—and being optimistic. Let us not forget slogans prevalent in the sixties: "Science and Technology for Economic Growth" was the central theme for the science policy in the OECD countries then. Serious doubts about science and technology appeared when it was realized that there are limitations to nature and its resources, when it became clearer and clearer that it is impossible simply to continue as before, impossible to go on in a continuation of the theme of the sixties. But what should be changed? Science and technology? People—men and women? Theological teaching? Or existing structures of society? The way of produc-

---

[1] *Anticipation*, No. 15, December 1973, p. 30.

tion? The existing international economic and also political order? What is crucial and what changes should be started?

It would be stupidly ambitious and egotistical of both East and West to lecture each other. We all will have to try hard to solve existing difficult and huge problems, those which we have in common and those which are specific to our individual situations. However, it is useful to bring forward some thoughts from the part of the world usually called the socialist countries—some thoughts on how to use science and technology and for what purpose, how to share world resources, and how to continue to exist on this planet.

Contemporary discussions among Marxists on limits to growth

Generally in the socialist countries and in Marxist thought the approach to science and technology is far more optimistic than in the industrialized West. The results of scientific and technological development are significant indeed. The amount of money spent on the development of science and technology in Eastern European countries is large and still increasing. Modern technology is crucial to the competition with the West throughout the world. It is also needed to satisfy the growing needs for consumer goods within socialist countries themselves. Let it be stressed at this point that in countries or societies where the material consumption is limited or poor, this material consumption becomes the concern of people and their central aspiration.

So it is easy to understand that the concept of limits to growth found no support in Marxist praxis and theory. On the contrary, this concept has been condemned as an ideological weapon against the growing economic and technological power of socialist countries. Indeed, the need for unlimited growth, immanent for the capitalist system, is also deeply rooted in existing socialist societies.

Marxists use several arguments to oppose the ideas of limits to growth. Different social structures, social goals and values realized in the socialist way of production, which is not motivated by profit, prevent crises, which are the result of disorganized, spontaneous development of the capitalist system and production, based on profit. The centrally planned economy can easily cope with future economic growth and technological development. Human creativity has in the past and will in the future always find ways to handle crises. The theoretical human ability to produce everything out of everything is growing faster than the exploitation of existing materials and sources of energy.[2]

We accept the view that unlimited economic growth and technological development in capitalist countries are primarily used to keep and enlarge the

---

[2]E. K. Fedorov and I. B. Novikov: "Problemy vzaimodeistvia čeloveka s prirodnoi sredoi", in *Voprosy filosofii*, No. 12, 1972; and I. S. Šklovsky: "Vselennaia, Žizn', Razum", Moscow, 1973.

power of capital, while in socialist countries economic growth and technological development are to be used to fulfil the needs of people. However, recently Marxists also are questioning whether it is really possible simply to ignore problems raised by the discussions of limits to growth.[3] Is it really possible to ignore the possibility of science and technology being misused as means of technocratic or bureaucratic manipulation of nature and its resources? Is it reasonable simply to ignore the fatal contemporary contradictions between social development and its natural, ecological preconditions?

It seems that although the social form of production has extreme importance, there are some objective conditions and ecological limits which cannot be simply abolished either by central planning or any other form of social control. Reservations have been also expressed about the assumption that human creativity can always find the way out. The reorientations of production and the way of life, which human creativity has achieved in the past, are more and more difficult and complicated. And they are not simply there, to be chosen; they have to be first found and then realized. The new solutions are often such that they produce more new problems than they solve. Often the problems are solved only on the surface, partially or temporarily, and later appear in a more powerful form and on a global scale. Besides, the technological development produces social problems, which are not to be solved by science. And even though the scientific and technological advance in principle would be capable of resolving all the negative consequences, it is still by no means certain that the solutions will be found in time. Negative consequences, especially those on the global scale, appear only after a period of time, so it is difficult to foresee them. It is difficult to foresee the negative consequences of the cumulative effect of different technologies which might not, individually, produce negative effects. Furthermore, it is theoretically impossible to know what man may create in future that might come into conflict with what already exists.

Similarities and differences between Marxist thinking and the concept of limits to growth

Marx and Engels saw the development of productive forces and the raising of productivity as the material precondition for the achievement of "the kingdom of freedom".[4] However, they did not see the growth of material production as the goal in itself. The goal of production in the future communist society is to produce the goods for life in quantities that enable everybody to fulfil his spiritual needs and carry out his social activities. The productive activity of people should be reduced to the necessary minimum, and

---

[3] A. Kirn: *Marx's Understanding of Science and Technology* ("Marxovo razumzvanje znanosti i tehnike"), Ljubljana, 1978; and B. Debenjak: *V alternativi. Marksistične studije* ("In alternative. Marxist studies"), Ljubljana, 1974.

[4] This is seen in many of Karl Marx's works, mainly *The Capital, The German Ideology, Misery of Philosophy*, and also in several of Engels's works.

this necessary minimum should be equally shared by all members of the community capable of producing. To Marx and Engels human needs are the result of natural, historical circumstances and the conditions of production. The material needs of the individual in the future communist society are not intended to be unlimited, but are conditioned by social, cultural and moral limits. So the idea, "to each according to his needs", should not be understood as meaning that there should be no limits to material needs. This maxim in no way means that everyone shall have unlimited material needs.

However, Marx's concept of the development of productive forces contains other elements which cannot so easily be brought into accordance with the idea of socially limited growth in material production. According to Marx, the spiritual and social development of man himself is in a permanent relationship with the development of the productive forces and depends on them. So, if material production were to become static and society simply reproduce itself (zero growth rate), sooner or later this would also set limits to human spiritual and social development. The unlimited development of human creativity is not possible if the material aspect of human life is to be limited. In a static, routine production situation, thinking would also soon become dogmatized. Marx's understanding of human productive activity did not take into consideration the possibility that obstacles might be placed in the way of man's action towards nature, and consequently also the changes in his own social nature. Nowadays also some Marxists think that humanity will have to limit and control its creativity in some aspects in order to protect its own existence.

We must specially emphasize another way, perhaps the principal way, in which Marx's, and Marxist, thinking diverges from the contemporary western ideas on the limits to growth. Western proponents of the concept of limits to growth usually overlook the fact that capitalist production decisively sharpens the present contradictions of exponential economic growth and adds to the problems arising from such growth. They also overlook the fact that different social relations can significantly sharpen or limit, if not completely eliminate, the consequences of the material level of contemporary production. Any reorientation or limitation of material production, without changing existing class structures, would in fact mean the perpetuation of existing social injustice and exploitation.

It is also an illusion to think that we can stop or master the growth of capitalist production by trying to change human values directly. To Marxists the decisive thing is to change social relations, which will in turn bring about a change of values. The advocates of limits to growth put the main emphasis on the distribution of goods. To Marxists the fundamental factor is the way of production. The importance of changes in the distribution of goods should not, of course, be neglected. But the condition for any really significant reorientation of production from production for profit to production for human needs lies in change of the way of production.

Marx and nature

Clearly, Marx did not consider the possibility that nature and its resources might appear as a factor limiting development. He did, however, recognize several negative aspects in the relationship between man and nature, particularly in connection with agricultural production and urban concentration in his own times. But to him, the destruction of the natural environment is the result of the disorganization inherent in the capitalist system and the capitalist way of production. Of course, he did not recognize the possibility that human productive activity could reach such a stage that no class would be able to consume fresh water, air, food. Marx's analysis of production was a social analysis, not an ecological one. In his view, however, and particularly in Engels's view, the man-nature relation could and should be harmonious in the communist society.

The relevant question for contemporary Marxists is if and how ecological principles place limitations on development and production in a socialist society. Is the natural environment of the planet large enough for a future communist way of production on the global level? Theoretically the answer should be positive. It should be possible theoretically to produce everything out of everything; the natural frontiers could be pushed from our planet to outer space, all wasteful activities could be avoided and all class accumulation and usurpation of goods could be abolished. If these notions were demonstrably possible, then there need be no fear that the existing capitalist way of production will use up the natural resources for the future communist society.

The way out?

It seems to several contemporary Marxists, at least in Yugoslavia, that if man wants to establish unity and harmony between himself and nature, he will have to renounce several of his existing goals and needs. He will have to change the present narrow evaluation of scientific and technological advances which places value mainly, if not exclusively, on the technical and economic aspects. It is essential that we start to reorganize production according to ecological principles. However, to Marxists it seems that this and other tasks can be more easily fulfilled in socialist societies where it appears easier to achieve common interests and ensure joint action. It must be admitted, however, that no system has so far developed adequate ways out of the ecological crisis. Even the existing socialist economy has not yet adapted itself to the requirements of ecology. In socialist countries, too, the technological advance has not been sufficiently socially guided and controlled to avoid the ecological crisis. The technological innovative process has hitherto been largely rationalized and controlled in relation to economic viability, productivity of labour, economic efficiency, etc. and not enough from the social and ecological point of view.

Many problems are similar, if not identical, regardless of whether we face them in capitalist or socialist countries. So we need as much international exchange of experience and cooperation as possible. However, while trying to find practical solutions, we should not fall into a kind of pragmatic confusion. The basic theoretical differences between the Marxist and the western approaches should not be forgotten. While the western approach tries to find solutions only within the existing capitalist mode of production, within existing social structures, Marxists believe that only basic changes in the existing capitalist way of production, change of social relations, the abolition of capitalist exploitation can ultimately lead out of the present crisis. Marxists believe that the present social and ecological crisis and its intensification in itself calls for and produces social changes.

The reshaping of social systems will not, of course, take place as an automatic result of the crisis. The crisis will, however, force—indeed is already forcing—people to take action to tackle the social origins of the crisis and to abolish obstacles preventing more complete, universal and long-term solutions. The quest for participation—not just consultation—in decision-making throughout the world, the ever-increasing realization that neither capitalist technocracy nor state bureaucracy can offer the solution, show clearly the direction that changes towards the future society must take. The transition must be not to a society of state bureaucracy nor to a society of transnational corporations, but to a state in which workers and people are joined together in working to fulfil their material and spiritual needs.

There is also another direction in which profound change must take place. The limited resources of our planet will evermore prevent any monopolization of nature and its resources. Increasingly, the whole of humanity will have to deal with nature and natural resources as a whole. We have heard several times at this conference about the idea of sharing natural resources. Natural resources of our planet can, of course, only be shared, only become the property of humanity as a whole, when the products and existing wealth are also shared by all humanity. Unless this condition is fulfilled, any idea of sharing resources is simply another form of justifying the exploitation of the peoples of the developing countries. So while we do indeed need a universal approach to natural resources, we can only arrive at it by fundamentally changing the existing international economic and political order.

* * *

It would probably be a waste of time to discuss whether Marxists or non-Marxists are in possession of the truth. It is surely more useful that progressive people and organizations concerned with the present situation—and the WCC is surely such an organization—begin to take action.

There is no disagreement on the need to strive for more freedom, more democracy, more participation. For Marx, the development of the productive forces, and therefore the development of science and technology, should serve the liberation of all working men and women, to enable them to enjoy their social, economic, cultural, civil and political rights; and also to enable them to participate in deciding on all social affairs, what to produce, how to produce it and how to share the fruits of production.

There is no disagreement on the fact that the arms race, particularly the nuclear arms race, with the permanent possibility of a nuclear apocalypse, is endangering any existing and future way of production or social system, whether capitalist, socialist, or communist, and promises only suffering, death and the perpetuation of different forms of domination. There seems to be no disagreement on the need for a more integrated world and more international stability. This can be achieved only through the strict respect of the right to self-determination and through fundamental change in the existing international economic order—and of course, by the elimination of situations such as apartheid around the world, which are a shame and a crime against humanity.

In many cases it is not even necessary to try to discover what to do. In many cases men and women, peoples and nations are clear enough about what they want to be done or do not want to be done. But very often, unfortunately, it is the will that is lacking!

A Christian View from the German Democratic Republic

HEINO FALCKE

I speak as a theologian from the GDR, one of the most advanced industrial countries of Eastern Europe. Not being a Marxist specialist, I cannot offer here an authentic presentation of my country's Marxism. But I welcome the opportunity of giving an account of the way Christians in the GDR look at the problems of science and technology in their socialist society. My church's Church and Society committee, of which I happen to be Moderator, has already done this in some detail in a paper which you will find published in *Anticipation* (No. 26, June 1979). Here I shall have to limit my remarks to a few main points.

We have defined the social task of Christians in our country as that of a critical and constructive participation. In other words, we are cooperating in the difficult effort to develop a socialist society at the frontier dividing the two German states, the East from the West. At the same time this participation is a critical one, and the question we ask ourselves is how the humanity to which Jesus Christ calls us may be achieved in practice. This also enables us effectively to counter the assumption that the Church in our country is faced with the stark choice between complete conformity and flight into the catacombs.

What does a critical yet constructive participation on the part of Christians in our country mean for the theme of this conference?

The scientific, technological revolution is increasingly finding acceptance in the GDR. We find here positive approaches in both theory and praxis, but also difficulties of a practical and ideological kind. If we are to meet our responsibilities we must look at both sides of the coin.

I would like to illustrate four problem areas.

1. Social justice as social goal

Socialism is nothing if not a programme of social justice. In questions of the scientific and technological revolution and its consequence, socialism holds a watching brief for questions of essential social changes and just social structures. It insists that only a *just* society can be a "sustainable" society. The difficult question facing our conference is whether the ideals of justice and "sustainability" can really be integrated in an ecumenical social ethic. If they can, this would help to stimulate interest in this programme in the GDR.

In the matter of development policy, too, the GDR takes the view that just social structures are the foundation of sound economic development. Our question, however, is whether our society is not doing far less than it should be doing, and whether we have yet realized that socialism must also be achieved in the North-South relationship as well. We were impressed by a statement made by Julius Nyerere: "Socialist governments and parties in Europe must carry over into the international arena the struggle they have waged and are waging in their own countries for equal rights and opportunities. They must recognize that, viewed from the international angle, it is their nations which are the rich ones and the exploiters, and act accordingly."

What does this mean for our churches?

• The sense of solidarity with the distant neighbour who has fallen among thieves must be intensified in our congregations. This will mean measuring our level of material consumption against the level of the developing countries and not against the higher level of western society, and realizing that we are the rich nations summoned to act justly. We must, as Brother Roger of Taizé says, make our life "a parable of mutual sharing".

• We must prepare the ground in public awareness so that solidarity may increasingly become a principle of economic policy even at the cost of effort and sacrifice.

• We must advocate disarmament because military expenditure is both the biggest obstacle to the establishment of justice and the most serious threat to the ecosystem.

2. The incorporation of science and technology in the social processes

Here I want to refer to the more theoretical questions of science and technology touched on at the beginning of our conference, and I ask for patience and understanding from those for whom the practical issues are more urgent.

Socialist society integrates science and technology in socio-ethical and political responsibilities. Marxism is critical of the thesis that science is neutral; it analyses its entanglement in class interests. The division of knowledge and action into sub-systems which, though perhaps rational in themselves, are inter-related in an irrational way, is an expression of human alienation. An attempt is made to solve this problem at the theoretical and practical levels. At the theoretical level, the natural and social sciences are integrated into the ideological system of dialectical materialism. The aim here is to achieve a total view. At the practical level, science and technology are included in the overall planning of society which knows it is called to achieve human purposes.

What is the significance of this for a Christian view? As Christians we endorse this intention. We cannot join forces with a positivistic critique of the ideological system, since here the problem of values remains unsolved. Jesus Christ does not permit us to separate truth and love. He is at one and the same time the truth, love, and therefore life. In his letter to the Romans and his first letter to the Corinthians, the apostle Paul speaks of the mind being enslaved to the desires. Translated into social ethics, this means that it is enslaved to social interests. To arrive at a true understanding which serves the community, it must be liberated. What significance has this for our understanding of scientific truth? A Christian critique of the Marxist system can only be achieved on the basis of a common intention to find a concrete synthesis of the True and the Good.

At present we have no public dialogue on these theoretical problems. But as Christians we must prepare ourselves for such a dialogue and develop a theology which is capable of dialogue. With this dialogue in view I want to formulate a few questions which Christians in our country—both scientists and theologians—are asking:

- Can there be a successful synthesis of the True and the Good in an ideological system based exclusively on the scientific approach to reality but excluding the religious experience of reality?
- Can the synthesis of the True and the Good be found today otherwise than in systems which are open for dialogue? This applies to cooperation between science, ideology and religion, but also to our multicultural world. Only in dialogical structures can the freedom and responsibility of science achieve a creative synthesis.
- Is it only the entanglement of science and technology in class interests that must be criticized? Do not other assumptions and attitudes which underlie the scientific technological revolution need to be brought into the open so that they may be examined critically? I mean, for example, the objectification of nature with a view to manipulating it, and faith in the feasibility of all things in the interests of human power. In the name of Jesus Christ, who used power as a means of service, we shall have to criticize the modern cult of feasibility. The critique of political economy must be broadened to include also the critique of the technological reason. In practical terms, this means

that we who are Christians must stand by those who are suffering from the negative consequences of the technological production process. We shall not achieve the concrete synthesis of the True and the Good unless we pay attention to, and draw attention to suffering with a view to its transformation and alleviation. The synthesis of the True and the Good will be found on the *via crucis* and not on the *via triumphalis* of the feasibility of all things.

3. Relationship between economy and ecology

Increasing attention is being paid to ecology in our society. This was also quite clear, for example, in the discussion our group had with the GDR Secretary of State for the Environment shortly before we left. This ecological awareness has its ideological basis in Marxism as dialectical *materialism*. Marxism recognizes that there is an indissoluble inter-relationship between humanity and society, on the one hand, and nature on the other. In this respect, a Christian theology which considers the human person solely in terms of soul, mind or personal relationships has much to learn from dialectical materialism. Karl Marx wrote in *Das Kapital*: "No society, not even all contemporary societies together, are owners of the earth. They are only tenants and must hand it on as good stewards to future generations." Here Marx shows himself an able interpreter of the biblical command to man to rule earth. Perhaps we also have something to learn from Marx to help us obey this command more effectively in practice. Prof. Daly (see Chapter 12) has defined "sustainability" as justice between present and future generations, and in this he has this quotation from Marx to support him.

Marxism sees the economy within a conditioning framework of ecological factors. Prof. Pavel Oldak of Novosibirsk has presented a model for this in his bio-economic system which is reproduced in the preparatory readings for this conference (see *Faith, Science and the Future*, Chapter 19).

While our state does aim at economic growth, rejecting the idea of zero growth, the growth it seeks (1) is not the result of any inherent capitalist dynamic, and (2) is intended to satisfy human material *and* cultural needs. This includes the need for a healthy environment.

We have good and internationally recognized legislation on the protection of the environment. Furthermore, central planning makes it possible to enforce ecological common sense in the economic process. Nevertheless, we have a great many practical problems.

Our state is not an economic island. Dependence on the world market and general technological development and the economic rivalry between East and West mean that a considerable economic effort is required of us. The population is largely influenced by western consumer standards, pressing for a higher standard of living and measuring the worth of the social system chiefly by its economic efficiency.

Ecological measures are thus compromises, and economic pressures are often given priority. The ideological line is that only economic growth can provide the means to pay for the expensive ecological measures. There is also an almost unshaken confidence in the capacity of technology and its development to deal with the ecological problems. Long-term ecological problems (such as the depletion of resources) take second place to current difficulties.

What must Christians do?

• I believe we must learn to understand the state's practical problems and the limits to its scope for action. Cynical criticism which contrasts the ideological claims with the realities and turns its back on both is not helpful. We have to help to improve the practical application of the theory, and here we have real, if limited, possibilities for action and participation.

• Above all, we must arouse awareness of ecological problems among our congregations, not only so that our generation may have a better environment, but so that the earth may be habitable for coming generations. In doing so, we must be careful not to create a sense of doom and paralysing pessimism. Jesus Christ did not preach, "Repent for disaster is at hand"; he preached, "Repent for the Kingdom of God is at hand". That means the enticing possibility of a new and meaningful life, freedom from fear, courage for action. The Faith and Order Conference at Bangalore in 1978 said: "The Christian hope is a resistance movement against fatalism." From this attitude Christians can draw the motivation to join with unflagging patience in our society's efforts for ecological reason in practice.

• In this respect our Christian motivation can go a long way with the Marxist one. For us, however, there is another aspect. The environment must be preserved not only for humanity's sake but because it is God's creation. As such it has a dignity of its own and, in the light of God's promise, a hope of its own. We hope not only for the emancipation of humankind, but also for the emancipation of nature.

4. Socialist way of life and Christian living

Ecological questions relate back to ethical questions. While ecological problems call for structural changes, they also require a reorientation of attitudes to the quality of life. But what is quality of life? Even at this conference I have heard more questions than answers on this subject.

Discussion of this question has been going on for a number of years in our country under the heading "the socialist way of life". No conclusive definitions have yet been given. What is meant, however, is life which has meaning, a more human way of working and producing, personal development based on cultural as well as material needs.

This opens up a wide field for dialogue between Christians and Marxists. What are the real human needs, and what is their order of priority? Marx believed that religion would be made superfluous if people had a meaningful life in this world. Is there not a greater danger of stifling to death in material interests? The injunction to "seek the Kingdom of God and his righteousness" does not appear in the list of material and spiritual needs, yet this is the way in which the needs of the neighbour will be met. We Christians will have to conduct this dialogue first and foremost through our practical action. What ultimately counts here is what the apostle Paul called the "demonstration of the Spirit and power"; in other words, a life in the freedom of faith, in the practice of love and the strength of a hope which is equal to all crises.

The Role of Sciences and Technology in Shaping Our Future: Introduction to a Hungarian Contribution

KAROLY PRÖHLE

The background of my statement is thirty years of communication between Christians and Marxists in Hungary—a communication which was not only a dialogue, but much more a sharing in our common tasks and a cooperation in promoting the development of our society. We have had to overcome very critical situations and tensions, but now we enjoy considerable fruits of this cooperation. Nevertheless, we are very critical of our results. Critical means for us self-critical. Christians as well as Marxists are very self-critical, because we feel the depressing weight and confusing interdependence of present worldwide problems and we see our modest and incomplete contribution to their solution. We cannot speak here for Marxists, but we as Christians can make some comments on the basis of our experiences with Marxism and Marxists.

It is well known that conditions are different in the different socialist countries. The question is whether these differences are valued rightly. It is obvious that conditions for socialism, for example historical traditions, geographical situation, size of land and population, resources in raw materials and energy, level of culture, science and technology, and many other factors were and still are very varied. But in our understanding, in spite of all these differences, all the socialist countries are on the way to realizing socialism; so they have much more in common than it sometimes appears. And socialism as a whole is progressing into more and more integration.

With regard to the problems of a more just, participatory and sustainable society, we should pay more attention to some facts concerning socialism as it is being realized in socialist countries:

1) the growing gap between rich and poor may be a reality in most parts of the world, but not in the socialist countries; wealth and poverty have almost disappeared;
2) the distribution of material and cultural goods is much more just than in the most parts of the world;

3) production is not oriented towards profit but the needs of the people, and this sets limits of growth and gives directives for production and consumption;
4) growing participation in education, cultural goods, organizations integrated in public life, economics and society makes more and more possible real participation in planning, in criticism and in decision-making;
5) sciences are understood as natural sciences and social sciences in close unity and inter-relation with one another.

Marxists, of course, retain their ideology that in the socialist society Christianity together with religions should disappear. We do not share this consequence and forecast of Marxism. Our faith and hope, our missionary service and our participation in building up socialist society, are based on our living Lord to whom has been given all authority in heaven and earth. Therefore we should not only teach people but first of all exercise ourselves to observe all that He has commanded. And so we serve, act and live in our society in the hope and conviction that our Lord is living and abiding with us always unto the end of the world.

Reactions and Comment

The responses to these addresses, as the conference developed, were closely related to the responses to the addresses of Herman Daly and C. T. Kurien (Chapter 12). For the most part, the conference did not engage in any systematic debate between ideologies of market and socialist systems. It tended, rather, to concentrate on the big problems of justice, participation and sustainability—usually acknowledging and often emphasizing that ideologies and social systems deeply affect perceptions of issues and possible solutions. Thus ideology and social systems came to be factors that coloured all discussion in the conference.

Furthermore, as participants raised the issues of ideologies and social systems, the context was far less the traditional relation of "East and West" (socialist and market economies) than of "North and South" (industrialized and developing economies). That shift of emphasis was not new in WCC discussions. But in any comparison of recent WCC documents with early ones (for example, the first assembly of the WCC in Amsterdam, 1949), the change of emphasis is noticeable.

Part Three
Particular Problem Areas

12. Economics of the Just and Sustainable Society

Introduction

Many discussions in earlier plenary sessions had been pointing towards this session. In the years of preparatory work leading to the conference, the issue of the relationship between economic policies and the aims of justice and sustainability had won considerable attention (see "The Conference Theme and its Evolution", in Chapter 1). The omission of the word "participatory" in the title of this plenary session was not a subordination of that accent; it was rather an acceptance of the importance of participation, along with a recognition that many international debates were, rightly or wrongly, setting up an opposition between justice and sustainability.

Participants had already seen the findings of the 1978 Zurich consultation on Political Economy, Ethics and Theology (*Anticipation*, No. 26, June 1979). They had noted that the book *Faith, Science and the Future* included chapters on the economic issues by Wassily Leontief of the United States, Pavel Oldak of the Soviet Union, and Theodor Leuenberger of Switzerland.

For this session the conference called on three speakers: Herman Daly, professor of economics at Louisiana State University and a well-known critic of current policies of economic growth; C. T. Kurien, Director of the Madras Institute of Development Studies and an influentical figure in the WCC; and Diogo de Gaspar, Brazilian economist, recently on the staff of the WCC and now with the World Food Council in Rome. It was expected that Daly and Kurien would present differing positions on the international debate. De Gaspar was asked to speak specifically on issues of food.

The Ecological and Moral Necessity for Limiting Economic Growth

HERMAN E. DALY

Two basic errors are often made in thinking about economic growth in the future. One is the error of *wishful thinking* (assuming that because something is desirable it must somehow also be possible). The other is the opposite error of *technical determinism* (assuming that just because something is possible, it must be desirable).

Traditionally technologists have tended towards technical determinism, and moral reformers have been prone to wishful thinking. But this is no longer so clear-cut. Today we find technologists passionately and wishfully committed to their unproved technical dreams. Is the nuclear power industry, for example, characterized more by technical determinism or wishful thinking? Social reformers on both the left and the right are often so committed to their visions of social justice via abundance (a world of middle-class American consumers in a classless society?) that they eagerly accept every promise of cornucopian technology from nuclear power to genetic engineering and space colonization, revealing a blindness to the social consequences of technology that becomes indistinguishable from technical determinism.

It is possible to avoid these errors. Fortunately, not everything desirable is impossible, nor is everything possible undesirable. The two sets do intersect. We need, however, to be sure that economic growth does not push us out of the intersection—that in chasing the desirable we do not crash headlong into the boundary of the possible, and that in following the technical impetus towards "the effecting of all things possible", we refrain from crossing the boundary out of the set of all things desirable. Section I of this paper, on ecological limits to growth, considers the first danger; and Section II, on moral limits to growth, considers the second. Section III briefly suggests some measures to ensure that we stay within both sets of limits.

I. The ecological necessity of limiting economic growth

Much is heard today about the problem of running out of accessible *non-renewable* resources. Actually, the more basic problem is with *renewable* resource systems and the destruction of their capacity to reproduce. A reduction in the sustainable yield capacity of a renewable resource system, such as forests, fisheries, grasslands, and croplands, is a far more serious matter than the depletion of a non-renewable resource. The latter is, after all, inevitable in the long run. The former is not inevitable (except in the astronomical long run). Any permanent reduction in renewable carrying capacity means fewer and/or less abundant lives will be lived in the future. This reduction should be minimized if we aspire to be good stewards of God's creation.

Although renewable resources are the crucial ones to protect, their destruction is not independent of the rate of use of non-renewables. There are two ways in which the too-rapid depletion of non-renewables contributes to the destruction of renewables. First, high rates of depletion result in high rates of pollution of air and water which directly threaten biological resources. Second, and more importantly, rapid use of non-renewables has allowed us to reach and sustain temporarily a combined scale of population and per capita consumption that could not be sustained by renewable resources alone. As these non-renewable resources run out, the danger is that we will try to maintain the existing scale and rate of growth by over-exploiting our renewable resource base.

For a sustainable economy two things are necessary: first, a renewable resource base; second, a scale of population and per capita consumption that is within the sustainable yield of the renewable resource base. We have a resource base of forests, fisheries, grasslands, and croplands on which mankind has almost entirely lived until the advent of industrialization some two hundred years ago. We are still dependent on these natural systems, but we have increased their short-run productivity with subsidies of non-renewable and fossil fuel and minerals.

Even with the aid of such large subsidies there is good evidence that the global per capita productivity of each of the four natural systems has peaked and is now declining:[1]

1) forest productivity as measured by cubic meters per capita per year peaked in 1967 (at 0.67 cubic meters);
2) fisheries productivity, as measured by kilograms of fish caught per year per capita, peaked in 1970 (at 19.5 kilograms);
3) for grasslands we look at annual per capita output of wool, mutton, and beef; wool peaked in 1960 (at 0.86 kilograms); mutton in 1972 (at 1.92 kilograms); and beef in 1976 (at 11.81 kilograms);
4) croplands productivity as measured by kilograms of cereals per capita per year peaked in 1976 (at 342 kilograms).

Trend is not destiny, and it is conceivable that some of these peaks will be surpassed, especially the most recent ones. But these levels of productivity were attained in the first place only with the aid of large fossil fuel and mineral subsidies to mechanization, irrigation, fertilizers, insecticides, and transport. It is difficult to believe that existing levels of output per capita can be maintained, much less surpassed, as we deplete the easily available petroleum, and as world population continues to grow. Annual world oil output per capita rose from 1.52 barrels in 1950 to an all-time high of 5.29 barrels in 1977. In 1978 it fell to 5.23, and it is quite likely that 1977 will prove to have been the peak year for oil consumption.

---

[1] For a summary of the situation and relevant statistics, see Lester R. Brown: "Resource Trends and Population Policy: a Time for Reassessment". *Worldwatch Paper* No. 29, May 1979, Washington, DC.

"CONSUMING TOMORROW'S SUNSHINE"

Mankind is the only species that does not live entirely on the budget of solar energy income. All other forms of life live off the produce of the surface of the earth where current sunshine is captured by plants. Only man digs "for riches couched and hidden deep in places near to hell", as Ovid puts it. Our rapid consumption of energy capital to supplement our energy income, that is, our consumption of not only today's sunshine, but also the stored sunshine of paleozoic summers, has thrown us out of ecological balance with the rest of creation. To the extent that we over-exploit natural systems and reduce their capacity to trap the energy of sunlight, we are in effect consuming tomorrow's sunshine as well as today's and yesterday's. I would *not* draw the conclusion that all terrestrial minerals should be left in the ground "close to hell", or that mankind should renounce industrialization. But I think we must conclude that there are limits to how fast such exhaustible resources should be used, and that we are in danger of reducing the carrying capacity because we have used mineral wealth too rapidly and built up too large a scale of population and per capita consumption to be sustained by our renewable resource base.

Faced with this situation there are two responses: (1) to define our sustainable-yield through-put or aggregate biophysical budget constraint and live within it, allowing technology to devote itself to increasing the efficiency with which we use the given through-put; (2) allow technology to devote itself to increasing the total through-put, with no recognition of a limited biophysical budget or through-put. The first response is the one proper to a creature charged by his Creator with the duty of stewardship for creation. The second response is that of modern Promethean paganism and modern growth economics. The latter view further assumes that all the world will follow the US, into the age of high mass consumption in which "growth becomes its normal condition. Compound interest becomes built, as it were, into its habits and institutional structure."[2] Such a vision, implicit or explicit, underlies most of the economic development theories and policies of today. But it is a wishful thought. As Nobel laureate chemist and underground economist Frederick Soddy pointed out long ago: "You cannot permanently pit on absurd human convention such as the spontaneous increment of debt [compound interest], against the natural law of the spontaneous decrement of wealth [entropy]."[3]

AN IMPOSSIBILITY THEOREM

The starting point in our thinking about economic development should be an impossibility theorem: that a US-style high mass consumption economy for a world of four billion people is impossible to achieve, and even if it could

---

[2] W. W. Rostow: *The Stages of Economic Growth*. Cambridge University Press, 1960, p. 7.
[3] *Cartesian Economics*. London: Hendersons, 1922, p. 30.

be achieved it would be very short-lived. Even less possible is an ever-growing standard of consumption for an ever-growing population.

As a simple intuitive demonstration of the impossibility theorem consider the following. If it requires roughly one-third of the world's annual production of mineral resources to support that 6% of the world's population residing in the US at the standard of consumption to which it is thought that the rest of the world aspires, then it follows that present resource flows would allow the extension of the US standard to at most 18% of the world's population, with nothing left over for the other 82%. Without the services of the poor 82%, the "rich" 18% could not possibly maintain their wealth. A considerable share of world resources must be devoted to maintaining the poor 82% at at least subsistence. Consequently, even the 18% figure is an overestimate.

But, it will be objected, the answer is simply to increase total world resource flows. By how much would such flows have to increase to bring world per capita levels up to US per capita levels? By a factor of about 6 or 7, it turns out.[4] But this refers only to current production. To supply the rest of the world with the average per capita accumulation or "standing crop" of industrial metals already embodied in existing artefacts in the ten richest nations would require more than sixty years of production of these metals at 1970 rates.[5]

Neglecting the enormous problem of capital accumulation, for how long could the biosphere sustain even the sixfold increase in the through-put of materials and energy, much of which would be required just to maintain the miraculously accumulated capital stock? Already existing through-put levels are damaging life support capacity. A sixfold increase would be highly destructive. Furthermore the sixfold increase is a gross underestimate, not only because it neglects the problem of past differences in accumulation between rich and poor that must be made up, but also because it neglects diminishing returns. A sixfold increase in net, usable through-put implies a much larger increase in gross matter-energy through-put as we are forced to use poorer grade ores from less accessible places, and to dispose of ever larger quantities of waste. The gross through-put will increase much faster than the net, and it is the gross through-put that affects the environment.

The recognition of the long-run aggregate biophysical budget constraint is imperative. Equally imperative is the discipline to keep the scale of popula-

---

[4] Let M be the factor, R the annual world mineral production; 4 billion is the world population; 210 million is US population, then:

$$\frac{M \cdot R}{4 \times 10^9} = \frac{0.33R}{2.1 \times 10^8} - M = 6.35$$

[5] Harrison Brown: "Human Materials Production as a Process in the Biosphere". *Scientific American*, September 1970.

tion and per capita consumption within the biophysical budget. The ecological necessity of limiting economic growth at some level is irrefutable, and the evidence that current levels are unsustainable is persuasive. If one wants to evade the obvious conclusion that economic and demographic growth must be limited, then one must put one's faith in technological miracles. Even if one believes that such miracles will be possible in the future, does not common sense require that we limit the growth of scale while waiting for the second coming of Prometheus?

II. The moral necessity of limiting economic growth

From the impossibility theorem just discussed it follows that the total number of person-years of industrially developed living is limited. A number of important and difficult ethical questions arise.

How will the limited number of person-years of developed living be apportioned among nations? Among social classes within nations? Among generations? To what extent should present luxury be limited to permit more lives in the future? To what extent should sub-human life be sacrificed in exchange for more person-years of developed living? If a man is worth many sparrows, then we must take it for granted that a sparrow's worth is not zero. How many sparrow-years are worth one person-year? How many sparrow-years are worth the difference between one person-year of luxurious living and one person-year of frugal living? Should the burden of scarcity be made to fall more heavily on the present or the future? On the standard of consumption or on numbers of people?

Probably the main value of such questions lies more in their tendency to inspire humility rather than in any prospects for an answer. But lest one think that such questions can be ignored, it should be noted that varying answers have already implicitly been given at United Nations conferences in Stockholm, Bucharest and Rome. The leaders of overdeveloped countries seem to be saying that the burden of scarcity should fall more heavily on numbers, especially of the poor. Let the poor limit their populations. The leaders of the underdeveloped countries seemed to be saying that the burden should fall on the high consumption of the rich. Let the rich limit their per capita consumption. Both sides seemed willing to pass as much of the burden as possible on to the future and on to sub-human life. Let the future have fewer people, reduced per capita consumption, and fewer sub-human species.

The old Marxist class conflict between capital and labour has been softened by rapid economic growth. Struggle over relative shares is less intense when the absolute income of each class is increasing. But growth based on rapid resource depletion constitutes exploitation of the future. To the extent that we refrain from exploiting the future we sharpen the class conflict within the present generation. Ethical questions of fair distribution within one generation must be considered simultaneously with questions of equity between generations. In this three-way struggle the future has the great disadvantage of not-yet-existing. But it must be of some weight in a democratic society that future people greatly outnumber present people. If the present is to consume less for the sake of the future, then the rich of the present must bear most of the burden. All that can reasonably be asked of the poor is that they limit population growth while continuing economic growth up to a sufficient, not luxurious, level. The rich must limit population growth also, and reduce per capita consumption from luxury towards sufficiency.

"THE GREATEST GOOD FOR THE GREATEST NUMBER"?

I for one must confess that I do not know how many person-years of future life are worth one Cadillac, nor how many sparrow-years are worth the difference between one person-year of luxurious living and one person-year of frugal living. One hesitates even to raise such questions for fear that some econometrician will get a grant of public funds to build a model which maximizes a weighted sum of years lived by all species from now on, using the current market price fetched by the skins of each species as weights, and discounting by the interest rate on treasury bills! The best I can do is to offer a reconsideration of an old rule of right action which has played a large role in economics: the utilitarian or Benthamite rule of "the greatest good for the greatest number". There are three problems with the dictum:

1. *The definition of good:* In applying the rule economists have substituted measurable "goods" for the unmeasurable "good". The rule has become "the greatest production of goods and services for the greatest number". For very poor societies such a reduction of good to goods may be defensible, although even that is debatable. For an affluent country such a reduction is absurd. Even this reduced form of the dictum runs into two further problems.
2. *The problem of double maximization:* As is well known, only one variable can be maximized at a time. An increase in product can be had in exchange for a reduction in numbers, and vice versa. The dictum contains one too many "greatests". For one of these "greatests" we must substitute "sufficient". Which of the greatests should be substituted?
3. *The definition of number:* Does "number" refer to the population simultaneously alive now (or at some future date), or to the cumulative number ever to live over time? Usually it is taken as those currently alive, even though Bentham may have thought in terms of cumulative number ever to live. We might also ask whether number should count sub-human species in some appropriate way.

To meet these objections I would suggest the following reformulation as a general rule of right action: "sufficient per capita product for greatest number over time". In this reformulation we define number as number over time and suggest some appropriate consideration for sub-human life, but beg the question of defining "appropriate". We retain the economists' substitution of goods for the good in the interest of operationality, but apply to it the condition of "sufficient" rather than "greatest". Since production cannot be considered "the good" it should not be maximized. Production is clearly a good thing up to a point, but beyond some sufficient level further production no longer contributes to the good, and even begins to detract. By substituting sufficient for greatest we avoid the logical fallacy of double maximization and recognize that goods represents a greatly reduced form of "the good" and does not merit maximization.

Difficult as it is, we can at least have some idea of what is a sufficient per capita income for ourselves and for others not too unlike us. But we have no clue to what God considers a sufficient number ever to live in his creation over time. How long the world lasts is God's business, not ours.

DEFINING SUFFICIENCY?

It should be unnecessary to add that "greatest number over time", far from implying unlimited population growth, absolutely requires that the population of each generation be limited to the carrying capacity. "Thou shalt not destroy the capacity of creation to support life" is a logical extension of "thou shalt not kill". The setting up of some maximand such as production in the pursuit of which we destroy carrying capacity seems to be the modern form of idolatry, as well as poor stewardship.

The dictum "sufficient per capita product for the greatest number over time" is no magic philosopher's stone for giving easy solution to the difficult questions raised earlier, but it does seem a better principle of right action than that of the growth economy, which urges "greatest per capita product for the greatest number now". The latter principle sins against both logic and Christian ethics, and probably against Jeremy Bentham as well.

The concept of sufficiency plays no role in modern economic theory. To define sufficiency one must ask "sufficient *for what*?" The answer is "sufficient for a good life". The notion of sufficiency leads us back to the basic question of philosophy and religion: "What is a good life?" In its quest to become a positive science, economics has stifled this question and attempted to cut free from all religious and philosophical issues that could not be solved deductively or empirically. With consideration of the good life thus ruled out, there was no possibility for the issue of sufficiency to arise. Therefore learned men were led to concern themselves even more strenuously with satisfying their appetites, yet without raising the ever more obtrusive question of whether the appetite itself was excessive. Appetites can be excessive only in relation to sufficiency, which remained undefined because its definition would require some reference to the taboo concept of a good life. This is a ludicrous situation. However difficult or utopian it may appear to be to introduce sufficiency into economic theory and practice, it is even more utopian to think that economics can get along without the concept.

III. Some steps towards living with limits

An important step towards getting the concept of sufficiency into economics would be to recognize a long-run aggregate biophysical budget constraint—something like the ecologists' notion of permanent carrying capacity. It would refer to that level of through-put which the ecosystems of a country could continue to supply to the economy on a sustainable-yield basis, and the waste products of which could be taken back by the ecosystem in a sustainable way. In other words the supply of both low entropy matter-energy inputs and the service of assimilation of high entropy waste outputs must be restricted to a level sustainable by the ecosystem.

Therefore, three kinds of interdependent limits must be institutionalized. First, the real biophysical budget must be recognized and given a financial counterpart. I have suggested either a depletion quota auction or a national ad valorem severance tax as effective and efficient means of limiting the through-put flow. Second, the need to limit population has long been apparent and many schemes suggested. I will not pursue that issue here. We need a third institution for limiting the range of inequality in per capita resource consumption. Simple minimum and maximum limits on individual income would restrict inequality without implying a jealous quest for flat equality.

Throughout I have spoken of per capita resource consumption rather than standard of living or quality of life. Limiting resource consumption certainly does not foreclose all possibility of improving the standard of living. It merely directs our efforts towards improving efficiency and away from increasing the scale of resource through-put. Efficiency cannot increase forever, but we still have a long way to go in that direction.

Sufficiency has still not been defined. We have only argued that the concept is necessary and that even the vaguest definition is better than ignoring it. Schumacher attempts a definition of sufficiency along the lines of St Ignatius Loyola. The goal of man is salvation. Man should make use of the resources of the rest of creation just so far as they help him to attain this goal, and should withdraw from their use just so far as they hinder him. That may be more a restatement of the problem than an answer, but at least it focuses our attention in the right direction.

My own view is that we in the United States have some withdrawing to do. We must limit our resource consumption for our own spiritual welfare as well as for ecological reasons. Probably it will be enough of a challenge for now to stop growth in our resource consumption scale, which is sufficient if justly and wisely used. We will never seek greater justice and wisdom in resource use as long as we believe that we can submerge all inequalities in a sea of absolute abundance.

A "THIRD WAY"

This vision of ever-growing abundance has been the common ideal of both capitalism and communism. Wishful thinking and technical determinism transcend ideologies. Capitalist and communist economic theories both put growth in first place. One of the first Christian thinkers to seek a third way, neither capitalism nor communism, was G. K. Chesterton. Towards the end of his losing battle for "distributism" (as he called his third way), he made the following reflection: "I now realize... that what we have taken on is something much bigger than modern capitalism or communism combined. I realize that we are trying to fight the whole world; to turn the tide of the whole time we live in; to resist everything that seems irresistable...

"For the thing we oppose is something of which capitalism and collectivism are only economic by-products... It is so vast and vague that its offensiveness is largely atmospheric; it is perhaps easier to defy than to define. But it might be approximately adumbrated thus: it is the spirit which refuses Recognition or Respect."[6]

Chesterton goes on to argue that if men refuse to recognize the natural boundaries inherent in their created beings, and refuse to respect their Creator's transcendence, then they have nothing left to recognize and respect except their own desires and their own ability to satisfy them. Economic growth unconstrained by natural limits or considerations of sufficiency (growth-mania) is a direct result of the spirit which refuses recognition or respect. Recognition of the limits inherent in our created being and respect both for our Creator and the sub-human part of his creation are the first and most important steps towards a just and sustainable economy, and offer the best possibility for a reconciliation between capitalism and communism.

A Third World Perspective

C. T. KURIEN

The Planning Committee of the conference has asked me to deal with self-reliance and economic growth in developing countries within the context of the continuing ecumenical discussion on a just, participatory and sustainable society. I get the impression that there is an implicit assumption that of the three adjectives—just, participatory and sustainable—the most important or at least the most urgent is "sustainable". This is reflected in the Planning Committee's poser to the participants in the discussion:

"Assuming that there is a limit to the earth's capacity to supply continuing worldwide economic growth and constantly expanding standard of living for all people, Christian ethics demand that the rich world's material growth should taper off while the poor world continues to grow. Do you accept the underlying assumption? If so, what is the nature of the economic system which could deal with this situation? In what ways would this system challenge the traditional economics of the capitalist and socialist world?"

I cannot claim to have any special competence in the area of Christian ethics. I am willing to accept that Christian ethics demands justice, but I am not sure that justice is based on the principle of arithmetic average. In any

[6] "The Issue of the Indiscriminate". *G. K.'s Weekly*, 8, 9 March 1929, 411.

case, as a student of economics and of society, I know also that more growth does not necessarily mean greater share to the deprived (in spite of the oft-repeated dictum that when the cake grows, everyone can have more), and that more growth and less growth are not brought about by merely passing resolutions to that effect. If I had more time at my disposal I would have entered into a discussion of these aspects. But I am constrained to skip them and go directly to the "sustainable society".

Slogans that reflect a pampered minority

A new social order has been a major theme of the ecumenical movement almost from its inception, and the sustainable society is the latest manifestation of that urge. It is a response to the "limits to growth" uproar of the early seventies. I have tried to analyse why the limits to growth theme has become such a box-office hit. After all, it stated a very simple and obvious proposition that because of the finiteness of resources, unlimited growth is not possible. I believe it hit the headlines for two reasons.

The first is that this simple proposition was uttered by the scientist-oracles of the modern times who relied on the latest computers to arrive at this statement of the shape of things to come. It will be interesting to examine the social psychology that results in a near absolute faith in scientists and their modern crystal balls. But I cannot do it now.

My second reason is related to the political economy of the affluent nations, particularly the affluent capitalist nations of the West. As the material abundance of these nations grew after the Second World War, growth became the national creed as never before in history. It came to be accepted also that steady growth could be sustained only through equally steady wasting of resources. In the name of economic progress, profligacy became the chief national virtue with the mass media as its main propagators. Increasing use of resources came to be thought of as the symbol of social progress. It is reported that the Senate of the United States went on record in the late sixties with a sense of national pride, I presume, that the people of the country (just a 7% of the world's population) had used up in the decade of the sixties more resources than the entire humankind in all previous history. It is this grand American dream of endless expansion and ever-growing affluence that was disturbed by the limits to growth oracle. The oracle spoke about the finite resources of the planet earth, but the message was clear: the American way of life cannot be sustained in America itself and in other parts of the world where tiny islands of affluence had emerged in vast oceans of plain living.

May I submit that the limits to growth slogan and its antidote, the "sustainable society", are both reflections of the anxiety of a pampered minority that its way of life is being threatened. This was probably not clear when the Americans held on tenaciously to the dream of the two-car "average" family, but in the summer of 1979 when gas stations have to be closed down systematically, big cars have to be abandoned out of necessity, and people who were always on the move have to stand in lines for gasoline, there is no doubt what the writing on the wall means. The future shock has come, shockingly different from what it was forewarned to be.

Nor is this all. The clever manipulators of capitalism are still making profits, from trash, from scarcity, through pollution, through anti-pollution—and above all through their propaganda that private affluence is still necessary and possible. For the law and logic of capitalism is accumulation and more accumulation, and converting the limited resources of the spacecraft earth into private affluence and accumulation is not prohibited by the rules of the game. Capitalism today confronts a major dilemma: by its *raison d'être* it must grow, accumulate and expand; but nature now sets limits, and makes it impossible for it to pursue its vocation. The "sustainable society" is a naive alternative put forward by innocent economists who like to feel that their science has a remedy for any problem related to resources.

But of course the advocates of "sustainable society" claim for it very noble motivations. According to some of them, reduction in the rate of utilization of the resources of the earth today is a duty that the present generation owes to the future generation. This sudden concern with the generations yet to be born could have been interpreted as an indication of the maturity of the human race. This would have been so if the same concern were shown about the plight of the generations that are with us today. Otherwise one is justified in making a profane paraphrase of St John and saying: If you claim to be concerned about the unborn humanity that you cannot see, but show no regard for the humanity that you can see around you, then you are a liar. It is a small affluent minority of the world's population that whips up a hysteria about the finite resources of the world and pleads for a conservationist ethic in the interests of those yet to be born; it is the same group that makes an organized effort to prevent those who now happen to be outside the gates of their affluence from coming to have even a tolerable level of living. It does not call for a divine's insight to see what the real intentions are.

Anxieties not real for the vast majority

The advocates of the sustainable society concept try desperately hard to cover up the lie by proclaiming that the concept is internationally applicable and that, in the interest of a global sustainable society, the rich nations must reduce their growth and the poor nations must accelerate theirs. To me it appears to be a very jejune argument. For one thing, I do not believe in any prescription about "growth", whether it is to increase growth or to decrease growth, which does not also spell out the social processes that will make that prescription operational. Growth is not a number to be manipulated at will, but a societal phenomenon showing clearly the marks of the social fabric on what is being produced, how and for whom it is produced.

I must also insist that the anxieties that underlie the sustainable society concept are not real for the vast majority of human kind. Let me make this contention concrete with reference to the pattern of living of people of my own country. According to the latest information available, the per capita monthly expenditure of people in the rural areas of India (80% of a total population of some 650 million) is Rs.53 with Rs.39.7 spent on food and Rs.13.3 spent on non-food items. A more detailed breakdown will give a clearer picture of the pattern of life of these vast multitudes. Of the approximately Rs.40 spent on food, cereals claim Rs.23, milk and milk products Rs. 3.8, pulses Rs. 2.0, vegetables Rs.2.0., edible oil Rs.2.0, sugar Rs.1.7, meat, fish and eggs Rs.1.4, spices Rs.1.3, beverages Rs.1.2, and fruits and nuts Rs.0.6. The major items of non-food expenditure are clothing Rs.3.6, fuel and light, Rs.3, tobacco and intoxicants Rs.1.5, durable goods including footwear Rs.1.0, and miscellaneous goods and services Rs.4.2. I can assure you that the main item under the miscellaneous category is not gasoline! According to prevailing exchange rates the US dollar is equal to about Rs.8, the British pound approximately Rs.17 and the Russian rouble about Rs.10. On this basis you can convert the figures I have given into currencies you are familiar with to get a mental image of the conditions of living of some of your fellow people. Please remember also that the figures I have mentioned are averages, and possibly 75% of the population comes below the average. Similar figures can be given from many other countries of the Third World also, which really constitutes two-thirds of the world's population.

Usually these figures are quoted to show how utterly poor the bulk of humanity is, and that must be accepted as a fact. But there is more to it. You will notice how little of the so-called "scarce resources" of the earth enters into their consumption patterns directly. Even indirectly the only scarce non-renewable resource on which their lives depend is land for cultivation. This means that even if all the petroleum were to be exhausted, all the coal and copper were to be used up, *the poor would survive*. While it is a truism that the fittest will survive, there is no reason to believe that the fattest are also the fittest. In reality, as in Pharoah's dream, the opposite may well be the case. I do not for a moment imply that the bulk of humanity must be kept at such miserably low levels. I shall come back to this issue later. But if it is true that the vast majority of human beings are far removed from the threats posed by "limits to growth", in whose name are we conducting our "sustainable society" discussions?

Since I have been asked to refer specifically to growth in developing countries, may I draw your attention to a few more aspects of life and change in my own country? The population of India, according to the 1951 census, the first after Independence, was 355 million, and everybody, particularly experts from the West, considered the country vastly "overpopulated". In those days few dared to believe that 30 years from then the population of that already dangerously "overpopulated" country would be 700 million. But it is. During the same period food production also increased from 55 million tonnes to close to 130 million tonnes. This too has been quite an impressive performance. And here is a paradox for those who take only an arithmetic approach to growth. No other period of Indian history has witnessed such pronounced increase in population; yet in no other 30-year period has there been a more or less steady increase in per capita income in the country! And to those who mechanically proclaim that growth is good for the poor, may I point out that that impressive record of growth and increase in per capita income did not benefit the bottom 40%, but went to fatten further those at the top.

One more puzzle. Recently when the new popular government came up with a New Strategy of Development to eradicate poverty and unemployment, the target of food production for 1983 was set at 145 million tonnes, increasing the daily per capita availability of food from 0.52 kg in 1978 to 0.57 kg in 1983 because it was scientifically calculated that the *demand* for food (not the *need* for food) would not exceed it.

How do we interpret these apparently bizarre phenomena? Do we say that India still continues to be part of that mysterious Orient beyond the rationalities of science, the logic of modern economics, and now the ethics of the ecumenical movement? Or do we say that words like "growth" and "sustainable society" are empty, though emotive, and that therefore one cannot discuss them effectively unless one puts content into them?

I have already put *a* content into the concept of the "sustainable society" as the term is now being used in western circles. To repeat, it is my contention that it reflects little more than the neurosis of the members of the Club of Affluence because their hitherto protected domains are being threatened. But as those who claim hegemony over the whole world, they naturally project their fears as a phenomenon encompassing the whole of human kind.

Socialist counter-heresy

If it were understood in these terms, it would not have become necessary for the socialists of the world to come up with the counter-heresy that all talk of the finiteness of physical resources is just capitalist propaganda, and that under socialism unlimited growth is both possible and necessary. No one can deny that the increase in the production of material goods is a necessary condition to move up from the realm of necessity to the realm of freedom. But socialist dogma misrepresents this proposition when it is argued that an increase in the abundance of things is also a sufficient condition for freedom, and that the more things a society has, the closer it is to becoming genuinely free. In relation to things a socialist society certainly differs in many ways from a capitalist society, but that does not prevent a socialist society from becoming a slave to material abundance, or from falling into the error of curbing the spirit of the human being as a means to have more things to set one free! To pretend that this danger does not exist in a socialist state is to become blind to what history, including contemporary history, has to show.

I must return to the main theme—just, participatory and sustainable society. I am sure all of us want it. But how and where? Stone walls do not a prison make, says the old adage; neither do emotive adjectives make a society. How, then, do we *make* a just, participatory and sustainable society?

I submit that we do not achieve it either through technical calculations of sustainability supplied by scientists and experts or through theoretical assertions about justice, put forward by philosophers and theologians. What determines whether a society is just or will be sustained is the *actual* pattern of participation in its affairs by its members. It means, for instance, that in a capitalist society a just, participatory and sustainable society is not achieved primarily through the arithmetic of sustainability, but by realizing that the so-called institutionally neutral market mechanism is very much an ally of those who own and control resources and that its operations will make the vast majority of people effectively non-participants when it comes to questions on how resources are to be utilized. In a socialist country it means recognizing that a mere legal socialization of the means of production does not ensure justice unless provisions are made for effective participation in economic and political decision-making processes by all members of society. And in countries like mine where millions of people linger at the survival level, and an increase in the growth of goods and services is a necessary condition for human dignity, it means recognizing that growth cannot ensure freedom and justice without the willing participation in it by the masses who alone must decide what must be produced and how much.

Effective participation by *all* members of society in the social processes does not come about without effort in any part of the world; in most instances it will call for sustained struggle. Just and sustainable societies will emerge in our lands if we too join in these struggles when we return to our homelands.

Economics and World Hunger

Diogo de Gaspar

In memory of a very dear friend, Luis Carlos Weil, who gave me the opportunity to join the ecumenical movement and from whom I have learned so much about it.

I should like to start by stating some very well known facts which give shape to our debate. If no major event happens, the population of the earth, which in 1850 was 1,262 million, and in 1975 was 3,968 million, will in the year 2000 probably be 6,254 million. Of this population, in 1950 34% were living in developed regions; in 1975 that figure went down to 29%; and in 2000, it is expected to go down to 22%. The population in less developed regions, therefore, was 66% in 1950 and 71% in 1975; in the year 2000, it is expected to be 78%.

It is quite clear that the minority, living in the developed parts of the world, at this stage consume about 75% of the world's resources. They control about 88% of the gross world product, 80% of world trade and investment, 93% of its industry and almost 100% of its scientific and technological research.

Vertical and horizontal proliferation

I am using these figures to explain that I am not going to talk about growth. Borrowing terminology from the section that deals with atomic energy, I want to speak about vertical and horizontal proliferation. My contention is that within the framework of this conference we might reaffirm the true faith: that the horizontal proliferation of science and technology will become the major correction of the past and the main task of the future.

So far, growth theory has been the terminology and world-view that corresponds to a concept of historical triumphalism, and most history has been written by and about the triumphalists. In fact, we have a world that is a museum of history: we have coexisting systems and phases of history at the same time in different geographical areas. What I mean by horizontal proliferation is the spread of enough science, enough wealth, enough technology that humankind can catch up with history and rise from the levels of poverty that C. T. Kurien has described so dramatically. Perhaps such a change will respond to the main concerns of Herman Daly—not through a process of very logical, very rational, very cool decision-making, but through a major struggle in the near future.

Growth in the traditional way will probably curve down at its peaks among small groups of the world, giving place to a horizontal growth in the spreading and sharing of wealth, ownership, and science and technology. The pressure of population will probably be the dynamic element calling for that major change in the world. In present-day discussions in official circles, this is called a new international economic order.

Perhaps one of the Christian sins is the perversion of the concept of charity from its original form, so that now governments can borrow this perverted Christian concept in order to shape mechanisms of "aid" where no responsibility exists, where the decision to give remains with the wealthy. They decide how much to give, what for, when, in which form. And they ask their so-called recipients to be gracious and not raise any further points.

Thinking of two concerns of this conference, food and energy, we see that at this stage food, worldwide, is a major asset in the hands of the developed countries. After the Second World War there was a tremendous concentration of food production in the north-western region, which today produces about 80% of the wheat consumed outside that region. Energy is no more in the hands of the industrialized countries, but in those of a new group of countries that finally raised their consciousness and started using oil in order to develop themselves. The non food-producing countries and the non oil-producing countries—the vast majority of the world today—are caught, as our African brothers say, under the fight of two elephants. And when two elephants fight, the grass pays for it.

Food: distribution, production and security

I have been asked to speak about food. You have an extremely well informed chapter on the subject in the preparatory book for this conference (*Faith, Science and the Future*, Chapter 10). I want to point out that, to tackle the issue within the world context just set forth, there are three interacting issues: distribution, production and security.

There are more hungry people in the world now than there have ever been. More than 1,000 million may not get enough to meet their energy calorie requirements. And over 450 million of these, or a quarter of the population of the developing market economies, are estimated to suffer from serious undernutrition. Over 60% of them live in the most seriously affected countries, mostly in the Far East, and the majority are rural people.

For many, hunger or undernutrition means diminished ability to work, cope with infection and other environmental stresses, enjoy the normal satisfactions of life, raise and educate healthy children. Hunger, the result of deprivation of food in adequate quantity, is one—and by far the most widespread—manifestation of the nutrition problem. Inadequate dietary quality results in various forms of malnutrition, which affects children more than any one else. Every year in developing countries 50 million children die from malnutrition and disease, as compared to half a million in developed countries. In the poorest countries, of those children who survive, between one quarter and one half suffer from severe or moderate protein energy malnutrition.

Hunger and the various forms of malnutrition all constitute specific manifestations of the overall problem of inadequate nutrition. Although the distinction among the forms is not always clear-cut, their consequences can be measured in terms of both human suffering and the drag on socio-economic development caused by their effects on mortality, morbidity, mental and physical development, creativity and productivity. Poverty is the common cause of all of them—except, of course, overnutrition mainly associated with affluence. But in the context of efforts to reduce poverty, different specific measures are required to deal with the various manifestations of nutritional inadequacy.

Hunger is essentially a food problem, the solution of which will require both greater production and improved distribution of food. Governments can take immediate interim measures to complement and support the necessary long-term development efforts.

Raising the food intake of the over 450 million severely undernourished to the level of their nutritional requirements would involve the equivalent of 40-60 million tons of wheat per year. This is no more than 3-5% of present world cereal consumption, or 10-15% of the cereals now being fed to livestock in the developed countries.

Longer term prospects need to be investigated in the dynamic setting of population growth, estimated food supplies and inequalities in food distribution. Present food supplies could adequately feed the world's entire population if they were more equitably distributed. Distribution according to need would probably be the least expensive way to eradicate hunger. Food production would then need to increase at only about the rate of population growth. Such statements are theoretically sound but not very realistic. Any attempt to approach the problem as one of food production only would be similarly unrealistic. To reduce undernutrition significantly requires efforts of both production and distribution.

Food distribution patterns in market economies depend largely on three factors: income and its distribution, the price of staple foods, and the relation of growth in caloric consumption to growth in income (income elasticity of demand for calories). This last varies greatly, reflecting social and cultural factors influencing consumption.

Interaction of these factors and the likely impact on nutrition by 1995 have been analysed by the World Bank in the case of five major countries: India, Pakistan, Bangladesh, Brazil and Morocco. Assuming no change in income distribution (although evidence from a number of countries suggests that it may have worsened in recent years), the study concludes that only under the most optimistic and perhaps least likely conditions (high average per capita income growth and stable food prices) would hunger be significantly reduced by 1995. Even then, there would be over 150 million people in these five countries whose diets would not fully contain sufficient calories. Low income growth and slightly increasing food prices—not an implausible assumption—would combine to increase hunger steadily.

This and other analyses all point to the same conclusion: present policies will not solve the hunger problem. A solution requires reorientation of policies with a thrust towards achieving food security for all social groups everywhere, now and in the future. This will require (1) fundamental long-term development efforts with a special focus on the food problem, (2) interim measures to arrest the increase of hunger, and (3) immediate relief for hundreds of millions now suffering from undernutrition. It will also require improved understanding of the linkages between national responsibilities and international cooperation.

The specific measures that could effectively reduce nutrition-related health hazards are an issue of intense debate. However, experiences in greatly varying countries, developed and developing, suggest that it should be possible to reduce greatly malnutrition well in advance of the fruition of fundamental long-term efforts. It is a recorded fact that during the last World War, when rationing was introduced, for instance, in the UK, the population was in a better nutritional position than when purely market forces were in control.

The technologies for increased food production are well known. There is a great deal to be done yet, but this is one of those areas where horizontal proliferation can give quick results, provided that the known technologies are adequately absorbed and adapted for local uses. Kurien mentioned the expanded production of food in India. But, as he said, it does not solve the distribution problem. India, after three or four years of good harvests, has some 20 million tons of reserves of grain; but the general level of nutrition of the population has not yet been altered.

The spreading of these technologies will require huge amounts of capital. The investment requirements for agricultural technology for the period covering 1975 to 1990 in only 36 countries of Asia, Africa and Latin America—including water resources, irrigation, land settlement, roads, disease eradication, fertilizer, seed, mechanization and research extension—are estimated to be of the order of $98,890 million. This capital needs to be generated—and shared.

This conference has chosen the most crucial issues of our time: the three basic forms of energy—faith, food and oil.

Reactions and Comment

The concerns of de Gaspar for the food problem won wide assent in the conference. The debate between Daly and Kurien evoked major discussion in this plenary session and in the coffee breaks and continuing conversations. Among the questions raised were these:

1. Was the argument between Daly and Kurien really as sharp as it seemed to be? Since Kurien agreed that the impossibility of unlimited growth was a "simple and obvious proposition", did he not join Daly in rejecting the "growthmania" of Rostow and others? Did Daly not agree with Kurien's attack on the "grand American dream of endless expansion"? And did they not concur in their criticisms of both conventional capitalist and conventional socialist theories of growth?

2. Although Daly said that "the rich of the present must bear most of the burden" of change and that the United States in particular must withdraw from its excessive consumption, did he show any way of making his proposals operational? And if not, was his argument (in Kurien's word) "jejune"?

3. Did Kurien, in showing India's rising agricultural productivity, take account of what Daly called the subsidization of agriculture through non-renewable resources? Would "the poor" really survive if all the petroleum and petroleum-based fertilizers were exhausted? Had John Francis earlier supported Kurien's position when he said that "the economic trauma that is to come" may be hardest on industrialized countries (Chapter 10)? Had Liek

Wilardjo challenged Kurien's position when he said that "the poorest countries have been hardest hit" by the energy crisis (Chapter 9)?

4. Can Daly's concern for the future be embodied in social policies without hurt to living poor people in the present world?

5. Was Kurien right that the conference considered "sustainability" more urgent than justice and participation? Or did sustainability, as some participants argued, get the least emphasis of the three?

6. What might either Daly or Kurien make of de Gaspar's reckoning that about $100 billion would be required for the horizontal proliferation of agricultural technologies in 36 countries over 15 years?

The discussion of these questions continued in many sections and was a special concern of Section VIII, "Economics of a Just, Participatory and Sustainable Society". Eventually the conference recommended that, since work on these issues was still "in an early stage", the WCC "continue the work begun at the 1978 Zürich Consultation on Political Economy, Ethics and Theology" (see recommendations coming from Section X, Volume 2).

13. Energy for the Future

Introduction

The Working Committee on Church and Society over the past several years had conducted studies in two selected areas of scientific-technological change: energy and biological sciences (emphasizing genetics). They were chosen both for their intrinsic importance and as examples of problems that called for new ethical thinking in the churches. The Working Committee therefore included these two areas in plans for the world conference, scheduling plenary sessions on them and organizing sections to deal with them.

The prior studies on energy took shape at the WCC conference on Science and Technology for Human Development (Bucharest, July 1974). That meeting led to an Ecumenical Hearing on Nuclear Energy in Sigtuna, Sweden (June 1975), where the WCC called on eminent scientists with clashing opinions to work together with representatives of the WCC. The papers for that hearing and the findings were published in *Anticipation*, No. 21, October 1975, and in the book *Facing up to Nuclear Power*, edited by John Francis and Paul Abrecht.[1]

As the public debate and the discussions of member churches mounted, the Working Committee on Church and Society continued its work, both in studying the issues and in organizing the project "Energy for My Neighbour". With the authorization of the Central Committee of the WCC, it presented a position paper to the International Atomic Energy Agency (Salzburg, 1977). This paper (*Anticipation*, No. 24, November 1977) relates energy to "the struggle for a new and more just international economic order". It calls for "the widest possible discussion of issues, because every human being has a voice and a stake in those issues". It recognizes nuclear energy as "one of several possible options for the future in many countries", but insists that its availability should not "diminish the search for alternative, long-term, safer forms of energy". It warns that "the maturity of the nuclear energy system is not yet such as to justify its worldwide application", and it calls

---

[1] Edinburgh: St Andrews Press, 1976, and Philadelphia: Westminster Press, 1976.

special attention to the risks of the fast breeder reactor. Finally, it asks all people to recognize "that they are not God, that their power has its limits, that not all problems yield to technological solutions, that humanity must learn to live with nature as well as to harness its resources".

Later, at the request of the Central Committee, Church and Society organized a major consultation—a follow-up of the Sigtuna hearing and subsequent activities—on Ecumenical Concerns in Relation to Nuclear Energy at Bossey, Switzerland, in May 1978. The sixty participants, including scientists, theologians and church leaders from many parts of the world, differed widely in their opinions about nuclear energy. Their report and some of the addresses given at Bossey are printed in *Anticipation*, No. 26, June 1979.

Soon after this consultation, the Working Committee on Church and Society, meeting at Erfurt in August 1978, summed up its findings to that point. It was consistently concerned about the whole set of issues connected with energy, but it gave special attention to the controversies about nuclear energy. In a summary presented to the WCC Central Committee at Kingston, Jamaica (January 1979), it sought to put the nuclear debate in a technical, economic, social and theological context that would do justice to its complexity. Saying that nuclear energy could neither be accepted nor rejected categorically, it concluded: "It is a conditional good, subject to reasoned acceptance under some circumstances and subject to reasoned rejection in others. Even where accepted there may be a point when we may have to say: 'Thus far and no further'." And it urged the churches to continue working on the issues, not foreclosing discussion by "silencing the variety of opinions" (*Anticipation*, No. 26, June 1979).

The documents coming out of this sequence of studies have been published in *Anticipation* (see Nos 20, 21, 23, 24 and 26). In addition, the preparatory volume for the 1979 conference, *Faith, Science and the Future*, included three chapters on the issues. Two of them constituted a debate: Chapter 7, "Energy: the Argument for Keeping All Options Open—Including Nuclear", and Chapter 8, "The Argument for Emphasizing Renewable Energy Sources". Chapter 9, "The Churches and the Debate about Nuclear Energy", was a narrative and analytical summary—far more detailed than the foregoing four paragraphs—of discussions on the issue in the churches and the WCC.

Thus the 1979 conference was in many ways a continuation of an already extensive process. It was in other ways a fresh event, with new voices entering in.

Participants came to the plenary session on 17 July with high expectations. The press and television cameras were more obvious than in most sessions. The three addresses had different purposes. Shem Arungu-Olende, an electrical engineer from Kenya and currently a member of the UN staff in New York, analysed the world energy situation in the manner of an international civil servant. In his presentation the specific problems of nuclear energy were a very small part of the total world problem. He emphasized the urgency of the situation in its many aspects: technical, economic, political and ethical.

The next two addresses were designed to constitute a debate—and they unquestionably did. David Rose, professor of nuclear engineering at MIT, advocated inclusion of nuclear energy among the sources for the near future. His address included projected slides and original cartoons. He distributed to the participants a long paper, of which only about half can be printed here. Jean Rossel, professor of physics at the University of Neuchâtel, Switzerland, argued against nuclear energy. His paper is printed with minor abridgment.

A fourth scheduled speaker, Vladimir F. Pominov of the USSR, was unable to be present. However, the earlier address of Bo Lindell on risk assessment (see Chapter 6) has major relevance to this plenary session.

An Interpretation of the Global Energy Problem

SHEM ARUNGU-OLENDE

As we look at the issue of energy in the world today, we are awed at its complexity. We are also surprised at how little is known about the important factors that bear on energy use. Our knowledge about energy resources is minimal at best. The paucity of knowledge is more pronounced in the case of new and renewable sources of energy, largely due to their diversity in nature and technology. Projections about future availability and demand are speculative and could be misleading as a basis for future policy analysis and formation.

We are also brought face to face with economic, social and environmental problems associated with the development and use of energy resources. And there are ethical issues related to the disparity in consumption between the developed and developing countries.

We know that global energy use will continue to grow, conceivably at a lower rate if corrective action is taken in good time. We also know that major resources, notably petroleum and natural gas, are soon running out. This should convince us that the time for the development of alternative sources of energy is now. It will not be an easy task. It will be costly in resources. But it has to be done.

Why is energy so important?

Energy, in one form or another, is required in practically all aspects of human activity. It has been said that the life of contemporary civilization is energy.

The role energy plays in the economic development and wellbeing of a country has generated a great deal of attention, especially in the light of the growing scarcity of such major resources as petroleum and natural gas. Assessment of the interdependence between energy and the economy, especially at the national level, has been undertaken for many countries with a view to developing methodologies for estimating future energy requirements. But this has been a difficult task; and the results have been inconclusive, for the relationship between energy and the economy is a complex one. Energy availability and use affect every facet of the economy in a manner that has yet not been clearly understood. To add to this complexity is the fact that energy is used in different forms; moreover, there are regional differences in energy use, and it also varies according to the time of the year and the time of the day.

The task is the more difficult for developing countries, where not all the facets of economic activities are included. A large proportion of these activities are concentrated in rural areas. Most of them have not been quantified; some are indeed non-quantifiable. Moreover, energy inputs for most activities in the rural (and, to a sizable extent, urban) areas are derived from the traditional, so-called non-commercial forms of energy, including wood and wood products, plant and animal wastes; these are not normally reflected in the analysis.

However, there are experts, especially in the developed countries, who point to the evidence of a causal relationship between energy consumption and economic development. But even they have become cautious about the exact nature and, in particular, the direction of the relationship.

The energy problem

That there is an energy problem is not in dispute. Suffice it to say that the nature of the energy problem is complicated, and different people or groups define it differently according to their particular interests and objectives.

Individuals are, for example, concerned with high prices and availability of petroleum products, growing scarcity and high prices of wood and wood products, limitation of travel and probable changes in life-styles.

Energy industries are concerned with increased exploration and production, as well as distribution, of energy resources and the extent to which government attitudes, taxes and regulations impact on these. They also see their problems as deriving from the climate of uncertainty generated by, so they claim, their government's lack of clearly-defined energy policies. In recent times the attitudes of consumers (or at least their perception of the role played by the energy industry in making the consumers' lives difficult) has been of concern to the energy industry.

Environmentalists, on the other hand, define the problem according to the negative impact that exploration, development, and use of alternative energy resources may have on the environment. They may, for example, be concerned with the reclaiming of strip-mined land in arid areas, the social impact of different modes of transporting coal, the health hazards of burning fuels.

Governments see the problem of unavailability of data; inadequacy of institutional framework for developing and implementing energy policy and programmes; the inadequacy of human and financial resources to develop conventional or alternative sources of energy, etc. They are also concerned about security of supply and the need to reduce overdependence on imported supplies. Oil-importing countries are constantly worried about the financial burden from importing oil at ever rising prices and the negative impact this has on their balances of payments, economic growth and development in general. Oil-exporting countries are concerned about how best to utilize surplus funds, especially in the light of spiralling inflation and the erosion of the purchasing power of the funds obtained from the sale of oil. Practically all governments lack a viable energy policy and an integrated energy development strategy that reflects the real needs of the country and that is in harmony with other developmental objectives.

Thus there are divergent views of the nature of energy problems. These divergent views must be reconciled, to the extent possible. Now is the time to develop a coherent framework within which various elements of energy issues and problems can be addressed.

Energy demand patterns

The demand for energy in the world has been growing steadily over the last decades in response to rapid industrialization, growth in population, rise in per capita income and standards of living, and concomitant increase in propensity to waste energy resources.

A closer look at the past consumption patterns leads to the following observations:

1. Except for breaks during the two world wars and during the depression of the 1930's, the growth in global energy consumption has been exponential, and the rate of growth of world energy consumption has been nearly the same except for the breaks. Furthermore, growth in energy demand since World War II has been constant at 5,03% per annum.

2. There has been a wide disparity of consumption levels in the developed countries, on the one hand, and developing countries on the other. Thus, 29 years ago the developed countries, with less than one fourth of the world population, accounted for 75% of total commercial energy, compared with only 5,6% for the developing countries. The situation has improved only slightly since that date. The disparity is even more glaring when per capita energy consumption is considered. In 1976 developed countries, on the average, consumed 15 times more commercial energy than the developing countries. Needless to say, there has also been wide disparity in consumption levels within developed countries and within developing countries.

3. There has been a steady increase in the consumption of petroleum and natural gas and concomitant reduction in the share of coal. Energy consump-

tion in developing countries has been accompanied by shifts away from non-commercial (traditional) forms.

4. Consumption of commercial energy has been growing at a much faster rate in the developing than in the developed countries.

5. Growth in electricity consumption has, on the average, been faster than corresponding growth in total energy; the fastest growth rates in electricity consumption have been registered in the developing countries.

Each of the above observations has important implications for future patterns of energy demand and supply, and for relationships between countries. One is led to ask the following questions: How long will or can global energy consumption continue to grow exponentially? If the apparent constant exponential growth rate continues, are there adequate energy resources—renewable and non-renewable, conventional and non-conventional, commercial and non-commercial—to sustain this kind of growth into an infinite future? What can be done to change the pattern of growth and what are the implications of such action?

Chances are that the disparities in consumption levels will continue long into the future. In any case, no concerted effort is being made, to the best of my knowledge, to correct the imbalance. If left uncorrected, this could very well be an area of potential conflict between developed and developing countries. The inequality in levels of energy consumption also coincides with inequalities in wealth and in levels of technological advances. These have historically been associated with domination by one region (the developed countries) of another (the developing countries); and genuine fears have been expressed against the apparently increasing disparity. These fears are likely to increase in intensity, especially as available energy resources become scarce, and they may herald the days of major international conflicts that could threaten our very existence. Could a more just distribution of energy consumption share be targeted and achieved? What are the implications of such an action?

It is, however, difficult to project how far into the future the shift away from coal to petroleum and natural gas will be maintained. It will undoubtedly be influenced by comparative price advantages of petroleum and natural gas in relation to coal and by technological advances that bear on availability, production, processing, conversion, and ease of use. The coming depletion of petroleum and natural gas has generated intense anxiety that should spark off concerted effort to develop coal and alternative sources of energy. Or it could heighten the potential for conflict between developed and developing countries and bring closer the time for the conflict. The shift in the developing countries away from traditional to conventional commercial forms of energy is likely to continue. It implies, at least partially, that the faster growth of commercial energy consumption in these countries will be maintained, a trend which is bound to aggravate the scenarios mentioned above.

A comment

The end-use patterns vary considerably from country to country, depending on the size, level and rate of economic development; structure and level of industries; customs and life-styles; and availability and form of energy resources. No adequate effort has been given to the assessment of end use of energy and its influence on energy demand. Hence very little is really known about the structure of energy demand and the exact nature of factors bearing on this, including their mode of interaction. This is a serious situation, especially in the developing countries. Consequently, projections and forecasts of future energy use have been little more than intelligent guesses.

Many such forecasts have been based on the relationship between energy and economic activity as reflected in the Gross National Product (GNP). The nature of this relationship is not clearly understood, and the extent to which it holds in the developing countries has yet to be established. Moreover, forecasts of economic growth are themselves subject to great uncertainty, especially as the time horizon increases, say, beyond 1990.

Many forecasts also emphasize the causal relationship which exists between demand and supply of energy resources. There is uncertainty on the energy resources mix, heightened by inadequate information on the extent of remaining petroleum and natural gas resources, their future prices, expected rate of exploitation of coal resources, technological advances and breakthroughs in the development of new and renewable sources of energy.

And yet, future formulation and implementation at the national, regional, or international levels, and indeed action at the industrial level, depend on our ability to make accurate energy forecasts. This is an area that needs special and urgent attention.

This comment is not intended to downgrade the importance of forecasts. Rather it is meant to point out important gaps that must be filled in order for the forecasts to play their crucial role. Meanwhile, as has been said, "if the best that can be achieved is a broad brush of the future, then action must be planned on this broad picture".

Assessing energy resources

The preceding discussions on the future demand for energy lead to an important question. Will there be sufficient energy sources to meet the expected exponential growth in energy demand? There is no unequivocal answer to this question. Much depends on a number of factors, many of which are not known with any level of certainty. First, as noted, the nature of exponential growth in demand and of projections about future energy use. Second, the extent to which demand can be managed through conservation and more efficient use of energy. Third, how accurately conventional energy resources, notably coal, petroleum, natural gas, water resources, uranium, thorium and non-commercial resources (wood and wood products, plant and animal waste, etc.) can be estimated. Fourth, the extent to which conventional as well as non-commercial resources can be further explored and developed—through the application of improved technical and management techniques. Fifth, the extent and speed of development of new sources and renewable sources of energy. Sixth, policies and strategies for the development and utilization of energy resources. Seventh, socio-economic, financial, environmental and institutional constraints. The list is by no means complete.

Looking at conventional resources, we find abundant coal. There are also significant quantities of petroleum and natural gas, and of uranium and thorium. Estimates of hydro resources place them as vast. But these are only estimates. And it is a frustrating exercise to make any sense of them.

First, there seems to be no agreement whatsoever among the experts on the extent of these resources; there are as many estimates as there are experts. Second, there are no universally agreed upon definitions of resources, thus making it virtually impossible to make intercountry or inter-regional comparisons. There is another important shortcoming: practically all the estimates are based on information received from the energy industries, and so far no independent means of verifying these estimates are available. Special efforts should be made to correct these shortcomings. More effort should also be directed, on a global basis, at making detailed projections on which policy decisions can be made.

Conservation

The case for conservation, that is, for improving the efficiency with which energy is used, is compelling; it can lead to less dependence on energy, especially imported energy, and thus improve the balance of payments of a particular country. But above all, it extends reserves and thereby allows for time to develop alternative resources, to accommodate environmental problems, and to make inevitable social changes more palatable and more manageable.

But there are costs in implementing conservation policies. These should be carefully evaluated and action taken on the best possible compromises.

Further development of conventional resources

There is scope for improved techniques covering a wide spectrum of energy activities including exploration, production/mining, processing/refining, conversion, transportation, distribution and use of energy resources. If successful these would substantially—directly or indirectly—extend existing resources. I should like to cite a few examples. First, more geological, geochemical and geophysical research and development should ensure better understanding of geological formations, and the use of advanced scientific techniques including better data interpretations should ensure a reduction in the margin of error. New drilling methods should reduce costs and enhance accurate assessment of the resources. More exploration, especially in remote on-shore and off-shore areas, should result in more discoveries.

Second, more comprehensive surveys of coal resources have yet to be undertaken in the developing countries. These could conceivably lead to the discovery of more coal resources.

Third, improved methods of determining sub-surface hydrology and the development of quicker and cheaper methods of examining geological conditions, in aid of the assessment of hydraulic resources, should be undertaken.

Fourth, enhanced recovery of oil is possible. Most oil wells are idle, not because oil is exhausted, but because oil is no longer flowing. More than 70% of oil *in situ* will remain because only a small fraction (25-30%) can be recovered with current techniques and technologies. Many methods are currently being tried, including water flooding, gas flooding, thermal recovery, hydrocarbon miscible flooding, carbon dioxide flooding, polymer flooding. While a number of these have improved recovery rates, none has done so with sufficient net energy gain at an economic price.

These are but a few examples. They could make a big difference. But the extent of this difference is unknown.

New sources of energy

Interest in new and renewable sources of energy has been growing steadily. Many sources are available: solar, wind, biomass, ocean waves, tidal and geothermal to mention only a few. There are also possibilities for developing new technologies for the exploitation of known resources such as coal, oil shale and tar sands.

Estimating the magnitude of new and renewable sources of energy is a speculative exercise at best. Not enough is known about some of them and about the technologies for exploiting them. Indeed the diversity of these resources in nature, as well as technologies, precludes their detailed treatment. But one thing is clear: they are expected to make a progressive contribution in the energy supply picture in the future. This will only be possible if concerted effort is put into their development. Further research and development are required to establish technical and economic feasibility of these resources and associated technologies and to establish their social acceptability. For some, e. g. geothermal, more research and development are needed to assess the extent of the reserve. Economic and environmentally acceptable methods of exploiting oil shale and tar sands have yet to be commercially proved.

Policy

Most experts agree that energy policy will play an important if not decisive role in national economies in the future. And yet few, if any, governments have an energy policy. There has been a lot of talk but little action. And this is to be expected. For devising a policy that effectively covers and accommodates energy is not easy. Energy covers such a wide range of economic and human activity. Energy policy needs to be integrated, covering all energy sources, and should itself form part of an overall economic and social policy of the country. It should try to identify the major issues, to harmonize conflicts with other sectors and within the energy sector, to adequately match short-term and long-term considerations, and to ensure that more difficult long-term considerations are not sacrificed for the seemingly simple short-term ones.

This is a big task, one that calls on substantial national resources, and one that must be tackled on a multidisciplinary basis. It should also recognize that some aspects of energy issues are international in character and should be treated as such.

Goals and objectives for energy resources planning and development must be clearly defined. Without them it would be difficult to determine whether or not the desired state has been achieved and to evaluate the viability and effectiveness of a particular option.

Transition

That fossil fuels are depletable is no longer in question. Petroleum and natural gas have been increasing their share of consumption. They are less abundant and will run out faster than coal. A post-oil era is thus inevitable and inescapable.

It is difficult to imagine what that era will be like. During the transition period, soon to begin, the whole world will be facing a profound challenge, the response to which will shape the future of society.

The impact of change will be magnified manyfold, for energy crises will come side by side with other challenges facing humanity. An example of such a challenge is the revolution that will be wrought in the work place, arising from advances in solid-state electronics and in computers, in particular the microprocessor. With its amazing powers of memory and computations, microprocessors have potential applications almost everywhere: in offices, universities, hospitals, industries, farms, etc. The initial impact will be felt in the industrialized countries—in particular on the white-collar worker- where it is expected to bring an organizational revolution comparable in magnitude to that resulting from the introduction of the assembly line to the blue-collar worker.

It has been said that this revolution will produce drastic population bipolarization, which would probably represent an end of the road to western civilization as understood. It will in all probability cause massive social and economic dislocation, alienation, and despair. Under these conditions, the full impact of the energy crisis will hit us.

But that will not be all. There are in everyday life types of anxiety that afflict us—about personal circumstances or human conditions in the universe. These, too, have been heightened in recent times, thanks partly to advances in and application of science and technology.

The importance of self-esteem, strong self-concept, sense of security, and stability have been emphasized by students of human nature. These qualities are difficult enough to attain under any circumstances; but under the stressful conditions that govern our present lives, or that our children are bound to face, it has become more difficult to feel secure and stable in a world that changes so rapidly.

It will take a special effort of faith to maintain a modicum of serenity in the face of such stressful conditions. But let us not lose hope. For it has been said that every period of crisis may be a prelude to disaster or to marvellous things ahead. For all we know, the turmoil of the present and immediate future stressful times may be the harbinger of a beautiful butterfly era of civilization ahead.

Concluding remarks

That fossil fuel resources will run out is an accepted fact; of these petroleum and natural gas have been estimated to go by the turn of this century. But there is no agreement on which alternative energy sources will take up the slack; indeed it is doubtful if adequate resources will be available. And yet long-term needs of the world call for increase in energy use.

The time to ensure our future supply of energy is today. Time flies—we cannot afford to vacillate. Decisions for the development of alternative sources must be made now. Concerted action must be taken now. In this, we must have the will to succeed.

It has been said: "No victor believes in chance." We cannot afford to leave the future of energy resources development and use to chance; we have no alternative but to win if humanity is to survive. We must plan. We must identify the major problem areas in energy exploration, development and use. We must strive to cooperate in the resolution of energy issues and problems, in the development of better technologies. We must have faith in our ability to overcome the odds, to survive.

Towards a Sustainable Energy Future

DAVID J. ROSE

Energy is ubiquitously important to both industrialized and non-industrialized countries, affecting the whole fabric of their civilizations. It involves issues that relate to resources, technologies, ownership and possession, end uses, environmental impacts now and later, social purpose, growth and no-growth, national and international stability, future visions of society, local and global justice, exploitive dominion vis-à-vis responsible stewardship, and more.

Such a wide variety of issues tempts discussants to apply a principle of selective inattention—pretending that a few parts of the problem were the whole of it. The investigator either selectively ignores areas whose study might invalidate his analysis, or assumes that difficulties associated with those parts will be overcome by some *deus ex machina*.

Among all these issues, some that need to be factored in from the start are:

1. The traditional resources of energy—chiefly oil and natural gas—are disappearing; the remainder are becoming increasingly expensive, and selectively out of reach of various countries.

2. The world contains about four billion people, and that number will increase with time, barring some convulsive catastrophe.

3. The route to industrial development followed by the presently industrialized nations cannot be followed by non-industrialized ones, under anything like the present distribution of energy resources, because of increasing cost and scarcity.

4. However, large supplies of fossil fuels remain—chiefly coal. But relying on coal has problems.

5. Continued use of fossil fuels at anything like the present rate—let alone at increasing rates—will in one or two generations cause severe global environmental and climatic problems, dwarfing any that we have experienced hitherto.

6. Patterns of energy consumption do not change easily in the short term, but in the longer term many opportunities exist to use energy more efficiently and rationally, most prominent in the industrialized countries, but also in less industrialized ones.

7. The energy problem contains sub-issues with different time perspectives, and the disparate responses required to suit different sectors and time perspectives often find themselves in opposition.

8. In the long run—say more than fifty years from now—the only major available energy options will be solar or nuclear power, each in various forms.

Can any world strategy—with variations to match local regions and times—take into account all these and other lesser issues? We should not automatically assume that any generally appealing solution exists; civilizations have collapsed in the past, failing to recognize that their central policies were internally inconsistent and self-destructive. Many early civilizations must have suffered energy starvation, although they apparently could not analyse the trouble.

Our present task is to seek for goals and methods that lead to a more just, participatory and sustainable society.

Resources and time perspectives

Short-term expedients may foreclose serious long-term options, and each nation must take great care that its accommodation to today's realities does not limit its scope in dealing with the more distant future. For example, strong emphasis on expanding domestic oil production may deepen our dependence on oil and intensify the harshness of the eventual and inevitable withdrawal. This is a special danger for countries that are now highly industrialized.

Financial and political institutions are more responsive to the short-term view, dictated by market rates of return and by electoral intervals, than to the longer and broader view determined by the depletion of world resources. The shortest meaningful time perspective for serious social decisions in the private sector is determined by normal market expectations of rate of return on investments. This leads typically to time horizons usually of five to ten years, in present industrial practice. Investments maturing later are relatively unattractive. Exploratory research aimed at very distant returns can be justified, but by normal market rules the cost must be low. The political sector has a similar time perspective, determined by the intervals between elections.

The next longer time perspective relates to new energy options: solar power, new and cleaner ways of using coal, more resource-efficient nuclear fission reactors and fuel cycles, nuclear fusion, and mature energy conservation technologies. This time varies somewhat depending on the technology but may take twenty years or more except under the most exceptional conditions and strong government incentives. Civilian nuclear power, for example, which was accorded remarkable federal priorities in the United States, was first seriously explored in the early 1950's and only by the early 1970's was well enough developed to contribute 2% of the nation's electric power. (But the industrial momentum built up during all that time led to a 12% contribution in 1978.) Such a development programme is clearly beyond the view imposed by the market.

This disparity between the economic and technological time perspectives leads to market exploitation of existing options and neglect—possibly foreclosure—of potential new ones. Governments can correct this imbalance by either underwriting the long-term development itself, as a non-market social good, or constructing appropriate market signals—tax and other incentives, regulations, and so on—to stimulate option development by the private sector. Governments do both.

Several even longer time perspectives are also important. The time it takes to deplete a particular energy resource should exceed the time it takes to develop and deploy alternatives or to adjust to doing without. Other important time perspectives are even longer. The urban and industrial infrastructures of civilizations, which heavily influence our energy use, can persist for centuries. Cities, for example, change fundamentally only over generations; most of them are presently designed to operate on oil and natural gas.

Rational utilization and increased efficiency

I will use the common term "conservation" even though it is inaccurate and often has the wrong connotation. The broadest questions about energy policy deal with the balance of emphasis between supply and conservation. In general, supply is relatively overemphasized, because the supply sector is simpler and better organized to receive and recognize rewards. Conservation tends to offer rewards that are received later in time by a diffuse and ill-organized population. Thus effective energy conservation requires either a strong public awareness or government financial incentives, or both.

Energy conservation consists of two different categories of activity. The first is relatively simple cessation of present waste, which should become more general as people are made aware of the costs of waste. The second category concerns deeper changes in the economic structure, the designs of what we use, and public incentives. It is here that we focus our principle attention.

Energy supply costs money and the marginal cost of energy increases as more is demanded; however, in the relatively pristine field of rational utilization and increased efficiency, much can be done, particularly in highly industrialized countries.[1] Related to energy conservation is the question of how energy use and GNP are related. In the short run, reducing energy consumed reduces GNP, but the long-term possibilities are much better. As capital equipment is retired it can be replaced by equipment designed to use less energy, generally at higher cost.

New homes, automobiles and industrial machinery can be built at much higher energy efficiencies. Detailed analyses suggest that, overall, energy used per unit of GNP could be as much as halved in 40-50 years, with negligible effects on GNP. This means that conservation incentives, including rising energy costs, could be structured so that by the year 2020 half as much energy as is now used would suffice for today's national total of goods and services; that is, the same amount of energy could accomplish twice as much.

The key to effective energy conservation is planning for the long term. Attempts to induce efficiency by replacing houses, cars and factories before they pass their useful lifetimes require that useful things go unused, which in turn generally implies increase in energy consumption and decrease in GNP growth.

Environmental catastrophe?

The chemical transformation of fossil organic materials—oil, coal, and to a smaller extent natural gas—has caused almost all the atmospheric pollution experienced today, much of the water pollution, and has been an important cause of illness and death. There are grave reasons for special concern about the impacts of certain energy sources, given current energy projections. Especially important are the hazards of fossil fuel combustion. Local and regional hazards, for example, arise from emissions of nitrogen and sulfur oxides and particulates, but by far the most worrisome global hazard is the prospective build-up of carbon dioxide in the atmosphere, in part as a

[1] See, for example, "US Energy Demand: Some Low Energy Futures", by the Demand and Conservation Panel, Committee on Nuclear and Alternative Energy Systems, US National Academy of Sciences. *Science*, Vol. 200, pp. 142-152, 14 April 1978.

result of fossil fuel combustion, in part as a result of global deforestation and the oxidation of humus in the ground beneath.

Carbon dioxide (CO_2) is an unavoidable consequence of burning carbonaceous material. Coal is the worst offender per unit of energy, though oil and natural gas, with about 65% and 50%, respectively, of coal's CO_2 emissions, also make important contributions.

Atmospheric CO_2 helps to regulate the temperature of the earth's atmosphere and surface. This happens because, although the atmosphere is transparent to the wave-lengths of incoming solar radiation, the CO_2 and water vapour in the atmosphere absorb the long-wave infra-red radiation (heat) reradiated from the earth's surface. They thus trap heat and raise surface temperatures; this is usually referred to as the greenhouse effect. Many analyses exist, and all of them are in general agreement: burning coal, oil and natural gas at present contributes about as much carbon dioxide to the atmosphere as does the present accelerated destruction of the world's forest biomass and humus (chiefly in the tropics). The present increase in atmospheric CO_2 is accurately observed worldwide. If present trends continue, the atmospheric carbon dioxide will double within two generations. Still in doubt is the actual effect on global temperatures, but almost all analyses predict an average warming between 1 and 5° C, with extra warming in the polar regions.

Government energy planning throughout the world virtually ignores this problem. But it presses now, because the fundamental changes that would constitute a remedy would take a long time. For example, global agriculture, by complicated geographic, social and institutional arrangements, matches crops to particular areas. Experience coupled with simple analyses show that total production decreases in times of changing climate, because neither the pattern of land use nor the fertility can change rapidly enough to accommodate. While the world energy problem is severe, the world food problem is even more critical, with fluctuations of a few percent in the global food production presently bringing misery to many.

These projections inform us that hard choices lie ahead, such as substantially reducing the combustion of coal, oil and natural gas worldwide, in the face of growing demand for them, especially by developing countries. The options of solar power, energy conservation (especially in industrialized countries) and nuclear power thus take on special significance. But the first and most difficult task may be to make people all over the world aware of the problem. No very effective global institutional mechanisms appear available to deal with such matters.

What are the long-term options?

Besides ever-increasing attention to frugal and efficient use, only two major classes of long-term options exist: solar power in several forms, and nuclear power. Geothermal and tidal power offer little, except at a few special places.

The fact that it will take a long time to develop and install solar or advanced nuclear power technologies, comparable to the time in which the classic fossil fuels must probably be phased out, creates a sense of urgency.

It is important to note that many of the most promising long-term options produce electricity as their most natural product. This fact bears strongly on the small-versus-large, diffuse-versus-concentrated debates now fashionable. All the nuclear systems are large; and while many of the solar technologies can be modular and small, the questions of interconnections and of back-up energy sources bring us back to the necessity of accepting substantial centralization. In all but the most primitivistic views of future society one finds increasing centralization of energy supply and delivery.

Solar power

Solar radiation is a diffuse source of energy and large amounts of materials are needed for collectors, storage devices, and so on. To build equipment that can capture and convert solar energy to useful forms requires capital investment embodying non-renewable resources that are far from free, even though sunlight itself is free. The real attractiveness of solar power, besides its ubiquity, is the relative ease with which it can be transformed for a number of uses. However, this attraction has often been oversold by various high-technology schemes.

Solar power includes not only direct conversion of sunlight, but also hydro-electric power, winds and biomass (organic matter). Discussions of this alternative thus tend to be extensive, since applications are diverse.

Low technology: The most immediately promising solar application is the production of low—and intermediate—temperature heat from about 70°C for domestic hot water to about 200°C for a variety of commercial, agricultural and industrial purposes. The simplest systems use flatplate collectors, while more advanced ones use mirrors or simple lenses to concentrate solar heat and provide higher temperatures. They will succeed if their design and construction are ingenious and simple enough to make them economically attractive. Another few years of rising oil and gas prices plus improvements in commercial solar systems should be sufficient for this technology to develop a strong commercial position, assuming that the systems' reliability turns out to be adequate.

High technology: In the past the solar energy programme concentrated on tasks with formidable (but interesting) science and engineering problems. At this extreme, we find advanced photovoltaic conversion schemes, such as the solar power satellite programme, the power tower concept and the ocean thermal energy conversion scheme. These are all very capital intensive and full of serious scientific and technical problems and they are unlikely energy options.

One of the most promising technologies is photovoltaic electricity generation, which is technically feasible in a variety of installation sizes ranging from the individual household to large central station generators.

Photovoltaic generators have in fact been marketed for specialized applications such as power sources for satellites or for electrical equipment in remote locations, where the high cost is justified. Wider applications must await either cost reductions of roughly an order of magnitude, for types in which the basic science is well understood (i.e. single crystals), or scientific development of potentially cheaper types (e.g. vacuum-evaporated thin films). A recent study by the American Physical Society[2] predicts that deployment of any such systems will be slow, for example 1% of US electric power by the year 2000.

Windpower devices occupy an intermediate status, neither high technology nor low, and like most other solar technologies should be regarded as augmenting conventional power supply.

Solar energy schemes require back-up sources of energy for times when the sun does not shine or when storage capacity is exhausted. There are many ways of providing storage. In the long-term the best form of storage is the production of fluid fuels that can serve as substitutes for hydrocarbons. A wide range of possibilities exists, ranging from electrolysis of water to generate hydrogen to various photochemical processes. This is an important and hitherto neglected area for basic research and exploratory development.

Nuclear power

This can be either fusion (the joining of hydrogen isotopes to produce helium in a super-hot plasma) or fission of heavy elements, chiefly uranium or plutonium.

The science of controlled fusion is fairly well understood, including schemes for containing the hot (100 million degrees or more) plasma in the middle of an evacuated space by using strong magnetic fields. The remaining (and larger) problems are technological: materials to withstand long-term bombardment by high energy neutrons, remote maintenance and repair of highly activated structures, handling and recovery of tritium which is highly radio-active and which must itself be replenished in the reactor (in this sense a fusion reactor is a breeder, but of tritium, not uranium or plutonium).

Those questions will not be answered in an engineering and economic sense before about AD 2000, so fusion can be looked upon as a possibility for the long-term, whose probability of being useful is still uncertain.

The debate about fission is much more intense, and sometimes proceeds with the finesse and charity of a duel in the dark with chain-saws.

What follows must be understood in the context of nuclear power incipiently withering away in the United States; new nuclear plants are still being built, but hardly any are being ordered, and all this well before the much-

---

[2] *Principal Conclusions of the American Physical Society Study Group on Solar Photovoltaic Energy Conversion*, chairman H. Ehrenreich. Published by the American Physical Society, January 1979.

publicized accident at the Three Mile Island plant. Electric utility companies are not ordering new plants or, having done so, cannot find adequate or timely resolution of environmental, technical and other licensing challenges. The problem is uncertainty about the social or regulatory acceptability of nuclear power, about whether the federal government will be politically able to resolve the nuclear waste problem, and so forth. These institutional difficulties are found in other countries as well.

The issues stated most often are (1) health hazards; (2) nuclear wastes; (3) accidents; (4) excessive cost; (5) environmental problems; (6) proliferation of nuclear weapons; (7) nuclear power as categorically evil; (8) the paradigm of high technology. These will now be taken up, wherein we will see in full operation the principle of selective inattention.

TABLE I: ESTIMATED U.S. EXPOSURE TO RADIATION FROM ALL SOURCES

CATEGORY OF US POPULATION EXPOSURE	US EXPOSURES *(breakdown)* *person-rems per year*	US EXPOSURES *person-rems per year*	ESTIMATED US CANCER DEATHS *per year*
1. Ambient exposures	19,800,000	19,800,000	3,960
a) cosmic radiation	9,700,000		
b) Th-232 series	4,600,000		
c) K-40 series	3,100,000		
d) U-238 series	2,400,000		
2. Medical and dental X-rays	14,800,000	14,800,000	2,960
3. Radio-pharmaceuticals	3,300,000	3,300,000	660
4. Technologically enhanced natural radiation	∿3,000,000	∿3,000,000	600
a) Rn-222 in natural gas	2,730,000		
b) coal-fired power stations	(see text)		
c) inactive uranium mines	70,000		
d) Rn-222 in LPG	30,000		
e) oil-fired power stations	15		
5. Fallout	400,000	400,000	80
6. Uranium fuel cycle (1976)	45,000	45,000	9.0
a) US population only	21,000		
b) occupational only	24,000		
7. Other occupational	4,400	4,400	0.9
8. Consumer products	6,100	6,100	1.2
TOTALS	NA	41,355,500	8,270

Source: "Radiological Quality of the Environment in the US, 1977", EPA-520/1-77-009, US EPA, September 1977; and the GESMO Final Report, NUREG-0002, Volume 105, USNRC, September 1976.

1. *Health hazards:* Radio-activity is the overwhelming concern. It can cause cancer and genetic changes. *Table 1*, prepared by my colleague Robert Marlay, gives comparative estimates to exposure from various sources. Those who worry exclusively about radiation hazards from normally or even somewhat abnormally operating nuclear reactors should stop using natural gas in their houses. The entry "see text" for coal-fired power stations refers to traces of radio-active materials (chiefly uranium and its decay products) in ash from power plants, which is made into cinder-blocks for construction, and for which the US Environmental Protection Agency tentatively estimates radiation doses far in excess of *any* listed in the table.[3] One hopes that there is an error in their estimate. But the largest health hazards of coal are not its radio-activity, but its biologically active pollutants: sulfur and nitrogen oxides, and many polycyclic aromatic hydrocarbons and other carcinogens and mutagens that would arise in conversion of coals to liquid fuels. Beyond this are the well-known health effects of coal mining, in which the morbidity and mortality per unit of energy far exceeds the deleterious effects in uranium mining.[4]

2. *Nuclear wastes:* Again, the worry is radiation and the threat of cancer and genetic defects. *Table 2* lists available lethal doses from various toxic substances, in amounts used in the US in 1975.[5]

TABLE 2: AVAILABLE LETHAL DOSES
FROM VARIOUS TOXIC SUBSTANCES IN THE U.S.

SUBSTANCE	LETHAL DOSES *(or potential deaths if the dose is uniformly administered)*
Radwastes age 100 years from an all-nuclear *electric economy*	10^{7}
Chemicals (as used in 1975)	
Barium	10^{1}
Arsenic	10^{0}
Chlorine	10^{4}
Phosgene	10^{3}
Ammonia	10^{2}
Hydrogen cyanide	10^{2}

[3] *Radiological Quality of the Environment in the US*, 1977 EPA-520/1-77-009, September 1977.

[4] See, for example, *The Hazards of Conventional Sources of Energy*, Health and Safety Commission Report of the British Government, April 1978; "Report of the AMA Council on Scientific Affairs: Health Evaluation of Energy-Generating Sources", *Journal of the American Medical Association*, Vol. 240/20, 2193, 10 November 1978; D. J. Rose, P. W. Walsh and L. L. Leskovjan: "Nuclear Power-Compared to What?", *American Scientist*, Vol. 63, 291-299, 1976.

[5] *Management of Commercially Generated Radioactive Waste*, Report DOE/EIS-0046-D, Vol. 1, Table 1.3.

The technology for disposal of nuclear wastes is in relatively good shape. For example, the Swedish proposal to encase them in lead and titanium jackets (and copper, if the spent fuel is to be entombed directly without any reprocessing) and then to emplace them in geologically stable granite formations with bentonite packing looks good. Eventually, disposal in the sea-bed may be even better; the North Pacific Plate appears to be exceptionally stable and geologically predictable.

We who worry about such matters should also worry about proposals for underground gasification or liquefaction of coal and/or oil shale, which would leave much vaster carcinogenic and mutagenic residues in highly damaged geologic strata, with much higher probability of leaching out and causing direct biological mischief.

3. *Accidents:* The Three Mile Island nuclear accident was very serious, and will lead to changes in specific technological items, in training of reactor and power plant personnel, in management and regulation of nuclear power plants, and perhaps even government ownership of large sectors of the US electric generating facilities—an arrangement common in most other countries. The event will probably cause an extension of the *de facto* moratorium on ordering new nuclear facilities in the US, but whether the moratorium becomes *de jure* cannot yet be foretold.

A principal lesson to be learned from TMI is that even though the general accident sequence had been foreseen in the US Reactor Safety Study[6], neither the human elements that exacerbated it nor the human ingenuity that prevented it from being worse were fully taken into account.

Substantial and rational efforts must be made to minimize the probability of such accidents, and to arrange the instrumentation and controls of reactors so that conditions are more readily and precisely judged and responded to. The hazard from nuclear reactor accidents (whatever it turns out to be) should be compared to the actual present deaths from its principal alternative—coal—which run 20-200 per large power-plant-year (the epidemiological data are poor) without stringent emission controls, and perhaps one-fifth as much with stringent controls.

4. *Excessive cost:* Nuclear power plants are expensive, but coal-burning power plants with emission controls are almost equally so, and the coal costs more than the uranium fuel. A principal reason why nuclear plants are not cheaper is that they have taken longer to construct and license, thus incurring increased expenses because of the payment of more interest during construction. One of the best-run electric utility companies in the US is the Commonwealth Edison Company in Chicago, Illinois. Rossin and Rieck[7] analyse

---

[6] Reactor Safety Study *("The Rasmussen Report")*. Report WASH-1400 (NUREG-75/014), USA, October 1975.

[7] A. D. Rossin and T. A. Rieck: "Economics of Nuclear Power". *Science*, Vol. 201, 582, 18 August 1978.

their nuclear and coal operations, and find that nuclear power is significantly cheaper.

5. *World environmental problems:* The big dangers are from coal, oil and natural gas, and the so-far unstated intergenerational cost of leaving future generations with very depleted resources of these materials, which are in any event better suited as chemical feed-stock.

6. *Proliferation of nuclear weapons:* Vertical proliferation, which means increasing the size or complexity of nuclear arsenals, has virtually nothing to do with civilian nuclear power. What we are concerned with here is horizontal proliferation, where a country not now processing nuclear weapons slides or sidles towards a nuclear weapons capability.

A country intending to build nuclear weapons that has no present civilian nuclear capacity would find it much cheaper and faster to build small dedicated plants than to build expensive civilian power facilities, and then try to subvert them. But the more serious problem is that an existing nuclear facility certainly makes the transition to weapons easier. Hence the present concern over the Non-Proliferation Treaty, IAEA inspections, control over use of nuclear fuel, etc.

But the other side of this logical coin is that if highly industrialized countries do not appreciably restrict their appetite for imported oil, and impose restrictions on nuclear assistance to developing countries, then the developing countries see themselves in a quandary, where they are shut off from too many energy options, through events over which they had no control. Thus regional autarchy, suspicion, and an attitude of go-it-alone (or with another supplier) builds up for installing nuclear power. Such attitudes, if commonly held, would lead to destabilization and enhanced danger of conflict. These matters have been discussed at length.[8]

An obvious though difficult resolution of this problem is to attempt to remove the reasons why nations want to build nuclear bombs in the first place. The list of countries quite capable of building nuclear weapons but not doing so is instructive: Australia, Canada, Italy, Japan, Sweden, Switzerland, Federal Republic of Germany, and probably a few more. Almost all are reasonably secure via international interdependence, and all have high enough standards of living to feel in no need to derail the international train of events in order to pick up pieces. The real key, then, lies in promoting a cooperative international interdependence (but not based on concepts of neo-colonialism); that in turn means paying more attention to the needs of the non-industrialized countries. More of that anon.

7. *Categorical evil?* The memory of Hiroshima and Nagasaki remains, and the shadow of ten thousand megatons darkens our prospects. But the

---

[8] D. J. Rose and R. K. Lester: "Nuclear Power, Nuclear Weapons and International Stability". *Scientific American*, April 1978, pp. 45-57.

evil lies not inherently in the phenomenon of nuclear fission or of any of the chemical elements, all of them parts of creation, but in the nature of man himself who, being given free will, can choose to build towards heaven or towards hell. In the present nuclear situation, I see both promise and peril, and the dangerous imperfection of man, susceptible to the sins of avarice, over-ambition and hubris. Despite these weaknesses, or perhaps because of them, I believe that resolution lies in seeking states of increasing grace and *caritas*, and accepting what is in creation with an attitude of thanksgiving, dedicating the use of these things to the good of all and not for selfish gain. In a sense, we are junior partners in creation, and should be careful stewards over the part of it entrusted to us.

8. *A paradigm of high technology, and therefore to be eschewed?* Jacques Ellul is correct that "techniques"—the more all-encompassing word he uses to describe man's works—can and often do have unfortunate unforeseen consequences, but the absolutist tendency implicit in such attitudes leads to other consequences just as unfortunate, or more so.

What to do?

We live in one world, though the parts be disparate. The industrialized countries could attempt to control the energy future of the world for their own use. But that would not even serve their own interest, except for a little while; once the civilization started to fall, as Rome did in the fifth century, they would lose the most because they had the most. The developing countries, with their generally lower energy use, have a more justifiable call on whatever low—and intermediate—technology-based resources exist. Apropos of this point, the developing countries used only about one-third as much oil in 1975 as did the US. A general social collapse affects them more poignantly because, living "so close to the ground", even a short fall brings them down to or below the level of existence.

The best strategy from many points of view would be for the industrialized countries to start a determined programme to reduce permanently their use of carbonaceous fuels—coal, oil, gas—via a combination of more rational and efficient energy use and a gradual accompanying shift to alternative energy resources. These sources are solar and nuclear; both will be needed, and both tend to be more electric-oriented than the present mix of fossil fuels. Such a shift dramatizes the problem of how to live with nuclear power, but the problem was with us anyway and would not go away, no matter what some might wish. If solar power eventually turns out as successful as we hope and nuclear power turns out to be unnecessary, so much the better; nuclear power will then wither away naturally.

The developing countries thus gain better interim access to oil and gas, which are more easily matched to their present economies than either nuclear power or the large solar schemes presently being developed (though many small ones are broadly applicable). As they develop, they too will need to shift to non-carbonaceous fuels; if everyone plans carefully, the build-up of carbon dioxide need not strain the global environment beyond our endurance. In all this, the developing countries should find it in their own interest to be energy-efficient also. If solar power wins here too, so much the better.

This strategy of the industrialized countries consciously switching their technological base could avert the global CO_2 catastrophe, in which everyone loses. It also goes a long way to making the developing countries full partners in the global enterprise. That is important to us all, because people in many developing countries see themselves as standing at the side of a railroad track, watching the train of the industrialized nations going by at ever-increasing speed, and they—the developing nations—being increasingly incapable of running alongside, let alone climbing aboard; then their only possibility to gain anything is to derail the train.

It is better and even in the interest of the industrialized countries to have everybody on board the train, and to plan to operate it for the long term.

Note: Parts of the discussion on time perspectives, conservation and solar energy are taken with permission from Chapter 5, "Energy", of the report *Science and Technology: a Five-year Outlook*, prepared by the National Academy of Sciences (USA) for the National Science Foundation, 30 March 1979, to be published by W. H. Freeman Company.

The Social Risks of Large-Scale Nuclear Energy Programmes

JEAN ROSSEL

In the 1950's and 60's, the development of the nuclear energy industry on a large scale had all the appearance of a broad and providential highway for the future progress of human society.

Having been personally involved in these early efforts in my own country, I shared the widespread feeling that this promise of abundance and material security opened the way to a new golden age. Even though atomic physicists were aware of unsolved problems, the social risks seemed perfectly acceptable in view of the benefits offered by a source of energy which was regarded as virtually inexhaustible. The official campaigns to convince people of the great advantage of nuclear energy for non-military purposes temporarily obscured the fundamental problem: the inseparable link between the peaceful fuel and the destructive explosive formed by uranium and plutonium. Discussion of the questions continued among specialists, particularly in the famous *Bulletin of Atomic Scientists*; among the general public, on the other hand, the attitude to the whole civilian nuclear problem was for a long time one of apathy.

It was only towards the end of the 1960's that critics began to make themselves heard—more and more of them, and more and more insistently—in the industrialized countries. The fact had to be faced that technical problems originally regarded as easily soluble—for example, perfect security in the operation of reactors, or management and disposal of radio-active wastes—defied any satisfactory and definitive solution. Also, new economic, political and social problems were becoming increasingly apparent. Significant evidence for this was provided by the Non-Proliferation Treaty.

Popular movements against the massive development of nuclear energy have now become a major element in the life of countries with an advanced technological structure, in which energy is produced and wasted to an ever-increasing extent. These movements, although they may often be misguided and not always inspired by constructive aims, are nevertheless based upon the solidly grounded positions of scientists and qualified specialists, many of whom have formed perfectly honest and credible associations, such as the Union of Concerned Scientists, the Friends of the Earth, and the Pugwash Movement, to mention only some of them.

It is therefore natural and legitimate to raise the question of the social risks resulting from intensive nuclear programmes. I propose to examine this question in terms of society as a whole, in a perspective which I hope will be illuminated by our Christian traditions.

Problems and risks of radio-active pollution

The distinguishing characteristic of the nuclear industry is in the exceptional nature of the wastes it produces: the beta and gamma radio-active fragments, residues of the fission chain reaction, on one side, and the unstable artificial alpha-emitting elements, heavier than uranium, which are formed by the capture of neutrons, on the other.

We are well aware that nuclear reactors did not create the phenomenon of radio-activity. The cells of living beings have always been subjected to the disturbing effects of the alpha, beta and gamma ionizing radiations from the natural radio-activity in our immediate environment and from the particles in cosmic rays. It is indeed the progressively established equilibrium between ionizing action—relatively unchanging throughout the ages—and the reaction of genetic mutation which, at least in part, has created the characteristics of the human species and its hereditary patrimony.

One of the most controversial biological questions at present is the attempt to determine whether populations subjected by geographical conditions to higher annual radiation doses than others (in a range from 120 mrem to 500 mrem, for example) show any real signs of degeneration as compared to what might be called the "average person". Even though these statistical studies are difficult and still subject to controversy, it seems clear that even small surplus doses cannot fail to have negative effects, both carcinogenic and genetic.

The nuclear industry produces concentrations of artificial radio-activity which are several tens of million times greater than those existing in nature. Even if perfect and trouble-free operation of atomic installations were to be assured, slow and steady pollution of the biosphere is inevitable in the generation of nuclear energy. At various stages in the fuel cycle, more or less well-controlled quantities of radio-active substances are regularly discharged into the air, water and ground, creating lasting contamination. Fuel reprocessing plants are particularly unfavourable in this respect. The assured protection of the biosphere against the infiltration of radio-active wastes for the next several thousand years is the most disturbing of the unsolved problems.

Among the more troublesome radio-isotopes, we may include tritium, carbon-14, krypton-85, iodine-19, cesium-137 and strontium-90, with half lives ranging from ten years to several million years (in the case of I-129), not to mention plutonium and other actinides. Estimates for twenty years from now predict a concentration of tritium four to five times greater than that occurring naturally, and difficulties are anticipated with Kr-85 and C-14. Despite regulations designed to assure maximum dilution and dispersion of the radio-active substances discharged, we are aware of high reconcentration factors—in the order of several thousand to a million—which occur in the food chain. The example of the Bikini Atoll, where the population was solemnly returned to its homeland and subsequently re-evacuated because of residual radio-active contamination of their environment, is significant.

Other instances of low-level irradiation doses which were believed to be free of any carcinogenic effect and which later gave cause for concern have now become known. These include the cases of the workers in the Hanford nuclear plant, the American soldiers who took part in operation "Smoky" in the 1950's, and the workers at the Portsmouth naval base in the US.

One could reasonably argue that the present-day medical use of ionizing radiations, such as X-rays for diagnosis and therapy, produce a collective dose of irradiation which is much greater than that attributable to the nuclear industry. This situation is quite different, however—first of all because the positive aspect of medical irradiation is indisputable and the means exist for reducing it greatly without diminishing the information obtained. Furthermore, once the instrument has been switched off, it produces no further effects and leaves no lasting pollution in the environment.

Our bio-genetic equilibrium is delicate. A slight disturbance, but one capable of causing a permanent shift, however improbable, is nevertheless a menace which cannot be ignored. In an international symposium on the biological action of low doses of irradiation (Lausanne, 1958) a seriously-regarded paper was presented which explained the disappearance of the giant saurians of the Mesozoic era by a slight rise in natural radio-activity which was fatal to the equilibrium of the voluminous organisms of these huge animals. I will not go so far as to extend this hypothesis by claiming that the excessive development of the nuclear industry and the radio-activity it produces will result in the disappearance of mankind from the earth, leaving it to the insects. We may nevertheless be concerned about the long-term effects of certain instances of light-mindedness which have assumed the force of law in international terms, in the framework of the International Atomic Energy Agency.

I am thinking of the "ALARA" principle, which states that supposedly harmful activities should be maintained at a level "As Low As Reasonably Achievable". Engineers in the nuclear industry have boasted to me of the great moral value of this principle. I am not so sure of it as they are, in view of the way in which our profit-oriented society defines the word "reasonably"—which will certainly come to mean nothing more than "economically acceptable". This state of affairs opens up some distressing perspectives, from the point of view of Christian ethical teaching, when it comes to limitations on security measures and the setting of so-called "acceptable" dosages of irradiation which are the logical consequences of this principle. The moral element underlying the principle is questionable indeed when it is proposed to define acceptable doses of irradiation for workers in the nuclear industry and for the general population in terms of the value of human life as expressed in dollars and cents. It is obvious, furthermore, that the security measures for the operation of nuclear plants are and will be in permanent conflict with what is regarded as "reasonable" in terms of economic output.

Without proposing at this point to examine the risks of serious accidents—by referring to the Rasmussen report and the criticisms made of it—it seems clear, taking into account the magnitude of the disaster resulting from a nuclear accident, that the risk is highly unacceptable since it is difficult to do anything to reduce severe radio-active contamination.

This is a problem of conscience which is a proper subject of reflection for communities inspired by the Christian ethic.

Problems of energy policy or the hazards of illusion

One of the burning problems of nuclear energy confronting us today, involving the future of industrialized society and consequently of human society as a whole, is that of massive recourse to plutonium for the production of energy by fission.

The accessible reserves of U-235 do not appear to be sufficient—especially outside the United States—to assure a sustained rate of nuclear development beyond the year 1990. Despite the reluctance of the American government, the reprocessing of spent fuel to extract residual U-235 and plutonium, followed by the construction of breeder reactors to make use of U-238, are inevitable for the long-term supply of nuclear energy.

The hazards of the proliferation of nuclear weapons are aggravated by the foregoing prospects. This menace should not, however, lead us to forget all the other hazards. There are other ways of obtaining nuclear weapons besides the use of commercial plutonium. The technological and political risks of civilian nuclear energy are significant in themselves and do not need to be considered predominantly in terms of the problems of modern warfare which, with or without nuclear weapons, threatens the survival of civilization.

There is total uncertainty as to the actual possibility of replacing petroleum to a sufficient extent and rapidly enough by nuclear energy based on fission. We are dealing here with an insidious but formidable social risk: that of committing ourselves to a development with irreversible and dangerous consequences which would in the end turn out to be a grand illusion. Future energy needs, which are evoked to justify the imposition of such a course, have so far not been evaluated by including in the reckoning the questionable structures and habits of our industrial civilization, which are based upon the systematic robbing of our planet's resources. Extrapolations of energy needs have been made, simply taking for granted the requirements of growth, accepting them as a dogma, and obeying ready-made assumptions which have not been subjected to adequate analysis and criticism.

No one can question that the amount of petroleum consumed by the so-called advanced countries is preposterous. The idea of making every effort to replace it without first of all reducing the waste is just as preposterous.

We cannot deny the need of developing countries for the technical means to produce more energy, provided these means do not simultaneously increase their dependence on the industrialized countries to an unacceptable degree. There is a serious lack of responsibility, however, in proposing a transfer of technology whose genuine efficacy is nullified in advance by the simultaneous transfer of wasteful methods. To propose the stabilization of society by maintaining and disseminating the patterns of thinking, the methods and the defective procedures evolved by the industrialized societies, constitutes a grave threat for the future.

Studies have been made by various independent experts of the development necessary for the nuclear industry if it is to take the place of petroleum without any change in our way of living. These studies (Lovins, Sonderegger) have been based on estimates of uranium reserves and fuel cycles from qualified sources in the electronuclear industry. Briefly, the argument is as follows: a 1,000-MW(e) LWR reactor has to operate for thirty years to supply the initial charge for a 1,500-MW(e) U-Pu breeder reactor. For optimal breeding, taking reprocessing into account, the number of plants must increase at the rate of 4.5% per year. In the year 2010, having completed the 4,500 LWRs which it would appear possible to run on the basis of the estimated reserves of U-235, we should have in operation by 2040 a total of 6,000 breeders. The total production of nuclear electricity would then amount to one-half of the energy now being produced by petroleum—in other words, 10% of the needs of that future period, based on a rate of growth in energy consumption of 3% per year.

It is obvious that such a gigantic undertaking is grotesque in terms of the results to be achieved. The effort required of our society to meet its gluttonous energy needs is like the efforts of the Danaides to fill their sieves with water. These are certainly not conditions which allow for a balanced and trouble-free society.

A civilization seeking to satisfy its exaggerated energy requirements by the present methods of megatechnology is, moreover, at the mercy of the extreme vulnerability of highly centralized production systems, a trend which is accentuated by the nuclear industry. A 1,000 MW(e) installation supplying electricity to a whole region constitutes a considerable risk both from an economic and a military point of view. The paralysis resulting from electricity blackouts, for example, can occur at any time. In addition, due to the great concentration of radio-active material in the core of each reactor and in the storage depots for spent fuel at the site of the plant, installations for the production of nuclear energy are a potential threat as targets for terrorist blackmail or military action.

In face of a development surrounded by such profoundly disturbing questions, there is no way for us to elude our responsibilities as scientists or as Christians.

The technological society and respect for mankind

For about the last two centuries, science and technology have played a dominant role in the building of modern society and have to a great extent supplanted the traditional values of the Christian world. In material terms, spectacular accomplishments have been made, in both the destruction and the conservation of humanity. The rational and quantitative element, culminating in the ideal of economic values and output, has steadily relegated the qualitative element to a secondary role in the conduct and organization of society. The triumphant scientific spirit of the nineteenth century and the first half of the twentieth has assumed the character of a new mind.

This deification of applied science, which is the root cause of the excesses of our civilization and the accelerated destruction of nature, is arousing increasingly violent reactions and criticisms which, in part at least, are undoubtedly justified. It is indeed surprising, in view of their remarkable efficiency in material terms, that science and its applications have not made it possible to construct a better balanced society.

We are compelled to recognize that after the Second World War the influence of the scientific and technical rationale has assumed a predominance and a scale that we can only regard as abusive. The scientific-technical spiral has assumed such power that it seems that the individual is no longer master of his destiny. He has surrendered his freedom of choice and delivered himself up to impersonal structures to such an extent that all responsibility is diluted and inspiration is absent.

Whether we like it or not, nuclear energy and its industrial organization, along with space exploration and its excesses, have become a sort of extreme expression of our simultaneously arrogant and fragile technological society. Rightly or wrongly, the nuclear industry now represents, in the eyes of the ordinary man who is still sensitive to traditional values, the quintescence of risks and dangers, difficult to assess and therefore all the more distressing.

It is easy enough to find examples of this boundless trend of expansion of science and technology in our megalomaniac society. One is concerned with the high energy physics of elementary particles and the reflections on this subject by Steven Weinberg, a theoretical specialist in this field. The pursuit of ever-increasing energies in order to gain a better understanding of the submicroscopic universe of elementary particles is evolving so rapidly that it will only be stopped in the end by the lack of resources in the countries putting up the funds to enable this effort to be pursued *ad infinitum*, for no voluntary self-limitation is possible. This confession seems clearly to indicate that no moderating element exists within science itself which is capable of halting it in its effort to recreate the material conditions of the original Big Bang or primeval fireball.

A number of economists and industrialists have drawn attention to the abuses and the disastrous consequences for the structures of society of a dehumanized technology whose excesses are beyond control. (We may refer, for example, to E. F. Schumacher in *Small is Beautiful.*) With increasing insistency, they are urging greater decentralization and the use of so-called "soft technologies", in particular to recover some of the vast amounts of energy now being wasted in what are known as the developed countries. Several industrial enterprises have effectively demonstrated the efficiency of these methods (heat exchangers, coupling between heat and electricity production, control of the energy efficiency of electric equipment, thermal insulation of buildings, etc.).

Estimates of the resources available through use of different renewable sources of energy derived directly or indirectly from the sun show that the world's needs for the next century could be entirely covered by these means, which are particularly kind to the environment and which encourage a structure of society more respectful of people and of human dignity.

It is not possible to examine in detail here the conditions required for the establishment of a stable society on this basis. For the pessimists and the advocates of intensive industrial centralization, such thinking is regarded as utopian. For others, among whom I count myself, it is less illusory than any social pattern depending mainly upon nuclear energy—and with enough open mindedness, imagination and inspiration, a civilization based on technology with a human face is not an impossible dream. We may even claim that it is probably the only truly viable solution for the next century.

Conclusions

To summarize the foregoing tentative and over-simplified considerations, the serious social hazards involved in the massive development of the nuclear industry may be considered on three levels:

1. The material and biological hazards are related to the special characteristics of radio-active waste. Through the extent and duration of its effects, it creates a whole new dimension of material damage, for example, in the event of accidents occurring at nuclear plants or storage facilities, whose security cannot be convincingly and acceptably demonstrated. Even assuming normal operations, the nuclear industry produces an inevitable increase in the radio-active level of the biosphere, constituting a serious threat to the biological integrity of living species.

2. We must add to these risks the ones which derive from dangerous illusions about the future of the world's energy economy, together with the threats implicit in the intractable political problems connected with the fission of uranium and plutonium — fuels and bombs alike. These open up the prospect of an unstable and fragile nuclear society in which freedom becomes completely impossible.

3. There are insidious but fundamental risks inherent in the very nature of the nuclear industry, dedicated as it is to gigantism and centralization and serving as the driving force in a society dominated by a technology of ever-expanding proportions. The intellectual equilibrium of the human community and its spiritual foundations are at stake in this dramatic evolution of a society which is perverting itself and turning its back upon the values on which it was built.

The Christian churches cannot allow themselves to be hypnotized by unreal prospects offered to the world by technocrats and politicians whose vision is dominated by a reckless confidence in science and technology pushed to their limits. Nature holds out to us, in its renewable and lasting reserves, the energy and materials we need to build a society which does not contain the seeds of its own degeneration.

The churches inspired by the Christian tradition must make a choice in conformity with the ethic that is based on respect and love, not only for our neighbours but for the whole of creation.

Reactions and Comment

The discussion following the addresses was one of the liveliest in the conference. It was obvious that many participants had come with strong commitments to positions — often sharply clashing positions — for which they wanted endorsement by the conference. Others were seeking information and understanding in order to decide what actions to support.

Among the many questions from the floor, one that was to have special significance came from Albert van den Heuvel, convenor of Section VI,

"Energy for the Future". Noting that Rose had referred to a de facto *moratorium on nuclear installations in the USA, van den Heuvel wondered whether the conference—which would obviously not agree on all issues—might agree in endorsing a moratorium as a matter of principle. Rose replied that the USA* de facto *moratorium was not worldwide and was not necessarily wise.*

Following the plenary session, concentrated discussion of the issues continued in Section VI, which had already begun working on the subject. During the following week there was also wide discussion outside formal meetings. A student caucus (see Chapter 1) asked the conference to reject nuclear energy.

Almost a week later the conference took up the issues in parts of two successive plenary sessions where it heard the report of Section VI. In accepting the section report and authorizing its publication, the conference—as in comparable actions on all section reports—did not necessarily endorse the report. But Section VI also prepared a resolution on which it asked conference action. The resolution—and a minority report dissenting from it—are printed in full in Volume 2. For the purposes of this volume, which records and summarizes plenary addresses and discussion, it is enough to say that the largest part of the resolution won general assent. There was endorsement of full discussion of energy issues in the churches and the publics of all countries, of the importance of changed and less extravagant life-styles and of a more just distribution of energy within nations and among nations.

Debate centred on the recommendation—in its final amended form—to "introduce a moratorium on the construction of all new nuclear plants for a period of five years", with the purpose of encouraging "wide participation in a public debate on the risks, costs and benefits of nuclear energy in all countries directly concerned".

The issues were joined in a spirited debate on the floor. Among the many arguing for the moratorium, John Francis of the UK called it "a limited pause" to allow various countries to examine kinds of reactors available, criteria of siting, etc. Ragui Assaad of Egypt said that the moratorium was "not an absolute stand on nuclear power" and did not regard such power as "intrinsically evil". Tunde Adegbola of Nigeria said that most of the Third World did not want nuclear plants. Gordon Edwards of Canada urged a shift of priorities for the "short and medium term" to conservation and renewable sources, without closing "the nuclear option". Numerous other speakers emphasized these same points or pointed to the danger of nuclear weapons. Although there were some signs of a total opposition to nuclear energy, the speeches from the floor repeatedly stated that the resolution did not mean that.

Speaking against the moratorium, David Rose of the USA and Max Setterwall of Sweden pointed to the dangers of fossil fuels and the economic-political risks in intensifying worldwide energy shortages. Ben Nwosu of Nigeria said that the moratorium would increase the tendency of industrializ-

ed countries to plunder the resources of the developing countries. Archbishop Kirill of the USSR warned that withdrawal from nuclear energy would turn his country from an oil-exporting to an oil-importing country. Other speakers, making variations on these same themes, said also that the moratorium would freeze the difference between those countries with nuclear energy (who could continue to produce it) and those countries without it (who would be forbidden to acquire it).

The debate extended late into the night and ended with a vote: 129 for the moratorium, 45 against, 21 abstaining.

The other controversial resolution opposed the extraction and use of plutonium as a fuel. The vote, with total numbers considerably reduced because of the lateness of the hour, was: 76 for the resolution, 32 against, 14 abstaining.

Again, readers are referred to Volume 2 for the complete texts of the resolutions.

14. The Biological Revolution: the Ethical and Social Issues

Introduction

New developments in biology, including genetics, was the second of the two problem areas—alongside energy—selected by the Working Committee on Church and Society for study in recent years and for attention at the conference.

An ecumenical consultation in Zürich in 1973 resulted in publication of the book *Genetics and the Quality of Life*, edited by Charles Birch and Paul Abrecht.[1] It included both preparatory papers and the findings of the consultation. The findings were also published separately by the WCC in a pamphlet under the same title, which circulated widely and led to further studies in various areas of the world. The preparatory book for the 1979 conference, *Faith, Science and the Future*, included a chapter on "Ethical Dilemmas in the Biological Manipulation of Human Life". This earlier work, along with the wide literature and public discussion of the issues, formed the background for the consideration of issues at the conference.

The two principal speakers were Jonathan King, associate professor of microbiology at MIT, and Karen Lebacqz, associate professor of Christian ethics at the Pacific School of Religion, Berkeley, California.

The title of the plenary session, "The Biological Revolution: the Ethical and Social Issues", showed an obvious intention to emphasize the social aspects of a subject that is often discussed primarily in terms of individual decisions. Even so, some participants were surprised that both addresses concentrated on the economic-political-cultural context of current scientific-technological changes and the decisions they require. The choice by the speakers was consistent with the emerging emphasis of the conference, and it was symptomatic of a wide concern in contemporary society and the churches.

---

[1] Potts Point, NSW, Australia: Oxford, and Elmsford, NY: Pergamon Press, 1975.

Two platform comments followed the addresses. Whereas King and Lebacqz had pointed to the hazards in biological research, especially within the prevailing social contexts, Gabriel Nahas of the National Institute of Health in Paris attacked directly the whole enterprise of genetic engineering as a dangerous and irreverent "warfare against nature". Traute Schroeder, speaking out of her experience in genetic counselling, described the ethical issues for both counsellors and patients in the counselling process.

New Genetic Technologies: Prospects and Hazards

JONATHAN KING

The spectacular record of thirty years

During the past thirty years we have witnessed extraordinary advances in knowledge of fundamental biological processes, particularly at the cellular and molecular level. Governments have invested major public funds in the training of biomedical scientists and support for biomedical research. The 1978 budget for biomedical research in the USA is about three billion dollars—a thousand times the federal expenditure on biomedical research in 1948.

In the US, these programmes had their origin in the pressing need for coordinated biomedical research to deal with the immense human damage suffered by soldiers during and after World War II. The federal funding of cooperative, organized research was highly successful and was continued after the war, after public pressure overcame opposition from the private medical sector.

The programme has led to the elucidation of the chemical structure of the genetic material, DNA; to the understanding of the organization of the genetic material in linear segments, the genes; to the recognition that genes constitute blueprints for the structure of protein molecules, which form both the building blocks and working parts of cells; to the understanding of the roles of the thin membranes that divide cells into different compartments; to the discovery of the organization and functions of the complex ribosomes, themselves composed of more than seventy different kinds of protein molecules, which serve as the factories for assembling new proteins according to the instructions of the genes.

The labours of tens of thousands of laboratory workers continue to reveal the extraordinary richness and creativity in the mechanisms by which living things reproduce themselves and interact with their environment and each other.

In the industrialized nations the major steps in cutting infant mortality, increasing the life-span, and controlling infectious disease occurred earlier in this century. These came from the economic struggles led by the trade unions for an improved standard of living, notably the shorter working day, higher wages and improved working conditions. They were aided by public health professionals, who fought for improved sanitation and water supplies, and control of food contamination, and through such measures eliminated cholera, diphtheria, scarlet fever and other scourges of the urban poor.

The more recently acquired understanding of the biochemistry of bacteria and viruses in human disease, and the development of tissue culture technology for growing cells and the viruses that infect them in the test tube, laid the basis for eliminating a further set of diseases: poliovirus infections in the 1950's, rinderpest virus (a major killer of African cattle) in the 1960's, and more recently the dramatic eradication of smallpox. Twenty years ago, in India alone there were 150,000 cases of smallpox and 41,000 deaths. These last two achievements depended on organized campaigns coordinated through the United Nations.

The scientific basis now exists for mounting research campaigns against viral diseases such as Rift Valley Fever in North Africa, yellow fever in Central Africa and hemorrhaggic fever in Asia. The scientific basis exists also for research campaigns against such widespread parasitic diseases as schistosomiasis, filariasis and one of its more tragic forms, river blindness.

Of course, many of these diseases are intimately associated with the particularities of the conditions of life—housing, local agriculture, water supplies and sanitation, and the level of nutrition. The development of the biochemistry and physiology of particular organisms does not substitute for the need to study the integrated ecosystem, as well as the social and economic conditions of human society. This knowledge of the inter-relationships among organisms is not well developed in industrial societies, with our focus on exploitation of resources rather than conservation. The development of indigenous scientific analysis, called for by Dr Odhiambo [see Chapter 9], is absolutely necessary to be able to make use of cellular and molecular biology.

For example, smallpox infected only humans, enabling all potential hosts to be identified and vaccinated. Many of the other viruses that affect humans can also live in other organisms, in insects or wild animals and other parts of the ecosystem. These cannot be eradicated by the same strategies used for smallpox.

Cholera provides another example: it is still a major problem in Calcutta, where it was first isolated in 1817. This is not because Indian scientists do not fully understand the microbiology of cholera, but rather because of the poverty that is partly the legacy of British imperialism.

Another major contribution of modern molecular genetics and cell biology is the recognition that much of human cancer is due to the damage to the genes of human somatic cells by external agents. These agents include certain industrial chemicals, such as aniline dyes, which cause bladder cancer, and vinyl chloride, a cause of liver cancer. They include also most forms of ionizing radiation causing, for example, leukemia among survivors of the holocaust of Hiroshima and Nagasaki, and those exposed to nuclear testing; bone cancer from strontium and plutonium; and other cancers from excess medical irradiation and, in the coming years, from exposure to nuclear waste.

These major breakthroughs have led to the recognition that much of human cancer is preventable. Unfortunately, powerful economic forces have a vested interest in the continued production and sale of these agents, so that the prevention of cancer involves a social struggle not so different from the ones earlier in the century for better working conditions.

Unfortunately we do not have a national health service or any system of comprehensive medical care in the United States. This limits our ability to realize the fullest fruits of our biomedical research. Without a comprehensive health care system, it is difficult to couple research to health care needs. When substantial advances occur, they are sometimes available only to economically advantaged groups. Farm-workers in Texas have an average life-span of 49 years of age, twenty years less than the national average.

Recombinant DNA technology

The growth of biological knowledge has been accompanied by the development of very sophisticated biochemical and genetic technologies. These technologies, which are today tools for the accumulation of knowledge of organisms, are also the tools for the genetic and biochemical modification of these same organisms.

The most dramatic and revolutionary of these technologies is recombinant DNA technology, or genetic engineering: the ability to incorporate segments of DNA—of genetic material—derived from one organism into the cells of another organism. The donor and recipient may be closely related (for example, two strains of bacteria) or they may be very different (for example, a mouse and a bacterium).

Members of the same species exchange segments of genetic material regularly; this is the biological basis of mating and sex—the exchange of equivalent segments of genetic material in the offspring of parents, generating new genetic combinations, which may prove advantageous in adapting to a changing environment.

However, exchange of genetic material between members of unrelated species is rare. Organisms adapting to different environments, to different niches, to use the ecologist's term, evolve different instructions, different genes. Exchange between such organisms is generally not useful and is rarely observed in nature.

Let me give an example of the use of recombinant DNA technology in biological research. Suppose I am studying how pancreatic cells produce insulin, and why liver cells do not. I might remove the pancreas from a mouse, and extract from the pancreas cells the long stringy DNA molecules that represent the blueprints for being a mouse. By treating these isolated DNA molecules with a special protein catalyst, a special enzyme, I can cut the DNA into shorter pieces, with the cut ends left sticky. Using similar techniques, I can isolate DNA molecules from a bacterium and chop it into small pieces, whose cut ends are also sticky. Usually this bacteria will be a particular species, derived from a bacteria common in the human gut, and called E. coli. On mixing the two tubes of DNA together, pieces of mouse DNA will join through their sticky ends with lengths of bacterial DNA. Such molecules, containing the genetic material of two different organisms, are termed "recombinant DNA" molecules.

These recombinant molecules can then be incorporated back into a living growing bacterium. When the bacterium divides, it reproduces its own DNA, and it also reproduces whatever piece of mouse DNA, whatever mouse genes, are incorporated into that bacterium. If we isolated a single such bacterium and incubate it in some beef broth, the next morning we will have a hundred billion daughter cells. Each of these will have an identical copy of the mouse gene. Molecular biologists speak of this as "cloning" a mouse gene.

Because bacteria, despite their complexity, are vastly simpler than a mouse cell, the techniques of chemistry and biochemistry can be used to study the mouse gene, and sometimes the protein whose structure it encodes. From these studies I might learn something about the signals involved in turning this gene on in some cells, and off in others. I might get some hint as to how the genetic information stored in the nucleus of a cell provides the blueprint for the three dimensional structure and the function of the cell.

This technology requires no more equipment than is found in a common college microbiology laboratory. It can be and is being used in a vast variety of research situations. Furthermore, using recently developed techniques, one can transfer in the other direction, and introduce DNA of a bacterium into a mouse cell. Similarly one can introduce DNA from one species of mouse into another, or transfer small segments of DNA from human cells into mouse cells, or into other human cells. Because of the hundreds of research laboratories using these techniques, experiments that are called "impossible" today turn out to be routine six months later.

Commercial exploitation and biological hazards

Though the scientific community generally views recombinant DNA technology as a feature of research, private corporations have moved rapidly to exploit it commercially, to produce for sale strains of economically or agriculturally valuable organisms. In addition to small venture capital firms, and practically the entire pharmaceutical industry, there have been substantial investments by transnational corporations such as International Nickel, Standard Oil, and Imperical Chemical Industries. A well-publicized case in the drug industry is Eli Lilly Corporation's plan to produce human insulin for sale to diabetics, by growth of strains of E. coli bacteria containing the gene for human insulin. Lilly believes that this will allow them to produce insulin more cheaply than their present process, in which bovine insulin is extracted from the pancreases obtained from beef cattle. The sale of insulin to diabetics is a $100 million dollar a year business.

There has been substantial debate over the deployment of recombinant DNA technology and its possible hazards. For example, though E. coli is a normal inhabitant of our intestinal tract, certain strains cause infantile meningitis and diarrhoea; other strains cause urinary tract infection in women, and serious bloodstream infection in hospital patients. Were such a strain to be synthesizing and exporting insulin, it could well cause additional damage.

To the extent that such strains might escape and establish themselves in some niche in the environment, they constitute a form of pollution. But such biological pollution is qualitatively different from other forms of pollution, such as heavy metals, oil or chemicals. Organisms reproduce themselves and cannot easily be removed from the ecosystem.

After considerable debate and controversy, the scientific community adopted guidelines requiring that recombinant DNA experiments use weakened strains of bacteria, which are unlikely to survive outside the laboratory, and that physical containment procedures be used, making escape even less likely. These guidelines are now referred to as the NIH (National Institutes of Health) guidelines. The controversy in Cambridge arose over the question of the adequacy of the guidelines, and whether it should be left to the scientists, or be overseen or supervised by the community and by laboratory workers. Cambridge and a few other communities passed ordinances making the guidelines mandatory, and they carry considerable weight for researchers. However, they do not apply to private industry or non-federally funded research. Laws regulating the activities of private corporations were proposed by a number of Congressmen, but were beaten back by the combined influence of the corporations and one wing of the scientific community. In Great Britain, however, the guidelines cover the entire country, and are strengthened by strong representation from the workers involved and through the Trades Union Congress.

Some observers have found it difficult to understand why scientists should be so concerned about the community imposing safety standards on laboratory work. Many of the constraints of safety are inconveniences, but they are relatively minor, as one can see by the rate at which work proceeds. However, safety procedures that are a minor inconvenience for ten millilitres of cells, have a very different impact on production of a thousand litres at the commercial scale. Safer procedures may substantially increase production costs and therefore reduce profit margins. If concerned scientists, citizens and workers demand strong safety standards, these will substantially increase the cost of production, which will in turn decrease profit margins. It may also result in a degree of community and worker control over the production process. Efforts to reduce profits or to get participatory control of production in transnational corporations often meet stubborn resistance.

There are human costs in new technologies, such as damage to the lungs of coal miners after the development of deep mining, or the induction of bladder cancer in workers in the British and German chemical industries, or lung cancer among uranium miners. These have generally been borne by the workers alone. In the case of recombinant DNA technology a movement has formed which insists that such costs be reckoned with from the beginning, as part of the production process, and not be passed on to an unwilling or unknowing population. It is not just costs-versus-benefit, but who gets the benefits and who bears the costs.

The attempt to protect capital investment and profit margins distorts certain features of the scientific process. A number of the corporations involved in exploiting recombinant DNA technology have obtained patents on organisms and processes. The scientists involved developed this work through public funding. They then entered into relations with the companies to patent developments which should have been the property of the whole population. Thus, in the recombinant DNA controversy some of the spokesmen calling for the unfettered (and unregulated) "search for truth" represented very different interests. Make no mistake: the controversy over recombinant DNA technology is not about freedom of enquiry; the debate is about regulating those who want to rashly exploit for private gain the fruits of knowledge which should belong to all peoples.

Agricultural and microbial productivity

In the future a very important and potentially socially productive application of recombinant DNA and other molecular genetic technologies is the development of new strains of plants and micro-organisms. The danger here is a familiar one to many of you: the strains developed in the industrialized countries will be designed for capital intensive agriculture, requiring chemical fertilizer, pesticides, and the destruction of any indigenous ecosystem. The most productive uses with respect to preservation of human and natural resources probably will in fact come from less manipulative technologies.

Thus in India, China and Pakistan, microbial technologies for converting manure and waste to clean gas for use in cooking, heating and transportation have been developed, taking advantage of existing bacterial strains. The residue provides a good source of fertilizer. Similarly in India, Burma and Nepal, there have been very successful projects to take advantage of strains of blue-green algae, which fix nitrogen, in fertilizing rice paddies, which provide half the world's food.

If the education and know-how does not exist to investigate and develop the features of local ecosystems, it will be difficult for the peoples of the developing countries to control imported technologies which rapidly introduce new strains of organisms, without proper investigation or consideration for the local reality.

A second danger derives from corporations moving production facilities for modified organisms from industrialized countries to developing countries, to escape regulation. Of course this would be done in the name of transfer of technology. The health hazards of recombinant DNA technology are much more acute in developing countries, where the conditions for spread of infectious disease still exist.

Human genetic engineering

The new biological technologies make possible the genetic modification of human beings. There is a great deal of very active research with small mammals, mice, rabbits, etc. both on introducing segments of DNA into these cells, and in analysing the DNA, as described earlier, by taking pieces out of the cells and cloning them in bacteria. Thus attempts are now being made to remove, for example, bone marrow cells, which form blood cells, from an animal, and insert into those cells the DNA segment coding for hemoglobin. If the added segment is incorporated into the cell, it can be transplanted back into the animal. This is a model for gene therapy of inherited blood diseases, such as sickle cell anemia and thalassemias.

The development of human *in vitro* fertilization, by Edwards and Steptoe, has vastly increased the potentialities for human genetic manipulation. In this case one can obtain in the test tube the earliest stages of a human embryo. By introducing DNA, or cells altered in the laboratory, into this early stage embryo, and then implanting the embryo back into the womb, one might introduce genetic change in most of the cells of the body, including the germ line cells. Thus the changes would be passed to subsequent generations.

Prior to the genetic manipulation itself, there will be vastly increased using of DNA technology to analyse physically the DNA of human cells. Some of this will be used for screening purposes, as in those rare cases where the change in the DNA and the relationship to disease is known, such as in certain rare inherited blood diseases. Instead of examining the blood itself in the mature fetus, one examines the DNA of the cells of the early embryo, or of the parents.

The use of genetic technologies on human beings will expand in the medical sector far more rapidly than any of us can accurately predict. They will bring alleviation of suffering to a small number of individuals, and they will also generate many moral and social dilemmas. Let me briefly touch on some of the complications.

In examining the DNA of different individuals, researchers will be confronted by the full range of genetic variation among individuals. What constitutes a genetic defect, and what constitutes genetic variation? Historically the values of many human genetically determined features, such as skin colour and hair character, were socially determined. What is a defect in one society is a desirable characteristic in another. At the biological level sickle cell trait is considered by some a genetic defect in the US. But in central Africa it is necessary for survival in malaria infested areas, rendering the blood cells resistant to the malarial parasite.

A second problem is the distortion of the true causes of human disease. Genetic engineering technology will focus attention on affected individuals and their genes. As a result, there is a strong tendency to lose sight of the agents that caused the damage in the first place: mutagens, carcinogens, radiation, etc. Our problems are not in our genes, they are in recreating a society in which the genes of individuals are protected from unnecessary damage.

Note that not all conditions resulting from damage to genes are inherited. If the egg is damaged, resulting in altered chromosome composition, as in Down's syndrome, this is not passed on to the next generation. Mongolism is not inherited, though it is due to altered chromosome abnormality.

Conclusions

The World Council of Churches should support every effort to expand and increase knowledge of the ecosystem, of the functioning of living things, and of their interactions with the environment, and of the effect of various forms of human society on these interactions. This knowledge must be available to all the peoples of the earth, and not just to a technocratic elite.

The most pressing area is the application of biological science to the ecosystems in the developing world. There must be efforts to solve some of these problems by biological technologies such as the development of better adapted strains of rice, corn and microbes. However, before this is done it is imperative that these biological systems first be studied, described and analysed, so that the manipulations are appropriate for the people who live there.

In the present situation a number of the most potent biological technologies are being developed by transnational corporations and institutions who subtly serve private gain rather than social and economic justice. To select what is needed will require very broad biological, ecological and agricultural education. The same lessons that many of the peoples of the world have learned with respect to the import of technologies of exploitation will have to be applied in the biological field.

The World Council of Churches should encourage participation of citizens in the decision-making processes surrounding the new biological technologies, whether on biohazards committees, protection of human subjects committees or other appropriate forms. Again, this will require substantial biological education and an investigation of environmental and occupational health. Appropriate liaison might be through the International Labour Office, the World Health Organization, and the United Nations Agency for Development.

In the area of human experimentation and genetic manipulation, the WCC should take an active role in ensuring that the development of very sophisticated technologies for helping a small number of individuals does not obscure the pressing need for eliminating the causes of disease and of genetic damage. An appropriate form might be a task force on protection of the genetic inheritance from environmental and social damage. This will require input into the setting of priorities in biomedical research, not just in the use of the technology that is developed. Otherwise we are deprived of the options of those technologies that were not developed. Thus we can transplant kidneys, but we cannot prevent kidney disease.

In closing, the problems of protecting our genes and of biological manipulation seem to me dwarfed by the danger of obliteration of future generations from nuclear war, and the danger to our genes from the plutonium and other deadly by-products of the production of nuclear weapons. I appeal to you as a scientist and biologist: do not allow this conference to close without speaking out as strongly as you can on the need for reversing the nuclear arms race that so deeply threatens future generations. Without the removal of this gravest of threats to human society, there will be no possibility of achieving the just, participatory and sustainable society that we all deeply desire.

Bio-ethics: Some Challenges from a Liberation Perspective

KAREN LEBACQZ

The task

In Lewis Carroll's delightful story *Alice in Wonderland*, Alice has a tendency to change size, not always at will. On one such occasion, the following dialogue ensures:

"Don't squeeze so," said the Dormouse to Alice.

"I can't help it. I'm growing," she replied.

"You've no right to grow *here*."

"Don't talk nonsense; you know you're growing, too."

"Yes, but *I* grow at a reasonable pace, and not in that ridiculous fashion."

These words describe all too accurately what many of us feel today in the face of the so-called "biological revolution": sitting next to something that appears to be growing at a ridiculous rate, we feel "squeezed" and are tempted to cry out: "You've no right to grow *here*." Wonderland, or bad dream? Current arguments posit one or the other: proponents hold out visions of miraculous cures for human ailments and new freedoms in human living, while opponents raise the spectre of Huxley's *Brave New World*. Perhaps the only thing on which both would agree is that developments in biomedical technology threaten to change the nature of our existence.

Rather than undertake a direct discussion of ethical dilemmas raised by biomedical research and technological capacity, I wish to raise a more profound question related to our sense of being "squeezed". The great church historian Ernst Troeltsch once said: "If the present social situation is to be controlled by Christian principles, thoughts will be necessary which have not yet been thought, and which will correspond to this new situation as the older forms met the need of the social situation in earlier ages."[1]

In the conviction that advances in biomedical technology require the development of "thoughts which have not yet been thought", I shall focus on the *way* we analyse ethical issues in biomedical arenas. That is, my concern will be methodological rather than substantive. In particular, I shall argue that the predominant western approach to bio-ethical issues suffers serious limitations and should be challenged in the light of some emerging ethical reflection, particularly that of feminist and liberation theology.

Bio-ethics: the prevailing approach

Most contemporary writings in bio-ethics share certain characteristics. While the following list would not apply uniformly, it does suggest the predominant characteristics of the field.

1. Decision-orientation

Like much current social ethics, both philosophical and theological, contemporary bio-ethics is largely decision-oriented. It focuses on such questions as: "Should we operate on this newborn infant with a congenital defect?", "Should we permit recombinant DNA research?" and so on. Indeed, most has been "crisis"-oriented, dealing not simply with action decisions in medical research and care, but with catastrophic events rather than routine questions about delivery of care.[2]

In short, we have focused on *doing the right thing*. This discussion of the right thing to do has resulted in increased clarity about the nature and meaning of some ethical dilemmas, some movement towards resolution of important ethical dilemmas in particular cases, and agreement about basic ethical principles applicable to certain bio-ethical dilemmas.

Nonetheless, the decision-orientation of contemporary bio-ethics has serious flaws. First, it tends to give the impression that there is *one* correct decision in every dilemma and that our only task is to find the "right" answer. It ignores the possibility that every possible action may embody some important values and that what may be at stake is not finding the "right" answer but choosing among competing values.

---

[1] Ernst Troeltsch: *The Social Teachings of the Christian Churches*, p. 1012. New York: Harper Torchback Edition, 1960.

[2] I have criticized this "crisis" approach in an earlier essay. See Karen Lebacqz: "Peter and His Doctor". *Journal of Current Social Issues*, Fall 1975. At the same time, I wish to emphasize that I have also tended to adopt the decision-orientation in my own writings in the field of bio-ethics. Thus, the purpose of this essay is not to assign blame to those who take such an approach, but to try to be cognizant of its limits.

Second, traditional normative ethics considers at least three questions: (1) which actions are right; (2) what makes a person "good" or virtuous; and (3) what constitutes the "ideal state" or structure of human society. The decision-orientation of contemporary bio-ethics focuses on the first of these. With some exceptions, two important aspects of normative ethics have been largely ignored.

2. Individualistic orientation

Most contemporary bio-ethics is also individualistic. It begins with the concerns of individual patients or physicians as they encounter dilemmas. Indeed, much contemporary bio-ethics takes as its starting place the "physician-patient relationship".[3]

This focus reflects the western, white culture from which such discussions originate, and is not adequate to explain the needs and experiences of most of the world. In many localities and countries, the major health questions have nothing to do with physicians and how they treat patients, but have instead to do with poor housing, inadequate sewage systems, and so on. In other localities, health care is provided through massive bureaucracies in which the primary problem may be that of getting *access* to a physician, not how one is treated once one finally sees her or him.[4] In a social structure where there is no access to physicians for major portions of the population, or in which one's "physician-patient relationship" comprises no more than 2% of one's medical and health care, a bio-ethics that takes the "physician-patient relationship" as normative is simply inapplicable. What is needed is an approach that focuses on systems and institutions and that takes seriously the entire web of relationships in the delivery of care, of which the presumed "physician-patient relationship" is only one.

3. Ahistorical approach

Partly because of the search for norms and principles that are generally applicable, bio-ethics as currently practised tends to be ahistorical. It is assumed that once the "right" answer is found, it will be correct for all similar cases; little discussion is given to the changing historical setting within which bio-ethical decisions are made and whether this setting might affect the

---

[3] While examples are legion, one of the best known is Paul Ramsey's important volume, *The Patient as Person* (New Haven: Yale University Press, 1970).

[4] I personally have not had a sustained "physician-patient relationship" with any single physician for more than 16 years; I find that my single most important problem is getting *to* the doctor—it routinely takes two hours of telephoning, two hours of waiting, and at least four contacts with clerks, receptionists, nurses, and others before I see the physician for what is generally a maximum of ten minutes. Since I am a relatively well-situated and well-educated health care consumer, I can only imagine how such problems might be multiplied for those who are less fortunate.

correctness of the decision. Resulting norms tend to be rigid.[5] While not all theorists agree with the "absolutist" position that, for example, rejects all abortion as unethical, most assume that once the proper "exceptions" are found, they hold irrespective of historical circumstance.

The "contextual" or "situational" approach to ethics, which gained popularity in the United States during the 1960's, attempted to correct this ahistorical rigidity by refusing to accept any "absolutes". However, in its own way it remains ahistorical: by failing to specify clearly *which* aspects of a situation or *which* historical changes make a difference, it also tends to focus on the immediate situation and loses any historical "bite". It leaves one with the impression that historical settings either do not matter at all, or that there is no way to sort out which do and which do not; thus, it fails to specify criteria for deciding which historical contexts are "morally relevant".

4. Scientific evidence as normative

Most bio-ethicists today operate out of the dominant western scientific world-view, in which science sets criteria for the acceptability of evidence. The results are, first, a minimizing of the value of individual or group experience, and second, a blurring of the value-laden nature of "facts" or data.

It is not uncommon, for example, to hear an ethicist say that the medical personnel or scientists must provide the "facts" or evidence in the case. While personal experiences are not totally ignored, they tend to be discredited: "feelings" are not an adequate basis for ethical decision-making; only logical analysis of "facts" will do. This tends to take the decision away from those most intimately involved, for they are often not in possession of all the data and are also inclined to be emotional in their responses.

Moreover, it tends to obfuscate the value-laden nature of data. Data are not value-free. We make choices about what to look for, how to measure what we find, and how to present it. Professional training determines to a large extent how we structure inquiry and how we interpret the results of that inquiry. In addition, prior value assumptions shape our interpretation and presentation of data. (E.g. is there a 50% chance of having a normal child, or a 50% chance of having a defective child? Note that the term "defective" is itself a value judgment, not a statement of fact.)

5. Grounding of norms

Most discussions of bio-ethical issues, particularly those by Christian ethicists, either accept a wide variety of grounding sources for norms or fail to specify the grounding of particular norms; there is also little discussion of the movement from theological presuppositions to particular norms.[6] For

---

[5] This is particularly a problem when norms are turned into governmental regulations. The norm "seek informed consent" still permits some flexibility; however, a law mandating informed consent does not permit the same flexibility.

[6] Several recent volumes attempt to address this problem. See Philip Wogaman: *A Christian Method of Moral Judgment* (Philadelphia: Westminster Press, 1976).

example, in his influential book *The Patient as Person*, Ramsey introduces a number of Judeo-Christian affirmations such as *hesed* (steadfast love), covenant (faithfulness), and the like. In his discussion of concrete issues, however, he turns to norms derived from medical sources such as the Nuremberg Code with its requirement for informed consent. The link between the two sources—if, indeed, there is any—is not clear, and it is often not clear how Ramsey incorporates his Christian principles into an otherwise Kantian perspective.

It is understandable, of course, that Christian ethicists working in the field of bio-ethics would incorporate a broad base for normative statements. Many operate out of a "natural law" tradition or approach in which they affirm as a part of their Christian belief a general set of norms available to all persons and not necessarily distinctive for Christians.[7] Moreover bio-ethicists must speak to lawyers, scientists, politicians, and others who do not operate out of a specifically Christian approach. It therefore behoves the Christian ethicist not to be overly narrow.

Nonetheless, the failure to specify the grounding for norms results in confusion and disagreement as to (1) what norms there are, if any; (2) which are applicable to the situation; (3) how they are to be interpreted, e.g. does "justice" require protection of the vulnerable or simply equal treatment?; and (4) how to weigh and balance conflicting norms, e.g. does the potential social good outweigh the requirement to seek informed consent in certain types of research or genetic screening programmes? In particular, we need to know whether it makes a difference to do bio-ethics as a "Christian" and, if so, what that difference is.

Challenges and alternatives

I shall here suggest some major alternatives to the prevailing mode of doing bio-ethics, drawing primarily on contemporary work in feminist and liberation theology.[8] I shall also indicate the sorts of questions that these

---

[7] For example, in his discussion of proxy consent for children, Richard McCormick argues that there are certain values that all human beings ought to uphold, and that therefore one may give consent on behalf of a child in order to foster those values. See "Proxy Consent in the Experimentation Situation". *Perspectives in Biology and Medicine*, Vol. 18, No. 1, 1974.

[8] Two words of explanation are in order here. First, much "feminist" theology *is* liberation theology and can be classified under that general heading. However, some feminist theologizing does not fit neatly under the liberation approach, and I have therefore chosen to specify that I am drawing from both types of theological thought as they are emerging.

Second, feminist and liberation theologies are not the only sources of some of the alternative insights and approaches specified here. A number of male theologians and ethicists from the dominant tradition have fostered one or another of these concerns, e.g. the Niebuhr stress on community, the work of Gustafson, Stanley Hauerwas, and others on character and virtue, James McClendon's stress on biography. Nonetheless, I shall take the theology from feminists and liberation thinkers as my baseline for this analysis.

alternative approaches would suggest, though it will not be possible here to answer these questions or to put them into full context.

1. Patterns of meaning and structural concerns

Liberation theologians and feminists are primarily concerned not with choosing the right action, but with structures and patterns of meaning.

I believe that this is partly why there has been little attention in these writings to bio-ethical issues, important though technological advances in biomedicine may be for the lives of women and other members of oppressed and disadvantaged groups. At a recent conference on Ethical Issues in Reproductive Technology: Analysis by Women, questions about whether *in vitro* fertilization is right or wrong were transmuted into questions about who holds the power to make such decisions, what the impact of all biomedical technologies combined is on the lives of women in this society, and so on.[9] In short, questions about what is right and wrong to *do* were ignored in favour of questions about the nature of the social structures and mythologies that support these technologies.

Other liberation theologians argue that it is not merely the shape of *particular* social institutions and structures that must be analysed, but the shape of the entire *age* or epoch. For example, Roy Sano argues that Asian American liberation theologians and people turn to apocalyptic rather than prophetic literature because apocalyptic literature gives a better base from which to observe the interweavings of the various powerful institutions.[10] Dussel argues that what is at stake is recognizing the shape of evil in any and all institutions.[11] Feminist theologians analyse the myths that undergird particular institutions by defining the "masculine" and "feminine" in society.[12] Thus, it is not simply particular institutions that are to be analysed ethically, but the thought structures, myths, and loyalties that permit those institutions to exist. The very shape of the scientific world-view may be at stake.

---

[9] Held at Amherst, Massachusetts, 24-29 June 1979.

[10] Roy Sano: "Ethnic Liberation Theology: Neo-Orthodoxy Reshaped or Replaced?" *Christianity and Crisis*, 10 November 1975. Others who are using apocalyptic literature and suggesting that it is the entire shape of the age that must be analysed and criticized include William Stringfellow: *An Ethic for Christians and Other Aliens in a Strange Land* (Waco, Texas: Word Books, 1973), and William Coats: *God in Public: Political Theology Beyond Niebuhr* (Grand Rapids, Michigan: William B. Eerdmans, 1974).

[11] Enrique Dussel: *Ethics and the Theology of Liberation*. New York: Orbis Books, 1978.

[12] See, for example, Jo Freeman (ed.): *Women: a Feminist Perspective* (Palo Alto: Mayfield, 1979); Anne Koedt *et al.*: *Radical Feminism* (New York: Quadrangle/The New York Times Book Co., 1973); Mary Daly: *Gyn/Ecology: the Metaethics of Radical Feminism* (Boston: Beacon Press, 1978); Sheila Collins: *A Different Heaven and Earth* (Valley Forge, Pa.: Judson Press, 1974); Mary Vetterling-Braggin *et al.*: *Feminism and Philosophy* (Totowa, NJ: Littlefield, Adams and Co., 1977); Rosemary Reuther: *Religion and Sexism* (New York: Simon and Schuster, 1974).

Applied to the biomedical arena, these insights would suggest some new questions to be asked: What images of health, disease, normalcy, womanhood, sexuality, etc. undergird the present delivery of health care and development of new biomedical technologies? Who or what are our current idols? Where are our loyalties? What is the relationship between the development of new biomedical technologies and nuclear power, communications technology, and so on? The primary ethical question has to do with the shape and inter-relationship of the dominant social structures and their impact on the lives of those who are oppressed. It is in part a theological question, having to do with our loyalties and whether we give our allegiance to anything other than God—even to the scientific world-view.

2. Story and community

As soon as one asks about patterns of meaning, one moves beyond looking at the specific decision to asking how that decision fits into the context of a life. The particular decision may either make sense or be muted in its total context within the person's life. Thus, questions of character, integrity, and virtue come to have central significance, and the telling and shaping of one's life story is crucial to the ethical task.[13]

The women's movement and feminist theology in particular have stressed the importance of life stories as the groundwork for theology. As women share their experiences, they locate patterns of meaning that emerge and give theological dimension. Theology and ethics, thus, are born of experience and its coherence in a life story.[14]

But this is partly because the interpretative framework brought to one's own life story has political significance. As women commonly put it, "the personal is political". This means that the entire context in which one interprets one's own story also matters. And so a concern for story and its patterns of meaning results in a concern for community. Indeed, it is often only when women are together in community that they make the transition from saying "I'm depressed"—an interpretative framework provided by the dominant western scientific world-view—to saying "I'm oppressed"—an interpretation possible within the context of a liberating community.

Applied to the field of bio-ethics, this concern for story and community would suggest that we ask not: "Should this woman have an abortion?" but:

---

[13] For example, in *Beyond Mere Obedience*, Dorothe Söelle describes the life story of a woman who broke many of the conventions of her day and whose life would probably be judged by most to include some unethical acts. Nonetheless, within the context of her total life, she has gone "beyond mere obedience" into a life of freedom, and she expresses some virtues and character that over-ride her particular misdoings.

[14] Sheila Collins is particularly emphatic on this point. See *A Different Heaven and Earth, op. cit.*, and "Reflections on the Meaning of Herstory" and "Theology in the Politics of Appalachian Women", in Carol Christ and Judith Plaskow: *Womanspirit Rising*. New York: Harper and Row, 1979.

"What is this woman's story? What are the interpretative frameworks that give meaning to her life? Does she have a supportive community? Is she oppressed? Will the abortion be liberating for her? Will it be community-building or community destroying?"

The concern for story and community that arises from feminist and liberation perspectives is akin to Ramsey's concern for covenant, Lehmann's focus on the koinonia, and H. R. Niebuhr's concern for accountability structures, in that it focuses on one's relationship within a group. However, I believe that feminist and liberation theologians are more true to the biblical perspective when they go beyond Ramsey, Lehmann, and Niebuhr to the point of seeing one's *identity* as in some way intimately related to that group. Ramsey talks about covenants between physician and patient as though no others need be involved, whereas women and members of oppressed groups argue that those in existence today have sufficient continuity with those of the past to be able to stand in their stead and receive what was their due. This is a radically different notion of identity and I believe that it is one of the contributions that a feminist or liberation theology might make to the field of bio-ethics.

3. History (or "herstory", as feminists say)

What has just been said makes it clear that feminists and liberation theologians also require a *historical* ethic—an ethic that takes seriously the oppression of people through time and asks: "Is something that was appropriate yesterday still appropriate today? Will it be appropriate tomorrow?" Yesterday's oppressions are not simply forgotten, but must be rectified today. Thus, for example, no interpretation of justice may be proffered that fails to account for retribution and compensation for past injury. Perhaps most important, this focus on history requires the rewriting of history, with a view to lifting up the role of women and other oppressed peoples—to locating the "fore-mothers" as well as the "fore-fathers" of current medical practice and technological innovation.

Applied to the arena of bio-ethics, this historical view would certainly preclude an absolute and unyielding "yes" or "no" to technological innovations. More important, however, it would require a second look at the history of development of biomedical technologies to ask how that history is perceived from the perspective of oppressed peoples, how it impacts on their lives and possibilities, and so on. One is tempted to suggest that from this perspective serious questions need to be raised about whether these technologies should be developed in the absence of basic nutritional, health, and medical care in "third world" countries.

4. Experiential approach

To argue for the importance of history, and for the re-claiming of one's story, is also to argue for new interpretative frameworks. Thus, new criteria for evidence are emerging. Scientific data are *not* the only source of meaningful interpretation; the life histories and shared experiences of oppressed groups are the primary "facts" to be considered. Most feel that only those who have had such experiences can communicate them accurately. Thus, there is a tendency to shift from a dependence on experts to a focus on the layperson.

This new approach also suggests that there may be numerous valid value systems, not one "right" approach. At the same time, as the above analysis has shown, the primary loyalty is always to those who are oppressed, and it is their interpretations and perspectives that are given most validity.

Applied to the ethical issues posed by technological advances in medicine and science, the questions become obvious: What is the experience of women who want desperately to become pregnant and are unable to conceive? Why do they want this so desperately—i.e. what in the system creates this need? How does the development of these technologies affect the chances for life and health of the "Third World"? And, perhaps most important, are these developments really "advances" at all? Finally, a participatory decision-making model, perhaps involving community as well as individual participation, might be called for with respect to each technology and to the scientific enterprise as a whole.

5. Sources for ethics

Since the question of norms is no longer the only question asked, the issue of grounding of norms is broadened to ask about sources of ethical insight. From the above, it is clear that a primary source for both feminists and liberation theologians is the experience of the oppressed group. Indeed, Cone goes so far as to assert that only those who are "black" can talk about God in the United States.[15]

Taking the experiences of the oppressed as central to the theological task has led some feminists to move beyond Christianity altogether, and to assert that the grounding for theological insight lies in women's bodies (e.g. menstruation and bodily cycles), dreams, and rituals.[16] Others retain a closer adherence to biblical insight, but with the proviso that the biblical message be measured and interpreted by the experiences of the oppressed.[17]

Serious questions remain for feminists and liberation theologians at this point. Is there a different norm or ethic for each group? Or is there only one ethical system, but that one discernible only by the oppressed? Is there a "natural law" or insight into ethical stances and norms provided by the natural (e.g. women's bodies)? Until such methodological questions are addressed systematically, the impact of these new approaches cannot be fully

---

[15] James Cone: *A Black Theology of Liberation*. New York: J. B. Lippincott, 1970. It is not clear whether "black" refers to skin colour necessarily or whether those of like spirit but different skin colour might be "black".

[16] See essays by Plaskow, Goldenberg, Washburn, and Christ in *Womanspirit Rising, op. cit.*

[17] See essays by Trible, Fiorenza, McLaughlin in *Womanspirit Rising, op. cit.*

assessed. It is difficult to know thus far what the impact on bio-ethics might be of new approaches to the source of ethical insight.

Conclusions

It is not the rate of growth of biomedical technologies *per se* that makes us feel "squeezed". Rather, it is the threat they present to the meaning structures of our world. This essay is submitted in the hopes of initiating the task of creating "thoughts which have not yet been thought" and which will meet the social situation of our day. Wonderland, or nightmare? Much depends on our perspective. Will we open that perspective to the challenge of the oppressed and incorporate into the doing of bio-ethics the message of liberation theology?

Genetic Meddling
A Response by Gabriel Nahas

I will comment briefly on the question of recombinant DNA and genetic engineering, which has also been called "genetic meddling". I believe that we are dealing here with an ethical problem more fundamental than one in public health or corporate profit. The main question is whether we have the right to put an additional fearful load on generations yet unborn—to let mortal men, be they scientists, make such an enormous, far-reaching decision as the creation of a new form of life.

One must consider the irreversibility of what is being contemplated and performed. Erwin Chargaff has denounced what he calls an attack on the biosphere, unthinkable to previous generations. One cannot recall a new form of life after it has been created. Should man, even *homo scientificus*, be trusted in the haphazard creation of new forms of life? Are we right in getting ready to mix what nature has kept apart?

The consequences will survive their mortal creator and his descendants. The worst is that our own generation will never know those consequences. The relationship between bacteria and higher forms of life is still poorly understood. They are in one form or another waging a constant warfare against each other. By blindly transforming this relationship we may be throwing a veil of uncertainty over the life of coming generations.

Are we not irreversibly risking the evolutionary wisdom of millions of years in order to satisfy the ambition and curiosity of the new entrepreneurs of the scientific establishment? Are we not losing sight of the slow process of evolution, that patient pilgrimage of man on earth, so beautifully set forth by

Teilhard de Chardin who describes in *Le devenir humain* the future of man moving in the midst of "the divine milieu"?

As Chargaff said, this world is given to us on loan. We come and we go. After a time we leave earth and air and water to others who come after us. My generation has been the first to engage under the leadership of the sciences in a destructive colonial warfare against nature. The future may well curse us for it. The wilful interference of man with the homeostasis of nature, of creation, is an act which betrays a fundamental lack of faith. Scientific imagination has also its pathology, and the urge to change irreversibly the biosphere may be one of its manifestations.

My life has been marked by two immense and fateful discoveries in science: the splitting of the atom and the recognition of the chemistry of heredity, DNA and its subsequent manipulation. It is the mistreatment of the nucleus that in both instances lies at the basis: the nucleus of the atom and the nucleus of the cell. In both instances I have the feeling that science has transgressed a barrier that should have remained inviolate.

Two biblical verses come to my mind: "You shall walk humbly with your God", and "There is a time to live and a time to die". For those who remain behind we should leave a creation which is not altered profoundly from its natural evolutionary course. Where are we going? Today, the cure of genetic disease; tomorrow, the experimental improvement of the human character through the administration of psycho-active molecules? The scientist should stop playing God and listen to what God has to say in preserving his creation and its evolution into the distant future.

Issues in Genetic Counselling
A Response by TRAUTE SCHROEDER

As a medical doctor and a human geneticist, I am involved in genetic counselling daily. To complement the papers of Dr King and Dr Lebacqz, I will mention some of the ethical conflicts that emerge in our everyday practice with people in need.

During the last 10-15 years, genetic counselling has become an important field in preventive medicine. The general population is using this opportunity more and more, especially when severe diseases have already occurred in the family. The book *Genetics and the Quality of Life*, edited by Charles Birch and Paul Abrecht, describes the major conflicts and problems in this field.

In 1974 the abortion laws in the Federal Republic of Germany were extended. Abortion is legally allowed within the first 12 weeks of pregnancy for so-called social reasons. It is also legal for medical and genetic reasons up to the twenty-second week of pregnancy. Similar laws have been introduced in many countries. The law leaves the final decision to the mother, in line with Dr Lebacqz's discussion of "identity and her story". In the FRG we now have about 35 genetic counselling units.

Genetic counselling means:

— listening to the problems of our patients; Dr Lebacqz has already mentioned that we should try to get detailed insight into the patients' outlook on life and understand their feelings and anxieties;
— reconfirmation of the diagnosis of an inherited or non-inherited disease in the family;
— ascertainment of the risk of whether or not, or to what degree, the patient and/or offspring will suffer from the same disease;
— discussion with patients about the risk and their reaction to it, including information about modern methods of detection, available in selected cases, such as prenatal diagnosis by amniocentesis or fetoscopy.

The genetic counsellor is necessarily involved in decision-making. He should be very much situation-oriented and he has to build a very close physician-patient relationship. There is no question of a ten-minute interview: genetic counselling usually requires between one and two hours per session.

The ethical conflicts concern the genetic counsellor as well as the patient. In the absence of new bio-ethical norms, the counsellor tries to present scientific data but he realizes that these data are not value-free. I fully agree with Dr Lebacqz that each case should be treated individually and cannot be subject to rigid norms, since there is never a perfect solution. This means that counsellor and patient always face ethical conflicts.

Amniocentesis and selective abortion is not the general solution for health problems and family planning, but nevertheless it is one possible way for a very few parents to avoid having a child with a severe inherited disease or malformation. It should be imperative for human geneticists to continue the research for improved treatments of inherited diseases, so that in a number of cases prenatal diagnosis leading to selective abortion will no longer be necessary.

In Germany—and in other countries, of course—the mass media continue to propagate the image of the perfect child under the heading "responsible family planning". The biological norm is a human being with a beautiful body, intelligent and mentally well-balanced, without genetic defects. Many young couples demand genetic counselling with written guarantees of a perfect child. They do not even want to accept the risk of anomalies connected with every pregnancy, and they definitely would not accept a low-account risk for malformations like cleft palate. Hemophiliacs demand selective abortion of their daughters because they carry the defective gene, although they themselves are healthy.

Most people do not realize that we all pass a number of defective genes on to the next generation. The Christian idea that suffering is a part of our lives is no longer recognized in western society. In other societies this idea is still alive, and the problems connected with genetic counselling, prenatal diagnosis and selective abortion are therefore quite different.

What will and can the churches do to teach and support Christians, within a society which starts defining personal health at a level that excludes minor anomalies? Let us see the danger of destruction which lies in the programme of prenatal diagnosis and selective abortion, and also legal abortion for social reasons. Although modern medical technology offers these possibilities, we should not have to take and misuse them on the grounds that abortion has become a minor medical affair and the elimination of the unwanted seems to be the solution to a problem.

Reactions and Comment

Time in the plenary session was quite inadequate for any intensive discussion of the many issues raised by the addresses and platform comments. Among the several observations from the floor, the one that raised most discussion in succeeding days was that of Fr Vitaly Borovoy of the Russian Orthodox Church, who was concerned that the ethic of Lebacqz seemed too situational, with insufficient attention to enduring criteria of judgment. There was no major response in the plenary session to the provocative position of Nahas. That, along with many other items, had to be turned over to the considerations of Section IV on "Ethical Issues in the Biological Manipulation of Life".

The report of Section IV to the plenary session the following week led to further discussion. The conference recommended adoption of international guidelines for all work in recombinant DNA. And after extensive debate and amendment of the original proposal from Section IV, it recommended that the WCC Working Committee on Church and Society "establish a continuing body to deal with ethical, theological, social and legal problems arising from (a) abortion of genetically defective fetuses; and (b) AID, donor egg and embryo transfer". It further voted that this study group consist of people of different theological positions and disciplines with at least 40% women and more if possible. The full text of these and other recommendations appears in Volume 2.

15. The Gathering and Processing of Information

Introduction

In planning the conference, the Working Committee on Church and Society invited the host institution, MIT, to provide the programme for one plenary session. The invitation was extended through David Rose, a member of the Working Committee and a professor at MIT, and the subject of the meeting was left to Rose to work out with his colleagues. The decision was to arrange a session on the topic of the gathering and processing of information. Three members of the faculty at MIT were the speakers.

If anyone had expected that the MIT speakers would present a united front against the critics of high technology, they were surprised. The three speakers generated almost as broad differences among themselves as existed on the floor of the conference.

David Staelin, of the Department of Electrical Engineering and Computer Science, spoke on the benefits of terrestrial satellites, emphasizing both the possibilities and realities of international cooperation. His address depended in large part on slides showing the earth from satellites. It has been impossible to reproduce those photographs in this book, so the address is regrettably truncated.

Thomas B. Sheridan, professor of engineering and applied psychology, spoke on the role of computers in modern industrial societies. While advocating many uses of computers, he emphasized the ways in which they alienate people from their work and from other people. He appealed for human control of computers for human purposes.

Joseph Weizenbaum, professor of computer science, made the most resounding attack of the day—perhaps of the entire conference—on the "toxic" element in modern science since the time of Francis Bacon. He called on the world's religious people to press for the detoxification of science—and, as the most urgent immediate example, the reduction and eventual elimination of nuclear weapons.

Terrestrial Satellites for Human Welfare

DAVID H. STAELIN

The space age was born abruptly in October 1957 when the first earth-orbiting satellite, Sputnik, was launched by the Soviet Union. In 1958 the United States followed with Vanguard, Explorer and Score. Today at least nine other nations have now manufactured entire satellites or significant portions thereof, and this number continues to increase as the technology is internationalized.

The civilian use of space has grown very rapidly, and now encompasses applications such as meteorology, earth resources, space science and communications. More than 102 nations have established ground stations for operational communications satellites, and as costs decrease this group will grow.

Although the number of nations building satellites is still limited, essentially all nations can now use such data directly or indirectly. For example, several of the operational weather satellites now carry automatic picture-transmission equipment which enables inexpensive ground equipment to receive almost instantly images of the weather obtained from the satellite as it flies overhead, all without payment of any money for the satellites themselves. For the approximate cost of printing and mailing, any nation can now purchase copies of any photographs obtained from the United States Landsat Earth Resources Satellites. Some satellites launched by other nations or international groups are similarly providing data for public use.

Space science is also increasingly an international activity and the results are widely discussed and shared by all. Even in the military sector, where the data are generally not shared, the increased mutual awareness of activities by various nations serves to reduce the probability of surprises and the incentives for covert hostile strategies. Since 1957 thousands of satellites have been launched, of which a significant fraction have been civilian payloads designed to enhance human welfare through communications and increased understanding of our global environment.

Weather satellites

The first weather satellites to routinely provide images from space produced such interest that they have been followed by several series of satellites carrying a variety of cameras. Most such cameras operate in the visible or the infra-red portion of the electro-magnetic spectrum, and provide either high-resolution images from low earth orbit or whole earth images from a stationary position in synchronous orbit.

Such photographs are available worldwide and enable weather forecasters to see precisely the forms of large weather systems as well as the development and character of smaller, more intense, storms such as hurricanes.

An example of the utility of such data is the experience in Bangladesh in October 1978. The United States government, in cooperation with industry, installed a ground station in Dacca, and one day after it began receiving data from US, Japanese, and Soviet weather satellites, it tracked a storm in the Bay of Bengal towards a predictable landfall. The populace was evacuated without any loss of life, whereas tens of thousands have died in the past when such storms struck without warning.

Infra-red cameras yield photographs both day and night, and microwave imaging systems can even produce images by penetrating the overlying clouds to map the underlying precipitation, humidity and atmospheric temperature structure.

Such quantitative sounding data are only just now beginning to be incorporated in routine weather forecasts. Much work and several years will probably be required before the value of this data can be fully appreciated, although it is already improving forecasts in data-sparse regions such as the South Pacific and the Indian Ocean. International cooperation in the collection and dissemination of such weather data is surely one of the brightest aspects of international cooperation in space for human welfare. Typical of this effort is the year-long Global Weather Experiment (GWE), which began in December 1978 under the auspices of the Global Atmospheric Research Program (GARP); more than 140 nations will participate in the GWE, the largest scientific experiment ever initiated.

Earth resources satellites

Although many of the early military satellites carried cameras capable of photographing significant geographic and man-made features, it was not until the Landsat satellite was launched in 1972 that such images became generally available to anyone for the approximate cost of photographic copying and distribution. Landsats A and B have 80-metre resolution, and Landsat C yields 40 metres. These satellites carry both visible and infra-red cameras, and can revisit any spot in earth every 18 days

Applications of this data have included monitoring and sometimes the management of agricultural production, desertification processes, water resources, rangeland, forests, urban and regional land use, marine and coastal resources, and environmental factors. The data have also supported disaster warnings and relief, and have been used for general cartographic and thematic mapping applications.

In addition to the usual methods for requesting data, some countries are erecting Landsat ground stations to receive the data directly. Nations that have agreed to operate such stations include Argentina, Australia, Brazil, Canada, Chile, India, Iran, Italy, Japan, Sweden and Zaire. France has decided to proceed with its proposed Earth Observation Satellite SPOT, the Federal Republic of Germany will fly a Zeiss camera on the Shuttle, and the Soviet Union has flown multispectral cameras on Soyuz-22, Salyut 6, and Meteor-2, 1976-1979. Increases in such activity can be anticipated.

Camera images at several wave-lengths (from a multispectral camera) can be combined by computer to yield a classification map for terrain. Similar data can highlight zones of change—for example, zones which are changing into residential areas. The extent and nature of certain crop diseases can also be identified.

Even more advanced sensors operating over a wide spectral range are now being developed. These instruments typically operate at wave-lengths ranging from the ultraviolet to the microwave. An interesting example is the electrically-scanned microwave radiometer (ESMR) which has mapped polar sea ice with 20-km resolution for over two years; the data have been used operationally for ship navigation, and scientifically to improve understanding of the geophysical processes which control these important regions of the globe. Another example is the SEASAT radar which has mapped selected regions of the globe with 40-km resolution and has permitted storms at sea and sea ice to be monitored as never before, particularly in those zones which are systematically shrouded by clouds.

Communications satellites

The most vigorous commercial use of satellite technology has certainly been in the area of communications satellites. In 1960, two years after Sputnik, the Courier satellite recorded and retransmitted radio messages to earth, and in 1962 TELSTAR began operations. The first communications satellite to operate in synchronous orbit such that its position would remain essentially stationary in the sky was SYNCOM I, launched in 1963.

In 1961 an agreement to form an international satellite organization was signed. This group, INTELSAT, launched its first satellite "Early Bird" to provide international service in 1965; it could carry 240 voice channels or one TV channel. Approximately one hundred nations are now members of INTELSAT and operate one or more ground stations. This is in addition to some nations which are members of the Intersputnik group, such as the USSR, Cuba, Mongolia, and countries in Eastern Europe. INTELSAT now carries over half of the world's transoceanic communications. Its $200 million revenues arise mostly from telephone traffic together with a small amount of data transmission and television. Ownership resides 27% in the USA, 7% in Africa, 6% in Asia, 12% in Latin America, 7% in the Middle East, and the rest in Europe and elsewhere, all in proportion to the use made of the facilities.

In most advanced countries the satellites provide primarily high-capacity international circuits, and perhaps the internal distribution of television and other signals to local cable or broadcast centres. In some countries satellites are also playing a major and growing role in internal communications because of the lack of well-developed terrestrial facilities. Countries making significant use of the INTELSAT system for domestic communications include Algeria, Brazil, Malaysia, Norway and Saudi Arabia.

A possible future development is the direct broadcasting of television signals to villages or even individual homes. The ultimate impact of increased cultural unification of the urban and rural centres of large third world countries is difficult to predict, as is the result of further improvements in communications between nations.

How the role of communications satellites evolves will depend partly upon the wisdom of the participants in the 1979 World Administrative Radio Conference, which will assign frequencies and orbital positions to various governments and services.

The technology employed on most present satellites seriously limits the number of satellites that can be operated in synchronous orbit without mutual interference. The allocation of this limited resource could pose a serious problem. Fortunately advanced technology provides an opportunity to remedy these problems, but it has not yet been determined how to make allocations which will efficiently and fairly encourage such progress.

Conclusions

The impact of satellite technology is similar to that of its predecessor technologies; it merely provides electronic transportation instead of physical movement. Just as ocean-going sailing vessels and aircraft each contributed to increased understanding of our natural environment and of all the world's peoples, so does the growing list of satellites used for communications and for monitoring weather, natural resources, and man's impact upon his world. All technology requires wisdom in its application in order to avoid adverse effects, but the rewards can be very great. Growing population pressures, limited natural resources, and the ability of one nation's commercial activities to affect another's (through air or ocean-borne pollution, meteorological effects and other means) all magnify the importance of satellite technology and its ability to reveal environmental truths and to unite the world's peoples in friendly communication and cooperation.

Computer Control and Human Alienation

THOMAS B. SHERIDAN

What do computers control now, and what are the possibilities for the future? What about robots? What forms of interaction between computers and people are likely, and what are the implications? Is alienation a prospect, and if so, what forms will it take? In Part I the status and trends of computer control technology are discussed. Part II comments upon the social implications.

I. Status and trends of computer control technology

Micro-electronic technology and computer control

By any standard the development of micro-electronic computer technology is remarkable. It is almost the only thing which is becoming cheaper at the same time as it becomes more powerful, more sophisticated, and uses less energy. The economic drive behind micro-electronics is huge and becoming more so. Within the decade micro-electronics has found its way into communication, transportation, health care, banking, politics, the arts and the home.

Computers started out centuries ago as clever and intricate clockwork and parlour game mechanisms devised by skilled craftsmen. They evolved through a number of stages: electromechanical relays and adding devices; passive electrical resistor-capacitor-inductor circuits; vacuum tubes; individual transistors; and finally the stage of thousands of subminiature solid state computational and storage elements formed on a single plastic "chip" the size of a small coin. These micro-electronic chips themselves are now made by automatic machinery.

Computer control has evolved over centuries from ideas of mechanism design and then of mechanical regulation. This history includes many "open-loop" machines which, when turned on, operated with no feedback, i.e. with no measurement of the environment to compare what was actually happening with what was desired. But even centuries ago there were primitive "closed-loop" devices such as simple vane mechanisms which keep windmills pointed towards the wind. Later came more elegant feedback mechanisms such as the steam engine flyball governor, a device which reduces steam as speed increases and automatically regulates engine speed to a mechanical setting, as well as the common home heating thermostat. Only much later came the surge of theory and sophisticated technology which was motivated by World War II and the first electronic computers.

Computer control presently pervades many kinds of human activity. Certainly military equipment, space vehicles and commercial aircraft are packed with micro-electronic computing devices. Microcomputers have invaded production of automobiles. They are now spreading through our hospitals, e.g. in CAT scanners (Computer Aided Tomography for radiation diagnosis of cancer), various patient monitoring systems in intensive care units, automated laboratory analysis and computerized patient record-keeping. Large factories, chemical plants and nuclear reactors are extensively computer controlled, so that most of the jobs previously performed by dozens of workers no longer exist. Wires from sensors and actuators now funnel to central control rooms where one or a few technicians sit, mostly inactive, monitoring rows of similar-looking dials, watching computer control systems manage the plant, waiting for something to happen which the computer cannot handle—and trusting that if it happens they are able to deal with it.

HUMAN SUPERVISORY CONTROL

As computers increasingly take over the continuous "in-the-loop" decision-making from humans, humans are assuming supervisory functions over computers. The trend in the design of industrial plant control rooms is worth noting. At present most of these control rooms have walls and panels covered with switches and knobs and lights and meters, each dedicated to a single function. The operator must walk around the room to do his job. Newer control rooms for chemical plants and nuclear reactors have a much smaller console at which the operator sits. He uses general purpose controls (keyboards on which the operator can ask the computer for any of a variety of measurements or analyses or actions to be performed) and general purpose displays (TV screens under computer control capable of showing almost any information the operator wants in any format—diagrams, status reports, etc.—with a rich assortment of symbols and in living colour). These techniques give the human operator much more flexibility, and reduce still further the number of people required. The operator becomes more of a manager, a supervisor of computers which themselves may be monitoring and controlling hundreds of separate sensor-microcomputer-effector control loops.

Five roles may be identified for the new human worker as computer-supervisory-controller: (1) planning what operations are to be done; (2) teaching or programming the computer system to do the appropriate tasks in the desired manner; (3) monitoring the automatic execution of the task while occasionally making adjustments; (4) taking over in case of emergencies, which includes diagnosis of abnormality, resort to a special shut-down or alternative operating control modes; (5) gaining enough understanding of the system to be able to empathize with and trust it, or to implement sufficient redesign that this trust is warranted. These functions are not unlike those of any other supervisor. The difference is that here the subordinates are computers and not people.

But now the computer is insinuating itself into a supervisory role also, that of expert diagnostician and adviser. In one manifestation, that identified with "modern control", the computer has inside itself an ongoing normative model of the salient events in the actual plant under normal circumstances. This model is continuously fed the same input signals as drive the machinery. If the predicted response of the computer's internal model deviates too far from the actual response of the machinery, there is evidence either of a significant external disturbance or a structural change in the plant—either of which is an abnormality which must be attended to. Assuming a valid model and performance, the computer usually is better able than a person to diagnose what has gone wrong and what to do about it, especially if speed is essential. However, the internal model may have some deficiencies. Thus, even while such "internal model" diagnostic systems often constitute much of what is called "optimal control", and at lower levels of control are authorized to go ahead and implement their own advice, at higher levels of control they are designed merely to give advice to the human operator.

How far to automate and trust to automatic control, and when to rely on the operator's judgment? This question arouses much debate in technical circles, but at the moment computer control systems are gaining ground. The list below describes a series of levels among which the systems designer must decide. In the nuclear industry, for example, the prevailing assumption is that human operators are not to be trusted at all during the first few minutes of a major emergency where the events are likely to be different from anything they have ever seen before. Therefore emergency systems are designed to be completely automatic for a ten minute period; the operator is expected to watch but keep his hands in his pockets. The industry has been debating whether ten minutes is long enough; it is likely to extend the present "ten-minute rule" and impose still further restrictions on human prerogatives. In the Three Mile Island accident the currently available evidence suggests that the operators took two hours to piece together a correct diagnosis of what had happened. Whether the computer could have made a better decision depends, of course, on what information it would have had. It certainly would have been quicker.

Computer control with human supervision is also the trend in commercial aviation. Seldom these days do pilots fly their airplanes in moment-by-moment fashion with their hands on the control wheels. They have become

LEVELS OF AUTOMATION IN DECISION-MAKING

100% human control ↑

1. Human considers decision alternatives, makes and implements a decision.
2. Computer suggests set of decision alternatives, human may ignore them in making and implementing decision.
3. Computer offers restricted set of decision alternatives, human decides on one of these and implements it.
4. Computer offers restricted set of decision alternatives and suggests one, human may accept or reject, but decides on one and implements it.
5. Computer offers restricted set of decision alternatives and suggests one which the computer will implement if human approves.
6. Computer makes decision and necessarily informs human in time to stop its implementation.
7. Computer makes and implements decision, necessarily tells human after the fact what it did.
8. Computer makes and implements decision, tells human after the fact what it did only if human asks.
9. Computer makes and implements decision, tells human after the fact what it did only if it, the computer, thinks he should be told.
10. Computer makes and implements decision if it thinks it should, tells human after the fact if it thinks he should be told.

↓ 100% computer control

button pushers, or "flight managers", with duties vis-à-vis their computer control systems (called "avionics") which are essentially the same as the five roles outlined previously. The newest commercial aircraft give the pilot, among other things, a complete picture of all neighbouring aircraft (so-called "cockpit display of traffic information"). The pilot now has a rich variety of control options. He can ask the aircraft to go to a certain altitude, heading or speed and hold until further notice. He can push some buttons and ask a gyroscopic system to fly the aircraft to within half a mile to any combination of latitude and longitude on the face of the earth. More and more aircraft are using regularly a computer "autoland" system which lands the aircraft without the pilot touching the controls. The passengers cannot distinguish the computer's landing from the pilot's, and mostly are not aware that they are being landed automatically. The autoland system can function when ceiling and visibility are very poor (though in the US such "zero-zero landings" are not yet authorized).

Fifty or more years ago there was great concern among managers to make workers more productive. This motivated Frederick Winslow Taylor and others to develop "scientific management" techniques to enhance worker efficiency (and, according to historians, to minimize worker creativity). Many of Taylor's ideas are still practised, but many have been criticized for being inhumane or ineffective. Today there is a resurgence of interest in man-machine efficiency and "mental workload", motivated by a new concern. This is the worker's or pilot's ability to make sudden transition from passively watching the computer do its routine job to actively coping with a major emergency. There is no generally accepted way of measuring "mental workload" or "mental stress" under such rapidly changing circumstances. Yet we continue to retain human operators in computer control systems, apparently assuming human operators are capable of taking over in emergencies where computers cannot cope. Researchers in the man-machine systems field are now questioning whether this is a reasonable expectation.

Robots

A robot is a computer-controlled machine of a special sort. It generally has one or more mechanical arms capable of manipulating physical objects, though sometimes the hand and/or tool is carried by structures which slide relative to one another and do not resemble human arms in their design. Sometimes the robot has wheels or other means to move about. Usually it has some kind of visual sensing (e.g. a TV camera) and/or some type of tactile or force sensing. These motor and sensory components are connected to a computer which is capable of being programmed so that the robot will perform actions based on its own sensory information as well as its stored programmes.

Robots are a reality. They are now performing routine or hazardous industrial jobs such as welding, spray painting, and assembly on the production line or the retrieval of parts from warehouses. Their use is motivated simply by their lower cost and their reliability compared to human workers. In Detroit they sometimes work side by side with automobile production workers. They can also be put to work around the clock, do not need rests or lunch breaks, and (claim their manufacturers) are quicker, stronger, more precise and more dependable than are people. (Also, they do not talk back or go on strike.) Whereas 15 years ago robotic theory was only an idle curiosity, today there are booming markets (a robot costs upwards of $25,000), a variety of professional societies devoted to robotics and established courses in universities. The Japanese are probably the current leaders in the development of robotics for industry, with the US a close second.

Quite clearly what has brought on the sudden boom in industrial robots are powerful and cheap computers. Through proper sensing and control techniques a "smart" robot can outperform a "stupid" (no sensors, not much computer) robot with ease.

The industrial robot can be programmed to do a variety of tasks. It can produce a small batch of one kind of product, then a small batch of another kind. A robot can also be made to perform several different tasks on one part. Finally the robot can handle a variety of parts coming down the assembly line intermixed. It can visually recognize each type of part and unerringly perform operations appropriate only to that part—a task which may be very confusing to a human worker. Robot vision and manipulation capabilities still fall short of their human counterparts in certain situations, but the robots are getting better each year.

When the task to be performed is not so well defined as it is in manufacturing, or if it is not so repetitive, control by computer alone may be inadequate. At least intermittent human participation through remote control may be necessary. In using robots to replace divers in the deep ocean (the robot is relatively insensitive to depth), the human operator may see what the robot sees through closed circuit TV and send his commands over wires. This is also the case in the nuclear hot lab or reactor, in deep mines, in construction, or in outer space. A robot which a person controls remotely (extending his own eyes and hands in space) is called a "tele-operator". The newest tele-operator contains a computer capable of interpreting some of its own sensory information and deciding upon and executing some of its own actions, while it is intermittently monitored and reprogrammed by remote control. If it runs into trouble, or if there is a time delay in communications (as there is with sending signals to space vehicles or planets), the tele-operator has sufficient wits to do the proper thing until it receives a proper update from its master.

Teaching or working with a smart tele-operator is not unlike teaching a small child a motor skill. The satisfaction and frustrations are strikingly similar. And the use of language is similar. In my own laboratory we have a tele-operator which the operator can command by typing strings of natural-language-like statements. Alternatively the operator can take the tele-operator's hand and guide it through some task, saying, in effect: "Do it like this, only faster", or smoother, etc. With either type of instruction the teleoperator will remember perfectly and perform the task when asked.

The use of robotic devices to aid the physically handicapped is an obvious challenge. The primary problems are not technology *per se*, but those of cosmesis (satisfying the natural craving of people to appear normal) and participation by the person in control of the robot. If the use of robotic technology looks too bizarre and unnatural, the handicapped person will not accept it. If it is physically attached to the person, as a prosthetic hand or arm or leg, cosmesis is very important and the user may tolerate having little or no actual function. If the device is physically separate from the person, acting as a mechanical servant or nursemaid, the primary need is for the handicapped person to be able to make it do what is desired.

Prosthetic arms and legs now use electromyographic signals (faint electrical signals produced by muscle contractions which would have helped control the limb were it there) in elegant ways. Micro-electronics are particularly promising for prostheses because of their small size, low energy consumption and low cost. A recent artificial leg development at MIT by Dr D. Grimes uses a computer to recognize from muscle and limb measurements which mode the user intends (e.g. level walking, up ramp, down ramp, upstairs, downstairs, stand, sit) and triggers a programme to make the prosthetic leg behave properly for that mode.

Electronic banking and communication

A popular theme for science fiction is that of the giant computer taking over control of the world. This scenario is not very likely. However, it is likely that computers will mediate not only industrial production and transportation and health care systems, as discussed above, but also other human services such as banking and communications.

Large banks already have computerized much of their record keeping and usually maintain duplicate computers simultaneously monitoring the same transactions. For a large bank to process cheques by hand is now unthinkable. However, bankers admit to their fears of what may happen after more and more responsibilities are given over to the computers and the technicians who run them, when one day the dual computers fail at the same time—or are made to fail by clever but malevolent people. Nevertheless, we seem to be proceeding apace towards more and more credit card use, "instant cash" and other banking arrangements which depend upon centralization. Not far away some prophets foresee the era of electronic funds transfer and the total obsolescence of cash as we now know it. The US government has already invested in serious assessment of this. All transactions would be made by credit cards, with instant validation, debiting and crediting executed over telephone lines to a central computer. The technology is mostly in place. What is holding us up, some say, is sentimental attachment to our old-fashioned notions about using cash.

Communication is already highly computerized, though the average telephone user or TV watcher is not aware of the intricate electronic logic which mediates satellite, microwave and cable channel multiplexing operations. A new and rapidly growing form of communications is the computer messaging network, wherein each of a large number of participants has a computer typewriter terminal which communicates over long distance telephone lines to any of several centralized computers. The user simply dials a local number which is a network "port" (there exist many such commercial networks with ports in major cities). He types in a code to get to the appropriate central computer, types in another code to specify the type of service (or messaging) he wishes to use, and reads the text from the computer (or types text to the computer). The services include tele-conferencing (wherein different persons can add statements to, or read selected sections from, a "conference proceedings"), "word processing" (computer-aided text storage and editing), sending a message to one or a large group of persons simultaneously, etc. Initial experiments are already being run on an "electronic journal" for which papers are written, edited, submitted, referred, revised, printed, read, and discussed entirely over the computer messaging network without any use of printing or mailing.

The examples of computer control cited above represent a cross-section. Many similar trends in computer control could be cited—in the office, in the kitchen, at the supermarket check-out counter and elsewhere.

II. Implications

These various examples have in common the idea of highly organized and centralized control—by some combination of people and computers. The human components in the system necessarily have a great dependence upon the computers, but the reverse is also the case. Both authority and responsibility become shared, and accountability becomes diffuse. While both human operators and computers wield great power, neither can easily be blamed if a small error develops into a large catastrophe. Sophisticated computer-aided back-up and emergency procedures can be added to the system, and incredible feats can be demonstrated which no old-fashioned bumbling bureaucracy of human workers could ever accomplish by itself as, for example, in the lunar and planetary space projects, military weapons systems and nuclear plants. The new bureaucracy is smooth, powerful and instantaneous. The old organization was cranky and inefficient but had room for lots of human-to-human interaction, adaptiveness, creativity, participation and sharing. The new organization—with interpersonal interactions mediated by computers—is, I assert, alienating. I use the word in a very general sense, and it needs some explanation.

Alienation

What computers are good at and what people are good at tend to be different. Computers have good memories, are fast, repeatable and reliable, but are not creative or adaptable to novel situations. People have poor memories, are slow, seldom do things the same way twice, and are unreliable, but they are definitely adaptable and creative. Computers are a different race from people. From one point of view it is a wonderful ideal to design systems wherein these two can complement one another—to wed their talents.

For some persons, however, dealing with computers in computer terms is intimidating. Serious engagement or wedding seems miscegenous, and interaction with the new race raises all the problems of racism. What factors make control by computers, these efficient and dutiful servants, alienating?

1. A first is that some people persist in comparing themselves to computers and worrying about their own *inferiority in rote tasks*. We all know people who pride themselves in being good computers; we have many such people at MIT. They are bound for disappointment if they expect to win this contest against the computer.

The time is here, I believe, to celebrate those ways in which people are not computers, and let computers take over those jobs where they clearly outperform us. A person can still pull the computer's plug. We may have to work at maintaining that privilege, however.[1]

2. A second alienating factor is the tendency for computer control *to make the human operator remote* from what he is ultimately doing. The worker or human operator, under the new supervisory regimen, is becoming more and more spatially remote from the objects being manufactured, from the banking transactions, or from the patient in the hospital. His actions are becoming desynchronized in time from the final shaping of the goods and services being produced. He no longer handles the things-in-process directly, but has artificial sensors which feed information to computers which in turn digest it and present the human operator a summary of what it, the computer, thinks he should know.[2]

It may seem a waste of effort to give the worker information about the end results of his work. Excuses are often given by managers: workers are not interested; the system is too complex; too much feed-back would be distracting. I believe that under most circumstances not only greater satisfaction but also improved performance will result by attention to reducing the worker's growing sense of remoteness from what is going on at the other end of his machine.

3. A third factor in alienation, surely related to and resulting in part from remoteness, might be termed *deskilling*. Skilled machinists, typesetters, laboratory technicians, food processors, and aircraft pilots are "graduating"

---

[1] One is reminded of the cartoon of the worker in the large automatic factory who starts to pull the plug on an errant computer, only to find his wrist suddenly grasped and pulled back by a large robotic hand.

[2] It is little wonder that the B52 pilots, supervising sophisticated computerized flying machines from tens of thousands of feet above the rural villages of Vietnam, had so little empathy with what was taking place below.

into button-pushers and machine-tenders. Their sensory-motor skills, acquired over decades and contributing much to their own dignity and image of themselves, are being lost through atrophy. They are presumed to be prepared to take over from the computer when necessary; in fact they are anxiously aware that they may not be up to it.

The reaction to these indignities by both romantics and Luddites may be an effort to turn the clock back, to get rid of computer control and return to manual craft. I doubt that such a strategy will work in the economic competition. Button-pushing is not so bad if it does not become the only contribution the worker can make.

4. A fourth factor, closely related to the third, has to do with our system of formal education and with C. P. Snow's two cultures. It is the greater *access* to information and power by the technologically literate minority as compared to the technologically illiterate majority (including, usually, both machine tender and the user of the products or services). The technological literate in this case includes the computer designers and programmers and their technical management. Curiously, the normally powerful but non-technical group such as financiers, lawyers and politicians feel themselves increasingly at the mercy of the technical elite. The top manager's sometime boast, "I hire and fire PhD's", is sounding more defensive. At the middle level of this particular pyramid are the workers who could benefit enormously were they better equipped by their formal education and were their managers willing to be a bit more flexible in allowing them access. At the bottom of the pyramid—the layers of which are not all that well defined—are the undereducated and older segments of the society who simply cannot keep up, have no understanding of the computer-based society and its concomitant concepts of probability, feedback control and artificial intelligence, and have no access to credit cards, home terminals and the like.

Clearly we must work at improving our educational systems to prepare citizens to participate in a computerized society without adversely compromising traditional goals of education.

5. A fifth aspect of alienation, closely related to both remoteness and access, is *mystification*. A most elegant statement of this attribute of computer control was made by the MIT mathematician and "father of cybernetics", Norbert Weiner. In a book written shortly before his death (in 1964), *God and Golem Inc.*, he compares Golem, the mythical half-man, half-beast of Hebraic tradition, to the computer. It is easy to attribute magical properties to the computer. Our pop culture encourages us to do so at every turn. But there is the great danger of trusting and attributing too much wisdom to the computer, and believing that its understanding of some programmed instructions is what its programmer intends. The computer may have a different understanding since, having no cultural empathy with its programmer, it does not assume the rich contextual fabric which underlies all person-to-person communication. If the computer is interconnected in a control system

with fast and powerful machines, the end result of this excessive trust can be disaster.

Fingers can be pointed in many directions: advertising; military and industrial security; plain snobbism and arrogance by the technological elite—all of which foster the mystique of a computer control panacea without telling the full story and revealing the limitations. These institutions and individuals may see it in their own best interest to pose as magicians. Happily a counterforce is growing, but the best strategies for demystification have yet to be worked out.

6. The previous discussion leads naturally to the next contributive factor in alienation, *higher stakes in decision-making*. The tendency is towards ever larger, more complex, more capital intensive, more centrally and more tightly computer-controlled systems where the costs of failure are large, though the probabilities of failure may be small. Military systems, nuclear plants and air traffic control systems are examples. On a day-to-day basis, such a system may run reliably and smoothly—minor failures within the system are automatically circumvented. "Fail-safe" is the ideal, and usually it works. But there is always a low probability of complete breakdown, and that failure may be spectacular. Reliability analysts know how to cope with the minor or low-cost failures whose frequencies of occurrence are known because they do happen from time to time and there is some experience, some basis for statistics, even some objective grounds for those sometimes offensive measures like "statistical deaths" and the "value of a life". However, they do not know very well how to cope with the improbable, high-cost events. It is relatively straightforward to gather statistics on an "unk" or "known-unknown". But what gives the analyst nightmares is the "unk-unk", or "unknown-unknown": he does not know where his ignorance lies, and that a certain variable or situation is critical. Consequently, he has no basis to judge even his degree of confidence. As systems get more complex, they invariably have more "unk-unks" to torment the reliability analyst.

The responsible position here would be to look openly and dispassionately at all available objective evidence, including statistical deaths, and then without apology feed into the computer-aided decision process the subjective factors which derive legitimately from human culture and intuition. We expect each other to make important personal decisions, such as the choice of a mate or a career, on mostly subjective grounds. Yet in business and public decision-making we seem to be ashamed of the subjective, attributing it either to ignorance or to dirty politics. There are encouraging signs within academe and government that this is beginning to change. A new respect for subjectivity is emerging. We owe it to ourselves to become more intellectually honest and explicit about combining the objective and subjective, affirming the value of both.

7. A final basis for alienation is *phylogenesis*. This has to do with the fact, or the threat, or the perceived threat, that the race of intelligent machines is gradually becoming more powerful than men. This dis-ease has

historical precedents, for other events in history have diminished man's image of himself: the computer is simply the most current. Mazlish,[3] Tribe,[4] and other writers have discussed the computer as a "fourth discontinuity" between man and all other nature which is being abridged, a fourth insult to man's right to position himself at the centre of the universe. The first insult was that of Copernicus; man's realm is not discontinuous from the rest of the physical universe. The second insult was that of Darwin; man is not a clear discontinuity in the animal forms. The third insult was Freud's; man is not above base instincts and drives. The question of the fourth discontinuity is whether man is ultimately any more or better than the machine. The question is ever more thrust upon people in their encounters with the computer.

Within computer science circles, no one seems comfortable with the question. Most scholars do not believe technology *per se* to be capable of exerting any more domination over man than man designs and programmes into it. If there is a culprit, it is surely man himself.

Machine productivity and human productivity

For one reason or another the puritan work ethic is out of fashion: hard work is no longer seen as the avenue to salvation. Letting our machines do our mental as well as our physical work—as much as they can take on—seems increasingly to be the norm.

From a strict energy or cost efficiency viewpoint, automatic control is often the obvious choice over human control, whether the task is to pump water in a rural village in an underdeveloped nation or to control a nuclear plant. Take, for example, the case of pumping water. Considering the relative energy efficiencies of the human body compared to those of a small gasoline engine (calories out relative to calories in) and the relative prices of calories for the two (assuming the humblest of foods for the person and fossil fuel price increases of orders of magnitude), the machine still comes out ahead.

For human execution of control tasks which are of great scale and complexity, in addition to the energy inefficiencies of the human body, there are the enormous inefficiencies of the management, organization and communication of an army of human workers. By contrast, new micro-electronic logic takes very little energy and exhibits fantastic speed and reliability.

By more subtle criteria, however, computer control systems do not fare as well. While it is true that human institutions are not known for their ability to change, they, like their members, are self conscious, whereas machines are not. Human institutions are continually re-examining their own goals,

---

[3] B. Mazlish: "The Fourth Discontinuity". *Technology and Culture*, Vol. 8, No. 1, Winter 1967.

[4] L. Tribe: "Technology Assessment and the Fourth Discontinuity: the Limits of Instrumental Rationality". *Southern California Law Review*, Vol. 46, No. 3, June 1973.

whereas computing machines, even the most adaptable and intelligent ones, are still guided ultimately by the criteria programmed into them.

Any large-scale technology, once set in place, is difficult to alter. The national highway system is an example: one does not easily abandon all that concrete to an altogether different mode of transport. The same goes for nuclear reactors and large industrial plants. Once established, they tend to go on producing whatever they produce—using whatever resources they use—whether or not there remains a real need for that product. The sheer size and complexity of the technology provide a kind of technological inertia, and this is compounded by the inertia of human institutions. Those whose interests are served by that production will do all they can to protect that market. This self-fulfilment of the productive process is one aspect of "autonomous technology" described by Ellul,[5] Winner[6] and others. The automatic factories are so good at making widgets that we are charmed, and we do all we can to cooperate with the production miracle. Further, we can sell the widgets to each other and spur the economy.

It is little wonder that the followers of E. F. Schumacher's *Small is Beautiful*[7] are growing in number. This "appropriate technology" movement, with its emphasis on ecological sustainability and community self-reliance, flies in the face of much of what large-scale computer control is now all about, with its centralization and dependence on the technological elite. It is a movement to watch. But make no mistake. The "AT" advocates are not anti-technology, and they too recognize that much of the new microelectronic computer technology, with its low dollar and energy costs, may provide an effective route towards harnessing the sun and doing other things they deem desirable. The institutional base for the technology is not cottage industry, however, and therein lies their dilemma.

The ultimate criterion for how computers shall be used is subjective. I am not sure the technologist sufficiently appreciates this. Man has always been a tool builder, and he is not likely to stop. We will have our computers, but our subjective sense of what is right and beautiful and consistent with a just and sustainable society, and contributes most to human fulfilment, ought to dictate our use of these exotic new tools with their enormous potential. Productivity in human terms should prevail over productivity in machine terms.

Thus, as computer control grows, along with enhanced capability and apparent magic by the new machines, we are likely to see some alienation and suffering by people. In response there is but one strategy open to us—to ensure that the man-machine interaction offers humanity and dignity. We must strive: to make evident and celebrate what people are that computers are not;

---

[5] J. Ellul: *The Technological Society*, translated by John Wilkinson. New York: Alfred A. Knopf, 1964.

[6] L. Winner: *Autonomous Technology: Technics-out-of-Control as a Theme in Political Thought*. Cambridge, Ma.: MIT Press, 1978.

[7] New York: Harper and Row, 1973.

to provide people with better feedback on the results of their own inputs to computer systems to reduce their sense of remoteness from what is going on; to find new ways for operators to participate constructively beyond button-pushing; to educate for a new literacy to allow more people to understand and participate in a computerized society; to demystify whenever possible; to affirm the role of subjective inputs into the computer-aided decision and control process; and to hold the designers and programmers of computers accountable, not the computers themselves.

Technological Detoxification

JOSEPH WEIZENBAUM

In another place—and, it now seems to me, almost another time—I wrote that "much of what we today regard as good and useful, as well as much of what we would call knowledge and wisdom, we owe to science". I then added: "But science may also be seen as an addictive drug. Not only has our unbounded feeding on science caused us to become dependent on it, but, as happens with many other drugs taken in increasing dosages, science has been gradually converted into a slow acting poison." Reading these words years after I wrote them, I am now surprised that I did not take the next obvious step, that is, to talk about our intoxication with our science and our technology.

Permit me to remind you that the word "intoxication" comes from the Greek *toxicon* which means arrow poison. To be intoxicated is to have ingested a poison in a dosage sufficient, according to a good dictionary, "to excite or stupify to a point where physical and mental control is markedly diminished". Significantly, the dictionary gives an alternate definition, namely that to intoxicate is "to excite or elate to the point of enthusiasm or frenzy".

Who can deny that it is precisely excitement, elation, enthusiasm, and especially frenzy which characterize modern western society's involvement with its science and technology? To be sure, the myth that we practise science purely in order to gain knowledge for its own sake continues to be maintained. But when one recalls the manner in which the United States of America committed itself to putting a man on the moon, to name only one example, then the characterizations just mentioned cannot help but leap to mind. The project was dressed up as promising to lead to the discovery to crucial secrets which, once unlocked, would lead to the deepest insights into the origin of the universe, i.e. as a search for knowledge for its own sake. But the excitement it generated—and which President Kennedy's speech was intended to generate—and the enthusiasm shown by the American public and the technical community had much more to do with the "space race" in which America and the Soviet Union were and still are engaged than with any scientific goals. Moreover, a truly scientific project would have been allowed to set its own pace, to proceed with a leisure which might allow thought and reflection to determine intermediate goals and strategies. But the American President himself set the frenzied pace when he announced that the result intended would be achieved "within this decade". Another American President, Richard Nixon, greeted astronauts returning from the moon with the words that this was the most exciting moment in his life—as if the purpose of this enormously expensive and dangerous undertaking had been to provide excitement for the people of the United States and for their President.

With every day that passes more than a billion dollars is spent worldwide on scientifically refined instruments of death; every day the United States adds three hydrogen bomb warheads to its arsenal; every day young men and women, many of them trained at MIT, exercise their God-given intelligence and ingenuity to bring the targeting mechanisms of missiles ever closer to perfection. And every now and then America's so-called First Lady "christens"—just think what that word means!—a submarine about whose weapons systems her husband, the President, boasts that they can in a few minutes wipe out life (though not necessarily property) in every major city in the Soviet Union. Clinical insanity! Utter madness! Who can, in the light of such facts, deny that we are rapidly losing—have perhaps already lost—physical and mental control over our society?

An addicted society

One can be intoxicated, that is affected by the ingestion of toxins, without being addicted to that toxin. We may speak of addiction only when the affected organism has undergone physiological changes which cause its body to be dependent on the toxin. Anyone can get drunk, but not every drunk is an alcoholic. I assert that our society has, in fact, become organically modified by our massive ingestion of the worst fruits of our science and technology. We are not temporarily stupefied by it, our loss of control is not merely momentary, nor is what afflicts us merely a sudden compulsion. I say this because the signs of addiction are everywhere around us. Massively distorted perceptions of reality abound. We euphorically embrace every technological fix proffered as a "solution" to every human "problem" which we have, of course, first converted to a technological problem. The most visible monuments to our world-view are our preoccupation with speed, with power, with quantity, and above all the enormous, gigantic, colossal *hubris* of much of our scientific community. (Just recall that the "blame" for the recent misadventures of the Skylab satellite was pinned on the misbehaviour of the sun—too many flares—not on any miscalculation on the part of scientists or engineers!) These conditions reflect organic lesions in our society—they are too deep and they have been with us too long to permit us to dismiss them as merely temporary aberrations.

I am an information scientist. In this world, this insane asylum, in which it would be considered a violation of trust were I to speak merely simple truths to you after having been invited to address you on the basis of my credentials as a scientist, I am obligated to back my assertions by reference to the field in which the illusion that I know more than you may be credibly maintained. Let me therefore support what I am trying to say here in terms involving information processing, computers, and so on.

Increasing abstraction

The toxin which has invaded us is, as seen from the perspective of an information scientist, fundamentally *abstraction*. The word abstraction means to draw away from. Science, in order to function at all, must practise abstraction in that it must *necessarily* simplify, deal with idealized models, in other words, draw away from reality. And science, idealization, abstraction are good and useful, as I have already said—in proper dosages, that is, and even then only when compounded by wisdom gained from many other perspectives. But what began to happen, beginning roughly with Bacon's observation that knowledge is power, and at first very gradually and then with ever-increasing rapidity, is that the very success of science has induced us first to confuse the abstract with the real and then to forget how to make the distinction at all. Our increasing loss of contact with reality is illustrated by, for example, the march of abstraction with respect to the products of human labour and of human labour itself. People once traded their labour directly for goods. Then money became an abstract quantification of human labour. Then cheques and other financial instruments became abstractions for money. Now we approach the so-called cashless society in which electrons racing around computers and beyond any human being's ability to sense become abstractions for financial instruments. An observer from another planet will see people labouring in order to optimize the paths of electron streams flowing on their behalf in computers unseen and incomprehensible.

Perhaps the most pervasive evidence for the phenomenon I am trying to describe is our substitution of peoples' *images* for their real persons. This applies not only to individuals, for example, to candidates for political offices and other so-called celebrities, but to entire populations. America's war on Vietnam was fought largely to impress various "audiences"—the word comes straight from the Pentagon and from our State Department. The *image* of the United States was at stake, not the lives of real people. Things are treated no differently: an American Secretary of "Defence" (I put that last word in quotes because it is an Orwellian lie), Melvin Laird, once asserted that American hydrogen bombs were not weapons of destruction but "bargaining chips" of which America had to have a great many so that it could "disarm from a position of strength". This is a logical extension to world scale of the already well-established military principle that often villages have to be destroyed in order that they may be saved.

At still another and deeper level, the reduction of authenticity to imagery serves to stupefy the collective consciousness of the people—just as intoxicated minds are stupefied—so as to render unnoticeable much more subtle manipulations of reality, even more profound drawings away from reality. I have in mind the corruption of everyday language, hence of the creative imaginations of speakers of everyday language, through the illegitimate raising of science-based metaphors to the status of common-sense truths. It is, for example, now commonplace to hear of people being programmed. In this way does the notion of an abstract machine—and one that fascinates the general public almost to the point of hypnotism—become that of a human being. And once we accept that human beings are machines, merely symbol manipulators and information processors, then the final step, namely the deliberate initiation of a programme to alter the course of biological evolution in such a way that the human species is replaced by "silicon-based intelligence", can be announced by the most eminent scientists—for example, by Dr Robert Jastrow, head of NASA's Goddard Space Flight Center—without alerting anyone that what is being talked about is not merely the death of the human species, in short literally genocide, not merely the death of God, but the murder of God!

Steps in technological detoxification

It seems to me obvious that what is now needed is an energetic programme—at least for the western world—of technological detoxification. I would say that such a programme should involve at least the following four steps:

1. We must admit that we are intoxicated with our science and technology in roughly the way I have here sketched, that, in other words, we are deeply committed to a Faustian bargain which is rapidly killing us spiritually and will soon kill us all physically.

2. We must muster the courage and the will to insist that we can recover. My own view is that we cannot recover except with the help of a miracle. But then miracles do happen these days—consider that wrought by Mrs Corrigan and Mrs Williams of Ireland, two simple women who managed for a time to stop a vicious civil war. Our task as individuals is to behave in ways that prepare the soil for such miracles, for example by being good to one another. At the very least we must avoid behaviour which tends to poison that soil; for example, we ought not to work on instruments that kill people.

3. We must make the decision to withdraw from our addiction. We must, for example, decide affirmatively to halt the Orwellian corruption of our languages; we must decide that life is better than death. We teachers must decide to teach, mainly by our own example, that authentic living, not life by abstract formulas, is possible.

4. Finally, we must strive to live first this very day, then the next day, and so on one day at a time. In the world we can but gradually wrest away from the framework of abstractions upon abstractions we have erected; in the real world, in a world peopled by genuine human beings, not images; in a world in which the value of word and deed inheres in the word and deed itself, not in the engineered applause of some abstract audience.

I am aware that these four prescriptions are very general. I think they may serve as guides to actions, but lest I be misunderstood, permit me to make some very specific proposals.

Nothing is a more concrete nor a more dangerous manifestation of our confusion of the abstract with the real and of the madness of the logic which then leads to murderous policy consequences than the ongoing international arms race. It is perhaps merely a grim joke, but I think it points up a tragic reality, that the foundation of the so-called defence policy of the NATO alliance is officially called MAD, an acronym for "mutual assured destruction". The first and most urgent step in the detoxification process ought therefore to be our withdrawal from the myth that ever more numerous and ever more powerful weapons of mass destruction offer any security whatever to the peoples of the world. I do, and let me be very explicit about this, argue for worldwide and total nuclear disarmament and, as a citizen of the United States, my personal position is that my country ought to begin that process unilaterally if necessary. However, as a first step and in line with the prescription that, in the initial stages of detoxification, one attempts to master one day at a time, I plead here only for the small step that we stop adding to our already enormous nuclear arsenal. And I want it to be clear as well, especially to this audience, that while I believe the destruction of the world nuclear stockpile to be a practical necessity, I think it even more important that everyone, especially the world's religious organizations, understand it and press it as a profoundly moral matter. Their failure to do so would, in my view, justify their indictment as co-conspirators in genocide and the murder of God.

On what appears at first glance to be a much less serious plane but is, in fact, also crucial to the mental health of our civilization, I would say that we in the West must stop the insane consumerism whose principal manifestation is the invention of products followed by the creation of a need for them. There are thousands of relatively trivial examples of what I am talking about. But as a computer scientist I am keenly aware of the virtually paradigmatic role the computer plays in this respect. The computer in our society is in large part a solution in search of problems. The mentality which breeds and nourishes this condition is precisely the same which converts human and political problems to technical problems and then proposes technical solutions. One effect of this conversion, and it is not always unintended, is that it distracts attention from real conflicts and from real clashes of interests. There is an almost worldwide initiative, for example, to introduce computers into schools. But once the abstract characterization of the educational process in information theoretical terms is ripped from in front of one's eyes, once the reality of what is happening in, for example, American secondary schools is exposed, then it becomes clear that the problems facing educators everywhere are political, financial, spiritual. Not least among the causes of these problems, in America at least, is that such a large fraction of our energy and wealth is invested in killing machines. What I propose is that we begin to learn to assess our situation first and then, *and only if our assessment reveals problems of a technological nature*, bring our technology to bear.

Science is an extremely tiny keyhole through which the world may be viewed. What it reveals about the world is, to be sure, enormously important and of course useful. But science provides no moral criteria for the behaviour of scientists as scientists or as ordinary people. You, the representatives of organized Christianity, make some claim of commanding such criteria. Help us if you can, *if you dare*, to detoxify our spirit and to stop the spoilation of the habitat of God's children.

Reactions and Comment

The addresses, as was often the case in the plenary sessions, prompted many more questions than could be handled in the time available. Some delegates asked whether the introduction of computers did not come more from political than from technical motivations. Others wondered whether corporations prefer computers because they are easier to control than human labourers. There were questions about unemployment that might be expected to follow from the increasing use of robots, and about the invasion of privacy by computers and information systems. One questioner asked about the validity of government censorship of incoming television programmes that might destroy local cultures.

Several participants questioned whether international political realities and inequalities of power did not make the use of satellites less beneficient than Staelin hoped. The acrimonious debates in the 1979 World Administrative Radio Conference, coming several weeks after the WCC conference at MIT, confirmed his predictions that the role of communications satellites would depend partly upon the "wisdom" of participants in that conference.

16. Disarmament

Introduction

In the year of planning prior to the conference there was frequent discussion of war and armaments in relation to "Faith, Science and the Future". Obviously, war throws a great threat against any conceivable human future; equally obviously, science and technology have much to do with the nature of modern war, and preparations for war pre-empt and finance much of the energy going into technological research. So the conference could not ignore war and armaments. But the WCC has a major programme on militarism, and it seemed foolish and perhaps a little arrogant for this meeting to try to do in two weeks what that programme was doing over the years. Therefore the initial plans called for Section IX to deal with "Science/Technology, Political Power, and a More Just World Order", but did not include a plenary session specifically on the issue of peace and armaments.

As the time of the conference drew closer, in an atmosphere of great international public concern about armaments, it became obvious that a conference on faith, science and the future could not do its job without giving some pointed attention to the relation of science and technology to military preparations and actions. When Philip Potter in his opening address (Chapter 2) emphasized "the acceleration of arms production and of the arms race", that was taken as a signal that the WCC would consider it appropriate for this conference to take up and speak on the issue.

Many of the major addresses gave attention to the theme. Hanbury Brown pointed out that the majority of scientists do work "largely controlled by governmental agencies serving national, military and civil interests" (Chapter 3). Jerome Ravetz spoke of the "cosmic obscenity of weapons of mass annihilation", and Manual Sadosky condemned both the waste and the terror of "preparation for war" (Chapter 6). Jonathan King, speaking on genetic technology, concluded his address by pleading for a conference statement on "reversing the nuclear arms race" (Chapter 14). And Joseph Weizenbaum, advocating "worldwide and total nuclear disarmament", urged as a first step a stop to enlarging "our already enormous nuclear arsenal" (Chapter 15). In the students' plenary session (Chapter 18 in this book but earlier in the actual programme) Tim Aukes of the Netherlands spoke on technology and militarism. The response to these and others made it evident that the conference wanted to declare itself on the issue of armaments.

David Rose, professor of nuclear engineering at MIT and a member of the WCC Working Committee on Church and Society, brought to the Steering Committee a request, on behalf of several concerned delegates, for a plenary session on disarmament. He further pointed out that specialists with great technical knowledge were available at MIT and Harvard. The Steering Committee welcomed the proposal and schedule a special plenary session on the eighth day of the conference.

The *ad hoc* group which requested the plenary session presented a proposed resolution for consideration by the conference. Metropolitan Gregorios, who chaired the session, explained that the resolution could be discussed in this session but could be voted on only in a later duly-called business meeting. A team of eight speakers addressed participants from the platform. Three of their addresses are printed below: those by Philip Morrison, professor of physics at MIT; George Kistiakowsky, professor emeritus of chemistry at Harvard University; and Archbishop Kirill, Rector of the Leningrad Theological Seminary.

Among the other speakers Ninan Koshy of India, a member of the WCC staff, reported on the WCC programme on militarism. W. Mutu Maathai of Kenya, remembered for her earlier eloquent address in appreciation of science (Chapter 3), called on the great military powers: "If you want to commit suicide, don't insist on taking us with you." Kazuyo Kishimoto of Japan reported on the anti-militaristic position of the United Church of Christ (Kyodan) in Japan. O. A. El-Kholy of Egypt (see Chapter 8) warned that the Third World, formerly by-standers in the big armaments race, was joining the "unholy club" and misusing its resources. Jimmie Woodward, of the United States and the World YWCA, gave examples of action programmes by local churches. Jan Evert van Veen of the Netherlands spoke of the theological imperatives for peace.

Metropolitan Gregorios, before calling for general discussion from the floor, requested comments from Roger L. Shinn, professor of social ethics at Union Theological Seminary in New York, and from Hugh Montefiore, Bishop of Birmingham in the United Kingdom. Excerpts from their comments are printed below.

The Nature of Strategic Nuclear Weapons

Philip Morrison

For more than forty years, I have as student and teacher tried to understand the atom, the nucleus, fields, gases. For five years of that time—in fear of a terrible threat to culture itself, from Nazi Germany—I was a very small cog, a man under thirty years of age, in a great engineering mechanism which left us the grim legacy of nuclear weapons. I was a loyal and a devoted cog, I admit it freely. But once I saw the air photos and then walked the ruins of Hiroshima, I came to the realization that we have a choice: cities or nuclear war. We cannot have both. I would like to explain why.

The destructive power of nuclear weapons

A weapon is called strategic when it is intended for and likely to be able to reach targets far from any battlefield, deep inside the territory of a potential opponent. The actual physical effects, however, are virtually the same as those of "tactical" nuclear weapons, which are oriented towards use against nearer battlefield targets up to some hundreds of miles away. The difference is more in the range of the vehicles which bring the weapons to the target and less in the nature of the weapons themselves. Strategic targets include some targets, such as great cities, which are of very large area; thus, strategic nuclear weapons sometimes possess greater explosive strength.

What a nuclear explosion does is to release a very large amount of energy with great suddenness *(Figure 1)*. The explosive energy yield is customarily

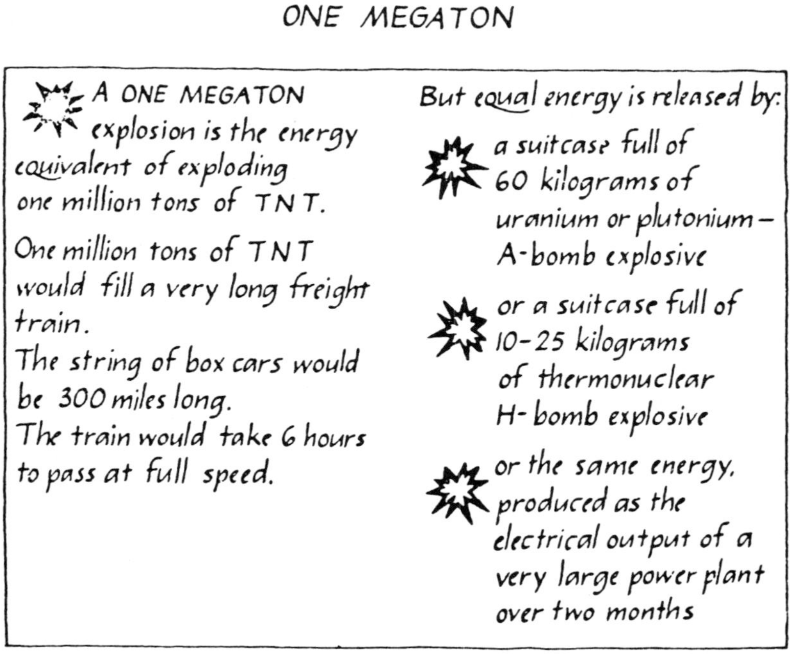

Fig. 1. The megaton — metric jargon for one million tons (of TNT) — has come to be the unit of energy release in large explosions. That same amount of energy can be released in different ways over different times.

described by a direct comparison to the amount of conventional high explosive material—TNT—which would release the same amount of energy. The word "megaton" (MT) is used to indicate one million tons of "TNT equivalent", which also equals 1,000 kilotons (kT).

Such large explosive yields as megatons are difficult to imagine. One way to imagine nuclear yields is to compare them with conventional war explosives; the total explosive energy spent by the United States during the eight years of war in Vietnam was equivalent to about six megatons. The nuclear energy yield of weapons held by the United States strategic forces today, in comparison, can be estimated as some 7,000 megatons total.

The effects of nuclear weapons can better be understood by comparison with large natural disasters such as tidal waves or earthquakes. The earthquake energy, for example, which shook down the city of San Francisco seventy years ago can be estimated as some 10 to 12 megatons equivalent. But nuclear attacks would be carefully arranged to take place in close proximity to the works and the homes of human beings; they would occur, not once in a great while, as for big natural disasters, but rather hundreds or thousands of times within hours *(Figure 2* overleaf*)*.

The blast pressure of nuclear explosions is similar to high hurricane winds which destroy structures and fling people and property about; the intense radiant fiery heat is like that of a volcanic eruption, which ignites fires in forest and city and burns exposed living flesh; the ground shock simulates the effects of an earthquake; a weapon exploded in a river or harbour raises enormous waves of water to roll over the shores—waves similar to tidal waves. In addition to blast, heat, shock and waves, nuclear weapons produce amounts of penetrating radiation unprecedented by any other phenomenon. This happens both at the time of the explosion and later, in the form of fallout, whenever and wherever the radio-active by-products of the explosion settle to the ground. This radiation can be life-threatening to organisms of all kinds, even though it is usually unperceived by the senses. The effect has no equally acute counterpart on earth (though it has in exploding stars).

Estimates of all these terrifying phenomena can be made more or less reliably, given the complex conditions of each event. Wind and temperature, terrain, bomb design, height of burst, air transparency, heat-reflecting snow or absorbing rain, and other such variables all affect the result of a nuclear explosion. The target structures—material, human and social—co-determine the effects as well on the actual targets. As a general rule, more damage can be done with several small weapons than with one large weapon *(Figure 3* overleaf*)*.

For ordinary civil targets, nuclear weapons are devastating. One modest warhead can cause heavy damage and catastrophic loss of life over many square miles, a sizable city district. On the other hand, a single warhead must come quite close if it is to destroy a buried, concrete- and steel-reinforced strong point, such as a missile silo. One has a better chance of destroying a

TYPICAL DAMAGE FROM A 40-KILOTON EXPLOSION

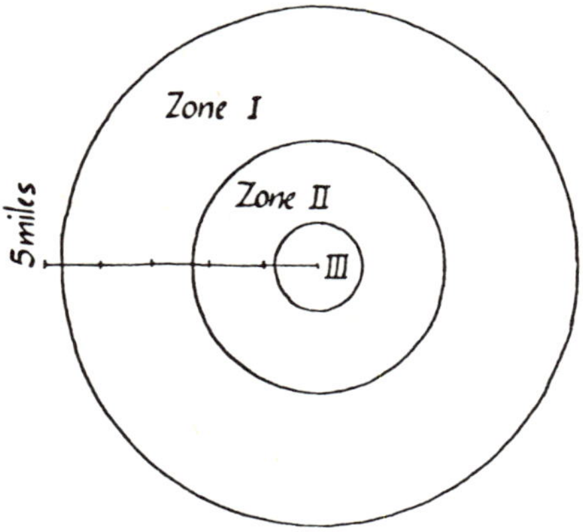

PHYSICAL DAMAGE	CASUALTIES
Out to 4.7 miles: General breakage of window glass, flying fragments, damage to weak structures. Out to 2.4 miles: Severe burns to exposed skin.	Zone I, 55 square miles. Chance of death grades from about 5% at outer edge of this ring to 40% near its inner edge. Deaths caused by flying glass, fires, building failures.
Out to 1.6 miles: Heavy structural damage to ordinary construction such as frame houses. Out to 1.4 miles: Ignition of clothing, light wooden pieces, etc.	Zone II, 14 square miles. Chance of death grades with distance from 40 to 60%. Deaths caused by fires, flesh burns, collapse of roofs & walls.
Out to .6 miles: Heavy damage to reinforced concrete structures: civic buildings. Out to .1 miles: Buried concrete & steel shelters and hardened missile silos made useless. Out to 200 feet: A crater of this radius is produced by an explosion at ground level.	Zone III, the innermost two square miles. 90% of persons present can be expected to meet death or grave injury through flying objects, collapse of whole structures, lethal radiation, thermal radiant burns, firestorm.

Fig. 2. The diagram maps the damage done by a 40-kiloton explosion at various distances from the point of impact. Plainly the variation is more or less gradual; the zone boundaries are rough classifications and refer to so-called prompt effects. Long-term effects, such as delayed cancers, would be in addition to the above calculations.

hardened silo with a low-yield but highly accurate weapon than with a high-yield but inaccurate weapon.

With test data, and with the experience of the two Japanese cities which were attacked with weapons of yield between 10 and 20 kilotons, it is possible to estimate the nature and number of casualties in a nuclear explosion as a function of the distance from the explosion.

Figure 2 shows potential damage relatively close to a nuclear explosion. There is also considerable threat to life at great distances from the burst. The fission product dust from an explosion drifts downwind, decaying as it drifts, and falling to the surface. Wind speed and direction determine this, as well as the height of burst, the nature of weapon, the nature of soil, and the weather. A typical elliptical downwind "plume" forms; people must either leave the area or find thickly shielded shelter before radiation exposure becomes fatal. Time and cover are crucially important. One may reckon that exposure to 300 or 400 rads (a unit of radiation exposure) will cause death in half the persons so exposed under the limited therapy available in disaster; the others will recover after some weeks of serious illness, though many among them may still develop malignant tumours many years later.

A wind speed of 15 miles per hour downwind from a 1-megaton nuclear explosion on the earth's surface yields a plume some 60 miles long by 10 miles

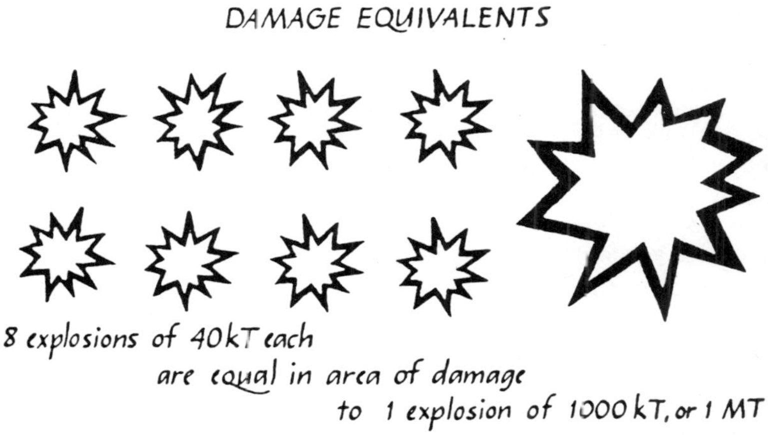

Fig. 3. Energy alone is not the only measure of an explosion. Very big explosions overdamage—even vaporize—the centre of the explosion, wasting energy. Hence the area of serious damage for typical targets increases more slowly than in proportion to the energy release. This has given rise to a rule of thumb here illustrated: the damage area of smaller explosions is expressed in terms of the number of 1-megaton explosions which would produce the same nominal area of damage. As shown, eight 40-kiloton explosions are about equivalent to one megaton in damage area, although it requires twenty-five 40-kiloton explosions ($25 \times 40{,}000 = 1{,}000{,}000$) to yield the energy of one megaton.

wide; within this early plume, humans will be exposed to 500 rads within a few hours even behind the shielding provided by a brick residence. The plume lengthens, widens, and dilutes. Evacuation would be prudent at least within an area 200 miles long by 30 miles wide within which a dose lethal to half the exposed people might be accumulated.

A conservative estimate predicts that the residents over 2,000 square miles have a substantial risk of radiation death or incapacitation. A similar area will be contaminated past safe use for a long time.

It seems probable that among the survivors who are lightly exposed many—perhaps one-tenth—will suffer radiation-induced tumours delayed over the decades after exposure. An estimate based on various exposures, including those at the Japanese cities, suggests that about one delayed malignant tumour can be expected for each 5,000 person-rads of exposure, with a similar number of genetic defects in the offspring.

There are global risks, as well, although they are poorly known. There exists at present worldwide fallout from 200 megatons of fission yield produced by all past atmospheric nuclear tests, now much decayed. The full explosive nuclear power now held by the United States alone might raise that by some 25 times. If that megatonnage were to be used, one would expect about ten million induced tumours worldwide in this generation and several times that number of genetic defects passed on to the future. The ozone layer worldwide would be seriously affected by a many-thousand megaton strike; this would place crops, plankton and forests at risk, a risk now believed repairable but, obviously, not known for certain to be so.

A number of populous nearby powers have a large stake in the matter of any future nuclear war, for the fallout is not likely to be spread with complete uniformity. Just as the countryside downwind from a military target or city will receive a very heavy plume of fallout, so China and Japan lie downwind from most of the planned impact sites for American weapons. They face serious danger, as does Atlantic Europe.

On the other hand, even the tens of millions of delayed tumours and genetic defects add only a fraction to those expected from natural causes among the world's four billion people. Although the safety factor is not as large as prudent public health officials might hope for—perhaps we are safe by a factor of only 100—it appears that all-out nuclear war with the present weapon stocks would not end human life worldwide as far as fallout effects are concerned. Whether some unforeseen subtle consequences for the climate or the ecology might turn out to be fatal is one more uncertainty of this grotesque situation.

Nuclear disarmament and deterrence

The logic of nuclear deterrence is still cogently expressed in the metaphor of two scorpions in a bottle, coined decades ago by nuclear physicist Robert Oppenheimer. True, times have changed. Several toxic centipedes now scurry around the two scorpions, and a number of other smaller creatures dream of acquiring stings. When only one scorpion had a sting, it thought of striking first, either in anger or to prevent the maturing of the other. But now a first strike would yield little gain to either, for the other can always strike back, at least so long as it possesses a sting which will survive the initial attack. This accounts for the rising importance of hidden weapons, like those under the seas, which are sure to survive a first strike. Given their secure, strongly toxic stings, the two scorpions are mutually deterred if they choose to survive. The ironic phrase employed to describe this stand-off is "mutual assured destruction" (often abbreviated MAD): the population of each side is held hostage to the other, with no means of defence. The world remains in that terrifying state of deterrence today, as it has for a quarter of a century.

Nowadays, there is a new idea about how nuclear weapons could be utilized, explicit in the US. Holding the great final stinger in reserve, one scorpion can yet punish the other by small, well-aimed stings in foreparts or legs, less than fatal, counting that the other will not risk mutual destruction by swinging the deadly tail. Might even enough of these pricks somehow weaken the great tail itself, before it is brought into final self-destructive use? Maybe. Such thinking has rationalized a great proliferation of small nuclear warheads, able to strike extremely close to any known target spot, and thus able to destroy military targets which are safe from more distant but larger explosion because they are of unusually strong construction or even buried deep underground.

We see no justification whatever for such profound risks. We will show that the deterrence of nuclear exchange—the posture of the two scorpions—is the only justifiable use for nuclear weapons; but this certainly depends on an air of reason and restraint inside the tensely balanced bottle. Our sense of timely action is to begin to reduce the venom of the stings while they remain deadly. The point is not at all who has the bigger sting, but that the stings are mutually fatal.

The tables and calculations of the previous pages should carry the grim argument plainly enough. The numbers can tell only a portion of the truth; the rest is a more human tale, a tale of families and crops and treasures of the world's culture exposed to apocalyptic terror, with one new Horseman called Radiation.

No sane leader ought to expect gain from the use of nuclear weapons. It seems probable that the world's leadership, which has for almost forty years carried us all up an escalator of potential damage, remains confident that it can still control unacceptable use of the weapons, and seeks to derive from their mere possession only the political benefits of prestige, power, veiled threat and "superiority", without actual use. Our fear is plain: such self-confidence in those with power is a defiance of history. Once it was called *hubris*; it remains a courting of the judgment of fate. The only safe way is to wind the danger down.

Some proposals

The arms race grows out of new developments now as much as it once did from size of forces. We believe American security may often be placed at higher risk—rather than at lower risk—by the increase in speed of nuclear response, by a new type of nuclear weapon, or by a gain in missile flexibility, even when it is our own. We therefore propose qualitative restraint, in addition to quantitative reductions:

1. A comprehensive ban on all nuclear weapons tests by treaty, to be negotiated after the United States has declared a moratorium on its own testing. Such a test ban is today verifiable enough to meet any reasonable objections. The United States should moreover announce its intention not to be the first to use nuclear weapons, and perhaps should seek such an agreement internationally.

2. A halt forthwith to the development or deployment of new options for strategic nuclear offensive war. The B-1 bomber was halted in 1977, the Trident submarine missile system is in construction and a new mobile ICBM called MX is in development. These new weapons are not needed for a secure deterrent; worse, their presence is not always clearly distinguishable from a force intended for one or another kind of initiation of nuclear attack, a first strike, or a growing sequence of exchanges. Earlier the US set aside anti-ballistic missile defence; that was viewed both as ineffective and as an incitement to increasing and improving the deterrent forces of the opponent. The 1972 ABM Treaty halted one needless race.

Once in the years after Sputnik, around 1960, the experts told us of a Soviet missile gap. The gap was real enough, but it turned out to be the other way: Soviet ICBM development lagged years behind the US. As early as 1966 we were told of new astonishing Russian advances in the anti-missile defence. Multiple warheads were first claimed essential to penetrate the defence overseas. That too proved insubstantial; the flurry ended with US MIRVed missiles indeed bearing many warheads, even though ABM was absent. Several years later, the Soviets in turn deployed their many-headed missiles. Once again, they have matched US speeding technical initiatives. Where is the gain? In the end, they will likely be able to follow the lead of US technology anywhere it goes, eventually more or less reaching parity; but what sense is there in this unceasing escalation of risk and threat, we two scorpions in a bottle, each year improving our stings?

The United States is safe against rational attack while it possesses an assured undersea retaliatory deterrent. No force at all can make the United States safe against an irrational attack. On both sides fear, self-deception and the instability which grows out of an unending search for "superiority" open the larger risks of unreason and of miscalculation.

Those are the worst of all threats to American security. The time is ripe to wind down.

The Need for a Mass Movement

GEORGE B. KISTIAKOWSKY

Professor Morrison has given us a vivid picture of nuclear arms and the status of the current arms race, which is really in full swing even though there are tens of thousands of nuclear warheads already in deployment with one or another means of delivery. And yet we have on the books and really in force seven bilateral and international treaties on arms control, which are supposed to be restraining nuclear arms, and which have been signed after much effort over the last twenty years.

This is an odd situation. If you study these treaties, you discover that they were written not to stop the arms race but to set up rules for continuing it, rules that were preferred by the signatories. These rules are very definitely better than none, and I believe that arms control negotiations such as SALT II are to be welcomed because they reduce or postpone the threat of nuclear war. But they have not stopped the arms race, and they will not stop it.

To me, at least, there is convincing evidence that the governments in the present circumstances are unable to reach agreements that would stop the arms race and start disarmament, even though the parties and the individuals comprising these governments change from time to time. The forces within the countries which believe the rather primitive notion that force is better than anything else are too strong for that. And so clearly a new force for disarmament must come into play to change this trend.

Once before such a force was said to be in action: it was the mass movement against atmospheric weapons' tests during the fifties. It was instrumental in forcing governments to negotiate for comprehensive nuclear test bans starting in 1958. Unfortunately several events intervened, and only a partial test ban was concluded in 1963 which ended atmospheric nuclear tests but not the means of developing new warheads by underground tests. This treaty stopped the pollution of atmosphere by radio-active fallout and, therefore and most unfortunately, it has also led to the atrophy of the anti-nuclear mass movement of the fifties, because so much of it was concerned, and very legitimately, with the terrible health hazards from exposure to ionizing radiation from radio-active substances.

I am coming to the conclusion, because of the ineffectuality of the governments, that such a mass movement must be recreated. Any nuclear war, not only the all-out nuclear war, will produce so much radio-active debris that everybody—I mean virtually everybody in the world—will be exposed to some nuclear radiation. Perhaps this notion, if nothing else, will catch public imagination and bring people to be actively concerned with the threat of such war. Certainly we know from current events in this country and abroad that the far smaller danger of radiation from nuclear power plants has had an extraordinarily great public impact.

We who believe that the arms race must be stopped before it is too late will be helpless to achieve our aim until we enlist broad public support—in fact, a truly international mass movement to be dedicated to the liquidation of nuclear arms.

Christian Responsibility for Nuclear Disarmament

ARCHBISHOP KIRILL

I shall start with the concluding words of Jonathan King's excellent paper: "I appeal to you as a scientist and biologist, do not allow this conference to close without speaking out as strongly as you can on the need for reversing the nuclear arms race that so deeply threatens future generations. Without the removal of this gravest of threats to human society, there will be no possibility of achieving the just, participatory and sustainable society that we all deeply desire."

Disarmament, and nuclear disarmament in particular, is a most important, integral and complex part of the common process which can lead us to the creation of a just, participatory and sustainable society. Without reduction and limitation of the material means of warfare, and especially of nuclear warfare, it is impossible to lay the foundation for political decisions aimed at the strengthening of international security, and to free resources necessary for the solution of economic and social problems confronting mankind today.

However, there are serious difficulties on the way to nuclear disarmament. Those difficulties seem to operate on several levels. Some of these difficulties do not belong in the political sphere, but rather in the sphere of scientific-technological discoveries which can be used for the improvement of old systems of weaponry and for the production of new ones. Such a situation calls for especially persistent efforts towards the conclusion of agreements in this field as soon as possible.

The arms race is by no means an inevitable "fellow-traveller" of man in his development. It is generated by the interests and activities of concrete political forces and can be stopped by the opposing forces of the adherents of disarmament. The treaties and agreements which have been concluded bear evidence to the practical feasibility of disarmament measures in the present historical conditions.

Restriction and eventual elimination of the arms race

The problem of disarmament after World War II should be considered in relation to three stages in the balance of nuclear strategic forces and also in the international situation. The first stage embraces the post-war period until the 1950's. This stage was marked by US "nuclear monopoly" and by the beginning of the so-called cold war, as well as by the reserved attitude of western countries to negotiations on disarmament.

The second stage covers the period from the early 1950's to the late 1960's. On the one hand, this period was characterized by the erosion of US monopoly in atomic weaponry, by the development of thermonuclear weapons in the USSR, by the launching of the first Soviet satellite into orbit round the earth, by the gradual establishment of a Soviet-American military-strategic balance; on the other hand, it was characterized by the still continuing cold war, which often took the form of imminent danger to universal peace. Under these circumstances a certain progress in relations and ideas on disarmament took place.

The third stage, which started in the 1970's, is marked not only by military-strategic parity but also by the difficulty of renouncing cold-war thinking and by the introduction of the principles of peaceful coexistence into the relations of states in opposing systems. For the solution of disarmament problems, this third period can become a turning point in many respects.

At the present time three conditions can be identified as providing a possibility for the reduction in the arms race. First is the establishment of strategic nuclear parity. Second is the achievement of considerable political changes in international relations, conditioned by the practical application of the principles of peaceful coexistence. Suffice it to remember the peaceful solution of a number of complicated problems, the elimination of hotbeds of danger and the process of political detente with its great possibilities for the strengthening of common security. Third, as a result of scientific-technological development the formidable killing capacity of different types of armaments has considerably increased, and great success has been achieved in seismology, radiolocation, space exploration and other fields, which in many cases removes the problem of inspection—for long the argument against reduction in nuclear weaponry.

The inter-related influence of these three factors creates favourable conditions for the restriction and the eventual elimination of the arms race. It is obvious that these factors as such do not lead to a restriction of the arms race and to nuclear disarmament.

Increasing and diminishing the threat of nuclear war

Forces actively hindering this process continue to act. In the 1970's, along with the conditions favourable for nuclear disarmament there appeared trends augmenting the danger of world war. The first of these was the propagation of the concept of a "balance of power" or the so-called "theory of restraint". According to this concept, international, political and military detente is not the only alternative to the cold war, and international security may be provided through so-called "military systems". Parallel to this type of trend we find theories about the "acceptability" of limited nuclear wars. These concepts become particularly dangerous when they form the basis of concrete projects for a quantitative and qualitative arms race (e.g. the neutron bomb).

The second such trend was the dangerous development of certain local international conflicts determined in particular by the large scale involvement of certain great powers. Some of the participants in these conflicts are close to possessing atomic weapons or have begun producing them, e.g. certain countries in the Middle East and South Africa.

Such steps as the creation of regional systems of security, the creation of peace areas in different regions, stopping the supply of arms, the peaceful solution of local conflicts can contribute towards a favourable climate for disarmament. The development of political and military detente should be inter-related.

The limitation of strategic weapons is an important measure for diminishing the threat of nuclear war, and for strengthening peace and international security. Therefore, it is quite understandable that mutually agreed measures for the elimination of the nuclear arms threat and the elimination of the arms race, first of all, in offensive-strategic armaments, are the backbone of Soviet-American relations. However, this problem concerns not only the USA and the USSR, but all the nations of the world, because such agreements between these two countries raise the level of confidence between the two countries, and therefore influence positively the international situation as a whole, thus consolidating peace throughout the world.

Very important steps have been undertaken in the limiting of antiballistic missile defence systems, the restriction of offensive strategic weapons (SALT I, 1972), the treaty for the prevention of nuclear war (1973), the minutes to the treaty for the restriction of antiballistic missile defence systems (1974), and finally the treaty on the restriction of offensive strategic weapons (1979, SALT II), which is yet to be ratified. This last treaty (SALT II) is the most important measure to date for nuclear disarmament. It creates a barrier to further accumulation of the most destructive, expensive and resource-wasting weapons. The coming into effect of this treaty will contribute to the slowing down of the arms race and to the creation of conditions for the achievement of SALT III, which should envisage not only the limitation of arms but their elimination. It is worth noting that SALT II should influence favourably the international climate in general. This positive significance of SALT II was noted in particular in the joint statement issued by the representatives of the churches of the USSR and of the USA who discussed problems of disarmament in Geneva in March this year.

Importance of non-proliferation of nuclear arms

Nuclear non-proliferation is one of the most urgent tasks in the limitation of nuclear arms and the strengthening of international security. This problem is reinforced by the accelerating process of creation of scientific-technological and industrial nuclear potential in a growing number of countries, and in particular by the speedy development of nuclear energy and an international trade in nuclear materials, equipment and technology. The existence of countries where the influence of militarist circles on foreign policy is strong and where there is pressure in favour of the possession of nuclear arms, complicates the situation and increases the hazard of a nuclear war. Of cardinal importance for international security is the famous treaty of 1968, which not only limits nuclear proliferation but creates the foundations for international cooperation in the peaceful use of atomic energy. Over a hundred states ratified this treaty, and this testifies to the hopes of the majority of countries for peace and security based on the non-proliferation of nuclear arms. However, over thirty countries are not parties to this treaty, in particular, South Africa, France, Israel, the People's Republic of China and other countries who are very close to producing nuclear installations. Therefore it is important to increase the number of participants in this treaty in order to give it a universal character.

The conclusion by non-nuclear countries of control agreements with the International Agency for Atomic Energy is an urgent task for ensuring the non-proliferation of nuclear arms. In the majority of non-nuclear countries the use of atomic energy is under the control of this Agency. However, to date not all the non-nuclear states which signed the treaty have concluded control agreements with this Agency. Therefore it is necessary to strive for the conclusion of control agreements between the IAEA and all non-nuclear participating countries, as well as with countries which have till now avoided participation in the treaty, so that all nuclear activity can be brought under international control, thus preventing the secret production of nuclear arms. This task has become particularly urgent in the context of the accelerating development of atomic energy.

In order to create further conditions of non-proliferation, it is also necessary to strengthen control over the export of nuclear materials, equipment and technology. Strong guarantees are necessary to ensure that international cooperation in the peaceful use of nuclear energy should not lead to the proliferation of nuclear arms. Christians and all people of goodwill should give the strongest support to such efforts in order to strengthen the conditions for the non-proliferation of nuclear arms as an important link in the measures for the containment of the nuclear threat.

Another important measure is the general and complete cessation of nuclear arms testing. This problem is directly connected with the protection of the environment. Important measures have been undertaken in this field: the conclusion of a treaty banning nuclear arms testing in three spheres (1963), and the treaty between the USSR and USA on the limitation of underground nuclear explosions for all purposes (1976). First of all, these initiatives provided a strong preliminary basis for the restriction of the arms race; secondly, they prevented further massive pollution of the immediate environment by radio-active waste; thirdly, they increased expertise in the use of national technical means of control over the commitments to the prohibition of nuclear arms tests.

A halt to nuclear testing

The solution to the problem of a total ban on nuclear testing, which was welcomed by the 32nd UN General Assembly, actually envisages at least two urgent actions for the present time: first, the accession to the treaty of 1963 of two nuclear powers, the Chinese People's Republic and France, and the ratification of this treaty by Argentina and Pakistan; and secondly, the adoption of a moratorium on underground nuclear tests by the great powers, until all nuclear states have become parties to such a treaty.

What would the banning of all forms of nuclear arms testing mean in practice? First of all it would mean a limit to the qualitative improvement of these arms. The participation of all the states in such a treaty would lead to the final ending of radio-active contamination of the atmosphere and the surface of our planet, of the disturbance of seismic stability, of the pollution of underground waters and the destructive consequences of underground tests.

The ending of all nuclear arms tests would mean an invaluable contribution to detente and to mutual confidence among nations. It would be a stage towards the achievement of general and complete disarmament, particularly nuclear disarmament. It would contribute to a lasting peace and the development of cooperation among all peoples in the context of a new international economic order and a just, participatory and sustainable society. Such is the principal duty and aim of all Christians and people of goodwill at the present time.

Not only is there no longer any other alternative for avoiding a nuclear holocaust on earth. But for Christians and for Christian religious consciousness and theological understanding, the struggle for peace, the struggle for general and complete disarmament and the establishment of a just society are closely related and are based on the concept of salvation and the Kingdom of God. Salvation, peace, justice, liberation are the main characteristics of the Kingdom of God partially manifested in history. Of course, the Kingdom of God in its fullness will appear beyond history. But the Lord said that the Kingdom of Heaven shall be taken in strength (cf. Matt. 11, 12). So here, on earth, it is manifested in the creative effort of man, it matures as a plant growing from a seed, as a vineyard entrusted to the labourer, according to the Gospel parable. The Kingdom of God in its particular manifestations, problems and elements is "partially manifested" in history. This "partial manifestation" in history is a concrete fulfilment in time, bearing its maturing fruit. We call this fruit salvation. And the elements of salvation in its historical developments are (besides personal holiness) love, peace, justice, liberty. This salvation brought to the earth by Christ, these elements of the Kingdom of God proclaimed by him, have a universal cosmic character (cf. Matt. 28:19, Rom. 1:16, Rom. 8:19 ff., Phil. 2:11, Acts 10:36, Rom. 10:12).

This cosmic dimension of salvation is implemented in the vocation of the Church and all Christians to make manifest to all people the seeds, the shoots and the elements of the coming Kingdom and Lordship of God here, on earth, in time and in the development of the historical process. That Kingdom impinges on all levels and all physical aspects of human life in this world, on all concrete social, political, economic, racial and ecological phenomena.

This underlines once again the fact that one of the main problems of modern life is the question of nuclear disarmament as a concrete step towards complete and general disarmament.

I want to conclude with a quotation from the Geneva Consultation between the churches of the USSR and of the USA (March 1979) when they appealed to their governments and to all mankind: "There may be only one answer. There is no other answer and no other alternative—choose life".

International Agreements and Unilateral Initiatives A Response by ROGER L. SHINN

I find myself in very close agreement with Prof. Morrison's case, and I share his perplexities. If in the next moment I emphasize the perplexities, it is not to dim passion but to test the clarity of my reasoning and to be corrected if there are those here who can help me.

But first I should say that I share Prof. Kistiakowsky's unenthusiastic endorsement of SALT. I am perhaps less enthusiastic than Archbishop Kirill about it, because I think it is very inadequate. But I think the defeat of it would be very bad, and I have pledged President Carter personally that I will support it, in spite of the fact that I think it very deficient. My fear is that in the United States the opposition from militarists and the opposition or lack of support from pacifists will combine to defeat it.

Now I return to the point of Prof. Morrison that perplexes both him and me. We live in this tragic situation—this absurd situation—where, as he has said, the fact that two great powers are hostages to each other has done something to prevent the use of nuclear weapons. I reluctantly agree with him that "the deterrence of nuclear exchange—the posture of two scorpions—is the only justifiable use for nuclear weapons". When only one scorpion had the sting, it—we, the United States—used it. After a second scorpion had the sting, nobody used it.

I do not like that situation. I do not know what to do about it.

If the Soviet government—to imagine the absurd—were to employ me as a consultant, I would not urge them to disarm unilaterally. I would have to tell them that they cannot trust those folks across the Atlantic. I would recommend bilateral, not unilateral disarmament.

If you think I am faking this opinion for wicked purposes, I can at least give you evidence that I really believe it. When the United States had an overwhelming superiority in nuclear weapons, I wrote in *Christianity and Crisis* that the world would be safer when the Soviet Union got parity with us. That was a very unpopular opinion then. But I believed it.

For the same reason I would not today advocate unilateral disarmament for the Soviet Union or for my own country. My reason is not that the Russians are worse than we, but that we all have the same human failings. And this puts me in the perplexing situation.

I do endorse unilateral initiatives, and I quite agree with Dr Morrison on that point, also. If somebody warns me that such initiatives are a risk, I ask what risks we are taking now with our armaments. I would rather take risks for peace than risks for war.

But I am in this perplexing situation where, without dimming my passion for nuclear disarmament, I have to ask what set of devices might help two great powers to work together, when neither trusts the other and yet both have enough sense to distrust their destructive potential.

So I repeat that I want my country to take initiatives and risks for disarmament, but also to take steps towards agreement and parity in disarmament. On this issue I think I detect the one major difference of opinion within the panel itself. I would hope that Section IX might explore the issue and bring us its wisdom.

The Task of the Churches in the Debate About Nuclear Disarmament

A Response by Hugh Montefiore

Like Prof. Shinn, I was warmly in favour of this session on disarmament, because it seems to me that it is perhaps the first charge on the Christian churches to see what they can do to remove this great threat which overhangs the whole of humanity: the danger of nuclear holocaust. And I have, like others here, been deeply moved by what I have heard said, especially by our brothers and sisters from Kenya, from Japan and from Egypt.

I want to speak to the draft resolution which we have before us and, like Prof. Shinn, I guess that what I shall have to say will not be over popular. But I think it is important, sisters and brothers, that in a Christian assembly we should respect what each other thinks and that we should be concerned for truth as we see it. I think that as Christians we should have three aims: first, that these dreadful satanic weapons should never be used; secondly, that they should be reduced in number; and thirdly, that they should be dismantled and destroyed.

Now, the first stage. Like Prof. Shinn, I do not believe that the first stage (that they should never be used) can be achieved by unilateral disarmament. Because we have in fact a system of mutual deterrents, like it or not, rough equality or sufficient balance has prevented a pre-emptive strike because there is no advantage in striking first if the result is catastrophic to yourself. And to keep the peace, we need to keep the balance of deterrents—though, please God, not at the present level. To lose this balance is, I believe, to bring nuclear warfare closer, rather than to take it further away.

Secondly, how to reduce the nuclear arms race; then, how to dismantle and destroy nuclear weapons. Not, I believe, by pious appeals and platitudes; not, I believe, by inculcating terror about the results of these weapons, or even by pleading a position of powerlessness. No, I think we have to go deeper. I think we have to take away what brings them into being—to remove genuine fear on both sides of confronting blocs which create the need for deterrents. Because, unless that fear is removed, we will get nowhere. And how are we to do it? To remove injustice, aggressiveness, unreasonableness on *both* sides of opposing nuclear blocs; on both sides, to promote justice, understanding, detente, and confidence between opposing nuclear blocs. That seems to me the prime requisite, and it is nowhere mentioned in this draft resolution. This is the churches' prime task, as I see it, laid upon all: laid upon the churches of those belonging to countries of each opposing nuclear bloc; laid upon the churches of those who belong to neither, to those in a position of powerlessness.

I think that this primary task, is much tougher than passing resolutions which seem to me like platitudes and which cost us nothing. I fear that the draft resolution, unless it is amended—and may I say I hope it *will* be amended because I hope that this assembly may be able to pass a resolution worthy of the World Council of Churches—takes our minds away from the primary task of Christian churches for reconciliation and the removal of fears. And while I cannot vote against it because I agree with everything that it says, I cannot vote in favour of it because it seems to me (and I hope I will be corrected if I am wrong), superficial—and superficial documents, however well-intentioned, can be mischievous.

Reactions and Comment

Because the plenary session was already extending late into the evening, immediate discussion was limited. But comments, both in this plenary session and on the following days, touched on several points. Some speakers said that it was premature, even hypocritical, to talk about disarmament before correcting great injustices in the world. Some said that the nuclear powers should not ask for non-proliferation of weapons while maintaining their own. But a strong general consensus emerged for a resolution from the conference.

Metropolitan Gregorios suggested that a committee, including some members of the group proposing the resolution and some members from Section IX, revise the proposal in the light of the discussion and bring it back to a later plenary session. His idea was accepted by common consent.

On 22 July the revised resolution was presented in plenary session, with an announcement that it would be taken up for action the next day. On 23 July it was moved and seconded in a business session. After some amendments of detail, the conference adopted the resolution with an overwhelming affirmative vote, no dissenting vote and no abstentions, and the chair ruled that the adoption was unanimous.

The resolution, as adopted, is printed in Volume 2 of this report.

Part Four
Participation and Power

17. Possibilities of Political and Personal Action

Introduction

Part Four of this book comes from the later plenary sessions. After the exploration of the many issues of faith and science, set forth in the agenda, the conference looked at the realities of power and the practical possibilities of participation in relation to all such issues.

This chapter combines addresses from two plenary sessions. The first had the theme "Science and Technology as Power: Their Control and Use, and Their Just Distribution between the Rich and Poor Nations". The speakers were B. C. E. Nwosu, Chief Education Officer (Science) of the Federal Ministry of Education in Nigeria, and a member of the WCC Working Committee on Church and Society, and Rogerio de Cerqueira Leite, professor in the Institute of Physics, Universidade Estadual de Campinas, Brazil. Their addresses, in addition to presenting their own experiences and insights, brought to a focus themes that had been opened up by most of the speakers since the keynote address by Philip Potter.

The second and parallel theme was "Science and Technology as Power: Possibilities of Personal and Community Actions". Here three speakers from different parts of the world told of experiences in their own countries where concerned citizens had exercised some influence on the uses of technology in the public arena.

Kerstin Anér, Under-Secretary of State in Sweden, reinforced some of the themes that Jerome Ravetz had voiced earlier (see Chapter 6), as well as the feminist criticisms of technology from Rosemary Reuther (Chapter 4) and Karen Lebacqz (Chapter 14). She then described new uses of telecommunication in northern Sweden as an experiment, encouraged by government, in strengthening the influence of citizens upon technological decisions.

Thomas R. Berger, Justice of the Supreme Court of British Columbia, told of the inquiry he chaired on the routing of a projected gas pipeline in the Canadian north-west. The case showed the possibility of actions, under the highest government auspices, which encourage the participation of cultural and ethnic groups that have a great stake in the plans proposed by technological and economic elites that often neglect such groups.

Finally Jun Ui, a sanitary engineer on the faculty of the University of Tokyo, described the efforts of networks of individuals and small groups to oppose destructive pollution in Japan. Unlike Anér and Berger, who found some governmental support for the participation of citizens, Ui spoke out of the experience, familiar to delegates from many parts of the world, where citizens see governments as more the problem than the ally of citizens' groups. Speaking out of the Buddhist tradition, Ui also continued the inter-religious conversation begun earlier in the conference (see Chapter 8).

Just Distribution Between Rich and Poor Nations

B. C. E. Nwosu

The debate on science and technology as power is a long-standing one, and I do not wish to bore you with a repetition of familiar arguments. The African perspective on this matter has been covered by Dr Odhiambo earlier. However, I would like to stress one central point frequently made by representatives from developing countries. Science and technology is power, and the third world countries want to share this power. In saying that the poorer nations wish to share it, one is not unmindful of the abuse and misuse of this power. The students' report given during this conference gives illustrations of the abuse of this power by the developing countries both in the use of resources and in the domination of less privileged nations, societies, and groups within nations. Nevertheless, my thesis is that one of the ways of checking the abuse of power is by ensuring that those who do not have power gain access to it, or at least share in determining its use.

Models of technology transfer—the key to power

Developing countries are, in my view, experimenting with three models of technology transfer. The first involves the "purchase of technology". This model is predominant in countries which have abundant raw materials such as oil, copper, etc. Nigeria and Kenya are African examples. Under ideal conditions, purchase of technology implies technology transfers which are paid for in raw materials under cooperative agreements between the developing and the developed country, creating bonds of mutual interest. In this model the nation buying technology learns to manage, maintain, replicate and improve the acquired technology through research with varying degrees of assistance from the selling nation.

Some of the conditions for success of this model include: the need of the buying country to establish conditions which guarantee the success of the technology; the clarification by both nations of what is to be transferred; a systematic bi-directional exchange of information and ideas; the assessment of the technology; the creation of a supportive engineering programme, particularly maintenance engineering, in which both nations have to participate; and finally a fair price for the technology being acquired.

The above approach to development, if properly implemented, has many advantages. Visible progress, albeit highly localized, is achieved in a short time. Roads, bridges and ports are built in record time; big public buildings and universities and show-piece teaching hospitals are erected. Using conventional parameters there is significant growth! Those developing countries able to finance the purchase of these foreign technologies get a psychological feeling of possessing and/or sharing power. The citizens, at least the elite, have a new sense of pride. But a more critical look reveals a number of ambiguities and contradictions. First, power acquired is ephemeral. My country provides an example of how short-lived this power can be. Because of the active and progressive role Nigeria has recently been playing in African affairs, particularly in Southern Africa, the western world put a squeeze on the purchase of oil from Nigeria. Only the crisis in Iran saved the Nigerian economy from this stranglehold.

Secondly, the gross domestic product of the buyer country may increase, but the development of the majority of the citizens is found to change little. Moreover, the governments are generally vulnerable, as the elite becomes affluent and corrupt, for example from their collaboration with the transnational companies. Mercedes Benz cars and air-conditioners are found all over the main cities and provincial capitals. (Please note that the socialist countries also have state-controlled "export companies" that behave like TNC's.) This state of affairs results in alienation between the haves and have-nots within the same country.

Thirdly, the technology transferred in this model is neither indigenous nor self-sustaining. Indeed, it perpetuates dependence on foreign know-how and on countries from which such know-how originates.

Finally, there is a general lack of confidence in indigenous scientists and technologists. These scientists and technologists, who usually have studied in the developed countries of the world and generally obtained reasonable proficiency, feel frustrated that they are not able to make a meaningful contribution to the development of their own countries.

The second model is based on self-reliance. An attempt is made to maximize independence of action and of use of resources from the particular country which has taken this option. The major advantage of this model, if one examines the situation in a country such as Tanzania, is the feeling that here is a country that is willing "to cut its coat according to its cloth". There is a great degree of healthy nationalism and self-confidence arising from this approach. Also, it usually implies relevance in the choice of technology. Although growth by self-reliant techniques is slow, it is more permanent and can be self-sustaining. In short this is a most attractive model which has gained a lot of support in the World Council of Churches' circles (see the 1974 Bucharest Conference Report, *Anticipation*, No. 19, November 1974).

However, a critical evaluation of the self-reliant approach, in the African setting, shows that expected results are not easily achieved. One of the prerequisites of a successful implementation of the model of self-reliance is the establishment of either an "iron curtain", "bamboo curtain" or any other similar "curtain". Many of the African countries are so weak that they cannot even erect a "paper curtain". The poor African countries are not left alone to do their own thing. Powerful international salesmen of the transnational companies besiege the offices of the policy-makers. They present short-cut solutions to all problems. The governments soon discountenance the advice of their own experts. Secondly, the needs of most of these countries are so pressing and diverse that most genuine leaders lose patience with the self-reliant approach. In their own words, they want changes in their lifetime. Another difficulty is that scientists in these countries are usually too few and specialized to form a "critical mass" to make significant innovative technological changes in their society.

The third model constitutes the multilateral interchange through the United Nations system. The greatest believers in this model are the smaller countries. The advantage of the multilateral interchange of expertise through the UN system is that it seeks to reduce the influence of the super-powers and the highly developed industrialized societies. On the whole, most of the experts in the UN system are either drawn from the third world countries or from the relatively smaller countries of eastern and western Europe and Latin America. Psychologically these experts feel at home in the third world countries and are reasonably well received. Furthermore, the training programme provided by the UN agencies, through fellowships, attachments, etc., provides these countries with useful manpower for their development programmes. But the problem in this model lies with the UN system itself. You have Unesco, Unido, Unep, Unicef, Undp, etc., all chasing around the same country selling the same idea. For example, in the West African sub-region there are at least three different UN agencies covering the area of science education. Recently another agency, NEI, has been set up to coordinate these agencies! From my own rough estimates 75% of the budget of UN agencies is spent on secretariats, personnel emoluments and travel of experts, another 15% is spent on coordinating meetings, conferences and workshops. A country is lucky if 10% is used in concrete development programmes.

But the main problem is that, in the UN system, the role of the highly industrialized nations is only superficially reduced. These countries pay the piper and therefore call the tune, directly or by remote control. A good example of this is the IAEA, a UN agency in which I have had the privilege of representing my country on a number of occasions. Every year there is a larger vote in favour of the monitoring of the Nuclear Non-Proliferation Treaty (with the financial commitments that requires), while only a small percentage of IAEA funds are allocated to peaceful applications of atomic energy to medicine, agriculture and industry. All representations by the developing countries to the IAEA in the last ten years have been on this point, because it is this area of IAEA activities that is most relevant to them. But these representations have yielded only meagre results.

The hypocrisy underlying technology transfer in the nuclear field is all too evident. Most scientists and policy-makers in highly developed countries argue that it is dangerous to allow African countries access to nuclear technology, basing their point of view on the example of giving a small child fire to play with. But the advocates of this point of view come from countries that have developed nuclear power to the highest level, both for industrial purposes as well as for armaments, and have misused this power (in their careless management of waste products or in the continued development and proliferation of nuclear weapons). We from the less developed countries challenge these people to propose concrete plans they have for sharing, say, the commercial secrets of solar energy. All we have are the isolated experiments of a group of idealists in Kumasi and Kano—the so-called Intermediate Technology Group.

Strategies of action

Science and technology is power. It is power to do good. It is also power to do evil. The poorer nations are poor only in technology, not in their culture. Therefore they have no option but to seek the power which technology confers. They have a duty to provide for their teeming populations as well as guarantee their security, be it national, sub-regional or regional. These countries need to control their destiny. The question is, how do they proceed? There are decisions which these nations must take by themselves. These are:

1. Every country, however small, must make up its mind about its national goals. These goals must be determined by its citizens, seizing their own destiny, unaware of what is happening elsewhere in the world, unintimidated by the major advances in science and technology in the developed countries.

2. Every developing country should establish a science education policy that starts from the grassroots and that is both humane and culture-bound. Such policies must combat the outmoded attitude that science is superior to what is termed "superstition" and that the customs of our people are outmoded. Students from the very beginning should understand that their individual development is based not only on the physical factors, which science caters to, but also on intellectual and spiritual factors which affect their lives significantly. An understanding of the spiritual aspects of their life should include their history, art, culture and customs. All the same, a mission-oriented, creative and innovative science curriculum has to be introduced at the primary education level. The emphasis must be the democratization of education for all citizens, including the handicapped.

3. Developing countries should seek to keep all their technology options open. In formulating their science and technology policy they need friends.

They have to choose their friends wisely. Any country that tells you that nuclear energy is bad but refuses to share with you the secrets of commercial solar energy or of other alternative technologies should not be taken seriously. Any country that sits on thousands of megaton bombs and harasses you about the dangers of nuclear proliferation should not be considered a friend.

4. We welcome the efforts of the churches to work out the implications of justice and fair play in the development and distribution of technological capability. Where they help technologically powerful countries to look at their technological capability in terms of their world responsibilities, they become the friends of developing countries. And churches in our developing countries should reciprocate by helping our governments and peoples to achieve the requisite use of such power and to resist the inevitable temptation to misuse it. Thus there can be the development of an ecumenical solidarity—one which is not based on illusions or false expectations, but on the real struggle of the developing countries for justice and participation in the distribution of power.

Technology and Oppression

ROGERIO DE CERQUEIRA LEITE

> "Commerce, as well as industry, is merely a branch of agriculture. It is agriculture that furnishes raw material for industry and for commerce and therefore provides for both... The nation that does not produce raw materials and limits production to industrial goods will be in a precarious and uncertain situation... Besides, this nation will always be dependent upon and submissive to those nations that furnish raw materials... The commerce among nations will be characterized by a situation in which those that furnish useful goods will take advantage over those that sell goods that are dispensable..."

This extremely lucid statement was made more than two centuries ago by François Quesnay, the first great French economist. It certainly appears to be quite reasonable, especially if we add minerals to the agricultural "raw materials". However, history has since demonstrated that it is rather the opposite of Quesnay's predictions that occurs. Countries that furnish raw materials have been dominated and exploited systematically by the industrialized nations.

Two instruments have been essential for the industrialized nations' success in subjugating the raw materials-producing communities. The first is a plurality of forms of colonialism, varying from classical colonialism to the subtle kind exercised through transnational corporations. The second instrument manipulated efficiently by the industrialized countries is the competition among the nations that sell raw materials in the international market.

Obviously, the effectiveness of these two instruments depends entirely on the incompetence of the leadership of the nations furnishing raw materials, a leadership incapable of reaching an understanding in the common interest. The only exception of some importance is OPEC, which after ten years of discussions was able to establish a policy of common interest. However, even this was possible only because the powerful transnational corporations in the oil area were the main beneficiaries and because a situation of dispute with Israel could be used politically for the prevention of an eventual unilateral action by one of the western industrial powers.

This was the first case of economic importance in which the price of a natural product was not determined by the production costs. In these last two centuries the advanced countries were able to ensure that the prices of raw materials in the international market were determined primarily by production costs. The intrinsic value was never taken into consideration. Today the industrialized powers would be happy to be able to buy oil from the Arab countries at no more than ten times the production costs.

Would it not be natural, therefore, to agree on the objective value, for instance, of iron ore for society before getting into a desperate price war that benefits only the advanced nations? The presence of transnational corporations in the exploration of natural reserves in developing countries further complicates the moral aspects of the problem.

The acute rationality of Quesnay's arguments generated such efficient instruments of control of international prices of raw materials. In reality, today one may "measure" the development of a nation by the ratio between its exports of industrialized goods and raw materials. Even the USA, which used to be considered rich in mineral reserves, presently imports 50% of the minerals it needs, including petroleum.

With the gradual evolution of the less developed countries, it is possible that they will begin to understand what Quesnay said more than two centuries ago: that there is an intrinsic value in raw materials and that only the communities that can produce them will be really independent. Perhaps that is why technology is becoming an efficient weapon in maintaining the *status quo*.

The initial phase of development attained by many of the less poor countries left them dependent on technology. And here, possibly not intentionally, the transnational corporations were very efficient. They maintained production of technology in the mother country, and fed to the foreign subsidiairies a minimum of technological prescriptions necessary to overcome indigenous competition. National industries, in order to compete with transnational corporations, have to acquire technology from the industrialized nations. There are, therefore, two different flows of technology from the developed world to the less developed countries. Both flows control the dependence of a given country. This mechanism already works spontaneously, but it may become a tool for the oppression of countries which rebel against the present economic order.

The apparent conspiratorial vision presented here is borne out by certain recent events. We shall consider here the Trilateral Commission, an organism founded with the intention of maintaining the present economic order in face of the growing "menace of the Third World". From the fourteenth document of the Trilateral Commission we obtain the following basic strategies:

1. *On the economic level:* Reinforcement of international capitalism through transnational corporations, and cooperation of all countries belonging to the capitalist system in seeking global solutions. The main obstacles to these prospects are considered to be the desire for autonomous national economies and the establishment of independent domestic policies.

2. *On the financial level:* Reinforcement of financial and monetary organisms and transnational private banks.

3. *On the technological level:* Transfer to peripheral countries of industrialization of the classical type, such as metallurgy, maintaining, however, the more advanced, more lucrative ones in the central countries. Of course, services will also remain in the developed world.

4. *On the political level:* Selection of countries which will be strongly tied to the central countries as satellites with certain privileges, including that of having their own sub-satellites. Rebel countries would be left on their own.

The Trilateral Commission is composed of some two hundred important personalities from Japan, western Europe and the United States, including President Carter and Messieurs Mondale, Brzezinski, Vance, Brown and Blumenthal, to mention a few, from the American side. In spite of that, it is not the Commission itself that unfavourably impresses conscientious leadership of the less developed countries. It is merely a symptom of the growing defensive attitude of the advanced countries towards the increasing demands of the underdeveloped world. This attitude may take several different forms. Consider nuclear energy, for instance. Advanced countries are more than willing to sell reactors to underdeveloped countries that do not need them. The insistence and strong support from governments of developed countries prompt us to guess that there is more than just a profit in the export of nuclear reactors to less developed countries. Indeed, a country that uses nuclear energy but is not self-sufficient in nuclear technology will be highly dependent. In most cases it will have to acquire enriched uranium and rely on the advanced nations for reprocessing. But most importantly, the technological dependence will tend to grow, since it is impossible for an underdeveloped country to perform any research in the nuclear field. This is the kind of situation that serves well the trilateral syndrome, since it increases dependency, while pretending that it serves the best interests of the less developed countries.

Community Involvement in Scandinavian Decisions

KERSTIN ANÉR

What does the citizen want and expect from science and its handmaiden, technology? And how does the citizen of today set about getting what she wants?

Science as magic

Science has always been magic. That is to say, it has promised to provide exactly the same things that magic did and does promise: the means to power, riches and love.

Military power. Economic resources. And the ability to keep your body young, healthy and attractive. That is what Mephistopheles agreed to provide Dr Faustus, and it is still what Big Science talks about when it talks to Big Government and Big Business.

People, however, used to be scared of their magicians. They did not trust their intentions, even when they trusted their powers. Today, after about a century and a half of unprecedented blind trust in good white magicians, we have discovered the cloven hoof again. There is nothing astonishing in this; the wonder is rather that the hoof stayed hidden so long.

The magicians don't like it, and nothing could be more natural. We have already heard a great deal at this conference of the same debate that goes on all over the campuses and in the mass media of the world:

- concerned citizens, on the one hand, blame the scientists for perhaps more than their share of the evils of this world;
- and the scientists cling to their innocence and cry out: we never meant any harm, we just put E, m, c and 2 together, and the bang is your business, not ours! *Our* business is pure mathematics, pure physics, pure chemistry—and may it never be of use to anyone! Science is the fairest flower of human intelligence and you are a barbarian if you meddle with us!

These arguments, which you can hear on any fine day on any campus, are most easily disposed of if you listen to the magi on the *same* campus any *other* day, when they are persuading private and public foundations to spend money on very, very promising lines of business indeed.

Science and politics

I will leave that controversy, for the moment at least. I assume we all know that in all fields of politics, or at least many of them, citizens are getting tired of being represented and are demanding to be heard instead.

All fields of politics—that is, of course, not quite true. An OECD report of 1978 asked a very pertinent question here: Why do *some* issues cause controversy and others not? Why are some groups of citizens so extremely active and others not at all?

In my own country we have a very handy explanation for this phenomenon: when one issue suddenly dips beneath the horizon of the media and another pops up, for its life of a fortnight or so, we all murmur: "Sweden is a very small country—there is only room for one opinion at a time!"

But when I see an OECD report wondering about the same thing, I feel I have to dig a little deeper. I should like to ask the advice of Prof. Amitai Etzioni, for instance, who wrote so well of the civil rights movements of the sixties and explained how an active society could come about: not among the most oppressed groups, but in the slightly less oppressed, with a certain margin of money and leisure, and enough motives for changing its mind. I should like to see a study of the same kind now. Is there really just the middle class love of a tidy lawn behind the environment movement, or the nostalgia of the mulch behind the organic food movement? Or should we perhaps go even further, to the sociologists of religion, for the explanation of the nuclear scare, the privacy scare—as we have seen them in various countries? Is it really only technology that so many of us are frightened of, or do deeper archetypes of horror rear their heads behind the atomic piles and the computers?

I do not say this to exculpate those who are really responsible for letting certain horrors loose on the world—and by that I mean the decision-makers, not chiefly their advisers. I only want to point out that just as the *myth* of science, the great white magician holding all the answers and all the powers in his hand, is a great part of the prestige and money-making capacity of science—just so the anti-science myth, while being equally unreasonable, is also very powerful. You cannot have it both ways. Science without its myth is just one set of tools which may be replaced and is not to be worshipped. Anti-science without its myths means just that—replacement.

But the myths are there, and will not go away. They are the strongest motive powers history knows, and indeed theologians should be experts on them. I think they could do science a great deal of good if they helped to disentangle the concrete benefits and disbenefits of science and technology from the celestial or devilish aura that surrounds them.

Then perhaps we could treat myths in the way apposite to them; and concrete political and technical questions in *their* way.

Let me now state briefly some of the most striking concrete demands that citizens make on science—and I am now describing citizens of that world which produces science, since that is the one I live in and know. We ask, for instance:

— that science, while defending us against old dangers, should not hit us with new ones—such as mutant genes, carcinogens in industry, nuclear radiation and catastrophes;
— that science should chiefly research those diseases we rich happen to be most afraid of, such as cancer, and not those which torture the poorer millions amongst us, such as tropical parasites and kwashiorkor;

— that science should give us unlimited powers over our reproductive lives—the pill, amniocentesis, genetic screening, test tube babies;
— that at the same time, all these new beautiful powers should be used *for* us, not against us; and since "us" means very different and conflicting groups, this demand is not and cannot ever be anything but political.

Man's power over nature has never meant anything but the power of some men over some others. So it is no use saying these questions are best left to the wise, the powerful, or the representative. They already have more power than is good for them.

The social base of science

But *can* science, or even technology, be made to obey the wishes of the people? Does not this run counter to its own nature? Is not science the service of Truth, naked and with a capital T? What has she to do with votes?

Well, the point is that *she is already voted on*. The kind of science and technology we have in this particular civilization is deeply marked by its social origin. It has three outstanding characteristics:
— it is chiefly and characteristically used for war;
— it is male-dominated;
— it is large-scale, brutal and death-centred.

The connection between science and war has been proved so many times and with so many figures that I need not bore you with it once again. As the Director of the Institute for Peace Research in Stockholm said last year: "The only significant limits on military R&D in the world are the amount of innovative capabilities of the Soviet and American peoples."

As for the male occupation of science, I am not complaining that 81% of the people at this conference are male, but that the values on which science and technology build are so male-dominated. Let me quote just two of my sisters on this.

First, Dr Diana Manning, Research Fellow at the Middlesex Polytechnic, England, says: "As an academic scientist myself, I am amused by the persistent attitude that women cannot be good scientists because they are too interested in people, they aren't able to cut themselves off from other aspects of life and devote themselves to a specialty, and so on. Yet those are just the qualities that are needed if science is to be used in the interests of society."

Next, Mlle Jacqueline Feldman, CNRS, of Paris, said at a recent Nobel symposium in Stockholm that the values of the male sex dominate in science and are considered better than the female ones. "Let us take the example of psychology. The current ideology says that women are better fitted than men to take care of children. But these jobs, however vital they may be to society, are of low status. So it is the scientist who will be asked to speak in an intellectual manner about the education of children. He will use in his language all the complicated words and complicated figures necessary to fit into an official scientific psychology. And then he will be the one who gets social recognition. Science thus takes away some of the prestige from the traditional role that women still had."

One particularly vicious example of how male values in science are translated into disregard for human beings of the wrong sex is the plight of women in agriculture in the Third World. Whatever agricultural science and technology trickles down to these farmers, it always stays with the *men*. In Africa, at least, men do very little of the actual work in agriculture. But they get all the machines, the large expensive tools, the education if there is any. Science and technology in the First and Second Worlds are not different in this respect! Think big, think male, and do not consider small beautiful! It is very hard on the women, who never get the simple cheap tools that would really help them.

An example from Sweden

I will finally give one positive example of how one can try to open the doors to real participation by the people concerned, in a new technological project. This concerns telecommunication and its application to regional development, and the experiment is being conducted in the far north of Sweden.

The idea is not new in itself. It is what the French call "télématique", and means communicating via computers, terminals, cable TV, telephones, in hitherto unseen and imaginative ways. This game is being played in the rich industrial countries in many places. But there, the big producers call the tune. They are looking for new markets and trying to prod societies into using their products in new ways.

The Swedish experiment is, as far as I know, the only one which starts from *the needs of the consumer* and asks: What would people like to have, what qualities of life do they lack which might conceivably be provided by new kinds of telecommunications? And then it tries to find out what this new technology would mean in terms of work, transportation, home life, education, leisure activities, social work, etc.

One of the things they think they have found is this: If you create a system of terminals, computers and computer lines, constructed so as to facilitate direct contacts between business and local administration inside one province, without having to go through a central bureau in the capital, this has certain effects. That province accumulates more political power, more information about its own problems, more opportunities of work within its own boundaries, and a stronger sense of community.

And if you give employees in the daughter companies of one large corporation the chance to talk and get together via computers, they will achieve more power in relation to their own managers, who always had this power of conferring together.

This particular experiment was initiated from above, from government agencies, but always in close cooperation with local and private organizations. That is the way we do it in Sweden, and I am not saying it is the only right way. (In our country, you can get a great deal done by fairly unorganized but continuous pressure on the elected representatives, even by quite small idealistic organizations. The system works rather well, chiefly because it is not new but has roots in the history and structure of the country.)

We have different ways, in different countries, of incorporating new ideas and embryonic new power centres in our old creaking machineries of government. Swedes believe in consensus, Frenchmen in orders from above tempered by elegant rhetoric, and Americans in adversary procedures. It is interesting to compare them, but very difficult to import any proceeding into a political system where it does not fit. What we should learn from each other is that mushrooms do break through asphalt, and that existing party systems are not conceived for eternity. New lines of difference, new ideological disputes start up and criss-cross party boundaries, and may very well one day make nonsense of them.

This does not mean that all systems of representation will become obsolete, only that we must start representing new ideas. I am not very scared of that. But I do think that the *prestige of science*, as the one and only truth, will be a more difficult threshold for the ordinary citizen to cross than the threshold of *government prestige*. The latter is getting quite shopworn everywhere.

But scientists can still say, as the former Chancellor of Uppsala University, Prof. Torgny Segerstedt, did at the Nobel symposium last August: "Before making up its mind, any government and any body of laymen must always consult scientists first. So one way or another, it is always the scientists who do decide."

However, if citizens take courage to go against such a dictum, they may find themselves heartened by the words of the Cambridge Review Board in its now famous pronouncement: "We wish to express our sincere belief that a predominantly lay citizen's group can face a technical, scientific matter of general and deep public concern, educate itself appropriately to the task, and reach a fair decision."

If that is the goal—and I think it should be—then let us debate how we should get there.

Technology Assessment in the Canadian Northwest

THOMAS R. BERGER

Science and technology confront us with choices whose consequences are not easy to foresee. We know that science and technology can change our world.

We used to think that the changes they wrought would be altogether benign. But in recent years another view has begun to take hold: that the advance of science and technology—especially large-scale technology—may entail social, economic and environmental costs which must be reckoned with.

The Mackenzie Valley Pipeline Inquiry

When the oil and gas industry proposed that a gas pipeline be built from the Arctic to the mid-continent, the government of Canada appointed a commission of inquiry to examine the social, economic and environmental impact of the proposal. The Mackenzie Valley Pipeline Inquiry (1974-1977) may well be unique in Canadian experience, because for the first time we sought to determine the impact of a large-scale frontier project before and not after the fact.

Arctic Gas, a consortium of Canadian and American companies, wanted to build a pipeline to transport gas from Prudhoe Bay across the north slope of Alaska and the northern Yukon to the Mackenzie Delta, where it would connect with a pipeline transporting gas from the Delta and then run south along the Mackenzie Valley to the Alberta border and thence to metropolitan centres in Canada and the United States (see map).

The Arctic Gas pipeline would be the greatest project, in terms of capital expenditure, ever undertaken by private enterprise anywhere. It would be a major construction undertaking across a land that is cold and dark in winter, a land largely inaccessible by rail or road, where it would be necessary to construct wharves, warehouses, storage sites, airstrips—a huge infrastructure—just to build the pipeline. There would have to be a network of hundreds of miles of roads built over the snow and ice. The capacity of the fleet of tugs and barges on the Mackenzie River would have to be doubled. There would be 6,000 construction workers required north of 60 to build the pipeline, and 1,200 more to build the gas plants and gathering systems in the Mackenzie Delta. There would be 130 gravel mining operations. There would be 600 river and stream crossings. There would be pipes, trucks, heavy equipment, tractors and aircraft.

We were told that a gas pipeline would result in enhanced oil and gas exploration activity all along the route of the pipeline. The government of Canada decided that the gas pipeline should not be considered in isolation. So it instituted an Inquiry to consider the impact if the gas pipeline were built and were followed by an oil pipeline.

What I have said will give you some notion of the magnitude of the Inquiry. I was to examine the social, economic and environmental impact of the proposed pipeline and energy corridor.

Public participation in the Inquiry

How could the public participate effectively in the Inquiry? The Mackenzie Valley and the western Arctic constitute a region as large as western Europe. Though it is sparsely settled (only 30,000 people live there), it is

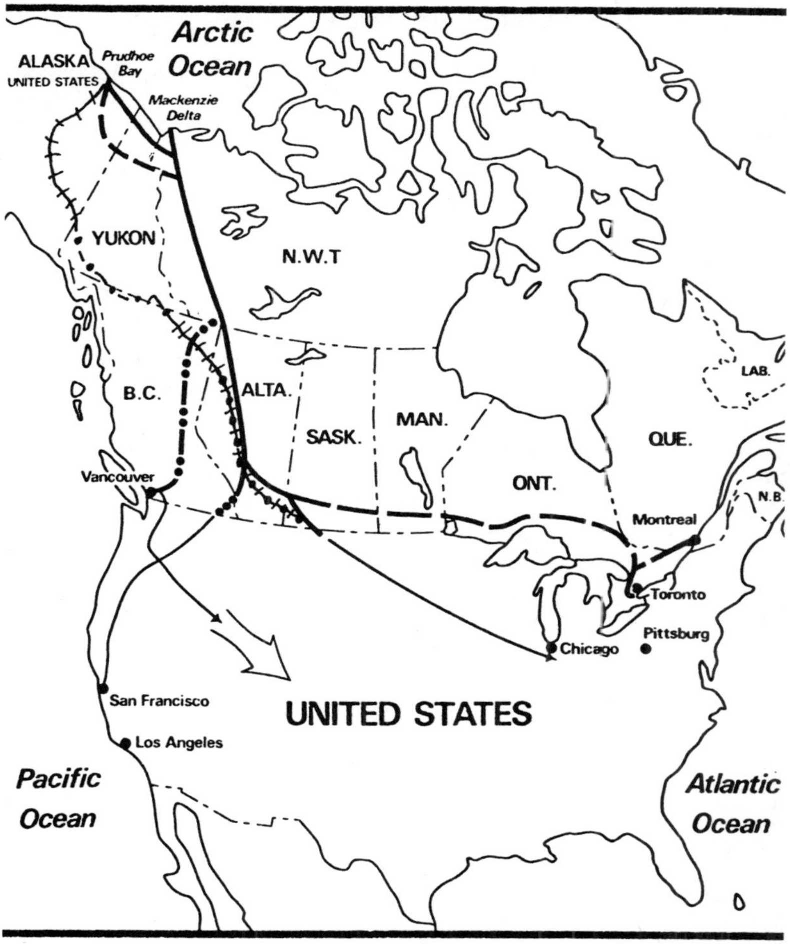

Arctic Gas System, Alcan Pipeline Project and Connecting Pipelines

————	Canadian Arctic Gas Pipeline Ltd. (via the Mackenzie Valley)	—··—··—	Westcoast Transmission Co. Ltd.
– – – – –	Alternative Route Across The Northern Yukon	—— ——	TransCanada Pipelines Ltd.
············	Alberta Natural Gas Co. Ltd.	————	Connecting Pipelines in the United States
++++++++	Alcan Pipeline Co./ Northwest Pipeline Corp.	+•+•+•+	Alberta Gas Trunk Line Co. Ltd.
—•—•—•	Foothills Pipelines (Yukon) Ltd. (via the Alaska Highway)		

inhabited by four races—white, Indian, Inuit and metis—speaking six languages—English, Slavey, Loucheux, Dogrib, Chipewyan and Eskimo. They were all entitled to be heard.

Governments have lots of money. So does the oil and gas industry. So do the pipeline companies. But how were the native people to participate? How was the environmental interest to be represented? If the Inquiry was to be fair and complete, all these interests had to be represented.

On my recommendation, funding was provided by the government of Canada to the native organizations, the environmental groups, northern municipalities and northern business, to enable them to participate in the hearings and to support, challenge, or seek to modify the project. These groups received $1,773,918. The cost of the Inquiry altogether came to $5,3 million.

I took the view that if these groups were to make their own decisions and present the evidence that they thought vital, they had to be provided with funds and there could be no strings attached. However, they had to account to the Inquiry for the money spent. All this they did.

Let me illustrate the rationale for this by referring to the environment. Arctic Gas carried out extensive environmental studies. But they had an interest: they wanted to build the pipeline. This was a legitimate interest, but not one that could necessarily be reconciled with the environmental interest. Funds were provided to an umbrella organization—the Northern Assessment Group—established by the environmental groups to enable them to carry out their own research and hire staff, and to ensure that they could participate in the Inquiry as advocates on behalf of the environment.

Other interests were also represented at the hearings. The result was that witnesses were examined and then cross-examined to make sure that the impact of an influx of construction workers on communities, the impact of pipeline construction and corridor development on the hunting, trapping and fishing economy of the native people, and the impact on northern municipalities and northern business, were all taken into account.

The usefulness of the funding was amply demonstrated. The funds supplied to the interventors, although substantial, should be considered in the light of the estimated cost of the project itself.

Formal hearings and community hearings

The Inquiry held two types of hearings: formal and community. The hearings went on for 21 months.

The formal hearings were held at Yellowknife, the capital of the Northwest Territories. In many ways the proceedings resembled a trial in a courtroom. We heard the evidence of the experts: scientists, engineers, biologists, anthropologists, economists—people from a multitude of disciplines, who have studied the northern environment, northern conditions and northern peoples. Three hundred expert witnesses testified. All the parties were represented: the pipeline companies, the oil and gas industry, the native organizations, the environmental groups, the Northwest Territories Association of Municipalities and the Northwest Territories Chamber of Commerce.

In recent years the government of Canada has carried out a multitude of studies on the north. These studies cost $15 million. The oil and gas industry carried out studies on the pipeline that we were told cost something like $50 million. Our universities have been carrying on constant research on northern problems and northern conditions. These reports were examined in public, so that any conflicts could be disclosed and parties at the Inquiry could challenge them.

At the same time, community hearings were held in each city and town, settlement and village in the Mackenzie Valley and the western Arctic. There are 35 communities in the region, the majority of them native. The people living in these communities were given the opportunity to tell the Inquiry—in their own languages and in their own way—what their lives and their experience led them to believe the impact of a pipeline and an energy corridor would be.

In this way we tried to have the best of the experience of both worlds: at the community hearings, the world of every day; at the formal hearings, the world of the professionals, the specialists and the academics.

In order to give people—not just the spokesmen for native organizations and for the white community, but all people—an opportunity to speak their minds, the Inquiry remained in each community as long as was necessary for every person who wanted to speak to do so. In many villages a large proportion of the adult population addressed the Inquiry. Some of the most perceptive presentations were given by young people.

The contribution of ordinary people

I heard from almost one thousand witnesses at the community hearings—in English (and occasionally in French), in Loucheux, Slavey, Dogrib, Chipewyan and in the Eskimo language of the western Arctic. They used direct speech. They seldom had written briefs. Their thoughts were not filtered through a screen of jargon. They were talking about their innermost concerns and fears.

You may ask what ordinary people can tell planners and policy-makers. The conventional wisdom is that a decision like this should be made by people in government and industry: they have the knowledge, the facts, the experience. The hearings showed that the conventional wisdom is wrong. We discovered that the judgment of planners and policy-makers at their desks in Ottawa and Yellowknife might not always be right.

The contributions of ordinary people were important in the assessment of even the most technical subjects; for example, the biological vulnerability of the Beaufort Sea, sea-bed ice scour and oil spills, life and importance of the caribou herd. These are complex, technical subjects but our understanding of them was nonetheless enriched by testimony from people who live in the region.

Their witness was of even greater importance in connection with the assessment of social and economic impact. The issue of native claims was linked to all of these subjects. At the formal hearings, land use and occupancy evidence was presented in support of native claims through prepared testimony and map exhibits. There the evidence was scrutinized and witnesses for the native organization were cross-examined by counsel for the other participants. By contrast, at the community hearings people spoke spontaneously and at length of both their traditional and their present-day use of the land and its resources. Their testimony was often painstakingly detailed and richly illustrated with anecdotes.

The most important contribution of the community hearings was, I think, the insight it gave us into the true nature of native claims. No academic treatise, no formal presentation could offer as compelling and vivid a picture of the goals and aspirations of native people as their own testimony did. In no other way could we have discovered their depth of feeling regarding past wrongs and future hopes, and their determination to assert their collective identity.

When you have such a vast area, when you have people of four races, speaking six languages, how do you enable them to participate? How do you keep them informed? We wished to create an Inquiry without walls. We sought, therefore, to use technology to make the Inquiry truly public, to bring the Inquiry to the people. This meant that it was the Inquiry, and the representatives of the media accompanying it—not the people of the north—that were obliged to travel.

The Northern Service of the Canadian Broadcasting Corporation broadcast across the north highlights of each day's testimony, both in English and in the native languages from wherever the Inquiry was sitting. The broadcasts meant that when we went into the communities, the people living there understood something of what had been said by the experts at the formal hearings, and by people in the communities that we had already visited. The broadcasters were, of course, entirely independent of the Inquiry.

The media served as the eyes and ears of all northerners, indeed of all Canadians, especially when the Inquiry visited places that few northerners had ever seen and few of their countrymen had even heard of. The Inquiry had a high profile in the media. As a result there was public interest and concern in the work of the Inquiry throughout Canada (see, for example, the work of the Interchurch Project on Northern Development, known as Project North). When its report, *Northern Frontier, Northern Homeland*, was made public on 9 May 1977, it became a best-seller.

Fundamental values

The pipeline issue confronted us in Canada with the necessity of weighing fundamental values—industrial, social and environmental—in a way that we had not done before.

The northern native people, along with many witnesses at the Inquiry, insisted that the land they have long depended upon would be injured by the pipeline and energy corridor. Environmentalists pointed out that the north, the last great wilderness area of Canada, is slow to recover from environmental degradation; its protection is, therefore, of vital importance to all Canadians. It is not easy to measure that concern against the more precisely calculated interests of industry. You cannot measure environmental values in dollars and cents. But still we had to face the questions: Should we open up the north as we opened up the west? Should the values of the past prevail today and tomorrow?

The north is immense. But within this vast area are tracts of land and water that are vital to the survival of whole populations of certain species of mammals, birds and fish. The northern Yukon is an arctic and subarctic wilderness of incredible beauty, a rich and varied eco-system: nine million acres of land in its natural state, inhabited by thriving populations of plants and animals. This wilderness has come down through the ages, and it is a heritage that future generations, living in an industrial world even more complex than ours, will surely cherish. I urged that the northern Yukon, north of the Porcupine River, be designated a national wilderness park.

If you were to build a pipeline from Alaska along the Arctic coast of the Yukon, you would be opening up the calving grounds of the Porcupine Caribou herd, one of the last great herds of caribou, 110,000 animals, in North America. In late August, as many as 500,000 snow geese gather on the Arctic Coastal Plain to feed on the tundra grasses, sedges and berries, before embarking on the flight to their wintering grounds in California, the Gulf Coast, or Central and South America. The peregrine falcon, golden eagle and other birds of prey nest in the northern Yukon.

The wilderness does not stop, of course, at the boundary between Alaska and the Yukon. The Arctic National Wildlife Range in north-eastern Alaska, contiguous to the northern Yukon, is a part of the same wilderness. So the future of the caribou, of the birds—of the whole of this unique wilderness region—was a matter of concern to both Canada and the United States.

Let me refer to another international resource, the white whales of the Beaufort Sea. For these whales—some 5,000 animals—the warm waters around the Mackenzie Delta are critical habitat, for here they have their young and here they stay until the calves acquire enough blubber to survive in the cold oceanic water. Nowhere else, so far as we know, can they go for this essential part of their life cycle.

I recommended that a whole sanctuary be established in Mackenzie Bay. Is this a practical proposition? Will it impose an unacceptable check on oil and gas exploration and development? We are fortunate in that the areas of intense petroleum exploration, to date, lie east of the proposed whale sanctuary, both offshore and onshore. A whale sanctuary can be set aside without impairing industry's ability to tap the principal sources of petroleum beneath the Beaufort Sea.

We in Canada have looked upon the north as our last frontier. It is natural for us to think of developing the area, of subduing the land, populating it with people from the metropolitan centres, and extracting its resources to fuel our industry and heat our homes. Our whole inclination is to expand our industrial machine to the limit of our frontiers. We have never had to consider restraint, to determine the most intelligent use of our resources. The question that we and many other countries face is, are we willing and able to make up our own minds, or are we simply driven, by technology and egregious consumption, to deplete our resources wherever and whenever we find them?

I do not want to be misunderstood. I did not propose that we shut up the north, as a kind of living folk museum and zoological gardens. I proceeded on the assumption that, in due course, we will require the gas and oil of the western Arctic, and that they will have to be transported along the Mackenzie Valley to markets in the metropolitan centres of North America. I also proceeded on the assumption that we intend to protect and preserve Canada's northern environment, and that, above all else, we intend to honour the legitimate claims and aspirations of the native people. All these assumptions were embedded in the government of Canada's expressed northern policy for the 1970's.

I sought to reconcile these goals: industrial, social and environmental. I proposed an international wilderness park in the northern Yukon and northeastern Alaska and urged that no pipeline cross it; but at the same time, I indicated that the Alaska Highway route, as a corridor for the transportation of Alaskan gas to the Lower 48, was preferable from an environmental point of view. This route lies hundreds of miles to the south and to the west of the critical habitat for caribou, whales and wildlife (see map).

I proposed a whale sanctuary in Mackenzie Bay, but I limited its boundaries to waters where no discoveries of gas or oil have yet been made. I recommended the establishment of bird sanctuaries in the Mackenzie Delta and Valley. Oil and gas exploration and development would not be forbidden, but subject to the jurisdiction of the Canadian Wildlife Service.

I advised the government of Canada that a pipeline corridor is feasible, from an environmental point of view, to transport gas and oil from the Mackenzie Delta along the Mackenzie Valley to the Alberta border. At the same time, however, I recommended that we should postpone the construction of such a pipeline for ten years, in order to strengthen native society, the native economy—indeed, the whole renewable resource sector—and to enable native claims to be settled.

The claims of native people

Virtually all the native people who spoke to the Inquiry said that their claims had to be settled before any pipeline could be built. It should not be thought that native people had an irrational fear of pipelines. They realized, however, that the pipeline and energy corridor would mean an influx of tens of thousands of white people seeking jobs and opportunities. They believed that they would be overwhelmed, that their native villages would become white towns, and they would be relegated to the fringes of northern life.

They realized that the pipeline and all that it would bring in its wake would lead to an irreversible shift in social, economic and political power in the north. They believed that the building of the pipeline would bring complete dependence on the industrial system and a future which would have no place for the culture they cherish.

Their tradition of decision-making by consensus, their respect for the wisdom of their elders, their concept of the extended family, their belief in a special relationship with the land, their regard for the environment, their willingness to share—all of these values persist within their own culture, even though they have been under unremitting pressure to abandon them. Their claims are the means by which they seek to preserve their culture, their values and their identity.

The emergence of native claims should not surprise us. After years of poor achievement in our schools, after years of living on the fringes of an economy that has no place for them as workers or consumers, and without the political power to change these things, the native people now want to substitute self-determination for enforced dependency.

Settlement of their claims should offer the native people a whole range of opportunities: the strengthening of the hunting, fishing and trapping economy where that is appropriate; the development of the local logging and lumbering industry, the fishing industry, and recreation and conservation. I urged that priority be given to local renewable resource activities—not because such activities are universally desirable, but because they are on a scale appropriate to many native communities, amenable to local management and control, and related to traditional values. But that need not exclude access to the larger economy, where large-scale technology predominates.

It will take time to limn these claims, especially their implications for native people entering urban life. Nevertheless, some elements are clear enough; for instance, native people say they want schools where children can learn native languages, native history, native lore and native rights. At the same time, they want their children to learn to speak English or French, and to study mathematics, science, and all the subjects that they need in order to function in the dominant society.

It is not only we in Canada who must face the challenge of native peoples with their own languages and cultures. There are all the countries of the western hemisphere, with their indigenous minorities—peoples whose fierce wish to retain their own common identity is intensifying as industry, technology and communications forge a larger and larger mass culture, extruding diversity.

The judgments we had to make were not merely scientific and technical. It is impossible—indeed, undesirable—to try to lift scientific and technological decisions out of their social and environmental, their moral and ethical context. In the end, no matter how many experts and computer printouts there may be, there is the ineluctable necessity of bringing human judgment to bear on the main issues.

Consequences of the Inquiry

I think a fuller understanding of the northern environment emerged during the course of the Inquiry. The proposals made for the creation of an international wilderness park in the Yukon and Alaska, for a whale sanctuary in Mackenzie Bay, and for bird sanctuaries in the Mackenzie Delta and the Mackenzie Valley, have attracted widespread support in Canada and the United States. The foundations have been laid for the development of a firm policy designed to protect the northern environment. In fact, the goal lies within our reach.

The government of Canada rejected the Arctic Gas pipeline proposal. Now Canada and the United States have agreed on the construction of a gas pipeline along the Alaska Highway route.

The Canadian government announced in July 1978 that it was withdrawing the northern Yukon, an area of 9,6 million acres, from new industrial development with a view to establishing Canada's first wilderness park, subject to traditional native hunting, fishing and trapping activities. The Carter administration has proposed that the Arctic National Wildlife Range on the United States' side of the international boundary should be designated wilderness. Canada has established a scientific committee on whales, which is examining the proposal for a whale sanctuary in Mackenzie Bay.

The decision not to build the Arctic Gas pipeline gives time to achieve a fair settlement of native claims in the Mackenzie Valley and the western Arctic—an opportunity to meet what I believe is Canada's greatest challenge in the north. Settlement will not be easy to achieve. There is a quite natural tendency for governments to look upon native claims as something which can be settled swiftly around the table, as a problem to be solved, as a clearing of the decks to enable large-scale industrial development to proceed. But for native people, their claims constitute the means to the preservation of their culture, their languages, their economic mode—the means by which they can continue to assert their distinct identity and still have access to the social, economic and political institutions of the dominant society. The settlement of native claims ought to provide, most important of all, for the collective fabric of native life to be affirmed and strengthened. The sense of identity of individual native people—indeed, their very wellbeing—depends on it.

This is an unusual, perhaps unprecedented outcome—a recognition that industrial goals do not at all times and in all places take precedence over environmental values and native rights.

Ethical dimensions of the future

The pipeline debate is, in one sense, over. But it has precipitated another debate, one about some fundamental issues which were thrown into relief by the pipeline proposals: the need of the metropolis for energy, the implications of the advance of the industrial system to the frontier, the protection of the northern environment and, above all, the rights of the native people. Canadians perceived in these questions something that was basic to them all: a broad moral and ethical dimension.

Since the Industrial Revolution we have thought of industrialization as the means to prosperity and wellbeing. And so it has been, to many people, and to many parts of the world. But the rise of the industrial system has been accompanied by a belief in an ever-expanding cycle of growth and consumption. We should now be asking whether it is a goal that will suffice. Should we and our children continue to aspire to the idea of unlimited growth? And, equally important, should the Third World aspire to this goal?

Our belief in an ever-expanding cycle of growth and consumption conditions our capacity and our willingness to reconsider the true goals of the industrial system. There is a feeling that we cannot pause to consider where we are headed, for fear of what we shall find out about ourselves. Yet events are pressing hard upon us.

In the last 15 years, world use of energy has doubled. North America now uses about five times as much energy as the whole of Asia, and per capita consumption is about 24 times higher. The United States each year wastes more fossil fuel than is used by two-thirds of the world's population. According to the Energy Research Project at Harvard Business School, the US uses a third of all the oil used in the world every day.

Certainly, if anything is plain, it must be plain that we on this continent shall have to get along with a smaller proportion of the world's energy and resources. This entails a reconsideration of conventional wisdom. I am not urging that we dismantle the industrial system. But I do say that we must pause and consider to what extent our national objectives are determined by the need for the care and feeding of the industrial machine.

To a large extent we have conditioned ourselves to believe that the onward march of industry and technology cannot and must not be impeded or diverted. Our notions of progress have acquired a technological and industrial definition. An ever-expanding cycle of growth and consumption is the secular religion of our time.

Our ideas are still the ideas of the mid-nineteenth century: the era of the triumph of liberal capitalism and the challenge of Marxism, the era of Adam Smith and the Communist Manifesto. Both of these creeds are the offspring of the Industrial Revolution.

Neither creed has yet come to grips with the necessity for rethinking the goals of the industrial system. Yet the consequences of large-scale technology out of control can be seen around the world: tankers cracking up on beaches; the ongoing destruction of the tropical rain forests of the Amazon; infant formula being sold indiscriminately in the Third World; the mining of soils in many countries.

Can the nations of the Third World achieve the levels of growth and consumption that have been achieved by the industrialized countries? If they cannot—if the consumption of natural resources at a rate necessary to enable them to do so (not to mention the concomitant increase in pollution) is not possible in a practical sense—then what? We have been unwilling to face up to the moral and ethical questions that this would raise for all of us.

A philosophy for the post-industrial era

We need a philosophy to sustain us in the post-industrial era, an era for which we have no name since we cannot yet discern its lineaments. I think we can venture some thoughts about it. There is no reason to suppose that it will necessarily mean a return to scarcity, a foregoing of abundance. Nor does it mean that the Third World must be relegated to a condition of permanent poverty. It would be a mistake to believe that the choice is growth or no growth. It is rather the rational application of industry and technology that we must pursue.

We cannot expect that within a week, a month, or a year, a new philosophy can be worked out in all its details. We must be prepared to begin on a small scale. Small can be beautiful, and that applies to theorizing as much as to anything else.

The intellectual challenge of comprehending the shape of the post-industrial era, of comprehending the lineaments of the moral, social and economic goals that will inform that era, will soon be facing us all.

So we stand on the leading edge of history, driven by forces that require greater and greater use of energy, and greater and greater consumption of dwindling resources. Can we change direction? Upon the answer to that question depends the future of each nation, of our environment, and of the world we know.

People's Participation in the Control of Environmental Pollution in Japan

JUN UI

Environmental pollution in Japan increased gradually during the high economic growth of the 1950's and 1960's and appeared explosively in the 1970's. The increase in environmental destruction was the inevitable result of a consistent government policy, oriented towards the protection of industry at the expense of the environment. Freedom to pollute the environment, the use of low wage labour, and highly protective trade barriers have been the three basic conditions upon which the high economic growth of Japanese industries has been based.

It is absolutely wrong to believe that pollution is only a minor negative factor to be expected from economic growth and, therefore, to be simply controlled by further applications of technology. The pollution and destruction of the environment in Japan is the structural base for high economic growth, and it cannot be controlled unless the whole structure of economic and political life is changed.

Recognition by the Japanese government of the extent of pollution damage in the 1970's was inadequate, and the pollution control laws that came to force were weak and ineffectual. The much praised air pollution control policy is mostly limited to the control of sulphur oxides. Further, the ambient limit criteria for nitrogen oxides were weakened in 1978 after industry came up with dubious arguments on the need for relaxing restraints. After 1970 pollution control policy was formulated under pressure from the pollution victims movement and public opinion, but was easily reversed under pressure from industry labouring under a so-called economic recession.

Industrial pollution is clearly an injustice to the public, but the government and the scientific establishment under its control have failed to recognize this simple but pervasive reality. As a result, governmental effort has concentrated only on the measurement of environmental factors. I do not deny the importance of such measurement; but a larger study of the damage resulting directly from structural and pervasive injustice has always been lacking.

As a result, even in Japan's classic case of environmental destruction, the Minamata Disease, we have as yet no reliable figures as to the actual number of victims. There have been tens of thousands of instances where the mercury levels in fish have been analysed, but even these results remain beyond the purview of the general public. The draft of the proposed legislation requiring environmental assessment of economic activity has been withheld for four years; for the foreseeable future, there is to be no parliamentary discussion on this draft. In a recent court action on limits to nitrogen oxide emissions, the government as defendant stated: "As these criteria have been determined through careful discussions with the highest authoritative experts, there is no room for the layman to doubt the policy outcomes." Such a statement clearly indicates the pervasive extent to which technocrats rule the situation.

The characteristics of pollution as a social problem

From the viewpoint of the victims of pollution, everything can be reduced to a very simple balance between the social power of the polluter and the victim. When the social power of the polluter is stronger than that of the victims, then pollution and destruction will increase without limit. When, with the help of public opinion, the social power of the victims becomes stronger, polluters are constrained to control the damage they do. Public opinion, administrative controls, the withholding of governmental protection, and the like, are all factors which can change this balance of power one way or the other. Pollution of a once viable environment and its continued destruction is a form of class injustice perpetrated by a stronger class upon a weaker class.

The structures of discrimination relative to environmental pollution are clearly evident in the ways in which damage is assessed. The victims of pollution are damaged in all phases of their lives, but such damage is expressed only objectively and in quantitative terms, relative to monetary and health damage. Modern scientific expressions, such as SO_2 levels, are only a very small part of a greater holistic reality. Polluters, and administrative organs which state that they are the impartial third party, generally only recognize the existence of pollution through the use of such quantitative and objective expressions. In extreme cases there is even denial that an environmental problem exists. It requires a heroic effort on the part of the victims' movement to force the polluter and the administrative organs involved to recognize the existence of the problem. And recognition of a polluted environment by the victim of the pollution is always a holistic synthesis. For many natural scientists who believe that objectiveness is the starting point of scientific inquiry, a holistic orientation is indeed very new and a great challenge. Environmental scientists must reflect this new social vision, and justice is a central component of any such work.

Empirical principles relative to pollution

The author has discovered that there are several empirical principles in the study of cases of pollution in Japan. These principles will be useful in determining effective action in the prevention of environmental degradation in other countries.

Environmental pollution as a social issue generally passes through the following four stages:

1. Beginning: The pollution problem is recognized by the local people and especially by the victims.

2. Continuation: The cause of the pollution is discovered as a result of study, which in many instances takes much time and effort.

3. Change: A smokescreen counter-attack on the part of the offending industrial polluter is mounted to obscure the cause, and so-called third party, neutral experts are used in this effort. In this situation the counter-attack stresses quantity over quality.

4. Finale: The information as to the true cause and the counter-attack smokescreen neutralize each other like acid and alkali, and the truth becomes obscured and then forgotten.

These four stages are like a four-part symphony with the allegro, andante, scherzo, and coda. Or, if you like, in oriental poetry these four stages are essential to the writing of a good poem. The only difference is that there is no decisive conclusion to the pollution problem.

The principle of the geometric mean

When a pollution issue comes to a head, at first the victims demand that the situation be restored to its original state and that the pollution be stopped. The polluter, of course, does not accept this; and a long process of argument and negotiation follows. The organization of victims evaluates the damage to them and the environment and requests a sum of money (A) as compensation from the polluter. The polluter responds with a sum (B) which in most cases is smaller than the sum demanded. Again, after very long negotiation, and in many cases with the intervention of the local politician or other men of power, a general and final compensation settlement is reached somewhere around the geometric mean of the two sums (A and B), which is the square root of A $\times$ B and not the arithmetic mean which is A + B divided by 2. This reality has a psychological basis. The degree of psychological compromise is measured by the logarithm of the sum and not by the numerical designation of the money involved. The geometric mean has very similar psychological distance from the initial proposals made by each of the two sides. In the processes of so-called political compromise, generally this principle comes into pretty common application.

It can be readily understood that when the polluter does not recognize his culpability, his proposal for compensation is very close to zero and, as a result, the final agreement is usually zero or a token amount.

Perpendicular or horizontal, the structural question

If the anti-pollution movement takes the apparent perpendicular reality of political structure at face value, and if the movement petitions first the lowest levels, such as the city, town or village, and then works its way upwards, things will end in frustration. The lower stages of government administration will always insist that the solution will have to be sought at a higher administrative stage. When the anti-pollution movement then repeats the petition at a higher level of government, all of its energy will be dissipated at the front desks of bureaucracy, resulting in a very small net effect for the movement.

When the movement refuses to accept the apparent reality of the political structure at face value, then the movement will be able to demand a true solution to the problem within the framework of local autonomy. Pollution problems are affected by many local factors and, as a result, the local autonomous bodies of government are the best locations for solutions to such problems; real understanding of the locality is to be found only at the local level. Thus, the seeking of a solution to a dispute over pollution and its consequences for the local population is a real test of the ability of the local government body.

Perpendicular or horizontal, the movement organization question

When an anti-pollution movement is organized along the lines of a well-ordered, vertical pyramid with a small number of leaders at the top, inevitably it will become inactive. One reason is that the small number of leaders can be easily bribed or immobilized through various forms of intimidation. As a result, even though there may be a desire on the part of the majority for continuing the effort, the whole organization becomes immobilized. For these very same reasons, most political parties and trade unions have been generally inactive throughout Japan's long history of environmental pollution.

On the other side of the coin, a network of independent, self-sustaining small groups and individuals can work together fairly effectively. From the viewpoint of the polluter, it is difficult to identify whom to bribe or intimidate. To bribe the entire network of groups would be too expensive. Such a network of ad hoc groups appears on the surface to be ineffective and weak, but in fact it works much more effectively by having a guerrilla movement characteristic.

During Japan's more recent modern history, the largest and most powerful people's movement, the anti-nuclear bomb movement, was divided into three factions through the intervention of the political parties, thereby losing power in 1963. This experience was a valuable lesson for many local ad hoc anti-pollution movements and helped to foster a very careful attitude towards cooperation with political parties.

My own ad hoc group, the Jishu Koza, is proposing the formation of a loose network of many socially concerned scientists around the world, with special emphasis on developing countries, so that there may be cooperation in overcoming environmental pollution. We are making preparations for an Asian Environment Society seminar and are ready to make use of our English language publication for this purpose.

The role of journalism in the formation of public opinion

In general, large Japanese newspapers and other organs of mass media have come to work in favour of the pollution movements and the victims, even though their management relies heavily on the massive commercial advertisement from large business and industry. Righteous indignation on the part of the frontline reporters forced the publication of pollution problems and issues with a high degree of accuracy, even though such new dissemination was in opposition to the policies of the mass media companies.

Even in the face of heavy pressure from the government, Korean journalists like Ton-a-ilbo campaigned against the dangers of pollution at a time when Japanese industries announced that manufacturing and processing facilities would be built in South Korea between 1975 and 1976. The reporting was effective in reducing the pollutional load that the factory would have produced. Similar activity is to be seen in Malaysia, Singapore, Thailand, and in other Asian locations.

The oriental concept of nature is that human life is simply a part of the total harmony. This concept provides a powerful basis for the conservation movement in Asia, although the concept has been compromised by westernization and industrialization. In Japan, fishermen in the Shibushi area of Kyushu Island declared: "Our choice is for a humble life under a blue sky, rather than beefsteak in the smog!" And with this statement they refused to accept an industrialization plan that would have reclaimed land from the coastal sea area.

Environmental pollution and the North-South relationship

By far the most visually graphic aspects of environmental destruction in Asia are the results of international trade in primary products and industry. The irreversible decrease in land productivity, brought about by monoculture, and the unplanned destruction of forest areas are typical cases of the irrational effects of the market price mechanisms that neglect the long-term social costs of exploitation. This problem can be solved only through cooperation and efforts of the exporting countries.

Secondly, polluting industries seeking low wages and areas where the pollution control laws are lax or non-existent are heading for the developing countries of Asia. We are trying to check the movement of such dirty capital into the developing countries, but this effort can only succeed when there is complete cooperation with the peoples' movements in the receiving countries. In the long run it is very dangerous for any government to increase its GNP at the expense of the health of its own people, especially when such a reality benefits the health of people in other industrialized areas of the world.

Thirdly, a new and more sophisticated trend has come into being since 1975. This is the export of pollution control technology and hardware from the industrialized countries. Quite expensive, capital intensive, and sophisticated systems of pollution control are being imported at no apparent cost to the developing countries, making such activity seem humanitarian. In fact, such aid not only promises new markets for the pollution control industries in the developed countries, but creates a future monopoly potential in the developing countries once the market has been established and the need created. In some industrialized countries like Japan, pollution control as public investment is a hotbed of corruption in which inadequate equipment at bloated prices is financed by the political slush funds of the party in power. This network of corruption can be easily extended to other Asian countries through the patterns of economic aid coming from Japan. The subway construction in Seoul, Korea, that was undertaken through Japanese foreign aid in the early 1970's, was a typical case of political slush fund financing, with the cost of the subway car being raised to a level 30% higher than the normal market price, the difference being paid back into Japanese banks.

The essence of pollution control is quite simple, and the experience underlying such control already exists in most developing countries. But these indigenous orientations are ignored for the sake of importing pollution control technology from the developed countries. If this trend is allowed to continue, the exploitation of developing countries will proceed to a new stage—from resource exploitation through trade capital, via labour and environment exploitation through industrial capital, to the systematic exploitation of the entire political and economic system by state-monopoly capital through aid systems which tie the developing to the developed.

What are the alternatives?

The final alternative is quite simple but not very easily attainable. States and regions must become independent in politics, economics and technology through efforts of self-reliance. In matters of environmental pollution, the most important point is to attain participation of the victim, as the most concerned and experienced party in the issue. The release of administrative information at this point has proved to be very effective, and this freedom of information is part of the common public domain in Sweden and the United States. This should be possible in most democratic countries.

In Japan, the realization of local autonomy is a realistic target for the movement. Even under a highly centralized government that retains as its basic task the protection of industry, there are opportunities for the participation of the victims and local inhabitants in the processes needed to solve problems relative to pollution. Once the effectiveness of such solutions is proved and published, there will be a widening of the circle of involvement. The largest obstacle is the fact that most politicians, whether conservative or progressive, do not easily welcome the participation of the people.

Few studies have been done on Asian agrarian communities and environmental pollution. In the past, the authoritarian character of the Japanese agrarian community frequently hindered the independence of individuals, resulting in many cases in the increase in environmental destruction, especially before the Second World War. Many social scientists believed that the dissolution of the agrarian community was an essential step in the modernization of Japan. Through this process, however, we also lost our traditional spirit of harmonious coexistence with nature. On the other hand, as can be seen with the communities of Shibushi and Usuki on Kyushu Island, traditional agrarian communities refused the importation of outside capital into their regions and have achieved some degree of self-reliance. The Kuala Juru case in Penang State, Malaysia, is another typical example of successful cooperation between an agrarian community fishing village and a consumers association in Penang City. It seems to me that the majority of social scientists in Asia, including Japan, are under the strong influence of a stiff and unbending Marxism or modernism and pay little attention to the actual social processes that develop in their own countries.

The countries that will occupy the centre of attention relative to problems of pollution in the coming decades are China and India. If China aims at unlimited economic growth, Japanese style, then the problems of environmental destruction may reach levels a hundred times as great as in Japan, because there are ten times the population and ten times less favourable natural conditions. How the Chinese agrarian society, with strong traditions of decentralization, will deal with pollution is of vital interest in view of the social system involved. In India, with its much more complicated social system, there is a discussion of appropriate technology within the discussions on social reform, and this is at a more advanced stage than in Japan. Incorporated in the spirit of Gandhism is a recognition of the relation between political liberation and economic and technical liberation. How Indian agrarian society will be able to liberate itself through self-reform without losing its traditional spirit will be of vital interest for the future.

The solution to issues of environmental destruction depends solely upon the achievements of the people as they work for self-education, self-organization and local autonomy. The degree to which these goals are achieved raises questions different from those where the concern is with industrialization and modernization.

Conclusions

To summarize my experience, I would like to try to answer three questions:

1. What has been my experience in encouraging wider public participation in evaluating particular forms of technological development?

People's movements are the key to pollution control and environmental conservation. For the scientist, the establishment of science of the people, by the people, and for the people is a central challenge. Such science has very different paradigms from those of modern science. Science becomes a kind of life science or service science. We need the cooperation of the religions to find a synthesized view of nature and to work for the liberation of the oppressed and the socially weak.

2. What can I recommend to individuals, groups, and communities seeking to protect themselves from the harmful effects of rapid technological change?

In Japan, as can be seen in the anti-pollution movements and in the anti-nuclear power movements, participation on the part of the people has been achieved only in the form of protest and resistance. Such might seem a rather negative orientation, but it was the only form of participation open, and it has been effective to some degree.

The largest obstacle to positive participation by the people in Japan has been the monopolization of information at the hands of politicians, administrative organs and industry. There are at least two channels where this information monopoly might be broken—in the diet (parliament) or the courts. But in general, change can come about more easily if action is taken in relation to the local instruments of government and the local courts in Japan, for the time being at least.

3. What are the weaknesses of government as they affect the ability to ascertain the social consequences of new technological developments?

The administrative methods of government allow only a very limited recognition of the extent of environmental damage. The inherent sectionalism and the dispersion of responsibility within the bureaucratic system, combined with social development models predicated on the development of industrialization, bring a certain blindness to the long-term need to protect humanity and all of nature. The result is a kind of modernized structural corruption in Japan.

The government in power is always disdainful of the people and attempts to maintain the people powerless by monopolizing information. The intellectuals within this government power structure, especially the scientists, cooperate with the government power as they seek to maintain their privilege above the people. As a result, science and technology wedded to centralized power finally loses its vitality and independence.

This is also the situation with respect to highly centralized political power systems in socialist countries, where it is quite the same as with capitalism. The socialist system and its theory has not established effective citizen participation in the making of policy, especially with regard to evaluating the uses of science and technology. The increase in environmental destruction in socialist countries is a direct indication of the fact that participation on the part of the people is crucial to a more humane technology.

I appeal to the people at this influential conference to consider the Japanese case, not as a special case but as an early warning sign of world environment. I appeal to the people to increase the channels of participation, in positive or negative ways, by mobilizing people's ability through formal and informal self-education.

Reactions and Comment

The addresses of Nwosu and Leite, along with earlier addresses on similar themes, spoke to issues that reverberated throughout the conference. There was some challenge to Nwosu's charge that socialist countries' "export companies" behaved much like transnational corporations, but Nwosu reaffirmed the similarity of behaviour.

On the fundamental issues raised by Nwosu and Leite, the responses—less obviously in the immediate plenary session than in the continuing work of the conference—were too deep and too diverse for any brief summation. They influenced the work of most sections, and they re-emerged in a later, special plenary session. Chapter 19 will say more about them.

The addresses of Anér, Berger and Ui came at an appropriate time. Many delegates, quite evidently, felt overwhelmed by the immensity of the issues they had been considering for more than a week and by their feeling of futility in meeting colossal problems. Their applause to these speeches showed their gratification at the news that some people in some places were actually influencing the direction of technological change. If, as one journalist later pointed out, the modesty of the victories still seemed incommensurable with the scope of the problems, that is itself a characteristic of the world situation in which the conference met.

18. The Student Presentation

Introduction

The importance of the student participation in the conference has already been mentioned (see "The Contribution of Students" in Chapter 1). The delegation of almost a hundred students began their work at a preliminary conference at nearby Wellesley College, then continued it at the official conference at MIT. Working long hours, often in sub-groups, they produced an extensive document on the issues they chose for emphasis (see Volume 2).

The students were invited to conduct a plenary session on 16 July. There, 13 students contributed to the entire conference something of the thought and elan of the shared experience of the larger body of students. Each spoke both as an individual and in a representative function; that is, each was chosen by the larger group of students to represent a region of the world, an interest, or the work of a sub-group that drafted part of the final report. Some gave the gist of a section of the fuller report. The excerpts of their addresses printed in this volume are designed (1) to point to the longer report in Volume 2 without repeating it unduly, and (2) to give some indication of the way in which the student presentation fitted into and influenced the work of the whole conference.

Like older participants, the students represented a diversity of experiences and opinions. Yet some of the dominant accents of the group are clear.

Genga Arulampalam of Sri Lanka moderated the meeting, introducing the speakers and conducting the discussion. The addresses are taken from transcriptions of tape recordings.

Scientific Education in Industrialized Countries
Joe Egan

Joseph Stalin once remarked that education is a weapon whose effect depends on who possesses it and at whom it is aimed. We science students agreed that in many respects present educational systems are weapons that ensure the continued domination of those in power. Our educational systems have institutionalized a set of values, then disguised the set of values in the garb of objectivity and technical rationality.

As participants in this conference, we students believe that our very presence here is an expression of the same kind of social power that resides at the heart of our educational systems. As in school, we are confronted here with a great problem. We then view the problem as observers and forget that we, too, are part of the problem, perhaps a major part of the problem.

That same social power is present in a form of education called technological determinism, in other words, the western model. We are taught that technology is simply gadgets and machines, that it somehow determines its own direction, as if it were a creature with a life of its own. We are taught that it advances unstoppably according to rational economic and technological laws. Since we are advised that there are no alternatives to current modes of technological development, we reach the distressing conclusion that there is no moral or ethical basis for social change. In this way technology is itself an ideology of legitimation, of justification.

We believe that technical and scientific education can be transformed from a destructive weapon to a constructive tool by a process of demystification. When we finally begin to separate technology from the ideology of technology, when we begin to question our own motivations for becoming and remaining scientists, then we will achieve an understanding far greater than any classroom experience could ever give us.

The Education of Scientists of the Third World

MARIE-CHRISTINE RAKOTONIRINA

Some of us at Wellesley decided to examine particularly the education of scientists of the Third World, since they exert a considerable influence on the evolution of their countries.

We found that the main reasons for students to study in the West are the following: (1) to raise their social status; (2) to achieve the prestige associated with the style of western education; (3) to benefit from the possibilities offered by scholarships.

All these reasons have to be seen in a socio-political context which makes the West highly attractive to third world students. In most cases this western education leads to the formation of an elite whose tendency is to pursue inappropriate technologies and to separate themselves from the people.

However, we found positive consequences, i.e. that once abroad, the third world students are sufficiently far away to analyse the situation in their own countries within a world context. Having discovered this, we suggest that foreign students' organizations become more active in ideological and social conscientization. These organizations should promote the cultural and social values of the third world countries; they should also enable students to analyse their own socio-political situation as well as that of their countries, and thus to define the role they must play in the development of their countries. Finally, they should educate students so that, on their return home, they will work for the community and not for their own interests, as they are taught in the West.

Technology and Cultural Alienation

RAGUI ASSAAD

Let me present the results of our discussion on technology and cultural alienation. The group agreed that the major cause of alienation is the economic system underlying technology, which is generally controlled by profit-seeking industries. Governments and political institutions contribute to this alienation by supporting these vested economic interests.

Even in industrialized countries, the majority of people and even some scientists are alienated by the implementation of high technology. In developing countries the alienation is compounded: existing social systems are dismantled and replaced by structures dependent on technologically advanced societies.

Another source of alienation is inherent in the change which necessarily accompanies the introduction of technology. Alienation will occur if the change is too rapid for society to be able to cope with its consequences. This is illustrated by the saying: "The soul cannot catch up with the body."

The materialistic outlook which leads to consumerism is also a major source of alienation. Materialism is the result of the economic system. A consumeristic outlook is infiltrating the Third World. The poor countries should have the power to decide for themselves how they want to use technology, while at the same time integrating it into their value systems. Participation is a vital aspect of this decision.

Now let me mention some of our strategies to conquer alienation. The first type can be overcome by increasing political awareness through community action with emphasis on political activity on the national level, and also by encouraging local church-related groups to gather and disseminate information about the activities of economic powers.

The second type of alienation, caused by consumerism, can be overcome by: (1) decentralizing sources of information; (2) directing scientific research towards the needs of the community; (3) consulting seriously with the users of technology, e.g. farmers and workers; (4) controlling advertising, which can create need for unnecessary items; (5) emphasizing appropriate technology, with which users feel comfortable and not mystified.

Women in Science

ROSEMARY NEFF

First, a personal remark: I had not previously been concerned with the question of women. But since our discussions at Wellesley I have concluded that it is vital to promote the discussion on the role of women in science.

Science is an almost exclusively male domain. This follows from a division of work which is reinforced by education: women take care of the family, men take care of progress. Women are generally restricted to certain social areas, e.g. pedagogy or paramedical sciences. However, men are taught from childhood to be interested in technology, mathematics and other scientific concerns. Women are not only under-represented, but are at a disadvantage in the field of science. In general, they are excluded from decision-making.

In the history of science the work of women researchers is hardly mentioned. The same is true in the history of the Church and its hierarchy. In order to change this situation women must seize and use the greater possibilities that exist in wider realms of life.

We hope that the WCC will really stand up for a just, participatory and sustainable society; that it will be a supportive community and undertake efforts to end discrimination against women; that it will open up equal possibilities for women to take part in the decision-making processes which concern all—men and women; and finally, that it will provide an education which furthers the abilities of all people. As long as women are excluded from the decision-making processes in science and the Church, the slogan of a just and participatory society remains a farce.

The Voice of the Poor

GUSTAVO BUESO MADRID

For this conference to be truly ecumenical, we believe that it should listen to the voices of all the churches all over the world. We feel that an important voice is missing—that of the Roman Catholic Church in Brazil, where names like Paulo Evaristo Arns, Helder Camara and Pedro Casaldáliga are symbols of the new Church.

Why a new Church? Because it has undergone a radical conversion. For centuries it has been on the side of the powerful, and now it has decided to be the voice of those who do not have a voice. It has taken the decision that its word will be the expression of the pains and aspirations of the poor. Even more, its word has to be heard by the poor.

Why this option? Because the Gospel is a word of faith and hope for the poor. It grows out of sufferings and hardships. We believe that this conference should pay attention now to these unheard voices.

Where is the voice of the poor in this conference? Perhaps we believe that the poor are stupid and incapable of expressing their needs. Perhaps we believe that our elites of intellectuals, scientists and theologians know more about the real needs of the poor than they do themselves. But we should never forget that these intellectual elites, with very few exceptions, are at the service of the powers who support the institutions for which they work.

If our world is frightened by looming crises—the threat of nuclear holocaust, of ecological holocaust, of total holocaust over oil—all this is the fault of the rich and powerful nations which, with the help of science and technology, have pushed us to this point. We must end this state of affairs.

We cannot hope that those in power will take the initiative. Power never ceases to be power. In accordance with the Gospel hope comes from the poor and the oppressed, because the biblical God is the God of the poor.

Secularization—and the Transfiguration of Human Life

AUGUSTIN NIKITIN

René Descartes once said: "I think, therefore I am." Now, however, people find themselves saying: "I consume, therefore I exist." Our regional group noted the gulf between technical progress and the moral perfection of human personality. However, technical progress alone is not the cause of this gulf, since the first fratricide was committed before the innovation of industrial production. With the aid of science and technology man masters nature, thus fulfilling the very task assigned by the Creator. Science and technology are a two-edged weapon, used for human good or detriment.

In our contemporary world and especially in East European countries one observes a process of secularization, which at first glance might be explained by scientific technological progress. However, such progress does not change the ontological essence of human nature. The rift between God and humanity occurred when the commandment concerning the fruits of the tree of good and evil was broken—in other words, with the use and exploitation of nature—contrary to God's design. This rift was mended through the redemption of the Saviour, who restored meaning to human activity, namely, to the continuing of the work of creation, transforming and transfiguring it. The confrontation between faith and knowledge, though leading to conflict in some historical periods, could now become an area of joint positive cooperation.

The present ecological crisis results from many factors. Although in Eastern Europe, in contrast to Western Europe, fundamentally different economic stimuli are at work, nevertheless there are common problems associated with the fundamental features of a scientific technical revolution. Extensive international cooperation is necessary, independent of religious, cultural and political views. The Church must always remind us of the sacred quality of human life, aspiring towards its transfiguration, based on the ontological solidarity of the whole of humanity, set in the image of the Holy Trinity. The Church must always act out of the love that it bears, defending the poor, the rejected and the hungry, drawing strength from its solidarity with them, since in every person it sees the image of Christ.

In view of these considerations we have formulated three questions we would like to offer for discussion: (1) How can one reconcile the historical teleological premise, according to which scientific technical progress must be seen as the expression of God's will, with the ever-growing secularization of society? (2) Where does one find the basic principles necessary for correlation between human freedom and reason, expressed in the dynamics of scientific knowledge *and* the intangible principles of the Christian faith? (3) How can one bring about a creative contact between the moral-ethical principles of Christianity and the scientific technical progress of our times?

If we do not discuss such questions, Einstein's prediction may well come true: if a third world war is fought with atomic weapons, then a fourth world war will be fought with wooden clubs.

The Contribution of the Church

CHRISTOPH STÜCKELBERGER

Our group on the role of the Church in technological decision-making discussed two main questions: (1) What is the specific contribution of the Church in technological decision-making? (2) What are the strategies for the Church?

With regard to the first question, we agreed completely that the churches need to be involved in decisions about technologies because technologies affect the way in which people live their lives. *(a)* In these decisions the Church must emphasize its vision of human beings and nature as the central concern, because of its belief in the Christian God who became himself a human being. *(b)* The Church must address those with power over technology and must ensure that those affected by technology are heard as early and as much as possible. The hopes, fears and desires of those affected are as important in decision-making as scientific and economic factors. *(c)* Because many technological decisions are the result of fear—we fear the adversary and therefore overdevelop armaments—the Church should struggle against the structures which create and maintain these fears.

The second question—what are the strategies for the Church—we considered on three levels. *(a)* There are many tensions inside the churches about whether they should speak as social institutions or only through their members as individuals. We believe that churches should not fear to speak as bodies, even though this may cause disunity. *(b)* The Church should take informative and educative actions, engaging in dialogue with the appropriate responsible institutions concerning the development of new technologies. *(c)* Where dialogue is not possible or successful, the Church should consider active protestation, for example, through official statements or even boycotts.

The Voice of the Pacific Region

AMELIA BOLALAILAI

The Pacific is still being used by some of the major powers as a testing ground for their nuclear weapons. As countries with small populations spread across a vast ocean, at a great distance from the centres of world power, we are considered to be the safest place for nuclear experimentation. But this experimentation is certainly not safe *for us*. Already we are on the way to becoming a radio-active paradise choked with nuclear weapons and wastes. Already people are suffering from exposure to nuclear radiation. The presence of the US Triton submarine in the Pacific makes us a potential target for nuclear weapons.

As a Pacific region we have protested, but our cries have been ignored. We have been told that these nuclear military installations would benefit us economically. We have also been told that "they" know what they are doing. All we know is that our environment and our lives are in danger. The Pacific Conference of Churches has appealed to other bodies and especially to the WCC to support us on this issue. We propose to this conference that it support the Pacific demand for a nuclear-free Pacific.

Technology and Labour

PETER RENDER

"Designed by computer. Silenced by laser. Built by robot." Those words are taken from an advertisement that is appearing all over Europe, an advertisement for the Fiat car company.

I hear the voice of the worker asking: Where am I? One difference between us students, at conferences like this, and the workers is that we can afford to spend hours in arguments forming grand ideologies. But we should spend our time talking about specific technologies, about these machines, not machines in general. We should be asking: Why this machine, who wants this machine?

We intellectuals should put our theory into practice. This does not mean organizing the working classes. The working classes can organize themselves. What they want from us is our solidarity. And this we can give by working in our own spheres, our own disciplines.

We can, for example, remove the falsification of history. For too long educators have told us very little about the history of trade unions. We must not let people grow up believing that the social and political powers have given all we have with willing hands.

Finally, those of us who are trade union members or support trade unions should work towards transnational unions. It is only through transnational unions that we will be able to fight the blackmail of transnational corporations.

Technology and Transnational Corporations

CAROL C. MAPONA

In the attempt to control and dominate the world, transnational corporations use technology as a tool of political and military power. For example, because of the TNC's the white racist minority in South Africa has the power to sustain apartheid and to control the economies of neighbouring countries. American and European TNC's and banks have enabled South Africa to develop the industrial capacity to produce its own weapons or to import weapons and oil to safeguard its economic and military hegemony. TNC's have licensed South African firms to produce military equipment (such as fighter aircraft), machinery and parts. No other African country has been given this right.

South Africa's military and economic power make it an effective sub-imperialist country, which can sabotage the economy of a neighbouring landlocked country like Zambia.

Because of TNC control over developing countries, I call on the political powers in those countries to think not only of themselves and the elite in society, but to show genuine concern for the welfare of their people by refusing to be manipulated by the TNC's.

Technology and Militarism

TIM AUKES

I would like to make some remarks about the spirit of the report of the group that discussed militarism and technology (see Volume 2).

The Church—and this implies mainly the community of believers—should not take it as a sufficient practice of Christianity to talk about problems, although we are pretty good at that. We ask the Church to develop strategies for political action on all levels of society.

The statements in our report may be judged as too trivial or cliché-like. But truth can be trivial, and even the most clear truth runs the risk of becoming a cliché when it has to be repeated over and over again, because the people and their churches do not want to act according to it.

The students have decided to present a motion to this conference dealing with the militarization of the world and the proliferation of nuclear power. Our hope is that the conference will take a stand against this ongoing process of domination, injustice and unsustainability.

The Self-Defeating Structure of this Conference

RUDY PRUDENTE

When students are asked to attend this conference, they are expected to be exciting, provocative and enthusiastic. And their presence is used to enhance the respectability of the conference: look how relevant we are because youth is involved! In fact, we students are no different from the rest of this conference. We are not exciting, provocative or enthusiastic.

At Wellesley College we had a challenging time of confrontation, thinking and interaction—despite the fact that the organization and structure of our conference was much the same as yours. We came alive only when a group of people decided not to be passive recipients of a predetermined and ecumenically packaged routine.

This conference was organized on a pattern of normal western bureaucratic practices: the way material is dealt with, the way topics are phrased, the format, the cultural assumptions on how arguments progress, and what conclusions constitute results. These cultural assumptions derived from the West are one factor determining what can come out of this conference.

Another aspect is the constituency. Inviting professionals who have a vested interest in the continuation of the prevailing systems of science and technology is rather like asking the South African government to examine alternatives to apartheid. It would seem imperative to include a substantial number of people who have suffered from the competitive educational system and the negative effects of western science and technology: for example, school drop-outs, more women, minorities, youth, the unemployed, factory workers, labourers and farmers.

The reality is that those who paid for this conference control the directions it takes. The results of this process are that the victims of western science and technology take second place, the deep crisis of prevailing academic methods is not faced, the necessity of developing alternative ways of doing science is ignored, limitations are placed on the range of issues and the depth to which they are discussed. Results will be pieces of paper, and strategies for action will be entirely within the framework of the dominant form of science and technology.

The context of science and technology is political. We should be talking about power. Surely this time we should listen to the voice of the oppressed, so that we do not offer improved health care to the poor when the technology they really want in order to achieve self-determination is guns to protect themselves from people like us.

Technology and Justice in Africa

ADWOAH SEIWAAH BONSU

The African group discussed the relation of science and technology in Africa to the problems of apartheid, racism, colonialism and neo-colonialism. It is obvious that western capitalism, using science and technology, has been employed to exploit and dominate the countries of Africa and elsewhere. Through this process indigenous technology has been distorted and destroyed. The result has been conflict and underdevelopment, and the continued domination of monopoly capital from Europe, America and Japan. The ruling classes of the African states, in alliance with international capital, have carried out economic and military atrocities against the people of Africa.

The search for a just society cannot be isolated from the need for participation of society as a whole. And the ultimate hope for the realization of the messianic promise presupposes the social harmony of the world.

In recognition of the urgency of the need for a just, participatory and sustainable society, we call on the WCC to continue to expand its assistance to the struggling peoples of Africa, particularly those in Southern Africa.

Concluding Comment by the Moderator

GENGA ARULAMPALAM

As the students here have made extremely clear, we view technology as part of a social process intricately entwined with political and ideological systems. Therefore, in many cases constructive action may necessitate the drastic alteration of such existing systems.

What we would like to see are scientists and theologians alike going out from here determined and willing to do something in order to bring about a more just, participatory and sustainable society. We must stop hiding behind pious platitudes and get down to constructive decision-making right here at this conference. To quote from the students' report: "It is time that most of us descended from the Mt Olympus of knowledge and abstraction, and engaged in the struggle of translating theory into practice."

Reactions and Comment

The immediate responses to the addresses came in discussion from the floor. The first questions, primarily from representatives from the Third World, challenged some of the students' statements. Students responded from the platform with enough zest and obvious enjoyment to throw into question Rudy Prudente's assertion that "we are not exciting, provocative or enthusiastic". Then Rubem Alves of Brazil congratulated the speakers for sparking the conference into vigorous dialogue.

In the following days most of the sections took up issues raised by the student presentations and the written report. In the conference design each section had a student vice moderator, so the students were easily able to get their ideas on the floor. As one example, the recommendation on "Nuclear Power and Nuclear Proliferation", though not adopted intact by the conference, influenced the final recommendations both on disarmament and on nuclear energy. On numerous other issues, both in section discussions and plenary debates, the student voice was persuasive.

Responses of and to the students continued after the conference. For example, the World Student Christian Federation Journal, *No. 3, 1979, contains written responses from the following student participants: Youssef Hajjar, Syria; Smith Za Thang, Burma; Ragui Assaad, Egypt; Tracy Gross, USA; Harold Brown, USA; and Chris Ledger, Australia.*

19. A Third World Protest

Introduction

One premise in organizing the conference was that national, social, economic and ideological differences were as important to the purposes of the conference as professional differences among scientists, theologians and the other vocations represented. A consequence was that the programme, organized in part around inquiries into topics (science, faith, economics, energy, biology, etc.), was also organized in part around regional and ideological groups (see especially Part Two, "Perspectives and Futures").

As the conference proceeded, it became evident that some participants thought it was dominated by the viewpoints of the industrialized societies that control technology. Others disagreed, pointing to the powerful influence of speakers from Africa, Asia and Latin America.

A group of delegates from the Third World began meeting and expressing their discontent. They approached the Steering Committee and requested a place on the agenda to state their concerns. Some members of the Steering Committee asked how such a meeting would differ from the earlier plenary sessions of the Third World (see Chapters 8 and 9) or from the substance of many of the conference addresses. Others wondered whether the sections, with many of their moderators and rapporteurs from the Third World, were expressing adequately Third World concerns; but preliminary reports from the sections varied. The Steering Committee concluded that the deep concerns of the group from the Third World should have a hearing in plenary session, and it rearranged the schedule to provide for such a hearing on the night of 22 July.

About thirty participants from the Third World sat on the platform. D. Enilo Ajakaiye, a Nigerian physicist and a co-president of the conference, read a two-page "Statement from Representatives from Africa, Asia, Latin America and the Pacific". She then asked that the statement be distributed to all participants (the statement, in its final revised version, is printed in Volume 2). Then Rubem Alves of Brazil, who had earlier addressed the conference (see Chapter 3), spoke as a representative of the group.

Biblical Faith and the Poor of the World

RUBEM ALVES

We know that many of you find it strange that the third world people are having the privilege of a plenary session. We must explain why.

We felt that a number of tensions have been building up due to the different concerns which bring us together here, and our different approaches to them. As a sort of duty of honesty, we want to share with you our concerns, our anxieties. These are the anxieties of those who come from the countries of the Third World and who have lived very close to the poor. Since we believe that the Gospel is a word of faith and hope addressed to the poor, and since the Holy Scriptures state unequivocally that the poor are those who more easily understand the Gospel, we believe their voice should be heard.

We are not poor. The poor are absent from this conference, and we understand why. Could they engage in meaningful dialogue with scientists, could they understand the wisdom of theologians? Obviously not. They do not belong here. Yet since they are absent, we will attempt to be their representatives and their advocates.

The poor must be heard. This is not a demand of the poor—they are weak and powerless. This is a demand which comes out of the very depths of our faith. We have been discussing faith, science and the future. If the poor were to speak, they would ask whose future we are talking about. This question might sound strange. Is it not obvious that we are concerned about the future of the world, the future of mankind?

The future: an improved form of the present?

Have you ever noticed that tigers have eyes in the front of their heads, whereas deers have eyes on the side of their heads? Do you know why? Tigers are hunters; deers are hunted. The questions that tigers put to their environment are different from the questions that deer put to the same environment. And when tigers begin to speak in general terms about the future of the animals, they obviously have in mind something quite different from the hopes of deer.

The sociology of knowledge has shown that our sense of the future is determined by our social, economic and political situation. The powerful want to preserve their power. For them the future has to be the development and perpetuation of their domination. Tigers cannot imagine a world dominated by deer.

The situation of the poor and oppressed is exactly the opposite. Their future must not be an improved form of the present. When domination is "improved", it is not abolished. The poor peoples of the world have been like deer, dominated, exploited, manipulated. It is not necessary to go through history in detail. You know very well what happened to the Mayas, the Aztecs, the Incas, the Indians of North America, the blacks, India under England, apartheid in South Africa. The domination goes on today under the auspices of the multinational corporations and the Trilateral Commission when it is not accomplished by direct military intervention.

The relationships between rich and poor nations have been disguised by means of ideological discourse. We used to say that the rich were developed and that the poor were underdeveloped nations. Later on, we stopped speaking about underdevelopment and we invented the term "developing nations". What does this jargon imply? It implies that both rich and poor are in a kind of race and that the rich are ahead. The poor have to catch up to become like rich nations. This is the goal for all. The problems of life, cultural consumption, and social organization of the rich are thus established as the unquestionable social goal, the future to be created for the poor. The rich never realize that they have become rich because of their exploitation of the poor and that the poor will never emerge out of their poverty if they continue to be exploited by the rich.

Indeed, the rich are willing to do things to the poor. As has been said elsewhere, the poor are running after the speeding train of the wealthy nations; and if the rich do not help them to board the train, the danger is that they will derail it. Yes, there is a help whose purpose is to preserve the patterns of power, economic growth, and consumption of the haves without altering in any way the relationships of domination.

The German sociologist Karl Mannheim said that those who criticize details bind themselves by the same critique to the whole as it is. It is the whole which must be brought to an end. From our point of view, the whole is the pattern of domination whereby tigers keep the deer under control. All the specific problems have to be considered as functions of this global structure.

The agenda reflects the priorities of the rich

Thus, as we have been speaking about the future of mankind we have indeed been speaking about the future of the rich, since the whole was not questioned. We spoke about science. We discussed its methods, its truth claims, its harmony and conflict with religion. Obviously the poor could not understand our discussions. They are not interested in them. Their problems are different: hunger, disease, pain, oppression. They work more, suffer more, live less. It is very easy for scientists boxed into their laboratories to dismiss the problem simply by saying that all the problems of the poor will be solved by science. But you know that science today has social existence only because it is supported by money. Without money, no telescopes, no microscopes, no research. But where does money come from? What are the reasons why those who control money, the military-industrial complex, subsidize science? To believe that science is the solution of the problem of the poor, one would have to believe that the military-industrial complex exists for the poor. It seems, on the contrary, that science has given solutions to the problems of the rich.

Indeed, science and technology have made a great impact on the nations of the Third World: cars, oil drills, plants, roads, televisions, gas stations, a fantastic expansion of the drug industry, the cigarette people, sophistication of armies, nuclear plants. Science has contributed to the strengthening of the local power elites. The rich have become richer, the poor have become poorer.

Indeed, the problem is not wealth. The problem is that the cultural fabric of our peoples and our political institutions are being destroyed. This becomes obvious if you see that there is a close relationship between the growth of militarism and the expansion of technology. Technology is transplanted to the poor countries either by the multinationals or by bilateral agreements. This transplant, however, is made under the condition that there will be political stability in the country. One must be assured that the deer will not rebel. The military function as the guarantors of stability.

We do not deny that epistemological and philosophical discussions about science are interesting. But we ask, if the poor and oppressed were to set the agenda would these be their priorities? Yes, the poor cannot understand the heights of our wisdom. But should we not as Christians be sensitive to the depths of their sufferings?

Out of painful experience

We have been talking about faith, and it is out of our understanding of faith that we are raising these questions. The eyes and words of faith as we find them in the Bible did not fall from the blue; they grew slowly out of painful experience of slavery, liberation, wilderness, pride and ruin, fear and weakness, defeat, exile, captivity, despair, longing, hope. We do not find here the eyes or the words of tigers, dominant classes, wealthy groups, victors. Here are the eyes and words of the dominated, the poor, the defeated ones. This is the reason why the biblical God is so biased for the poor and why so little hope is left for the rich. How difficult it is for the rich to enter the Kingdom! We do not find in the Bible any attempt at the scientific explanation of the world. God is not seen either through the mystery of the universe or through the mystery of life. On the contrary, it is the universe and life which are seen through the experience of the liberation of the oppressed. The oppressed are the place of revelation.

The biblical God is not a function of nature. The question as to whether the universe makes room for God is not raised once. The poor and the oppressed have experienced liberation in the past and are given hope for a new future. This is the only thing that matters. These words of hope grew out of the experience of liberation of the poor. They could understand them because it was part of their very being.

But does our theology grow out of the poor? Do the poor speak through our words? When we become concerned about making room for God in the physical universe or when biology becomes the model for our speech about God, have we not departed from the voice of the oppressed? Have we abandoned our tradition?

These are some of our concerns. We believe that, had the poor been heard, as our faith demands, we would have moved in a different direction. We bid you, therefore, to keep before your eyes in these last days here the image of the poor and dispossessed, so that all our decisions will be inspired by this vision.

Remember the dinosaur. He thought that he would survive by becoming big and strong. Small lizards survived—the dinosaur disappeared. It is time for the strong to realize that maybe they are going to disappear if they are not converted to the poor.

Reactions and Comment

Following the address of Alves, Metropolitan Gregorios called for discussion from the floor.

The initial discussion suffered from one confusion that skewed the issues. A representative of the group from the Third World had mistakenly delivered to the conference stenographic office for distribution an early draft of the group's statement, which differed significantly from the revised statement that had been read from the platform by President Ajakaiye. Many participants addressed their remarks to the statement in their hands rather than their memories of the revised version that they had heard.

The most important difference was in the opening declaration. The statement distributed to the participants described itself as a "Manifesto" and began: "We denounce science and technology..." The revision said: "We denounce the historical and current use of science and technology by industrialized and technically advanced societies, to serve military and economic interests which have brought about great sufferings to the people of the Third World." Several of the first comments from the floor attacked the unrevised form of the statement. Responding from the platform, Ajakaiye cleared up the confusion, explaining that she, as a professional scientist, could not possibly favour a denunciation of science.

In the first round of discussion from the floor, ten participants spoke. They came from Egypt, the Federal Republic of Germany, India, the Soviet Union, Trinidad, the United Kingdom, and the United States. Their comments showed a variety of agreements and disagreements with the document and with Alves' address. Then the Moderator called for replies from the panel on the platform. Several of the group made various points, including the following:

- *It would be valuable to have a conference in our world and to invite people from the industrialized world as a minority.*
- *We are not dividing the world into two groups: the good and the evil.*
- *We do not want a confrontation; we just want to be heard.*

A second round of discussion brought further comments from the floor and further responses from the platform.

Then the Moderator, Metropolitan Gregorios, proposed that the group be given the opportunity to revise the document, to whatever extent it saw fit, and to present it to a later business session of the conference, where it would have the same status as the reports from the ten sections. His proposal was accepted.

At a later plenary session a revised document was presented. As with the section reports, the conference was not asked to endorse the report but to accept it as the work of the group and to authorize its publication in the conference report. The conference voted to do so.

The discussion centring on this statement showed one of the differences of orientation and opinion that persisted throughout the meeting (see "Clashes and Consensus" in Chapter 1). While there was unanimous agreement on the ethical importance of the uses of science, there was a cleavage between (1) those who saw some importance in the issues of science and faith as responses to reality in appreciation and understanding, and (2) those who subsumed those issues under the issues of power and social consequences. The second group, even after the events reported in this chapter, felt that its message was not adequately appreciated by the conference as a whole. On the other hand, the first group felt that its valid concerns had been suppressed by a too quick translation of them into ideological and practical concerns.

Some representatives of the first group approached the conference leadership, asking for an opportunity to present their concerns in a plenary session. It was then late in the schedule. After examining the agenda and seeing the difficulties of scheduling another session, they agreed to withdraw their request.

The debate can be expected to continue.

Looking Forward

Introduction

The conference ended on a note of expectation as much as of conclusion. In the closing session Paul Abrecht, WCC Secretary for Church and Society, pointed to the sense of incompleteness about its work but saw in it the ingredients for continuing study and activity. "We tried too much," he said, "but that's what we should have done."

The closing act of worship included film, music from many cultures, prayers in many languages. The concluding meditation by Metropolitan Gregorios, "The Great Symbol", is printed below.

Since the conference, Abrecht and Gregorios reported on it to the United Nations Conference on Science and Technology for Development, Vienna, 19-31 August 1979. They also made a preliminary report to the Executive Committee of the Central Committee of the WCC, held in Geneva, 10-14 September. The WCC Working Committee on Church and Society met immediately at the close of the conference and will meet again in May 1980 to continue the work of the conference and of the programme that generated it. The Central Committee of the WCC will receive a full report in Geneva in August 1980. Through these channels the WCC will follow up the conference. Participants are following it up in many ways, both personally and in their professional capacities, in their various regions of the world.

The Great Symbol

PAULOS GREGORIOS

And a great symbol was seen in heaven!
A woman, wrapped around in the sun
The Moon beneath her feet
And on her hand a crown of twelve stars,
Pregnant, in labour pains, in agony to give birth!

And behold, yet another symbol in heaven!
A great dragon of fire appears,
With seven heads, each head with a crown,
The tail sweeping away a third of the stars of heaven
And hurling them down on the face of the earth!
The dragon confronted the woman about to give birth,
In order to devour the child as soon as it was born.
She gave birth to a son
Who was to reign over all with a sceptre of iron
Her child was snatched away to God and to his throne
While the woman fled into the wilderness.

Book of Revelation, 12:1-6

Those symbols are eloquent. In our tradition the symbol of the woman clothed with the sun stands interchangeably for three realities — for the Mother of our Lord, for the Church persecuted, and for the human race as a whole, in labour pains to bring forth the new humanity.

As the symbol for humanity, it speaks to our age in a new way. Clothed with the sun — let us imagine a future humanity sustained by solar energy. Her feet on the moon — that has come true in our decade: humanity has set its foot on the moon. And as for a crown of twelve stars — even in our own century we may manage to go beyond our own solar system. The next century may take us to a dozen stars which will be added to our crown.

But the important thing is that even with a dozen stars on our crown, the new humanity will still have to be born. With the sun harnessed, the moon colonized and space travel to a dozen solar systems established, humanity will still be great with child, in the pains of labour. And as it is about to give birth, she is faced by the fire-dragon, with enormous power capable of sweeping away a third of the stars in our galaxy.

That is where we are, already. The fire-dragon appears on the horizon, as the way to the sun and the moon and a dozen stars becomes clear through our science and technology.

We need to trust in God that the fire-dragon will not be able to devour the new-born humanity. God is more powerful than the fire-dragon with its star-sweeping tail. The new humanity, about to be born, is in God's hands, and its destiny is to be before the throne of God. But let us not make any mistakes with our science and technology and play into the hands of the fire-dragon.

May the blessing of God Almighty, Father, Son and Holy Spirit, abide with all of us, with our present humanity, and the new humanity about to be born — for ever and ever. Amen.

Appendices

The Conference Programme

WEDNESDAY JULY 11

All day	Arrival of participants
3.30 p.m.	Meeting of the Steering Committee

THURSDAY JULY 12

8.45 a.m.	Participants assemble in Kresge
9.00 a.m.	Opening worship led by Metropolitan Paulos Gregorios, Moderator of the conference Choral music by St Paul's Cathedral Men and Boys Choir directed by Thomas Murray
9.30 a.m.	First plenary session: Introduction and welcome Welcomes from Chancellor Paul E. Gray, MIT, Dr Claire Randall, and Cardinal Medeiros
11.15 a.m.	Address: "Science and Technology: Why Are the Churches Concerned?", Dr Philip Potter, General Secretary of the World Council of Churches
3.00 p.m.	Plenary session Address: "The Nature of Science", Prof. Robert Hanbury Brown. Comments by Prof. Rubem Alves and Prof. W. Mutu Maathai Address: "The Nature of Faith", Metropolitan Paulos Gregorios. Comments by Dr Rosemary Ruether and Prof. D. H. Verheul
5.45 p.m.	Reception by the MIT Corporation

FRIDAY JULY 13

9.00 a.m.	Morning prayers, Kresge Auditorium
9.15 a.m.	Plenary session: "Nature, Humanity, and God: Rethinking Christian Perspectives on Creation" Speakers: Prof. Charles Birch, Dr Gerhard Liedke and Protopresbyter Vitaly Borovoy
3.30 p.m.	Plenary session: "Science and Technology as Promise and Threat" Speakers: Dr Jerry Ravetz, Prof. Manuel Sadosky and Dr Bo Lindell
7.30 p.m.	First meeting of Sections

SATURDAY JULY 14

9.00 a.m.	Morning prayers, Kresge Auditorium
9.15 a.m.	Plenary session: "Future of Science and Technology: Perspectives in Developing Countries"
	Speakers: Dr O. A. El-Kholy, Dr Thomas R. Odhiambo and Prof. Carlos Chagas
3.30 p.m.	Plenary session: "Future of Science and Technology: Perspectives in Developing Countries"
	Speakers: Prof. Mahinda Palihawadana, Dr Nobuhiko Matsugi, Dr Fouad Zakaria and Dr Liek Wilardjo
7.30 p.m.	Second meeting of Sections

SUNDAY JULY 15

Morning	Conference worship in Old South Church, Copley Square
	Preacher: Dr John Habgood, Bishop of Durham, UK
3.30 p.m.	Third meeting of Sections
7.30 p.m.	Dramatic musical presentation: "Voices of Black Persuasion", National Center of Afro-American Artists

MONDAY JULY 16

9.00 a.m.	Morning prayers, Kresge Auditorium
9.15 a.m.	Plenary session: "Future of Science and Technology: Perspectives in Highly Industrialized (Market Economy) Societies"
	Speakers: Dr John M. Francis, Prof. Yoshinobu Kakiuchi and Prof. Theodor Leuenberger
3.30 p.m.	Plenary session: "The Debate about the Economics of the Just and Sustainable Society"
	Speakers: Prof. Herman Daly, Prof. C. T. Kurien and Dr Diogo de Gaspar
7.30 p.m.	Plenary session: Report of Science Students Conference

TUESDAY JULY 17

9.00 a.m.	Fourth meeting of Sections (opening with theological reflection on a biblical text)
3.30 p.m.	Plenary session: "Energy for the Future: Possibilities and Problems"
	Speakers: Prof. David Rose, Prof. Jean Rossel and Dr Shem Arungu-Olende

7.30 p.m. Plenary session: "The Biological Revolution: the Ethical and Social Issues"
Speakers: Prof. Jonathan King and Prof. Karen Lebacqz. Comments by Dr Gabriel Nahas and Dr Traute Schroeder

WEDNESDAY JULY 18

9.00 a.m. Fifth meeting of Sections (opening with theological reflection on a biblical text)

3.30 p.m. Plenary session: "Information Gathering and Processing: Power, Promise, and Peril"
Speakers: Prof. David H. Staelin, Prof. Thomas B. Sheridan and Prof. Joseph Weizenbaum

7.30 p.m. Plenary session: "Nuclear Disarmament"
Speakers: Prof. Philip Morrison, Prof. George Kistiakowsky and Archbishop Kirill, followed by brief comments from: Mr Ninan Koshy, Dr O. A. El-Kholy, Rev. Kazuyo Nishimoto, Dr W. Muta Maathai, Ms Jimmy Woodward and Mr Jan E. van Veen

THURSDAY JULY 19

9.00 a.m. Morning prayers, Kresge Auditorium

9.15 a.m. Plenary session: "Science and Technology as Power: Their Control and Use, and Their Just Distribution between the Rich and Poor Nations"
Speakers: Dr Heino Falcke, Dr Rogerio de Cerqueira Leite, Dr B. C. E. Nwosu and Prof. Ernest Petric
Announcement of Hungarian Churches' report to the conference

3.30 p.m. Sixth meeting of Sections (opening with theological reflection on a biblical text)

7.30 p.m. Seventh meeting of Sections

FRIDAY JULY 20

9.00 a.m. Morning prayers, Kresge Auditorium

9.15 a.m. Eighth meeting of Sections

3.30 p.m. Plenary session: "Science and Technology as Power: Possibilities of Personal and Community Action"
Speakers: Justice Thomas Berger, Ms Kerstin Anér and Dr Jun Ui

7.30 p.m. Ninth meeting of Sections

SATURDAY JULY 21

9.00 a.m.	Tenth meeting of Sections
12.45 p.m.	Excursion to Woods Hole, Cape Cod, Mass.

SUNDAY JULY 22

Morning	Worship in local churches
3.30 p.m.	Plenary session: Reports from Sections
7.30 p.m.	Presentation and discussion of statement by a group of third world representatives

MONDAY JULY 23

9.00 a.m.	Morning prayers, Kresge Auditorium
9.15 a.m.	Plenary session: Reports from Sections

TUESDAY JULY 24

9.00 a.m.	Morning prayers, Kresge Auditorium
9.15 a.m.	Plenary session: Reports from Sections
	Summing-up of the conference
6.00 p.m.	Closing plenary

WEDNESDAY JULY 25

Morning	Departure of participants

Directory of Authors

ALVES, RUBEM A.
Professor of Political Philosophy, State University of Campinas, São Paulo, Brazil. Author of *A Theology of Human Hope, Tomorrow's Child, Protestantismo e Repressão.*

ANÉR, KERSTIN (MS)
MP, Under-Secretary of State, Sweden. Former journalist and radio producer. Author of books on computer power, collections of sermons, articles on politics, science and feminism. (Lutheran)

ARUNGU-OLENDE, SHEM
Kenyan energy expert presently with the UN Center for Natural Resources, Energy and Transport, New York. (Anglican)

BERGER, THOMAS R.
Justice, Supreme Court of British Columbia, Canada; former Commissioner, Mackenzie Valley Pipeline Inquiry (Canada), and former Chairman, Royal Commission on Family and Children's Law, BC. (Anglican)

BIRCH, CHARLES
Challis Professor of Biology, University of Sydney, Australia, and Vice-Chairman, Working Committee on Church and Society. Author of *Nature and God* and *Confronting the Future*. Co-editor of *Genetics and the Quality of Life*. (Uniting Church)

BOROVOY, VITALY
Protopresbyter; Representative of the Moscow Patriarchate to the WCC, and Member of the Central Committee of the WCC. Formerly Professor of Church History at the Leningrad Theological Academy. (Russian Orthodox)

BROWN, ROBERT HANBURY
Fellow of Royal Society; Head of the Astronomy Department in the School of Physics, University of Sydney, Australia. Former Professor of Radio-Astronomy, University of Manchester, UK. Author of *The Exploration of Space by Radio* (with Ac.B. Lovell) and *Man and the Stars*. (Anglican)

CHAGAS, CARLOS
Dean, Faculty of Health Sciences, Federal University of Rio de Janeiro, Brazil. President, Pontifical Academy of Sciences. (Roman Catholic)

DALY, HERMAN E.

Professor of Economics, Louisiana State University, USA. Former Ford Foundation Visiting Professor at the University of Ceará, Brazil, and Research Associate, Economic Growth Center at Yale University. Author of *Steady-State Economics*. (Methodist)

EL-KHOLY, O. A.

Assistant Director General, Science and Technology, Arab Educational, Cultural and Scientific Organization, Cairo, Egypt. (Muslim)

FALCKE, HEINO

Dean of the Evangelical Church of Erfurt, GDR, and Chairman, Committee on Church and Society of the Federation of Evangelical Churches in the GDR.

FRANCIS, JOHN M.

Nuclear scientist. Now Government Administrator. Formerly with the UK Civil Nuclear Power Programme; Director, Society, Religion and Technology Project, Church of Scotland. Author of articles on science and public policy; co-editor of *Facing up to Nuclear Power*. (Anglican)

DE GASPAR, DIOGO

Brazilian economist. Formerly staff for the Programmes on Transnational Corporations and the New Economic Order of the WCC's Commission on the Churches' Participation in Development; now Assistant Director, Policy Development and Economic Analysis, World Food Council, Rome. (Roman Catholic)

GREGORIOS, PAULOS

Metropolitan of New Delhi, India. Chairman, Working Committee on Church and Society of the WCC. Member of the Executive and Central Committees of the WCC. Author of *The Human Presence: an Orthodox View of Nature*. (Orthodox Syrian Church of the East)

HABGOOD, JOHN S.

Bishop of Durham, UK. Formerly Principal, Queen's College, Birmingham; Vice-Principal, Westcott House, Cambridge; Demonstrator in Pharmacology, Cambridge University. Publications on religion and science. (Anglican)

KAKIUCHI, YOSHINOBU

Professor of Physics, International Christian University, Tokyo, Japan; former Member, Japanese National Commission for UNESCO, and Science Advisor, Ministry of Education. Author of *Science Policies in Japan*, and *On the Idea of Nature*. (Episcopal)

KING, JONATHAN

Professor of Biology, MIT, USA, specializing in research on the genetics of viruses; involved in the social issues of biological research.

KIRILL, ARCHBISHOP

Rector, Leningrad Theological Academy, USSR. Bishop of Vyborg, Vicar of the Leningrad Diocese. Member of the WCC Central and Executive Committees. (Russian Orthodox)

KISTIAKOWSKY, GEORGE

Professor Emeritus of Chemistry, Harvard University. Special Assistant to the President of the USA for Science and Technology, 1959-61. Former Vice-President, National Academy of Sciences. Author of *A Scientist at the White House*.

KURIEN, C. T.

Director, Madras Institute of Development Studies, India. Former Professor of Economics, Madras Christian College. Publications: *Poverty, Planning and Social Transformation, Economic Change in Tamil Nadu, Dynamics of Rural Transformation*. (Church of South India)

LEBACQZ, KAREN

Associate Professor of Christian Ethics, Pacific School of Religion, Berkeley, Calif., USA. Consultant to the National Institutes of Health. (United Church of Christ)

LEITE, ROGERIO C. C.

Professor, Institute of Physics, State University of Campinas, São Paulo, Brazil. Editor, *Folha de São Paulo*. Publications: *Technology and National Development, Thousand and One Nights of Multinationals, Nuclear Energy and Other Mythologies, Topics on Physics of Solid State, The Seven Plagues of the Brazilian University, Agony of National Technology*.

LEUENBERGER, THEODOR

Professor of Contemporary Social and Economic History, University of St Gallen, Switzerland. Author of *Bureaucratization and Modernization, The Powerlessness of the Citizen: Pladoyer for a Post-Modern Society, The Historical Compromise*. (Reformed)

LIEDKE, GERHARD

Pastor, Heidelberg, FRG. Formerly staff of the Protestant Institute for Interdisciplinary Research (FEST), Heidelberg. Publications on peace research, Christendom and militarism, theology and ecology. (United)

LINDELL, BO

Chairman, National Institute on Radiation Protection, Stockholm, Sweden. Chairman, International Commission on Radiology Protection since 1977. Delegate to the UN Scientific Commission since 1965.

MAATHAI, WANGARI MUTA (MS)

Associate Professor of Anatomy, University of Nairobi, Kenya; Chairman, NGO Environment Liaison Centre of the United Nations' Environment Programme. (Presbyterian)

MATSUGI, NOBUHIKO

Novelist. Former Assistant Professor at Momoyama Gakuin University, Japan. (Buddhist)

MONTEFIORE, HUGH

Bishop of Birmingham, UK. Publications: *Changing Directions* (ed.), *Nature, Man and God,* and *Nuclear Crisis* (ed.). (Anglican)

MORRISON, PHILIP

Professor of Physics, MIT, USA. Expert in nuclear weapons technology. Co-author of *The Price of Defence.*

NAHAS, GABRIEL

Director of Research on Pharmacology, Institut national de la santé et de la recherche médicale, Paris, France. Author of *Hachisch, cannabis et marijuana: le chauve trompeur.*

NWOSU, B. E. C.

Chief Education Officer (Science), Federal Ministry of Education, Lagos, Nigeria. Former Chief Scientific Officer, Natural Sciences Research Council, Lagos; Senior Lecturer in Physics, University of Nigeria, Nsukka. (Anglican)

ODHIAMBO, THOMAS R.

Director, International Centre of Insect Physiology and Ecology, Nairobi, Kenya. Former Professor of Entomology, University of Nairobi; Dean, Faculty of Agriculture, University of Nairobi.

PALIHAWADANA, MAHINDA

Professor of Sanskrit, University of Kelaniya, Sri Lanka. (Buddhist)

PETRIC, ERNEST

Professor, Faculty of Sociology, Political Science and Journalism, Ljubljana, Yugoslavia.

POTTER, PHILIP A.
General Secretary, World Council of Churches. (Methodist)

PRÖHLE, KÁROLY
Professor of Theology. General Secretary, Ecumenical Council of Churches in Hungary. (Evangelical)

RAVETZ, JEROME R.
Reader in the History and Philosophy of Science, University of Leeds, UK. Former Executive Secretary, Council for Science and Society, London. Author of *Scientific Knowledge and its Social Problems, The Acceptability of Risks.*

ROSE, DAVID J.
Professor of Nuclear Engineering, MIT, USA. Former Consultant to the US Congress, to US National Laboratories, and member of several studies by the US National Academy of Sciences. Former Director of Long-Range Planning, Oak Ridge National Laboratory, Tennessee. Co-author of *Plasmas and Controlled Fusion.* (Episcopal)

ROSSEL, JEAN
Professor of Physics, and Head of Physics Department, University of Neuchâtel, Switzerland. Former President, Swiss Physical Society; Vice-Chairman, Swiss Federal Commission of Radio-activity Protection. (Reformed)

RUETHER, ROSEMARY
Garret Evangelical Theological Seminary, Evanston, Ill., USA. Author of *The Radical Kingdom, Faith and Fratricide, New Woman/New Earth*, and other books. (Roman Catholic)

SADOSKY, MANUEL
Professor of Mathematics, Central University of Venezuela, Caracas. Former Professor at the University of Buenos Aires, and Vice-Dean, School of Science, University of Buenos Aires, Argentina.

SCHROEDER, TRAUTE M. (MS)
Professor of Human Genetics, Genetic Counselling and Prenatal Diagnosis, Institute for Anthropology and Human Genetics, Heidelberg, FRG. Publications on Cytogenetics and Human Genetics. (Evangelical)

SHERIDAN, THOMAS
Professor of Mechanical Engineering, MIT, USA. Co-author of *Man-Machine Systems.* (United Church)

SHINN, ROGER L.

Professor of Social Ethics, Union Theological Seminary, New York, USA. Author of *Tangled World, The Existentialist Posture, Wars and Rumors of Wars*, etc. (United Church)

STAELIN, DAVID H.

Professor of Electrical Engineering, MIT, USA. (Unitarian)

UI, JUN

Research Assistant, Department of Urban Engineering, Faculty of Engineering, University of Tokyo, Japan. Publications on pollution. (Buddhist)

VERHEUL, HENDRIK

Professor of Physics, Free University Amsterdam, Netherlands. Publications on Nuclear Physics. (Reformed)

WEIZENBAUM, JOSEPH

Professor of Computer Science and Engineering, MIT, USA. Author of *Computer Power and Human Reason: From Judgment to Calculation.*

WILARDJO, LIEK

Coordinator, APEID (UNESCO-ROEAC) Activities, Satya Wacana Christian University, Salatiga, Indonesia. Former Deputy Director for Academic Affairs, Satya Wacana Christian University. Former Senior Lecturer, Faculty of Electrical Engineering, Satya Wacana Christian University. (Reformed)

ZAKARIA, FOUAD

Chairman, Department of Philosophy, Kuwait University. (Muslim)

Inside front cover:
Conference participants assemble for Sunday worship in Old South Church, Boston. The preacher was Dr John Habgood, Bishop of Durham, England

Inside back cover:
1. Two of the organizers of the science students conference which preceded the main conference at MIT were Mr Peter Scherhans (left), a theological student from Heidelberg, Federal Republic of Germany, and Mr Janos Pasztor (right), a science student from Hungary studying at MIT

2. Bishop Paulos Gregorios, Metropolitan of New Delhi for the Syrian Orthodox Church of the East, was the moderator of the conference

3. Dr O. A. El-Kholy of Cairo, Associate Director General of the Arab Economic, Cultural and Scientific Organization, addressed the conference on the impact of science and technology in the countries of the Middle East

4. Dr Jonathan King, professor of microbiology at MIT, spoke on the dangers in the misuse of new biological discoveries

5. Dr Thomas R. Odhiambo, a well-known Kenyan scientist, spoke on the future of science and technology in Africa

6. Three key participants: (left to right) Archbishop Kirill, leader of the delegation from the Russian Orthodox Church, Archbishop Scott of the Anglican Church of Canada, Moderator of the Central Committee of the WCC, and Dr Philip Potter, WCC General Secretary

7. Prof. Karen Lebacqz of the Pacific School of Religion, Berkeley, California, speaks to the conference plenary session on the biological manipulation of life

8. A Marxist social philosopher from Yugoslavia, Prof. Ernest Petric, addresses the conference plenary session on the future of science and technology in socialist countries

9. The opening session of the conference at MIT: Chancellor Paul E. Gray of MIT welcomes the participants

Photos: Wendy Goldsworthy, Greg Moyer and John Taylor